CRITICAL SURVEY OF POETRY

Green Movement Poets

Editor

Rosemary M. Canfield Reisman

Charleston Southern University

SALEM PRESS

A Division of EBSCO Publishing, Ipswich, Massachusetts

ISBN: 978-1-42983-651-7

CONTENTS

CONTRIBUTORS

James Lovic Allen
University of Hawaii at Hilo

Andrew J. Angyal
Elon University

Todd K. Bender
*University of Wisconsin-
    Madison*

Nicholas Birns
*Eugene Lang College, The
    New School*

David Cappella
Boston University

David W. Cole
*University of Wisconsin
    Colleges*

Caroline Collins
Quincy University

Desiree Dreeuws
Sunland, California

John L. Grigsby
*Appalachian Research &
    Defense Fund of
    Kentucky, Inc.*

Kenneth Hada
East Central University

Sarah Hilbert
Pasadena, California

Tracy Irons-Georges
Glendale, California

Maura Ives
Texas A&M University

Philip K. Jason
*United States Naval
    Academy*

Jeffry Jensen
Pasadena, California

Sheila Golburgh Johnson
Santa Barbara, California

Rebecca Kuzins
Pasadena, California

Leon Lewis
*Appalachian State
    University*

Bernadette Flynn Low
*Community College of
    Baltimore County-
    Dundalk*

Perry D. Luckett
*United States Air Force
    Academy*

Sara McAulay
*California State University,
    Hayward*

Julia M. Meyers
Duquesne University

P. Andrew Miller
*Northern Kentucky
    University*

C. Lynn Munro
Belton, Missouri

Edward A. Nickerson
University of Delaware

Francis Poole
University of Delaware

Norman Prinsky
Augusta State University

Paul Siegrist
Fort Hays State University

Shelby Stephenson
Pembroke State University

Jonathan Thorndike
Belmont University

Rosemary Winslow
*The Catholic University of
    America*

ECOPOETRY AND NATURE POETS

Nature has long been a favorite subject of poets. Many cultures revere wilderness and have created whole mythologies surrounding life outside of civilization. Some believe that life in its original, purest form can only exist away from what man has created. There is a spiritual quality to the natural world that has drawn the earliest poets and modern man, a tug of the wild or a drive to return to what may be described as the source of all life. Facing the prospect of the earth's destruction, many contemporary poets have embraced the cause of speaking up for the very survival of the natural environment. Whether it is a lost cause, a noble cause, or a little of both, poets are determined not to remain silent as the earth continues to be polluted, ravaged, and torn apart.

One of the ancient masters of the nature poem was the eighth century Chinese poet Du Fu. As a Confucian scholar, Du Fu had absolute control of the poetry he composed. He is considered to be one of the greatest Chinese poets, having written more than one thousand poems on a vast number of topics. His work demonstrates his mastery of form and his preeminent ability to render serenity without effort. In countless poems, Du Fu employs the natural elements to symbolize human dilemmas, using water in all of its various forms as a symbol to create the appropriate mood. The seventeenth century Japanese poet Matsuo Bash{o} also reveled in writing about nature. He wandered throughout Japan, his travels inspiring him to compose some of the most miraculous haiku now known.

NATURE BECOMES THE IDEAL

As one of the leading English Romantic poets, William Wordsworth helped to usher in a revolutionary approach to poetry. The Romantic poets believed first and foremost in the value of the individual person and the inherent beauty of the natural world, necessitating a healthy respect for the goodness within both man and nature. In Wordsworth's famous preface to the second edition of *Lyrical Ballads* (1800), he states that man must strip off the influence of civilization in order to find his natural, more primitive state of being. This philosophy shaped Wordsworth's approach to his own poetry. He made it his life's work to write about the common man, somebody who lived in the rural areas away from the corrupting influence of cities. This concept has been considered naive or idealized, but at the time it was a powerful ideology that became extremely influential. One of his most brilliant poems is "Lines Composed a Few Miles Above Tintern Abbey," included in the 1798 edition of *Lyrical Ballads*. The poem was inspired by a walking tour that he took with his sister Dorothy. In it, he speaks of being a free man, connected to nature:

> Of aspect more sublime; that blessed mood,
> In which the burthen of the mystery,
> In which the heavy and the weary weight
> Of all this unintelligible world,
> Is lightened—that serene and blessed mood,
> In which the affections gently lead us on—
> Until, the breath of this corporeal frame
> And even the motion of our human blood
> Almost suspended, we are laid asleep
> In body, and become a living soul;
> While with an eye made quiet by the power
> Of harmony, and deep power of joy,
> We see into the life of things.

Several other Romantic poets were also nourished by what nature offered, including Samuel Taylor Coleridge, John Keats, and Percy Bysshe Shelley. Nature continued to inspire English poets from the mid-nineteenth into the twentieth century. Such poets as Gerard Manley Hopkins, Thomas Hardy, and William Butler Yeats also embraced the power of the natural world. During the mid-to-late nineteenth century in America, three towering writers directed their focus toward nature: Ralph Waldo Emerson, Henry David Thoreau, and Walt Whitman, who are remembered not only for their verse but also for their spirit and the tone of their work. As a poet, Emerson strived to bring purpose to the everyday in American life. For Whitman, poetry needed to be full of life and the spirit of America. He was not wedded to any particular poetic form; his poetry needed to be free to breathe. His *Leaves of Grass* is an American classic of epic proportions. The first edition was published in 1855, and for the rest of his life, he continued to expand it; as he saw America growing, so, too, did his poem. *Leaves of Grass* is a living testament to American life and landscape.

SPEAKING FOR THE ENVIRONMENT

Ecopoetry is a term that entered the lexicon in the final decades of the twentieth century. The increasingly popular wave of ecopoetry encompasses those poets who have made a point of deliberately emphasizing the ecological thread in their work. In his article "The Language of Habitat: An Ecopoetry Manifesto," published in the online *Octopus Magazine*, James Engelhardt claims that ecopoetry creates a "connection" with "non-human nature." It is not intended to merely "praise" nature or the ways that man can manipulate nature; these traditions must be discarded. The ecopoet should look to science for help in understanding nonhuman nature. With a greater understanding of how to recognize the forces of both culture and nature, it then becomes possible for the ecopoet to write an ecopoem that will at least attempt to connect the contradictions that exist in the world.

Some of the most noteworthy contemporary American nature poets are William Carlos Williams, Robinson Jeffers, W. S. Merwin, David Wagoner, Robert Bly, Wendell Berry, Gary Snyder, Donald Hall, and Mary Oliver. Each of these poets has written about the natural world in striking and profound ways. Never sentimental, their poems wrestle with the conflicts that exist between preserving nature and the encroachments of civilization. Berry represents the strong voice of the farmer, the father, the person who fights against the bloodthirsty corporation. A man of Kentucky, Berry has gained prominence not only as a poet, but also as an essayist and novelist. He has a strong connection with the land and is a fierce advocate for the survival of the small farmer. Bly, on the other hand, is a poet who believes in study, and his poetry is an outgrowth of his interests in mythology, psychology, and meditation. Since the 1960's, Snyder has focused on writing about how any relevant approach to living must also consider the role of the environment. For him, it has been, in a very direct sense, a lifelong pursuit. In both his poetry and his essays, Snyder is committed to the survival of the earth.

There are many more poets who have felt that the natural environment must be supported, promoted, and saved. Other American poets such as A. R. Ammons, Joy Harjo, Alice Walker, Raymond Carver, and Baron Wormser have written about the environment with profound eloquence. Whether they view nature as a symbol of beauty and freedom or as a neutral force that must be allowed to have its place in a coherent whole, poets from all continents have written forcefully and passionately about how humans must come to terms with their connection and responsibility to the earth.

Jeffry Jensen

BIBLIOGRAPHY

Bryson, J. Scott, ed. *Ecopoetry: A Critical Introduction*. Salt Lake City: University of Utah Press, 2002. A collection of essays concerning both literary and environmental issues in ecopoetry.

Elder, John. *Imagining the Earth: Poetry and the Vision of Nature*. Urbana: University of Illinois Press, 1985. A look at how poets see the natural world.

Englehardt, James. "The Language Habitat: An Ecopoetry Manifesto." *Octopus Magazine*, no. 9 (2007). A discussion of ecopoetry and its connection to science and nonhuman nature.

Felstiner, John. *Can Poetry Save the Earth? A Field Guide to Nature Poems*. New Haven, Conn.: Yale University Press, 2009. Discusses how poets of the past and present have attempted to speak with conviction in support of the earth.

Keith, W. J. *The Poetry of Nature: Rural Perspectives in Poetry from Wordsworth to the Present*. Toronto: University of Toronto Press, 1980. An overview of how poets have responded to the natural world around them.

Quetchenbach, Bernard W. *Back from the Far Field: American Nature Poetry in the*

Late Twentieth Century. Charlottesville: University Press of Virginia, 2000. A discussion of Robinson Jeffers, Theodore Roethke, Robert Bly, Gary Snyder, and Wendell Berry, and how each of them portrays nature in their poetry.

Spiegelman, Willard. *How Poets See the World: The Art of Description in Contemporary Poetry*. New York: Oxford University Press, 2005. A presentation of the various ways an observant poet can see the world.

A. R. AMMONS

Born: Near Whiteville, North Carolina; February 18, 1926
Died: Ithaca, New York; February 25, 2001

PRINCIPAL POETRY

Ommateum, with Doxology, 1955
Expressions of Sea Level, 1963
Corsons Inlet: A Book of Poems, 1965
Tape for the Turn of the Year, 1965
Northfield Poems, 1966
Selected Poems, 1968
Uplands, 1970
Briefings: Poems Small and Easy, 1971
Collected Poems, 1951-1971, 1972
Sphere: The Form of a Motion, 1974
Diversifications, 1975
The Selected Poems, 1951-1977, 1977
The Snow Poems, 1977
Highgate Road, 1978
Six-Piece Suite, 1979
Selected Longer Poems, 1980
A Coast of Trees, 1981
Worldly Hopes, 1982
Lake Effect Country, 1983
The Selected Poems: Expanded Edition, 1986
Sumerian Vistas, 1987
The Really Short Poems of A. R. Ammons, 1990
Garbage, 1993
The North Carolina Poems, 1994
Brink Road, 1996
Glare, 1997
Bosh and Flapdoodle, 2005
A. R. Ammons: Selected Poems, 2006 (David Lehman, editor)

OTHER LITERARY FORMS

Although A. R. Ammons (AM-uhns) is known primarily for his poetry, he also published reviews and essays. Central to an understanding of his work are "A Poem Is a Walk" and his short autobiographical reflection "I Couldn't Wait to Say the Word."

Ammons's several published interviews, especially one by Cynthia Haythe, give additional insight into his poetics. *Set in Motion: Essays, Interviews, and Dialogues* (1996) collects his most important writings about poetry.

ACHIEVEMENTS

Throughout a distinguished and prolific career, A. R. Ammons observed and presented the particulars of the world while projecting his longing for a sense of unity. He immersed himself in the flow of things, celebrating the world and the self that sees and probes it.

Ammons's work lies within the Emersonian tradition: He wrote from life without being a slave to any set poetic form. However, more than any other poet since Ralph Waldo Emerson, he developed a transcendentalism rooted in science and in a poetic that includes the self in the work. His epigrams, his short to moderate-length nature lyrics, and his long verse-essays are popular reading among poets.

His many awards include the Bread Loaf Writers' Conference Scholarship (1961), a Guggenheim Fellowship (1966), an American Academy of Arts and Letters Traveling Fellowship (1967), a National Endowment for the Arts grant (1969-1970), the Levinson Prize (1970), a National Book Award (1973) for *Collected Poems, 1951-1971*, an honorary Litt.D. from Wake Forest University (1973), the Bollingen Prize for Poetry for *Sphere* (1975), an Academy Award in Literature from the American Academy and Institute of Arts and Letters (1977), a National Book Critics Circle Award (1981) for *A Coast of Trees*, a John D. and Catherine T. MacArthur Foundation Award (1981), and the North Carolina Award for Literature (1986). In 1990, he was inducted into the American Academy and Institute of Arts and Letters. Ammons won the Lannan Literary Award for Poetry (1992), a second National Book Award (1993) for *Garbage*, the Poetry Society of America's Frost Medal (1994), the Bobbitt National Prize for Poetry (1994), the Ruth Lilly Poetry Prize (1995), and the Wallace Stevens Award (1998). Ammons is recognized as one of the most significant and original voices in twentieth century poetry.

BIOGRAPHY

A. R. Ammons was born Archie Randolph Ammons near Whiteville, North Carolina, in a house bought by his grandfather and situated on the family farm. The main book in the house was the Bible. Ammons's early experiences on the farm, working the land, helped shape his imagination. The self in his poems appears most frequently in relation to the natural world he knew as a child.

He was his parents' fourth child. Three sisters were born before him and two brothers after; one sister lived for only two weeks, and both brothers died, one in infancy and the other at birth. Ammons remembered the deaths of his brothers, saying that they accounted in part for the undercurrent of loss and loneliness in his work.

Upon graduation from high school in 1943, Ammons took a job in the shipyard in Wilmington, North Carolina. In 1944, he joined the U.S. Navy, spending nineteen months in service, including time in the South Pacific, where he began writing poems. Returning home after the war, Ammons attended Wake Forest College (his tuition paid for by the G.I. Bill) and graduated with a B.S. in 1949. That year he married Phyllis Plumbo and took a job as principal of an elementary school in the remote coastal community of Hatteras, North Carolina. From 1950 to 1952, he studied English at the University of California, Berkeley. In 1952, he took a position with his father-in-law's New Jersey medical glassware firm, a job he held for twelve years. He soon began to send poems to literary magazines, and in 1953, *Hudson Review* accepted two of them. His first book of poetry, *Ommateum, with Doxology*, appeared in 1955. Eight years later, *Expressions of Sea Level* appeared. In 1964, he began teaching at Cornell University. Other books of poems followed, and in 1972, most of his poems were published as *Collected Poems, 1951-1971*. *Sphere*, his poem of more than two thousand lines, published in 1974, gained for him the Bollingen Prize in Poetry for 1974-1975. Whitmanesque in its tendency toward democratic feeling, *Sphere* presents Ammons's aesthetic of continual motion and a musical affirmation of interdependence in the energy of all life. Ammons continued to be highly productive in his later years. *The North Carolina Poems* appeared in 1994; *Brink Road* was published in 1996; and his final book during his lifetime, *Glare*, appeared in 1997.

Ammons served for many years as the Goldwin Smith Professor of Poetry at Cornell University. In 1998, the university honored him with a celebration of his monumental achievement. He died from cancer in February of 2001, leaving behind his wife, his son John, and two grandchildren. Throughout his career, Ammons made frequent trips to eastern North Carolina, a place that figures prominently in his poems.

ANALYSIS

In one of A. R. Ammons's early poems, "So I Said I Am Ezra," from *Ommateum, with Doxology*, the speaker is whipped over the landscape, driven, moved by the natural elements. He is at once ordered and disordered, close and far, balanced and unbalanced, and he exclaims, "So I Ezra went out into the night/ like a drift of sand." The line is representative of Ammons's entire body of work, for it announces a search through language in an attempt to mean and to be clear, and failing to succeed completely in such clarity, the line ends by affirming a presence of radiance.

EXPRESSIONS OF SEA LEVEL

Ammons's poems have a tendency, like most contemporary poems, to take their own process, their own making, as a theme. Wanting to express something changeless and eternal, Ammons is constrained by his own intricate mortality. So in the title poem of *Expressions of Sea Level*, he presents the ocean as permanent and impermanent, as form and formlessness. He is interested in what humanity can and cannot know, giving full sway and expression to the ocean's activity: "See the dry casting of the beach worm/ dissolve at the delicate rising touch." The range and flow in Ammons's poetry, his search for balance, moved him to create his philosophical music, using a vocabulary drawn largely from everyday speech. He celebrates the need in every human being to discover a common experience in the least particular thing.

POEMS OF NORTH CAROLINA

Ammons attempts always to render visual details accurately. Some of the most moving poems in this regard are the poems inspired by his background in Columbus County, North Carolina. "Nelly Meyers" praises and celebrates a woman who lived on the farm where Ammons grew up; "Silver" records Ammons's love for and rapport with a mule he used for work. "Hardweed Path Going" tells of his life as a boy, doing chores on the farm, his playtime with a pet bird (a jo-reet) and a hog named Sparkle. These poems re-create Ammons's past, particularly his boyhood, which he renders in astonishingly realistic details.

CORSONS INLET

Ammons infuses the natural world with his own attuned sensibilities, acknowledging in the title poem of *Corsons Inlet* that "Overall is beyond me." The form of the poem is a walk over the dunes. What lives beyond his perception reassures, although he knows "that there is no finality of vision." Bafflement is a primary feeling in the poem, which may be studied for what it says about the relationship between logic and reason, imposed order and discovered order, art and life, reality and illusion, and being and becoming. "Corsons Inlet" concludes the walk/quest on the note that "tomorrow a new walk is a new walk." Ammons's desire to say something clearly, therefore, is not so much a search for the word as it is an attempt to find original ways to make and shape poetry.

TAPE FOR THE TURN OF THE YEAR

With *Tape for the Turn of the Year*, Ammons writes a long, narrow poem on adding-machine paper. The poet improvises and spontaneously records his thoughts and moods in what resembles a poetic diary. In one place, he praises how writing gets done, suggesting that doing it is almost its own practical reward, as the speaker acknowledges in another poem, "Identity," "it is wonderful how things work."

MAJOR THEMES

By the mid-1960's, Ammons's major themes had emerged, his sensibility oscillating between extremes: formlessness-form, center-periphery, high-low, motion-stasis, order-disorder, and one-many. One of his most constant themes has been the self in the work and in the world. He is concerned not only with the form of natural fact but also with form in the abstract sense, that is, with physical laws that govern the way individual entities act and behave. Ammons reaffirms the resonance of his subject, as in "The Eternal City," in which destruction must "accept into itself piece by piece all the old/ perfect human visions, all the old perfect loves."

Motion within diversity is perhaps Ammons's major theme. In "Saliences," from *Northfield Poems,* he discovers continuity in change. In "Snow Log," from *Uplands,* recognizing that nature's intentions cannot be known, he responds simply as an individual to what he sees in the winter scene: "I take it on myself:/ especially the fallen tree/ the snow picks/ out in the woods to show." In "The City Limits," from *Briefings,* a poem whose urban subject removes the speaker from nature, Ammons celebrates the "gold-skeined wings of flies swarming the dumped/ guts of a natural slaughter or the coil of shit."

COLLECTED POEMS, 1951-1971

Receiving the National Book Award in Poetry in 1973, *Collected Poems, 1951-1971* comprises most of Ammons's first six volumes, except for *Tape for the Turn of the Year* and three long verse-essays—"Extremes and Moderations," "Hibernaculum," and "Essay on Poetics." In "Extremes and Moderations" and "Hibernaculum," Ammons is a seer, lamenting humankind's abuse of Earth and appreciating the immediacy of a world that takes care of itself. "Essay on Poetics" considers the structural advantages and disadvantages of poetry. One reads this essay to appreciate more fully Ammons's views on writing.

SPHERE

In perhaps his major work, the book-length poem *Sphere,* Ammons explores motion and shape in a set form: sentences with no full stops, 155 sections of four tercets each. He relies on colons, perhaps suggesting a democratization and a flow. Shifting freely, sometimes abruptly, within a given stanza, phrase, or word, Ammons says, "I do not smooth into groups." Thus the book explores the nature of its own poetics, the poet searching everywhere for a language of clarity. In one place, he says that he is "sick of good poems." Wanting the smooth and raw together, Ammons reminds the reader that his prejudice against neat, traditional structures in poetry relates to the natural world where "the shapes nearest shapelessness awe us most, suggest the god." He regards a log, "rigid with shape," as "trivial." Ammons, therefore, makes his case for the poem of the open form as opposed to strong, traditional verses.

Ammons demythologizes poetics and language, while testifying to an Emersonian faith in the universe as flowing freely and spontaneously. At the same time, there is a counter feeling always working. He refers often to clarity and wants his poems to arrive and move forward "by a controlling motion, design, symmetry."

While he is writing the poem, commenting on it, writing himself into it, he shows his instinct for playfulness, for spoofing. This aspect of his work—the clowning humor—adds an inherent drama to his work, as critic Jerald Bullis has written:

> The tone of the poem or, I should say, of the voices of its "parts," ranges and range from that of the high and hard lyric, the crystalline and *as if* final saying, through a talky and often latinate professorial stance, to permutations of low tone: "bad" puns, catalogues that seem to have been lifted from a catalogue, and, in the example below, the high-pressure pitch-man tone of How-To scams: "Now, first of all, the way to write poems is just to start: it's like learning to walk or swim or ride the bicycle, you just go after it."

The poem goes on, praising the ability of humanity to write and to appreciate being alive.

Reverence for creation runs throughout *Sphere*, investing the work with a vision beyond and through the details of the poet's aesthetic. This religious strain has its source in Ammons's absolute reverence for the natural world. A religious vocabulary, then, is no surprise in his work and connects with his childhood, when church services and hymn-sings were dominant parts of his life. As in *Sphere*, he questions what is "true service," saying "it must be a service that is celebration, for we would celebrate even if we do not know what or how, and for He is bountiful if/ slow to protect and recalcitrant to keep." Ammons goes on to say, "What we can celebrate is the condition we are in, or we can renounce the condition/ we are in and celebrate a condition we might be in or ought/ to be in." Ammons fuses and plays on the relationship between creation and imagination, hoping and trying to discover "joy's surviving radiance." In the presence of this radiance—the hues and bends of Ammons's music—exist the crux of his aesthetic, his art and his being: the solitary man never surrendering as he is being imposed on and whipped about, as he writes in one of his earliest poems, "So I Said I am Ezra/ and the wind whipped my throat/ gaming for the sounds of my voice." However, the self is not dwarfed by the world. Ammons understands his moral and aesthetic convictions and will not cease to assert them. Such desire allows the visionary in Ammons constantly to discover new ways to see and understand his life. In this regard, key words crop up often: "salience," "recalcitrant," "suasion," "periphery," "possibility," tentative words that tend to illuminate or seek the proper blend in experience. So *Sphere* ends as it began, clear and free of all encumbrances except the spoken voice: "we're ourselves: we're sailing." The ending is right for the "form of a motion," the sense of wonder and uncertainty going on beyond the finality of the poem. Past, present, and future are one, and the poem and its end recall Walt Whitman's absorption into the dirt in "Song of Myself."

THE SNOW POEMS

In *The Snow Poems*, Ammons continues his experimental attempt to arrange a poetic journal, recounting in lyrical splendor the concerns of daily life, including details about weather, sex, and the poet's attempt to write and to experience a dialogue between the specific and the general. Ammons's work since the mid-1970's marks a return to the more visionary tendencies contained in his earlier terse, fierce lyrics of short or moderate length. "Progress Report" is an epigram from *Worldly Hopes*: "Now I'm/ into things// so small/ when I// say boo/ I disappear." The words flow in natural motion.

LAKE EFFECT COUNTRY

Lake Effect Country continues Ammons's love of form and motion. The whole book represents one body, a place of water, a bed of lively recreation. In "Meeting Place," for example, "The water nearing the ledge leans down with/ grooved speed at the spill then,/ quickly groundless in air." His vision comes from the coming together of the natural elements in the poem, rising and falling, moving and forming the disembodied voices that are the real characters in his poems: "When I call out to them/ as to the flowing bones in my naked self, is my/ address attribution's burden and abuse." "Meeting Place" goes out "to summon/ the deep-lying fathers from myself,/ the spirits, feelings howling, appearing there."

A COAST OF TREES

A major contemporary poem is "Easter Morning," from *A Coast of Trees*. Based on the death in infancy of the poet's younger brother, the poem is filled with reverence for the natural world, Ammons's memory ever enlarging with religious and natural resonances. "I have a life that did not become,/ that turned aside and stopped,/ astonished." The poem carries the contradictory mysteries of the human condition—death, hope, and memory—working together in a concrete and specific aesthetic. Presented in the form of a walk, "Easter Morning" reveals the speaker caught in the motion, as two birds "from the South" fly around, circle, change their ways, and go on. The poem affirms, with the speaker in another poem ("Working with Tools"), "I understand/ and won't give assertion up." Like Ezra going out "into the night/ like a drift of sand," the poet celebrates "a dance sacred as the sap in/ the trees . . . fresh as this particular/ flood of burn breaking across us now/ from the sun." Though the dance is completed in a moment, it can never be destroyed, because it has been re-created as the imagination's grand dance.

SUMERIAN VISTAS

Another major contemporary poem is "The Ridge Farm" from *Sumerian Vistas*. In fifty-one parts, the poem renders the farm itself on a ridge, on the edge of everything and nothing. Ammons's speaker joyfully resigns himself to the "highways" and the dammed-up brooks. The implication is that poetry—like nature—breaks through and flows, exploring the motion and shape of the farm's form. The farm itself is a concrete place wherein Ammons explores the nature of poetics and other realities.

THE REALLY SHORT POEMS OF A. R. AMMONS

In *The Really Short Poems of A. R. Ammons*, the poet continues his necessity to really see the natural world. That seeing becomes the poem; its motion, the story moving through the images. The form and subject move in a terse, fierce way as the poem discovers itself. In "Winter Scene," for example, the natural world changes radiantly when the jay takes over the leafless cherry tree. The landscape transformed, the poet notes what he sees: "then every branch/ quivers and/ breaks out in blue leaves." Motion formerly void of color brightens with vision and sway.

GARBAGE

Many consider *Garbage* to be a capstone of Ammons's maturity. Inspired by a massive landfill along Florida's portion of Interstate 95, this book-length poem continues Ammons's contemplation of and reverence for nature, this time positing the theme of regeneration following decay. It is a theme he applies to the human condition as well as to the sorry condition humanity has brought to nature. According to David Lehman, in his profile of Ammons published in the Summer, 1998, issue of *American Poet*, Ammons was attracted to the garbage mound for several reasons, including its geometry. Writes Lehman,

> The mound struck him as a hierarchical image, like a pyramid or the triangulation of a piece of pie. The pointed top corresponded to unity, the base to diversity. This paradigm of unity and diversity—and the related philosophical question of "the one and the many"—has been a constant feature of Ammons's work from the start.

GLARE

Ammon's penchant for stretching out his thoughts and words is nowhere as evident as in his 1997 volume, *Glare*. Comprising two sections, "Strip" and "Scat Scan," and written in his familiar couplet style, it is a work that is self-deprecating and spontaneous. Ammons speaks of "finding the form of the process," and critics have noted that his apparent ambition in *Glare* was "to make the finished form of the poem indistinguishable from the process of composition." In doing so, it reveals an immediacy of experience and thought, a kind of poetry in real time. In "Strip," he writes, "I have plenty and/ give plenty away, why because here/ at nearly 70 stuff has bunched up/ with who knows how much space to/ spread out into." The themes of "Scat" are harder to discern. Overall, he uses twisted proverbs and recalls Robert Frost's poetry to sum up his life.

OTHER MAJOR WORK

NONFICTION: *Set in Motion: Essays, Interviews, and Dialogues*, 1996.

BIBLIOGRAPHY

Bloom, Harold, ed. *A. R. Ammons*. New York: Chelsea House, 1986. This volume contains eighteen essays on Ammons's work, plus an introductory essay by Bloom. Among the contributors are contemporary poets John Ashbery, Richard Howard, and John Hollander. Perhaps the central theme of all the essays is that Ammons, like Walt Whitman, is a solitary self in the world.

Burak, David, and Rogert Gilbert, eds. *Considering the Radiance: Essays on the Poetry of A. R. Ammons*. New York: W. W. Norton, 2005. A collection of essays on Ammons's poetry, some of which were written by fellow poets.

Elder, John. *Imagining the Earth: Poetry and the Vision of Nature*. Urbana: University of Illinois Press, 1985. Elder writes about poets who remember and re-create Earth. His chapter on Ammons is called "Poetry and the Mind's Terrain." Elder's prose is clear and uncluttered; he presents Ammons from the fresh perspective of contemporary poets. Includes chapter notes and an index.

Hans, James S. *The Value(s) of Literature*. Albany: State University of New York Press, 1990. This book addresses the ethical aspects of literature by discussing three major American poets: Walt Whitman, Wallace Stevens, and A. R. Ammons. The chapter on Ammons is called "Ammons and the One: Many Mechanisms." In a concluding chapter, "The Aesthetic of Worldly Hopes," Hans speculates that one of the reasons poetry is not read widely in the United States is that it is "perceived to have nothing of ethical value inherent in it." What Hans calls "patterns of choice" exist in poems such as "Corsons Inlet" and "Essay on Poetics."

Holder, Alan. *A. R. Ammons*. Boston: Twayne, 1978. This introductory book-length study presents Ammons's life and works through *Sphere*. The text is supplemented by a chronology, notes, a select bibliography (with annotated secondary sources), and an index.

Kirschten, Robert. *Approaching Prayer: Ritual and the Shape of Myth in A. R. Ammons and James Dickey*. Baton Rouge: Louisiana State University Press, 1998. A mythopoetic study of each author that focuses on ceremonial strategies, this analysis examines the nature of Ammons's interest in ancient Sumerian as well as other traditions.

Schneider, Steven P., ed. *Complexities of Motion: New Essays on A. R. Ammons's Long Poems*. Madison, N.J.: Fairleigh Dickinson University Press, 1999. Essays by Helen Vendler, Marjorie Perloff, and other major critics examine the genre of the long poem as individualized by Ammons. Rationale, shape, structure, and strategy are explored, along with recurrent themes.

Sciagaj, Leonard M. *Sustainable Poetry: Four American Ecopoets*. Lexington: University Press of Kentucky, 1999. Along with Ammons, discusses and compares Wendell Berry, Gary Snyder, and W. S. Merwin and their treatment of nature and environmental concerns in their works. Bibliographical references, index.

Spiegelman, Willard. *The Didactic Muse*. Princeton, N.J.: Princeton University Press,

1989. Spiegelman's chapter on Ammons is called "Myths of Concretion, Myths of Abstraction: The Case of A. R. Ammons." Spiegelman ranges over Ammons's work, particularly the longer poems through *Sumerian Vistas*. Spiegelman's concern is the relation between poetry and philosophy. He contends that Ammons's dominant conceit is motion: his attempt to find that place where the conscious and unconscious move, yet stay. The book is important to any student who wishes to see Ammons's work within the larger context of contemporary poetry.

Vendler, Helen, ed. *Voices and Visions: The Poet in America*. New York: Random House, 1987. A companion to *Voices and Visions*, a Public Broadcasting Service television series. Calvin Bedient's essay on Walt Whitman discusses Ammons's *Sphere* within Whitman's energetic thrust out—toward a desire to create a motion within the American attraction for space, for going on, for expanding one's self in a larger world. The book contains pictures of poets, illustrations, notes on chapters, suggestions for further reading, notes on contributors, a list of illustrations, and an index.

Shelby Stephenson; Philip K. Jason
Updated by Sarah Hilbert

WENDELL BERRY

Born: Henry County, Kentucky; August 5, 1934

PRINCIPAL POETRY

November Twenty-six, Nineteen Hundred Sixty-three, 1963
The Broken Ground, 1964
Openings, 1968
Findings, 1969
Farming: A Hand Book, 1970
The Country of Marriage, 1973
An Eastward Look, 1974
Horses, 1975
Sayings and Doings, 1975
To What Listens, 1975
The Kentucky River: Two Poems, 1976
There Is Singing Around Me, 1976
Three Memorial Poems, 1976
Clearing, 1977
The Gift of Gravity, 1979
A Part, 1980
The Wheel, 1982
Collected Poems, 1957-1982, 1985
Sabbaths, 1987
Traveling at Home, 1989
Sabbaths, 1987-1990, 1992
Entries, 1994
The Farm, 1995
The Selected Poems of Wendell Berry, 1998
A Timbered Choir: The Sabbath Poems, 1979-1997, 1998
Given: New Poems, 2005
The Mad Farmer Poems, 2008
Leavings, 2010

OTHER LITERARY FORMS

In addition to poetry, Wendell Berry has written nonfiction, fiction, essays, and a biography of Harland Hubbard. He has also been the subject of numerous published interviews.

ACHIEVEMENTS

Wendell Berry first achieved regional and then national prominence as a poet, essayist, and novelist who writes about the small farmers of his fictional Port William community in northern Kentucky. As a poet, Berry has published widely since 1957, in small magazines, poetry volumes, private printings, and collections of his verse in 1985 and 1998. He won the Bess Hokin Prize from *Poetry* magazine (1967), an Academy Award in Literature from the American Academy of Arts and Letters (1971), the Jean Stein Award in Nonfiction (1987), the Aiken Taylor Award in Modern American Poetry (1994), the T. S. Eliot Award for Creative Writing from the Ingersoll Foundation (1999), the Thomas Merton Award (1999), and the Poets' Prize (2000). His major topics are the land, the family, and the community, especially the way that each has been affected by greed and indifference. Berry is a deeply traditional poet in theme and form, celebrating a timeless agrarian cycle of planting and harvest. He affirms a strong sense of place and ancestral inheritance, stemming from local family ties stretching back almost two centuries. His values are a curious blend of conservative and radical, combining a strong commitment to marriage and family with a pacifist stance and criticism of corporate exploitation of rural Appalachia. His voice is that of the farmer-poet, husband, father, and lover. For many readers and critics, he has reached the stature of a major contemporary philosopher.

BIOGRAPHY

Born in Henry County, Kentucky, on August 5, 1934, Wendell Erdman Berry grew up in a family of strong-willed, independent-minded readers and thinkers. His father, John M. Berry, was an attorney and a leader of the Burley Tobacco Growers Association. After attending the University of Kentucky for his bachelor's and master's degrees, Berry was married and taught for a year at Georgetown College in Kentucky. He then accepted a Wallace Stegner Fellowship in creative writing (1958-1959) at Stanford University. A Guggenheim Foundation award allowed him to travel to Europe in 1962 before he returned to teach English at New York University from 1962 to 1964. Berry wrote a moving elegy for President John F. Kennedy that won critical praise, and his first major poetry volume, *The Broken Ground*, appeared in 1964.

Berry and his family returned to Kentucky in 1964, when he was appointed to the English Department at the University of Kentucky in Lexington. He purchased Lane's Landing Farm in Port Royal in 1965 and moved back to his native county, where he has continued to farm and write. Berry has also served as a contributing editor to Rodale Press. He and his wife, Tanya (Amyx) Berry, raised two children, Mary and Pryor Clifford, on that farm.

ANALYSIS

Wendell Berry is a poet of deep conviction. Like Henry David Thoreau, he has felt a need to reestablish himself from the ground up by articulating the ecological, economic, and religious principles by which he would live, and by trying to live and write in accordance with those principles. He has striven to achieve a rigorous moral and aesthetic simplicity in his work by reworking the same basic themes and insights: the proper place of human life in the larger natural cycle of life, death, and renewal; the dignity of work, labor, and vocation; the central importance of marriage and family commitments; the articulation of the human and natural history of his native region; and precise, lyrical descriptions of the native flora and fauna of his region, especially of the birds, trees, and wildflowers. Expanding on these basic themes, he has included elegies to family members and friends, topical and occasional poems (especially antiwar poems expressing his strong pacifist convictions), didactic poems expressing his environmental beliefs, and a surprising number of religious poems expressing a deeply felt but nondenominational faith.

One finds in Berry's verse a continual effort to unify life, work, and art within a coherent philosophy or vision. Put simply, that vision includes a regional sensibility, a farming avocation, a poetic voice of the farmer-husband-lover-environmentalist, and a strong commitment to a localized environmental ethic. His most notable persona is the "Mad Farmer," though it is not clear why he is "mad"—does Berry mean passionate, exuberant, or merely eccentric? From childhood, Berry always hoped to become a farmer, and his verse celebrates the life of the land. His vision, however, is that of simplicity: of the land, of the community, and even of his art. In his literary works, Berry expresses nostalgia for the kind of small-scale, labor-intensive farming that was practiced in his region before World War II. His style of unmechanized organic farming is practiced today mainly by the Amish and the Mennonites. Berry has admitted that farming his hilly, eroded land has not been profitable, and while it may be ethically admirable to restore damaged land to production, it is generally not economically feasible without another source of income.

One senses in Berry's poetry a keen awareness of living in a fallen world, to be redeemed, if at all, through hard work, disciplined self-knowledge, and a gradual healing of the land. However, though he is a lyric poet, too often his lyrics do not sing: His muse is Delphic rather than Orphic, prophetic instead of lyrical. His verse is carefully worked and thoughtful but burdened at times by didacticism. The Berry persona is sometimes detached and impersonal, preoccupied with its own sensibility or with an environmental theme. His lyrics are often descriptive meditations in which little happens aside from the registration of impressions on the poet's sensibility. Still, the simplicity of his verse is often lightened by a sense of humor, a sense of proportion, and awareness of others. However, sometimes his lyrics seem sanctimonious or self-righteous. His verse echoes the rhetorical question of Robert Frost's "The Oven Bird"—"What to make of a diminished thing?"—and the answer is hard-won redemption.

Berry first published many of his poems in literary journals or small magazines or specialty presses, so that original editions of his works are often hard to find. His individual poetry volumes were published first with Harcourt Brace (*The Broken Ground*, *Openings*, *Farming*, *The Country of Marriage*, and *Clearing*) and later with North Point Press (*A Part*, *The Wheel*, *Collected Poems, 1957-1982*, and *Sabbaths*). The pieces in *Collected Poems, 1957-1982* are selected from each volume, but the collection is not entirely inclusive. He did add some important poems, such as the contents of the volume *Findings*, which was originally published by a small specialty press and is out of print.

Berry's poetry marks him as one of the most important modern American nature poets. His sense of the sacredness and interdependence of all life places him within the tradition of Ralph Waldo Emerson, Walt Whitman, and Henry David Thoreau. He is also one of the foremost American regional writers, insisting that his poetry be firmly rooted in a sense of place. His poetry reflects the same deep concern for the natural environment and for sound conservation and farming practices that is evident in his essays and fiction. His emphasis on marriage, family, and community allows him to affirm these necessary human bonds. His poems reflect his loyalty to his native region, his love of farming, his view of marriage as a sacrament, and his deep awareness of the beauty and wonder of the natural world.

ELEGIAC POETRY

Though Berry had been publishing poems in literary magazines and journals since the mid-1950's, his first critical recognition came in 1964, with the appearance of *The Broken Ground*, his first poetry volume, and *November Twenty-six, Nineteen Hundred Sixty-three*, his elegy for John F. Kennedy, which first appeared in the December 21, 1963, issue of the *Nation*. Berry's elegy, which was accompanied by woodcuts by Ben Shahn, has been called the most successful commemoration of Kennedy's death. Though written in free-verse form, Berry's elegy makes use of a traditional stanzaic organization and refrain and incorporates the traditional elegiac cycle of grief, mourning, the funeral procession, the interment, and the apotheosis of the subject's memory. Berry's interest in the elegy was also apparent in "Elegy," the opening poem in *The Broken Ground*. Other elegiac works include "Three Elegiac Poems" (*Findings*), "In Memory: Stuart Engol" (*Openings*), and "Requiem" and "Elegy" (*The Wheel*). Death is always present in Berry's work, but it is presented naturalistically, without a compensating carpe diem theme or renewal, except in the natural cycle of life.

THE BROKEN GROUND

The Broken Ground is a collection of thirty-one free-verse lyrics with a distinctly regional flavor, twenty of which were later included in his *Collected Poems, 1857-1982*. Many of these poems first appeared in *Stylus*, *Poetry*, *The Nation*, and *The Prairie Schooner*. This early collection introduces the Berry voice and some of his major themes: the cycle of life and death, a sensitivity to place, pastoral subject matter, and recurring images of water, the Kentucky River, and the hilly, pastoral landscape of north-central Kentucky. His language is terse, intense, and compressed, his style imagistic and at times almost epigrammatic. The stylistic influence of William Carlos Williams and the Orientalism of Kenneth Rexroth seem apparent in these early poems. Berry's sharp, sculpted images also recall those of his friend and fellow poet Gary Snyder. Some of the poems seem curiously detached and impersonal. They are animated by no great myths, legends, or events, aside from the figures of Daniel Boone and other early settlers. Instead, the poems are intensely private, detached, and descriptive. Although many of them are set in his native Kentucky, the Berry persona seems curiously detached from members of his local community beyond his family. One does not find the social engagement Williams shows in his Patterson poems, a warmth that came from his lifelong involvement as a local pediatrician. Instead, the Berry persona seems solitary and austere: too much the detached observer, quiet and understated, though perhaps not intending to project a sense of social isolation. The parallels with Williams are instructive: While Williams was a practicing local physician whose poetry often reflects his sympathetic understanding of his patients and their families, Berry presents himself as a working farmer whose poetry reflects his love of his work. What redeems Berry's poems is his love of farming and the rhythms of physical labor: its purposefulness, its physicality, and its tangible rewards, including a sense of psychological and natural harmony.

LOST PARADISE AS THEME

Berry's poems contain a mythic vision of a lost, primeval paradise, a fall from grace, and a guarded hope in work, discipline, and renewal. "Paradise might have appeared here," he announces in "The Aristocracy," but instead he finds a wealthy old dowager airing her cat. Like Robert Frost's pastoral world of a diminished New England landscape, Berry's Kentucky River Valley has suffered from neglect and abuse. The moments of grace are few—bird songs, the return of spring, the cycle of the seasons, glimpses of the natural order—and death is always present. Like Frost, Berry has chosen to make a "strategic retreat" to a pastoral world in which the poet-farmer can take stock of his resources, but his sensibility differs from Frost's. For Frost, the sense of diminishment came from the abandonment of farms in rural New England after the Civil War, while for Berry the sense of loss comes from environmental despoliation of the Cumberland plateau, first by careless farming practices and later by timber interests and the big coal companies. The villain in Berry's loss of paradise is the machine in the garden—modern technology—for which Berry never has a kind word.

Berry's version of the Paradise Lost myth centers on the massive environmental destruction by modern technology visited on the Cumberland region by absentee corporate owners. He has been radicalized by Kentucky's legacy of corrupt government and indifference to environmental concerns, which has left the region virtually a Third World economy, based on cheap, large-scale mineral extraction with little regard for the human or environmental consequences of pit or surface mining. The practice of strip-mining has been particularly devastating to the land and water resources, given the use of bulldozers and other machinery never contemplated when the rights to access the coal were sold a century or more ago. Living downstream from the despoiled hills and polluted creeks of Appalachia, Berry has seen at first hand the flooding and water pollution that have occurred on the Kentucky River.

THE KENTUCKY RIVER AND FINDINGS

As Berry recounts in *The Kentucky River*, the first white settlers who entered the Kentucky territory were unable to respond to the richness and abundance of natural resources except by exploitation. Hence, in "July, 1773," the first of the "Three Kentucky River Poems," young Sam Adams fires heedlessly into a herd of peacefully grazing buffalo at a salt lick, a clear parallel to the extensive hunting and killing done by early Kentucky settlers such as Daniel Boone, which soon changed the face of hunting in the area.

Not only did the publication of Berry's *Collected Poems, 1957-1982* permit the republishing of nearly two hundred poems from his previous eight volumes, many of which were by then out of print, but it also allowed him to select which poems he could retain and which he would drop from those early volumes. Among Berry's best early work was the sequence of three long poems from *Findings*. "The Design of a House" is about beginnings and intentions, the conscious fabrication of a dwelling and a marriage relationship that had previously existed merely as a vague dream or desire, and a wish to reestablish roots in one's native place. It becomes a nuptial poem, the speaker's dedication of his love to his wife, Tanya, and his daughter, Mary, and the continuation of their life together. The design of their house comes to signify the design of their family relationship.

The second poem in *Findings*, "The Handing Down," continues this theme of family and place, this time in terms of an old man's memories and reflections and his sense of satisfaction with the life he has led, as expressed through conversations with his grandson. The speaker in this poem recalls Jack Beecham, the protagonist of Berry's novel *The Memory of Old Jack* (1974). Both the poem and the novel have to do with an old man's preparations for death, his gradual letting go of life through the memories that run through his mind. The third part of *Findings*, "Three Elegiac Poems," commemorates the death of the old man, which the speaker hopes will occur quietly at home, away from the sterile coldness and isolation of hospital wards and the indifference of physicians.

CELEBRATION OF NATURE AND LAND

Openings, Farming, The Country of Marriage, and *Clearing* celebrate Berry's return to Kentucky and the satisfaction he found in taking up farming. After living in California, Europe, and New York City, he came to appreciate the possibilities of writing about his native region. Berry was particularly impressed with the hill farms of Tuscany, around Florence, which showed him that such "marginal land" might remain productive for many centuries with the proper care and attention. The quality of these farms led him to rethink the possibilities of hill farming in his native Kentucky. As he indicates in the autobiographical title essay in *The Long-Legged House* (1969), he kept feeling himself drawn back home, particularly to the small cabin built on the Kentucky River by his uncle Curran Matthews. After it was flooded, Berry moved this house farther up the riverbank and rebuilt it to create his writer's study.

Berry's poems in these middle volumes show a new depth of craft and responsiveness to nature. They celebrate the values of land and nature, family and community, marital love and devotion. They are quietly attentive to the cycle of seasons, of the organic cycles of growth and decay, of the subtle beauty of the native flora and fauna. As philosopher, visionary, and political activist, his "Mad Farmer" persona speaks out against war, wastefulness, and environmental destruction. He dreams of a new, gentler orientation to the land that will encourage people to cherish and preserve their natural heritage. He finds deep spiritual sustenance as he reflects on the beauty and fitness of the natural order and the richness of the present moment.

Berry's poems are broadly pastoral in orientation, but they reflect the Kentucky frontier tradition of pioneer homesteading and yeoman farming rather than artificial literary tradition. Some pastoral themes evident in his work include an idealization of the simple life, an implied city-country contrast, a yearning for a past "golden age" of rural life, a celebration of the seasonal tasks of farming life, a strong affirmation of small-scale, organic farming, and an identification of the poet with his native region.

OPENINGS

In *Openings*, "The Thought of Something Else" announces the speaker's desire to leave the city for country life, but first he must make peace with the legacy of the past, which he does in "My Great-Grandfather's Slaves." The next three poems are autumnal in tone, establishing the speaker within a seasonal cycle. In "The Snake," he comes upon a small reptile preparing for winter hibernation. The "living cold" of the snake, replete with its engorged meal, parallels the contented winter solitude of the speaker in the next poem, "The Cold." The starkly descriptive "Winter Rain" leads to "March Snow" and "April Woods: Morning," which resemble haiku in their delicate imagery. In "The Porch over the River," the speaker establishes himself in his riverside writer's cabin, like the classical Chinese poet Du Fu. In "The Dream," he imagines the surrounding countryside restored to its pristine beauty, unspoiled by greed or acquisitiveness. The tree celebrated in "The Sycamore," a venerable specimen whose gnarled trunk is scarred by lightning, becomes a symbol of natural resiliency. Like the tree, the poet wishes that he might be shaped and nurtured by his native place. "Grace" and "A Discipline" reflect the strength the speaker draws from nature, allowing him to withstand the destructiveness of his culture, in which people are at war with the environment, one another, and themselves.

FARMING AND THE COUNTRY OF MARRIAGE

Farming and *The Country of Marriage* are less solitary in mood. They introduce the colorful persona of the "Mad Farmer," an exuberant, Bunyanesque figure who flaunts social convention in "The Mad Farmer's Revolution" and "The Contrariness of the Mad Farmer," dances in the streets in "The Mad Farmer in the City," and—through his prayers, sayings, satisfactions, and manifestos—offers a wry and humorous commentary on Berry's own views as expressed in his books and essays. "The Birth," a dramatic dialogue, constitutes an interesting departure from Berry's customary lyrical verse. A group of farmers, up late with lambing on a cold winter night, unexpectedly come upon a couple and child who have taken sanctuary in their barn for their own nativity. Berry's poem captures the cadences and flavor of ordinary country talk, in which more is implied than said.

Berry's poems are noted for quiet attentiveness to surroundings, almost as if the speaker tried to make himself part of his habitat. His farmer persona is a keen naturalist, carefully observing the seasonal behavior of the birds and animals. His speaker is especially attuned to bird songs, and the variety of birds mentioned in his poems is notable— kingfishers, song sparrows, phoebes, herons, wild geese, finches, wrens, chickadees, cardinals, titmice, and warblers. Implicit in his poems is a sense of grace and renewal, a deep satisfaction and contentment.

Berry's relationship with his wife and children has been central to his task of renewal as a pastoral poet. An accomplished love poet, Berry has written many poems to his wife, Tanya, on the anniversaries of their marriage or to express his gratitude for their common life. For his children, too, Berry has written poems on their births, comings of age, and marriages, and on the births of grandchildren. In "The Gathering," the speaker recalls that he now holds his son in his arms the way his father held him. In "The Country of Marriage," farming and marriage serve as complementary and inseparable extensions of each other. Husbandry and marriage are recurring tropes in Berry's poetry, illustrated in clearing fields, sowing crops, planting a garden, tending livestock, mowing hay, and taking in the harvest. He celebrates farming as a labor of love, a work of regeneration and fecundity that is at once vital and procreative.

CLEARING

The poems in *Clearing* articulate Berry's sense of region and place. "Where" is a long pastoral meditation on the history and ownership of the fifty-acre farm, Lane's Landing, which the Berrys purchased between 1965 and 1968. The history of the farm provides a case study in attitudes toward stewardship and land use, from the earliest settlers to the developer from whom Berry bought the farm. The transition from wilderness to settlement to worn-out land rehearses an ecological myth of the fall from primeval abundance to reckless waste and decay. Berry presents the history of his farm as a parable of the American frontier and an indictment of the reckless habits that quickly exhausted the land's natural richness and abundance. "Where" is both a personal credo and a contemporary ecological statement of what needs to be done, both in terms of land management and in changing cultural attitudes toward the land.

A PART

Berry's next two poetry volumes, *A Part* and *The Wheel*, reflect in their titles his deepening ecological awareness. *A Part* includes short pastoral lyrics; some religious verse; translations of two poems by the sixteenth century French poet Pierre de Ronsard; "Three Kentucky River Poems," a narrative triptych based in part on historical accounts of the McAfee brothers' 1773 expedition into Kentucky; and "Horses," a verse tribute to the skills of working draft horses, in which Berry excoriates tractors and internal combustion engines for destroying the quiet pleasures of farming.

THE WHEEL

The Wheel takes its title image from the mandala, or "wheel of life," of which Sir Albert Howard speaks in his classic study *An Agricultural Testament* (1943), which influenced Berry's thinking about organic farming. This collection is a book of elegies of remembrance and praise, celebrating the continuities of birth, growth, maturity, death, and decay. An increasing self-assurance is evident in Berry's voice, a relaxed, self-confident voice free of anxiety. His verse forms also become more formal, with an increased use of rhyme and regular stanzaic form, though he still seems to prefer a short line.

"Elegy," one of Berry's finest poems, appears in this collection. A pastoral elegy, it is one of a series of three poems dedicated to Owen Flood, whom Berry honors as a teacher and friend. The first poem, "Requiem," announces his passing, though his spirit remains in the fields he had tended. "Elegy" pays tribute to the quality of Flood's life in eight sections, invoking the spirits of the dead to reaffirm the traditional values that Flood embodied: duty, loyalty, perseverance, honesty, hard work, endurance, and self-reliance. It reaffirms the continuity of the generations within a permanent, stable agricultural order. There is a sense of recycling human life, as nature recycles organic materials back into the soil to create fertile organic humus. The poem also celebrates human permanences: marriage, work, friendship, love, fidelity, and death. The dominant image is of life as a dance within the circle of life, implying closure, completeness, and inclusion. "Elegy" affirms farm labor as an honorable calling, true to the biblical injunction to live by the sweat of one's brow. The opening line of the poem reaffirms an implicit purpose in all Berry's work: "To be at home on its native ground." The poem honors the elders of the community who were the speaker's teachers, including Flood, and concludes with the affirmation that "the best teachers teach more/ than they know. By their deaths/ they teach most."

Another important poem in this collection, "The Gift of Gravity," reaffirms the life-sustaining cycles of sunlight, photosynthesis, growth, decay, and death. The poem announces its major theme, "gravity is grace," with the dominant image of the river of life and the return of all life to its source. There is an almost mystical unity conveyed in the opening lines: "All that passes descends,/ and ascends again unseen/ into the light." Two other poems, "The Wheel" and "The Dance," affirm the interlocking unities that knit the community together in festive celebrations of song and dance.

Dissatisfied with Harcourt Brace, Berry changed publishers in the early 1980's, moving to North Point Press, a small publisher in Berkeley, California. One immediate result was the issuing of his *Recollected Essays, 1965-1980* (1981) and *Collected Poems, 1927-1982*, which includes the better part of his first eight volumes of poetry.

SABBATHS

Sabbaths marks something of a departure in tone and style from Berry's earlier work. It is at once more formal, more structured, and more overtly religious in its sensibility. The forty-six poems in this collection were written over a six-year period, from 1979 to 1985. The poems are untitled, arranged by year, and identified only by their first line. There are quiet, restrained, almost metaphysical meditations that incorporate a number of lines from Scripture. Here Berry makes use of traditional rhyme and meter. These poems show a deep, nonsectarian religious sensibility, akin to the personal faith of the New England Transcendentalist poets, especially Emily Dickinson. Like Dickinson, Berry applies Christian tropes to nature to imply a natural religion. The many allusions to Eden, Paradise, worship, hymns, song, grace, gift, the Maker, heaven, resurrection, darkness, and light invoke a kind of prophetic vision of a new Earth, healed and reborn—a paradise regained. Berry again describes the primal fertility and richness of the Kentucky landscape before it was ruined by the rapacious settlers. His poems combine a moral awareness of a deep wrong done to Earth by human greed and ignorance with an ecological awareness of the need for a change that can come only from within individuals and local communities.

The overall theme of *Sabbaths* is the need for rest and renewal—both within human hearts and in the natural world. People need to take time away from their heedless ravaging of the environment to try to understand and appreciate Earth's beauty and strength. Berry calls for the cultivation of a different kind of sensibility—less inclined to impose human will on nature and more inclined to appreciate the natural world on its own terms, as a kind of heaven on Earth. Berry weaves many scriptural allusions into his poems, quoting from the Psalms, the Old Testament prophets, and the New Testament. The poems manage to convey a deep meditative sensibility without making any formal religious affirmations except by implication. The speaker comes across as a deeply thoughtful but independent spirit, reverent but unchurched. One finds in *Sabbaths* a new blend of spiritual and ecological awareness, a sense of life and of the land, as worthy of the deepest veneration. This meditative cycle of poems is extended in *A Timbered Choir*.

GIVEN

These poems were written between 1994 and 2004, late in Berry's career. The first three sections of the volume are most notable for "Some Further Words," which sets out in considerable detail Berry's most important beliefs, including that the world of nature outranks the domestic world of humans, that the rich are mostly thieves, that most intellectuals are (figuratively) prostitutes, that stockpiling weapons for war is not something that enourages peace, that health is not equivalent to medication, that science used by corporations is "knowledge reduced to merchandise," which is a "whoredom of the mind" and not progress, that machines should be gone, and that capitalism is fantasy (and the stock market fall should evoke "long live gravity!"). Rather, the poem endorses "old intelligence of the heart," as in love and respect for one another and everything else.

Part 4, "Sabbaths 1998-2004," fills two-thirds of the volume, and like *Sabbaths*, his 1987 collection, these new Sabbath poems are formal in structure and often overtly religious. For example, the fifth poem in "Sabbaths 1999" is a sonnet, celebrating both human, earthly love and the realization that such love is also eternal, religious love, which humans learn on reaching heaven. The natural world, of course, is a major element in Berry's religious vision, as in poem 5 of "Sabbaths 2000," in which the poet visits a favorite nature scene as "one of the thresholds/ between Earth and Heaven," where he can detach from himself and be free. Even in these religious poems, however, Berry continues to satirize the excesses of American capitalism, as in poem 4 in "Sabbaths 2001," with the "country smeared" because of human stupidity, with freedom unappreciated and unexercised, with the "idiot luxury" replacing true religious faith, and with beauty, closely associated with religious faith and love, sold in the marketplace. Also, in poems 6 and 9 of "Sabbaths 2002," modern technology in the form of boats on the river is again satirized, with the river "bedeviled" (word choice deliberate for its Satanic overtones) by the engines, which fill "the air with torment." Even more powerfully satiric are the post-September 11, 2001, Sabbath poems, including poem 3 from "Sabbath 2003," with its depiction of the "Lords of War," driven by greed and wrath, destroying any place based on "their willingness to destroy every place." The poet urges the alternative of "saying yes/ to the air, to the earth, to the trees" and to all living therein. Also, poem 7 of "Sabbaths 2003" satirizes the sworn defenders of freedom who are snuffing out freedom's candle while chanting praise for freedom. This poem also satirizes artists for creating art for art's sake while keeping their university jobs and literary awards and argues for no art if it "cannot speak freely in defiance/ of wealth self-elected to righteousness." With their important ideas conveyed by sophisticated literary techniques such as oxymorons ("silenced into song, blinded into light"), literary allusions (estranged hearts like Hemingway's "islands parted in the sea"), and metaphors (aged poet as gray heron, withdrawing in peace), Berry's Sabbath poems from 1998 through 2004 rank with the very best poetry.

OTHER MAJOR WORKS

LONG FICTION: *Nathan Coulter*, 1960, 1985; *A Place on Earth*, 1967, 1983; *The Memory of Old Jack*, 1974; *Remembering*, 1988; *A World Lost*, 1996; *Jayber Crow*, 2000; *Hannah Coulter*, 2004; *Andy Catlett: Early Travels*, 2006.

SHORT FICTION: *The Wild Birds*, 1986; *Fidelity*, 1992; *Watch with Me*, 1994; *Three Short Novels*, 2002; *That Distant Land: The Collected Stories*, 2004.

NONFICTION: *The Long-Legged House*, 1969; *The Hidden Wound*, 1970; *The Unforeseen Wilderness*, 1971; *A Continuous Harmony*, 1972; *The Unsettling of America: Culture and Agriculture*, 1977; *The Gift of Good Land*, 1981; *Recollected Essays, 1965-1980*, 1981; *Standing by Words*, 1983; *Home Economics*, 1987; *Harland Hubbard: Life and Work*, 1990; *What Are People For?*, 1990; *The Discovery of Kentucky*, 1991; *Standing on Earth*, 1991; *Sex, Economy, Freedom, and Community*, 1993; *Another Turn of the Crank*, 1995; *Life Is a Miracle: An Essay Against Modern Superstition*, 2000; *The Art of the Commonplace: The Agrarian Essays of Wendell Berry*, 2002 (Norman Wirzba, editor); *In the Presence of Fear: Three Essays for a Changed World*, 2002; *Citizenship Papers: Essays*, 2003; *Standing by Words: Essays*, 2005; *The Way of Ignorance, and Other Essays*, 2005; *Bringing It to the Table: On Farming and Food*, 2009; *Imagination in Place: Essays*, 2010; *Conversations with Wendell Berry*, 2007 (Morris Allen Grubbs, editor).

CHILDREN'S LITERATURE: *Whitefoot: A Story from the Center of the World*, 2009.

EDITED TEXT: *Blessed Are the Peacemakers: Christ's Teachings of Love, Compassion, and Forgiveness*, 2005.

BIBLIOGRAPHY

Angyal, Andrew J. *Wendell Berry*. New York: Twayne, 1995. A standard critical biography in the Twayne United States Authors series.

Berry, Wendell. Interviews. *Conversations with Wendell Berry*. Edited by Morris Allen Grubbs. Jackson: University Press of Mississippi, 2007. A collection of interviews in which Berry covers most aspects of his work and life.

Basney, Lionel. "Having Your Meaning at Hand: Work in Snyder and Berry." In *Word, Self, Poem: Essays on Contemporary Poetry from the Jubilation of Poets*, edited by Leonard M. Trawick. Kent, Ohio: Kent State University Press, 1990. Discusses Berry's early volumes as articulating a work ethic that is rooted in a person's interaction with a particular place, with a sense of community, and with an uneasy Christian sacramental vision.

Bonzo, J. Matthew, and Michael R. Stevens. *Wendell Berry and the Cultivation of Life*. Grand Rapids, Mich.: Brazos Press, 2008. An in-depth study that attempts to capture Berry's religious vision, arguing that the writer is the one person to whom contemporary Christians need to listen.

Cornell, Daniel. "*The Country of Marriage:* Wendell Berry's Personal Political Vision." *Southern Literary Journal* 16 (Fall, 1983): 59-70. Through a close reading of the poems in *The Country of Marriage*, Cornell offers a thoughtful examination of the thematic implications of Berry's pastoral metaphors. Cornell locates Berry within an agrarian populist tradition that defies conventional conservative or liberal labels.

Freeman, Russell G. *Wendell Berry: A Bibliography*. Lexington: University of Kentucky Libraries, 1992. This is the place to begin straightening out the history of Berry's nonstop, multigenre publishing career.

Goodrich, Janet. *The Unforeseen Self in the Works of Wendell Berry*. Columbia: University of Missouri Press, 2001. Goodrich argues that whether Berry is writing poetry, fiction, or prose, he is reimagining his own life and thus belongs to the tradition of autobiography. A fresh approach to Berry's literature.

Hicks, Jack. "Wendell Berry's Husband to the World: *A Place on Earth*." *American Literature* 51 (May, 1979): 238-254. Perhaps the best critical overview of Berry's earlier work. Examines the farmer-countryman vision in Berry's fiction. Hicks traces thematic connections between Berry's essays, poetry, and fiction.

Peters, Jason, ed. *Wendell Berry: Life and Work*. Lexington: University Press of Kentucky, 2007. This collection of essays focuses on Berry's values of agrarianism, family, and community.

Shuman, Joel James, and L. Roger Owens, eds. *Wendell Berry and Religion: Heaven's Earthly Life*. Lexington: University Press of Kentucky, 2009. A collection of essays examining Berry's religious point of view. The work is divided into four sections: "Good Work," "Holy Living," "Imagination," and "Moving Forward."

Andrew J. Angyal; Philip K. Jason
Updated by John L. Grigsby

RALPH WALDO EMERSON

Born: Boston, Massachusetts; May 25, 1803
Died: Concord, Massachusetts; April 27, 1882

PRINCIPAL POETRY
  Poems, 1847
  May-Day and Other Pieces, 1867
  Selected Poems, 1876

OTHER LITERARY FORMS

Ralph Waldo Emerson's *The Journals of Ralph Waldo Emerson* (1909-1914), written over a period of fifty-five years (1820-1875), have been edited in ten volumes by E. W. Emerson and W. E. Forbes. Ralph L. Rusk edited *The Letters of Ralph Waldo Emerson* in six volumes (1939). Emerson was a noted lecturer in his day, although many of his addresses and speeches were not collected until after his death. These appear in three posthumous volumes—*Lectures and Biographical Sketches* (1884), *Miscellanies* (1884), and *Natural History of Intellect* (1893)—which were published as part of a centenary edition (1903-1904). A volume of Emerson's *Uncollected Writings: Essays, Addresses, Poems, Reviews, and Letters* was published in 1912. A sixteen-volume edition of journals and miscellaneous papers was published between 1960 and 1982.

ACHIEVEMENTS

Although Ralph Waldo Emerson's poetry was but a small part of his overall literary output, he thought of himself as very much a poet—even in his essays and lectures. He began writing poetry early in childhood and, at the age of nine, composed some verses on the Sabbath. At Harvard, he was elected class poet and was asked to write the annual Phi Beta Kappa poem in 1834. This interest in poetry continued throughout his long career.

During his lifetime, he published two small volumes of poetry, *Poems* and *May-Day and Other Pieces*, which were later collected in one volume for the centenary edition of his works. Altogether, the centenary volume contains some 170 poems, of which perhaps only several dozen are noteworthy.

Although Emerson produced a comparatively small amount of poetry and an even smaller number of first-rate poems, he stands as a major influence on the subsequent course of American poetry. As scholar, critic, and poet, Emerson was the first to define the distinctive qualities of American verse. His broad and exalted concept of the poet—as prophet, oracle, visionary, and seer—was shaped by his Romantic idealism. "I am more of a poet than anything else," he once wrote, although as much of his poetry is

Ralph Waldo Emerson
(Library of Congress)

found in his journals and essays as in the poems themselves. In *An Oration Delivered Before the Phi Beta Kappa Society, Cambridge* (1837; better known as *The American Scholar*), he called for a distinctive American poetry, and in his essay "The Poet," he provided the theoretical framework for American poetics. Scornful of imitation, he demanded freshness and originality from his verse, even though he did not always achieve in practice what he sought in theory. Rejecting the derivative verse of the Hartford wits and the sentimental versifiers of his day, he sought an original style and flavor for an American poetry close to the native grain. The form of his poetry was, as F. I. Carpenter argues (*Emerson Handbook*, 1953), the logical result of his insistence on self-reliance, while its content was shaped by his Romantic idealism. Thus his cumulative influence on American poetry is greater than his verse alone might imply.

Expression mattered more than form in poetry, according to Emerson. If he was not the completely inspirational poet called for in his essays, that may have been more a matter of temperament than of any flaw in his sense of the kind of poetry that a democratic culture would produce. In fact, his comments often closely parallel those of

Alexis de Tocqueville on the nature of poetry in America. Both men agreed that the poetry of a democratic culture would embrace the facts of ordinary experience rather than celebrate epic themes. It would be a poetry of enumeration rather than elevation, of fact rather than eloquence; indeed, the democratic poet would have to struggle for eloquence, for poetry of the commonplace can easily become flat or prosaic. Even Emerson's own best verse often seems uneven, with memorable lines interspersed with mediocre ones.

Part of the problem with Emerson's poetry arose from his methods of composition. Writing poetry was not for him a smooth, continuous act of composition, nor did he have a set formula for composition, as Edgar Allan Poe advocated in "The Philosophy of Composition." Instead, he trusted inspiration to allow the form of the poem to be determined by its subject matter. This "organic" theory of composition shapes many of Emerson's best poems, including "The Snow-Storm," "Hamatraya," "Days," and "Ode." These poems avoid a fixed metrical or stanzaic structure and allow the sense of each line to dictate its poetic form. Emerson clearly composed by the line rather than by the stanza or paragraph, in both his poetry and prose, and this self-contained quality often gives his work a gnomic or orphic tone.

Although some of his poems appear to be fragmentary, they are not unfinished. They lack smoothness or polish because Emerson was not a lyrical but a visionary, oracular poet. He valued poetry as a philosophy or attitude toward life rather than simply as a formal linguistic structure or an artistic form. "The poet is the sayer, the namer, and represents beauty," he observed in "The Poet." With Percy Bysshe Shelley he believed that the poet was the visionary who would make people whole and teach them to see anew. "Poets are thus liberating gods," Emerson concluded, because "they are free, and they make free." Poetry is simply the most concentrated expression of the poetic vision, which all people are capable of sharing.

Thus Emerson's poems seek to accomplish what the essays announce. His poems attempt to reestablish the primal relationship between humans and nature that he sought as a substitute for revelation. Emerson prized the poet as an innovator, a namer, and a language maker who could interpret the oracles of nature. In its derivation from nature, all language, he felt, was fossil poetry. "Always the seer is a sayer," he announced in his Harvard Divinity School address, and through the vision of the poet "we come to look at the world with new eyes."

Of the defects in Emerson's poetry, the chief is perhaps that Emerson's muse sees rather than sings. Because his lines are orphic and self-contained, they sometimes seem flat and discontinuous. Individual lines stand out in otherwise undistinguished poems. Nor do his lines always scan or flow smoothly, since Emerson was virtually tone-deaf. In "The Poet," he rejects fixed poetic form in favor of a freer, more open verse. For Emerson, democratic poetry would be composed with variable line and meter, with form subordinated to expression. The poet in a democracy is thus a "representative man," chanting the poetry of the common, the ordinary, and the low. Although Emerson pointed the way, it took Walt Whitman to master this new style of American poetry with his first edition of *Leaves of Grass* (1855), which Emerson promptly recognized and praised for its originality. Whitman thus became the poet whom Emerson had called for in *The American Scholar*; American poetry had come of age.

BIOGRAPHY

Born in Boston on May 25, 1803, Ralph Waldo Emerson was the second of five sons in the family of William Emerson and Ruth Emerson. His father was a noted Unitarian minister of old New England stock whose sudden death in 1811 left the family to struggle in genteel poverty. Although left without means, Emerson's mother and his aunt, Mary Moody Emerson, were energetic and resourceful women who managed to survive by taking in boarders, accepting the charity of relatives, and teaching their boys the New England values of thrift, hard work, and mutual assistance within the family. Frail as a child, Emerson attended Boston Latin School and Harvard, where he graduated without distinction in 1821. Since their mother was determined that her children would receive a decent education, each of her sons taught after graduation to help the others through school. Thus Emerson taught for several years at his brother's private school for women before he decided to enter divinity school. His family's high thinking and plain living taught young Emerson self-reliance and a deep respect for books and learning.

With his father and step-grandfather, the Reverend Ezra Ripley of Concord, as models, Emerson returned to Harvard to prepare for the ministry. After two years of intermittent study at the Divinity School, Emerson was licensed to preach in the Unitarian Church. He was forced to postpone further studies, however, and to travel south during the winter of 1826 because of poor health. The next two years saw him preaching occasionally and serving as a substitute pastor. One such call brought him to Concord, New Hampshire, where he met his future wife, Ellen Louisa Tucker. After his ordination in March, 1829, Emerson married Tucker and accepted a call as minister of the Second Church, Boston, where his father had also served. The position and salary were good, and Emerson was prepared to settle into a respectable career as a Boston Unitarian clergyman. Unfortunately his wife was frail, and within a year and a half, she died of tuberculosis. Grief-stricken, Emerson found it difficult to continue with his duties as pastor and resigned from the pulpit six months after his wife's death. Private doubts had assailed him, and he found he could no longer administer the Lord's Supper in good conscience. His congregation would not allow him to dispense with the rite, so his resignation was reluctantly accepted.

With a small settlement from his wife's legacy, he sailed for Europe in December, 1832, to regain his health and try to find a new vocation. During his winter in Italy, he admired the art treasures in Florence and Rome. There he met the American sculptor Horatio Greenough and the English writer Walter Savage Landor. The following spring, Emerson continued his tour through Switzerland and into France. Paris charmed him with its splendid museums and gardens, and he admired the natural history exhibits at the Jardin des Plantes. Crossing to England by August, he met Samuel Taylor Coleridge in London, then traveled north to visit Thomas Carlyle in Craigenputtock and William Wordsworth at Rydal Mount. His meeting with Carlyle resulted in a lifelong friendship.

After returning to Boston in 1833, Emerson gradually settled into a new routine of study, lecturing, and writing, filling an occasional pulpit on Sundays, and assembling ideas in his journals for his essay on "Nature." Lydia Jackson, a young woman from Plymouth, New Hampshire, heard Emerson preach in Boston and became infatuated with him. The young widower returned her admiration, although he frankly confessed that he felt none of the deep affection he had cherished for his first wife. During their engagement he renamed her "Lidian" in their correspondence because he disliked the name Lydia. She accepted the change without demur. Within a year, they were married and settled in a house on the Boston Post Road near the Old Manse of Grandfather Ripley. Emerson was now thirty-two and about to begin his life's work.

The next decade marked Emerson's intellectual maturity. *Nature* was completed and published as a small volume in 1836. In its elaborate series of correspondences between humans and nature, Emerson established the foundations of his idealistic philosophy. "Why should not we also enjoy an original relation to the universe?" he asked. Humans could seek revelations firsthand from nature, rather than having them handed down through tradition. A year later, Emerson gave an address before the Harvard Phi Beta Kappa Society, an event that Oliver Wendell Holmes later called "our intellectual Declaration of Independence." In his address, which is best known as *The American Scholar*, Emerson called for a distinctively American style of letters, free from European influences. Invited in 1838 to speak before the graduating class of Harvard Divinity School, Emerson affirmed in his address that the true measure of religion resided within the individual, not in institutional or historical Christianity. If everyone had equal access to the Divine Spirit, then inner experience was all that was needed to validate religious truth. For this daring pronouncement, he was attacked by Harvard President Andrews Norton and others for espousing "the latest form of infidelity." In a sense, each of these important essays was an extension of Emerson's basic doctrine of self-reliance, applied to philosophy, culture, and religion.

His self-reliance served him equally well in personal life, even as family losses haunted him, almost as if to test his hard-won equanimity and sense of purpose. Besides losing his first wife, Ellen, Emerson saw two of his brothers die and a third become so feeble-minded that he had to be institutionalized. Worst of all, his first-born and beloved son Waldo died in 1841 of scarlet fever at the age of six. Emerson's melioristic philosophy saw him through these losses, although in his journals he later chided himself for not feeling his son's death more deeply. Despite the hurt he felt, his New England reserve would not allow him to yield easily to grief or despair. Nor would he dwell in darkness while there was still light to be found.

During these years, Emerson found Concord a congenial home. He established a warm and stimulating circle of friends there and enjoyed the intellectual company of Nathaniel Hawthorne, Henry David Thoreau, and Bronson Alcott. As his fame as a lecturer and writer grew, he attracted a wider set of admirers, including Margaret Fuller, who often visited to share enthusiasms and transcendental conversations. Emerson even edited *The Dial* for a short time in 1842, but for the most part he remained aloof from, although sympathetic to, the transcendentalist movement that he had so largely inspired. His manner at times was even offhand. When asked for a definition of transcendentalism, he simply replied, "Idealism in 1842." When George Ripley invited him to join the Brook Farm Community in 1840, Emerson politely declined. Reform, he believed, had to begin with the individual. Thoreau later rebuked him for not taking a firmer stand on the fugitive slave issue, but Emerson was by nature apolitical and skeptical of partisan causes. His serenity was too hard-won to be sacrificed, no matter how worthy the cause.

So instead he continued to lecture and write, and his essays touched an entire generation of American writers. Thoreau, Whitman, and Emily Dickinson responded enthusiastically to the appeal of Emerson's thought, while even Hawthorne and Herman Melville, although rejecting it, still felt compelled to acknowledge his intellectual presence. Lecture tours took him repeatedly to the Midwest and to England and Scotland for a second time in 1847-1848. Harvard awarded him an honorary degree in 1866 and elected him overseer the following year. His alma mater also invited him to deliver a series of lectures on his philosophy in 1869-1870. When Emerson's home in Concord burned in 1877, friends sent him on a third visit to Europe and Egypt, accompanied by his daughter Ellen, while the house and study were rebuilt with funds from admirers. He spent his last few years in Concord quietly and died in the spring of 1882. Of his life, it can be said that perhaps more than any of his contemporaries, he embodied the qualities of the American spirit—its frankness, idealism, optimism, and self-confidence. For the American writer of his age, all things were possible. If, finally, he was as much prophet as poet, that may be because of the power of his vision as well as its lyrical intensity, a power that suffused his prose and was concentrated in his poems.

ANALYSIS

Ralph Waldo Emerson's poetic achievement is greater than the range of his individual poems might suggest. Although perhaps only a handful of his poems attain undisputed greatness, others are rich in implication despite their occasional lapses, saved by a memorable line or phrase. As a cultural critic and poetic innovator, moreover, Emerson has had an immense influence through his essays and poetry in suggesting an appropriate style and method for subsequent American poets. He tried to become the poet he called for in *The American Scholar*, and to a degree, his poems reflect those democratic precepts. Determined to find distinctively American art forms, he began with expression— not form—and evolved the forms of his poems through their expression. Inspired by the "organic aesthetic" of the American sculptor Horatio Greenough, whose studio in Rome he visited in 1833, Emerson abandoned traditional poetic structure for a loose iambic meter and a variable (though often octosyllabic) line. Instead of following a rigid external form, the poem would take its form from its particular content and expression. This was the freedom Emerson sought for a "democratic" poetry.

Emerson's best poetry is thus marked by two qualities: organic form and a vernacular style; his less successful pieces, such as "The Sphinx," are too often cryptic and diffuse. These strengths and weaknesses both derive from his attempt to unite philosophical ideas and lyricism within a symbolic form in which the image would evoke its deeper meaning. "I am born a poet," he wrote to his fiancé, Jackson, "of a low class without doubt, yet a poet. That is my vocation. My singing, to be sure, is very 'husky,' and is for the most part in prose. Still I am a poet in the sense of a perceiver and dear lover of the harmonies that are in the soul and in matter, and specially of the correspondence between these and those." Correspondence, then, is what Emerson sought in his poetry, based on his theory of language as intermediary between humans and nature.

In "The Poet," Emerson announced that "it is not metres, but metre-making argument that makes a poem." His representative American poet would be a namer and enumerator, not a rhymer or versifier. The poet would take his inspiration from the coarse vigor of American vernacular speech and in turn reinvigorate poetic language by tracing root metaphors back to their origins in ordinary experience. He would avoid stilted or artificial poetic diction in favor of ordinary speech. This meant sacrificing sound to sense, however, since Emerson's "metre-making arguments" were more often gnomic than lyrical. As a result, his poems are as spare as their native landscape. They are muted and understated rather than rhapsodic, and—with the exception of his Orientalism—tempered and homey in their subject matter, since Emerson was more of an innovator in style than in substance. Emerson's "Merlin" provides perhaps the best definition of what he sought in his poetry:

> Thy trivial harp will never please
> Or fill my craving ear;
> Its chords should ring as blows the breeze,
> Free, peremptory, clear.

Emerson's poems fall into several distinct categories, the most obvious being his nature poems; his philosophical or meditative poems, which often echo the essays; his autobiographical verse; and his occasional pieces. Sometimes these categories may overlap, but the "organic" aesthetic and colloquial tone mark them as distinctly Emersonian. Two of his most frequently anthologized pieces, "Days" and "The Snow-Storm," will serve to illustrate his poetic style.

"Days"

"Days" has been called the most perfect of Emerson's poems, and while there is a satisfying completeness about the poem, it resolves less than might appear at first reading. The poem deals with what was for Emerson the continuing problem of vocation or calling. How could he justify his apparent idleness in a work-oriented culture? "Days" thus contains something of a self-rebuke, cast in terms of an Oriental procession of Days, personified as daughters of Time, who pass through the poet's garden bringing various gifts, the riches of life, which the poet too hastily rejects in favor of a "few herbs and apples," emblematic of the contemplative life. The Day scorns his choice, presumably because he has squandered his time in contemplation rather than having measured his ambition against worthier goals. The Oriental imagery employed here transforms a commonplace theme into a memorable poem, although the poet never responds to the implied criticism of his life; nor does he identify the "morning wishes" that have been abandoned for the more sedate and domestic "herbs and apples," although these images do suggest meanings beyond themselves.

"The Problem"

A thematically related poem is "The Problem," in which Emerson tries to justify his reasons for leaving the ministry, which he respects and admires but cannot serve. Perhaps because he was more poet than priest, Emerson preferred the direct inspiration of the artist to the inherited truths of religion, or it may have been that, as a romantic, he found more inspiration in nature than in Scripture. The third stanza of "The Problem" contains one of the clearest articulations of Emerson's "organic" aesthetic, of form emerging from expression, in the image of the artist who "builded better than he knew." The temples of nature "art might obey, but not surpass."

"The Snow-Storm"

This organic theory of art reached its fullest expression in "The Snow-Storm," which still offers the best example in Emerson's poetry of form following function, and human artistry imitating that of nature. Here the poem merges with what it describes. The first stanza announces the arrival of the storm, and the second stanza evokes the "frolic architecture" of the snow and the human architectural forms that it anticipates. Nature freely creates and humans imitate through art. Wind and snow form myriad natural forms that humans can only "mimic in slow structures" of stone. As the wind-sculpted snowdrifts create beauty from the materials at hand, the poem rounds on itself in the poet's implicit admiration of nature's work.

"Hamatraya"

One of the most intriguing of Emerson's poems is "Hamatraya," which contains an attack on Yankee land-greed and acquisitiveness, cast as a Hindu meditation on the impermanence of all corporeal things. In "Hamatraya," the crass materialism of his countrymen evokes Emerson's serenely idealistic response. No one finally owns the land, he asserts, and to pretend so is to be deceived. The land will outlive successive masters, all of whom boast of owning it. In the enduring cycle of things, they are all finally returned to the earth they claimed to possess. Emerson uses dramatic form and the lyrical "Earth-Song" as an effective counterpoint to the blunt materialism of the first two stanzas. His theme of all things returning unto themselves finds its appropriate metaphor in the organic (and Hindu) cycle of life. Hindu cosmology and natural ecology complement each other in Emerson's critique of the pretensions of private land-ownership.

"BRAHMA"

Another of Emerson's Oriental poems, his popular "Brahma," is notable for its blend of Eastern and Western thought. Here Emerson assumes the perspective of God or Brahma in presenting his theme of the divine relativity and continuity of life. Just as Krishna, "the Red Slayer," and his victim are merged in the unity of Brahma, so all other opposites are reconciled in the ultimate unity of the universe. This paradoxical logic appealed to Emerson as a way of presenting his monistic philosophy in poetic terms. The poem owes much to Emerson's study of the *Bhagavadgītā* (c. 200 B.C.E.-200 C.E.; *The Bhagavad Gita*, 1785) and other Oriental scriptures, the first stanza of "Brahma" being in fact a close parallel to the Hindu text. The smooth regularity of Emerson's ballad stanzas also helps to offset the exotic quality of the Hindu allusions and the novelty of the poem's theme.

"URIEL"

Religious myth is also present in "Uriel," which Robert Frost called "the greatest Western poem yet." Even if Frost's praise is overstated, this is still one of Emerson's most profound and complex poems. Again it deals with the reconciliation of opposites, this time in the proposed relativity of good and evil. Borrowing the theme of the primal revolt against God by the rebellious archangels, Emerson uses the figure of the angel Uriel as the prototype of the advanced thinker misunderstood or rejected by others. Uriel represents the artist as the rebel or prophet bearing unwelcome words, roles that Emerson no doubt identified with himself and the hostile reception given *An Address Delivered Before the Senior Class in Divinity College, Cambridge . . .* (1838; better known as *The Divinity School Address*) by the Harvard theological faculty. Uriel's words, "Line in nature is not found;/ Unit and universe are round; In vain produced, all rays return;/ Evil will bless, and ice will burn," speak with particular force to the modern age, in which discoveries in theoretical physics and astronomy seem to have confirmed Emerson's intuitions about the relativity of matter and energy and the nature of the physical universe.

"EACH AND ALL"

Emerson's monistic philosophy also appears in "Each and All," in which the poem suggests that beauty cannot be divorced from its context or setting without losing part of its original appeal. The peasant, sparrow, seashell, and maid must each be appreciated in the proper aesthetic context, as part of a greater unity. Beauty cannot be possessed, Emerson argues, without destroying it. The theme of "Each and All" perhaps echoes section 3 on beauty of his essay *Nature*, in which Emerson observes that "the standard of beauty is the entire circuit of natural forms—the totality of nature. . . . Nothing is quite beautiful alone; nothing but is beautiful in the whole. A single object is only so far beautiful as it suggests this universal grace." The poem "Each and All" gives a more concentrated and lyrical expression to this apprehension of aesthetic unity. The poetic images lend grace and specificity to the philosophical concept of the beauty inherent in unity.

"GIVE ALL TO LOVE"

Emerson's fondness for paradoxical logic and the union of apparent opposites appears in yet another poem, "Give All to Love," which initially appears to falter on the contradiction between yielding to love and retaining one's individuality. The first three stanzas counsel a wholehearted surrender to the impulse of love, while the fourth stanza cautions the lover to remain "free as an Arab." The final two stanzas resolve this dilemma by affirming that the lovers may cherish joys apart without compromising their love for each other, since the purest love is that which is free from jealousy or possessiveness. Emerson reconciles the demands of love and those of self-reliance by idealizing the love relationship. Some commentators have even suggested that Emerson envisions a Neoplatonic ladder or hierarchy of love, from the Physical, to the Romantic, to the Ideal or Platonic—a relationship that in fact Emerson described in another poem titled "Initial, Daemonic, and Celestial Love"—but the theme of "Give All to Love" seems to be simply to love fully without surrendering one's ego or identity. The last two lines of the poem, "When half-gods go,/ The Gods arrive," are often quoted out of context because of their aphoristic quality.

"THRENODY"

A poem that has led some readers to charge Emerson with coldheartedness or lack of feeling is "Threnody," his lament for the loss of his beloved son Waldo, who died of scarlet fever at the age of six. Waldo, the first child of his second marriage, died suddenly in January, 1842. Emerson was devastated by grief, yet he seems in the poem to berate himself for his inability to sustain his grief. In his journals, Emerson freely expressed his bitterness and grief, and he gradually transcribed these feelings into the moving pastoral elegy for his son. "Threnody," literally a death-song or lamentation, contains a mixture of commonplace and idealized pastoral images that demonstrate Emerson's ability to work within classical conventions and to ameliorate his grief through his doctrine of compensation. Some of the most moving lines in the poem describe the speaker's recollection of the child's "daily haunts" and unused toys, although these realistic details are later muted by the pathetic fallacy of external nature joining the poet in mourning the loss of his son.

"THE RHODORA"

Emerson's muse most often turned to nature for inspiration, so it is no accident that his nature poems contain some of his best work. "The Rhodora" is an early poem in which Emerson's attention to sharp and precise details of his New England landscape stands out against his otherwise generalized and formal poetic style. The first eight lines of the poem, in which Emerson describes finding the rhodora, a northern azalea-like flower, blooming in the woods early in May of the New England spring, before other plants have put out their foliage, seem incomparably the best. Unfortunately, the second half of the poem shifts from specific nature imagery to a generalized homily on the beauty of the rhodora, cast in formal poetic diction. Here Emerson's impulse to draw moralistic lessons from nature reminds us of another famous early nineteenth century American poem, William Cullen Bryant's "To a Waterfowl." This division within "The Rhodora" illustrates some of Emerson's difficulties in breaking away from the outmoded style and conventions of eighteenth century English landscape poetry to find an appropriate vernacular style for American nature poetry. Here the subject matter is distinctly American, but the style— the poem's manner of seeing and feeling—is still partially derivative.

"THE HUMBLE BEE"

"The Humble Bee" is a more interesting poem in some respects, in that Emerson uses a form adequate to his expression—a tight octosyllabic line and rhymed couplets—to evoke through both sound and sense the meandering flight of the bumble bee. As the poem unfolds, the bee gradually becomes a figure for the poet intoxicated by nature. Some of the poem's conceits may seem quaint to modern taste, but "The Humble Bee" is innovative in its use of terse expression and symbolic form. Its style anticipates the elliptical language and abbreviated form of Dickinson's poetry.

"WOODNOTES"

"Woodnotes" is a long and somewhat prosy two-part narrative poem that appears to be extracted from Emerson's journals. Part 1 introduces the transcendental nature lover ("A Forest Seer") in terms perhaps reminiscent of Thoreau, and part 2 describes the reciprocal harmony between humans and nature, in which each is fully realized through the other. The vagueness of part 2 perhaps illustrates Emerson's difficulty in capturing transcendental rapture in specific poetic language.

"CONCORD HYMN"

"Ode" ("Inscribed to W. H. Channing") and "Concord Hymn" are both occasional poems that otherwise differ markedly in style and technique. "Concord Hymn" is a traditional patriotic poem in four ballad stanzas that Emerson composed to be sung at the placing of a stone obelisk on July 4, 1837, to commemorate the Battle of Concord, fought on April 19, 1775, on land later belonging to the Reverend Ezra Ripley. The lines of the first stanza, now so well known that they are part of American national folklore, demonstrate that Emerson could easily master traditional verse forms when he chose to do so:

> By the rude bridge that arched the flood,
> Their flag to April's breeze unfurled,
> Here once the embattled farmers stood,
> And fired the shot heard round the world.

The images of the "bridge" and the "flood" in the first stanza ripen imperceptibly into metaphor in the poem's implied theme that the Battle of Concord provided the impetus for the American Revolutionary War.

"ODE"

Emerson's "Ode" is a much more unconventional piece, written in terse, variable lines, usually of two or three stresses, and touching on the dominant social and political issues of the day—the Mexican War, the Fugitive Slave Law of 1850, the threat of secession in the South, and radical abolitionism in the North. This open form was perhaps best suited to Emerson's oracular style that aimed to leave a few memorable lines with the reader. His angry muse berates Daniel Webster for having compromised his principles by voting for the Fugitive Slave Law, and it denounces those materialistic interests, in both the North and the South, that would profit from wage or bond slavery. Emerson's lines "Things are in the saddle,/ And ride mankind" aptly express his misgivings about the drift of American affairs that seemed to be leading toward a civil war. His taut lines seem to chant their warning like a Greek chorus, foreseeing the inevitable but being helpless to intervene. By the 1850's Emerson had become an increasingly outspoken opponent of the Fugitive Slave Law, and on occasion risked his personal safety in speaking before hostile crowds.

LEGACY

Despite his commitment to a new American poetry based on common diction and ordinary speech, Emerson's poetry never quite fulfilled the promise of his call, in *The American Scholar* and "The Poet," for a new poetics. Emerson wanted to do for American poetry what Wordsworth had accomplished for English lyrical poetry, to free it from the constraints of an artificial and dead tradition of sensibility and feeling. However, he was not as consistent or as thoroughgoing a poetic innovator as the Wordsworth of the "Preface" to the second edition of *Lyrical Ballads* (1800), who both announced and carried out his proposed revision of the existing neoclassical poetic diction, nor did he apply his theory to his poetic composition as skillfully as Wordsworth did. Emerson could envision a new poetics but he could not sustain in his poetry a genuine American vernacular tradition. That had to wait for Whitman and Dickinson. Perhaps Emerson was too much the philosopher ever to realize fully the poetic innovations that he sought, but even with their flaws, his poems retain a freshness and vitality lacking in contemporaries such as Henry Wadsworth Longfellow and James Russell Lowell, who were probably more accomplished versifiers. Emerson's greatness resides in the originality of his vision of a future American poetry, free and distinct from European models. It can be found in the grace of his essays and the insights of his journals, and it appears in those select poems in which he was able to match vision and purpose, innovation and accomplishment. His "Saadi" was no less a poet for the restraint of his harp.

OTHER MAJOR WORKS

NONFICTION: *Nature*, 1836; *An Oration Delivered Before the Phi Beta Kappa Society, Cambridge*, 1837 (better known as *The American Scholar*); *An Address Delivered Before the Senior Class in Divinity College, Cambridge . . .* , 1838 (better known as *The Divinity School Address*); *Essays: First Series*, 1841; *Essays: Second Series*, 1844; *Orations, Lectures and Addresses*, 1844; *Addresses and Lectures*, 1849; *Representative Men: Seven Lectures*, 1850; *English Traits*, 1856; *The Conduct of Life*, 1860; *Representative of Life*, 1860; *Society and Solitude*, 1870; *Works and Days*, 1870; *Letters and Social Aims*, 1875; *Lectures and Biographical Sketches*, 1884; *Miscellanies*, 1884; *Natural History of Intellect*, 1893; *The Journals of Ralph Waldo Emerson*, 1909-1914 (10 volumes; E. W. Emerson and W. E. Forbes, editors); *The Letters of Ralph Waldo Emerson*, 1939 (6 volumes; Ralph L. Rusk, editor); *The Journals and Miscellaneous Notebooks*, 1960-1982 (16 volumes); *Emerson in His Journals*, 1982 (Joel Porte, editor); *Political Writings*, 2008 (Kenneth Sacks, editor).

EDITED TEXT: *Parnassus*, 1874.

MISCELLANEOUS: *Uncollected Writings: Essays, Addresses, Poems, Reviews, and Letters*, 1912.

BIBLIOGRAPHY

Bosco, Ronald A., and Joel Myerson, eds. *Ralph Waldo Emerson: A Documentary Volume*. Vol. 351 in *Dictionary of Literary Biography*. Detroit: Gale/ Cengage Learning, 2010. Provides primary source documents, including reviews and assessments, concerning Emerson and his works by contemporaries and by persons writing after his death.

Buell, Lawrence. *Emerson*. Cambridge, Mass.: Belknap Press, 2003. A thorough and admiring biography that presents Emerson as an international figure.

Gougeon, Len. *Emerson and Eros: The Making of a Cultural Hero*. Albany: State University of New York Press, 2009. Argues that, for Emerson, Eros is the essential cosmic force that joins humanity and the universe, and that Emerson's writings are filled with this dynamic spirit.

Myerson, Joel, ed. *A Historical Guide to Ralph Waldo Emerson*. New York: Oxford University Press, 2000. A collection of essays that provide an extended biographical study of Emerson. Later chapters study his concept of individualism, nature and natural science, religion, antislavery, and women's rights.

Porte, Joel, and Saundra Morris, eds. *The Cambridge Companion to Ralph Waldo Emerson*. New York: Cambridge University Press, 1999. Provides a critical introduction to Emerson's work through interpretations of his writing and analysis of his influence and cultural significance. Includes a comprehensive chronology and bibliography.

Schreiner, Samuel Agnew. *The Concord Quartet: Alcott, Emerson, Hawthorne, Thoreau, and the Friendship That Freed the American Mind*. Hoboken, N.J.: John Wiley & Sons, 2006. Examines the relationship among Emerson, Henry David Thoreau, Nathaniel Hawthorne, and Bronson Alcott. Sheds light on the mind behind Emerson's poetry.

Waynem, Tiffany K. *Critical Companion to Ralph Waldo Emerson: A Literary Reference to His Life and Work*. New York: Facts On File, 2010. Contains a biography of Emerson, an alphabetical list of his works, and a chronology.

York, Maurice, and Rick Spaulding. *Ralph Waldo Emerson: The Infinitude of the Private Man—A Biography*. Chicago: Wrightwood Press, 2008. A thorough biography with a chronology and selected bibliography. Describes the reaction of Emerson to Walt Whitman and his writing of "The Poet."

Andrew J. Angyal

BRENDAN GALVIN

Born: Everett, Massachusetts; October 20, 1938

OTHER LITERARY FORMS

Brendan Galvin has written critical articles on Theodore Roethke, a number of reviews, and the controversial essay "The Mumbling of Young Werther: Angst by Blueprint in Contemporary Poetry" (published in *Ploughshares* in 1978). He has also published several short stories. His translation of *Women of Trachis* by Sophocles appeared in 1998.

ACHIEVEMENTS

In Brendan Galvin's work, a hard-won accuracy of statement and description stands in place of fashionable "poetic" ambiguities. His writing makes that of most other poets seem sloppy and vague. Galvin wrestles a clarity from language that makes attempts to paraphrase his lines not only futile but also ridiculous. The experience of his poetry is in the language; the experience is the language. Fresh diction and imagery are his hallmark, as are highly imaginative yet precisely appropriate figures of speech.

Galvin has refined his gift for language in many ways. Denotative accuracy and connotative subtlety are reinforced by his finely tuned sense of rhythm and sound. His lines break cleanly, splitting where meaning divides or where hesitation is a necessary part of the reader's experience. Almost every feature of Galvin's craft is functional. In his disciplined poems, "free verse" is a solved riddle. Galvin has known what to do with this freedom; there is little chance of mistaking his work for prose broken up into lines.

Galvin seems to have a special territory that he has made his own and in which he has no rival among his contemporaries. His ability to bring his gifts to bear on rendering a close look at a particular object, especially a natural object (or process), is unparalleled in his time. He has fashioned a distinct poetic idiom, alternately tart and tender, for this task of giving his readers a new chance to see the natural world and to feel themselves in it.

Galvin has given such an alert and sensitive account of the region he knows best—the coastal Northeast and particularly Cape Cod—that it has become truly known and almost mythically real. The animals of the shore and sea, the birds above, the climate and landscape, the cultural temperature of the small New England town—these are Galvin's province, and his song is the perfect translation of its wide range of sensations into language. To his lyric achievements, he has added three book-length poems that assure his place as a major storyteller in verse. Galvin's achievement has been recognized by National Endowment for the Arts Fellowships (1974, 1988), a Guggenheim Fellowship (1988), the Sotheby Prize from the Arvon International Foundation (1988), the Levinson Prize from *Poetry* magazine (1989), the inaugural O. B. Hardison, Jr., Poetry Prize from the Folger Shakespeare Library (1991), and the Charity Randall Citation from the International Poetry Forum (1994). In 2005, *Habitat* was named a finalist for the National Book Award in Poetry. Galvin won the Aiken Taylor Award in Modern American Poetry from *Sewanee Review* in 2006 and the James Boatwright III Prize for Poetry from *Shenandoah* in 2008. In April, 2009, he received Boston College's Arts Council Alumni Award for Artistic Achievement.

BIOGRAPHY

Brendan James Galvin was born in the Boston suburb of Everett, Massachusetts, and has maintained a strong identification with the history and flavor of New England. He received a B.S. degree in natural science from Boston College in 1960; one finds evidence of the trained eye of the informed naturalist everywhere in his work. Shifting to English studies in graduate school, Galvin earned an M.A. from Northeastern University in 1964, where he also began his teaching career.

In 1965, Galvin enrolled in a course of study at the University of Massachusetts that would lead to an M.F.A. in creative writing in 1967 and a Ph.D. in 1970. Although he had dabbled in poetry since the late 1950's, it was only after 1964 that Galvin charged himself with the serious pursuit of poetic excellence. The early results were impressive;

he had two poems published in *The Atlantic Monthly* in 1965. Still, Galvin's published output was small until 1970, after which a creative explosion seems to have occurred.

The late 1960's were busy years, busy in ways that allowed for poetry to be germinated if not harvested in publication. In 1968, Galvin married Ellen Baer, and the couple has raised two children. A one-year position at Slippery Rock State College in Pennsylvania (1968-1969) would inevitably cause some temporary dislocation of sensibility for a man so attuned to the Massachusetts coast. With the 1969-1970 academic year, Galvin began his long association with Central Connecticut State College. The chance for settled employment and the completion of his doctoral work seems to have freed Galvin's energies. His dissertation, which involved a close reading of Roethke's poems through the lens of Kenneth Burke, was also a stimulus to Galvin's direction as a poet. Of the poets of his generation, Galvin is the heir apparent to Roethke as a precise and loving recorder of the natural world. Much of what Galvin records is the Cape Cod area, where his Irish immigrant grandfather settled, known to Galvin from childhood. It is there that he would spend some part of each year.

Galvin's first two collections were chapbooks published in limited editions. These slim volumes of the early 1970's introduced some of his recurring motifs: the country-city dichotomy, the close observation of nature, the pain of history, the ethos of the New England town or neighborhood, the entrance into fantasy or dream. Galvin's first full-length collection, *No Time for Good Reasons*, recapitulated and extended these interests and revealed Galvin to be a most inventive fashioner of imagery and figures of speech. The same year that this gathering of ten years' work was published, Galvin won a fellowship from the National Endowment for the Arts. By now a tenured professor at Central Connecticut, Galvin had made for himself a secure position as a poet-teacher-critic but only the beginning of a national reputation.

In 1975-1976, Galvin took over William Meredith's courses at Connecticut College in New London as a visiting professor. By the next year, his second major collection, *The Minutes No One Owns*, was receiving acclaim. In it, Galvin's voice and vision grew more distinctly his own, and his range of subjects grew broader.

Galvin hit full stride and wider recognition with his next two collections: *Atlantic Flyway* and *Winter Oysters* both received Pulitzer Prize nominations, the latter making the short list. *Seals in the Inner Harbor*, easily as strong a collection as the Pulitzer nominees, rounded out a miraculous period of steady achievement and continued Galvin's tendency toward a greater openness, a fuller release of personality, begun in the preceding book.

Wampanoag Traveler represents a change of pace. This is Galvin's first book-length poem, a sustained narrative-meditation in the form of fourteen letters by an imaginary eighteenth century naturalist, Loranzo Newcomb.

In the consolidating gesture of *Great Blue*, the map of Galvin's dedicated journey of more than twenty-five years revealed the highest promontory of achievement. However, many of Galvin's critics (Dave Smith, George Garrett, and Thomas Reiter are among the exceptions) have not known how to deal with this poet for whom words really matter and for whom nature is not merely an abstract idea or a stirring in the blood. In the volumes that followed through the 1990's, Galvin's art climbed from strength to strength. After retiring from his post at Central Connecticut State University, Galvin continued his prolific output, shuttling between visiting writer posts around the country and his home in Truro, Massachusetts.

ANALYSIS

Brendan Galvin's work has been called passionless. The charge is groundless but understandable. The human figure, the domestic drama, does not loom in the forefront of Galvin's work. That is not to say that his books are not peopled, but certainly he has given less attention to the themes of love, sex, family, and self than is customary. Galvin often treats nature, the town and city, and humankind in the aggregate. Moreover, much of his work on animals—birds in particular— seems to be at the expense of humans: Direct or implicit contrasts between human and animal life are made to humans' disadvantage—"no bird violates another/ with the inflections of small print."

For Galvin, humans are only one center of interest in the universe through which he moves, and not necessarily the most important one. Through Galvin's work, one comes to learn that there is a passion in beholding the rest of creation, that his acts of attention—whether the subject be a heron, a thunderstorm, or "The First Night of Fall" (from *Great Blue*)—are more than intellectual exercises. There is a passionate humility and what might be called a passionate objectivity. There is a passionate giving of the full resources of his art to something other than himself. There is a passion felt, by the alert reader, seeping through the pressure that would control it. There is a passion in the acts of language that so rarely stoop to the mere naming of passions. There is a passion that leads the thing observed and the observer to become intertwined: "A small event at a time,/ sleep comes to the weedy pond/ at the top of your mind." There is drama enough, too, in the small events that Galvin records so well. Small or large, the events to which he is attentive diminish, with sanity, the human ego: "I know the wind and more/ is beating down the centuries,/ and while I sit the tides go on/ rearranging the earth."

In three of Galvin's earlier books, there is a recurring character named Bear who is, one assumes, the more earthbound side of the poet's nature. Galvin's Bear is another version of the metaphor found in Delmore Schwartz's "The Heavy Bear Who Goes with Me," for while Schwartz seems only embarrassed and victimized by the body's clumsy pursuit of its appetites, Galvin has a friendly feeling toward the pull of the instinctual. He records, sympathetically, Bear's difficulties with artists, intellectuals, high-toned women, and all of the mind's subtleties. Bear seems to have the last word; something about him is more anchored in this world than in the world of abstraction, even while this world remains a mystery. Bear's senses do not fail him, but his mind gets in the way.

"THE ENVY OF INSTINCT"

In "The Envy of Instinct" (from *The Minutes No One Owns*), Galvin develops the theme of human beings' separation from the rest of nature, a theme that he never leaves for long. The poem begins with the speaker asking, "Earth, air, or water,/ which are we natural to?" The problem is that there is no easy answer. Is a steel and glass skyscraper a natural habitat for humans? The speaker is out running in his paltry human way, "one foot/ before another." It is as if this human running were not the real thing or were an activity that the human animal was not—or was no longer—fit for. The runner knows that before he reached this place "a deer clicked off/ the distance like a caliper." Such movement, he realizes, is true running.

Under the strain of this now unnatural exercise, the runner seems to break down into his more primitive animal parts:

> My heart beats red
> as the pouch
> of a horny frigate bird.
> My lungs are sponges
> working for more air.

The speaker wonders which of the many distinctions between humans and the lower orders is the crucial one: speech, perhaps, or the complexity of his nervous system. He is amazed at the freedom that the absence of reason allows. A bird he sees skimming along the shore "could go without reason/ to Venezuela tomorrow." By contrast, the complexity of human life is felt to be a series of unsatisfactory compromises, a collection of disparate and trivial indulgences of the mind.

The poem concludes with an earnest yet comic longing for "the energy ants save the world with." Galvin would store it up until he had enough of it to redirect natural history so that humanity became a properly subordinate phase, not a thing unto itself: "A decimal at a time, to carry off/ whole silos, nudging the origin/ of species my way."

"RUNNING"

In "Running (from *The Minutes No One Owns*), the speaker is reduced by exhaustion to the status of a mere physical presence. The keen celebrant of nature, observing while he runs, seems to be casting off his human difference and becoming suffused with the essential physicality of existence. One might think of Eugene O'Neill's *The Emperor Jones* (pr. 1921) turned into a true comedy. Galvin's skill at capturing this process is impressive: "By mile four/ I'm only the framework a breeze passes through." At the end of the run, there is a chant of victory in the blood, a half-silly song of belonging: ". . . my pulse begins its/ shorebird glossolalia. It says/ dowitcher coot yellow-legs/ brant bufflehead knot." The catalog of birds' names is a self-mocking description of the runner's delirium as well as that echo in the blood that joins him, for the moment, to his fellow creatures.

"THE WINTER RUNNER"

An earlier poem, "The Winter Runner" (from *No Time for Good Reasons*), gives the humans-in-nature interest a mythic dimension. This poem is told in the third person, depicting the runner (an American Indian, perhaps, or a hunter) as a small figure crossing a richly evocative terrain that changes constantly. There is no war between the mind and the body here, but rather a vital harmony. Galvin finds just the right words to bring mind and object together: "the low hills afterthoughts/ between the sky and sea." Looking over the runner's shoulder, the reader shares direct sensory experience: "the orange, thumbnail tip of sun/ and last fruits of day: eelgrass softening/ from tan to plum." This poem is distanced in a bygone golden age; even though the imagination can re-create it, such a state is an illusive goal for contemporary humans. That is Galvin's complaint.

ATLANTIC FLYWAY

Galvin's naturalist's eye and conservationist impulse in both theme and language are clearly visible in "Pitch Pines" from *Atlantic Flyway*. In "Pitch Pines," Galvin alludes to John Brereton (or Brierton) and Bartholomew Gosnold, two Englishmen who followed Giovanni Verrazano's path across the Atlantic and in May, 1602, founded a short-lived colony on an island off Cape Cod. Brereton's *A Briefe and True Relation of the Discouerie of the North Part of Virginia* (1602) is the record of that voyage. In imagining Brereton's view "from Bartholomew Gosnold's deck," Galvin reveals not only his growing interest in regional history but also his love of names. An opportunity to get the sounds of "Bartholomew Gosnold" into a poem is not to be missed. This historical interest is felt elsewhere in *Atlantic Flyway*: in "Homage to Henry Beston," in two poems about old maps, and, in terms of family, in the Irish American focus of "1847" and "Himself."

"Pitch Pines" begins by sketching the unpromising appearance of trees that are "blown one sided/ by winds salted out of the northeast." The unusual use of "salted" in this passage is characteristic of Galvin's spare diction, gaining richness through compression and suggestion. These pines are derelicts of trees, with "limbs flaking and dying/ to ribs, to antlers and spidery twigs,/ scaly plates slipping off the trunks." The sharp picture is accompanied by a sharpness of sounds: plosive consonants—*b, k, p, g, t,* and *d*—allowing the reader to hear the branches breaking and striking the ground. Nothing about the pitch pines is hopeful. They are "blamed for a history of cellar holes" and they "thin out by dropping sour needles/ on acid soil." Although the sound patterns are less aggressive here, one should note the high density of repeated sounds in these phrases: in "history of cellar holes" the bonding on *h, s, r,* and *l* sounds is accompanied by a pleasant modulation of vowels; in "dropping sour needles/ on acid soil" the *d, r, s,* and *l* links are carried along Galvin's movement up and down the vowel scale. Galvin's skillful manipulation of sounds and rhythms continues as he describes the result of the pines' pollination: "a shower/ that curdles water to a golden scum."

At this point, the poem's perspective becomes historical. Brereton, the reader is told, had known a Cape Cod "timbered to its shores/ with hardwoods." The demand for buildings and ships, however, began the process of denuding the cape. The swamp cedars were "split to shakes" or used for foundations "while sheep cropped/ elm and cherry sprouts/ and plows broke the cleancut fields." Birch, maple, elm, beech, and oak were all put to use as firewood for various enterprises, notably the iron and glass industries, "till the desert floundered/ out of the backlands and knocked/ on the rear door of towns." Only the ugly, useless pitch pines were left, unlikely survivors of the "brushfire" of progress.

"Pitch Pines" raises the question of the price of progress, but it does so in a way that avoids the usual harangue associated with such subjects. The facts, as Galvin selects and presents them, are left to speak for themselves, and they speak with an eloquence born of restraint. The tenacious pitch pines are a stunted note of hope; they remind readers that whatever they see around them in nature is what is left after the toll of humanity's actions has been taken. (One might compare this poem to Galvin's earlier "Ward's Grove," in which the rhetoric is more heated; the poem includes the splendid simile of "the oil derrick offshore like Triton's middle finger.")

Atlantic Flyway contains some of Galvin's most imaginative poems of small-town life. "Shoveling Out" and "Hometown" evoke a bracing nostalgia for the flavor of growing up in these comfortable places where a mixture of boredom and dread gives life a special balance: "we lived with that town/ like a man lives with a trick heart" ("Hometown"). Most of these poems of the small town, like much of Galvin's achievement, use the device of the catalog or inventory. Item by item, his strategic accumulation of telling details reaches out for a total vision: The parts are important, but the whole is more than their sum.

Galvin's vision of the small town is particularly clear in "Defending the Provinces." This poem begins with a contrast between the scale of city and town. The paralysis induced by the city's infinite range of choices is set against the security of the small town's confined and simpler patterns. Galvin presents the image of a man spinning around on a city street corner with a "shopping bag in each fist." His dizzying, anonymous dance (perhaps the bags are hiding liquor bottles) takes him "through all the compass points/ until he falls." The speaker may fall on the Main Street of his town, but this street only allows the choice of north or south, and the townspeople "know my name/ and drive me home."

Galvin then identifies the small-town ethos with the sixteenth century art of Pieter Brueghel (the elder), noted for his country landscapes and his renderings of peasant life and folk wisdom. The city's representative becomes Jackson Pollock, the nonrepresentational twentieth century artist noted for his frenzied canvases produced by dripping the paint and allowing for random effects.

Clearly enough, Galvin is no partisan of cities. As cultural meccas, he finds them sterile. As places for human interaction, he finds them lacking in human scale and warmth. If the values of a small town in New England are provincial, a defense of the provinces is one that he is willing to undertake. Still, he admits that the logic of the case is limited. There are certain, seemingly trivial, things that people simply "have to know" to appreciate the town—and if they know them, they do not need the argument. A brief catalog of the things one has to know includes: "You have to know/ what a Chrysler marine engine/ is doing in the Widow Wood's front yard." Knowing such things, one belongs; and belonging, after all, is what matters.

The poem goes on to celebrate, in an affectionately humorous vein, the provincial outlook itself. Readers hear how the townsfolk tout the good weather and excuse the bad, or even glorify it: "Next day, since it makes a good story, we will say/ we saw minnows swimming in roadside puddles." Galvin gives his readers a special brand of boosterism, talking about "skies the color of Boy Scout Troops" in a way the Chamber of Commerce people would if only they could. He asks readers to join him in writing the president, requesting the evacuation of "the Big Apple" so that it can be planted with kudzu. Then all Americans, including the lost city-dwellers, can make a return to the small town. Here, cleansed and ready to experience provincial epiphanies, they will be able to see and relate how "one star/ over the bay seemed to move closer."

No Time for Good Reasons

Galvin's poetry of place is not only a poetry of landscape and nature description; it is also a poetry of community. In *No Time for Good Reasons*, Galvin presents uncannily accurate slices of small-town life in poems such as "Rookie's Place" and "Stealing the Christmas Greens." The reader who attends to this group of poems—"The Paper Route" and "Assembling a Street" are others—will find a large cast of small-town characters and a judicious selection of scenes and events presented with loving patience. In many of these poems, Galvin asserts or suggests the special kind of shared knowledge that defines a community and that outsiders can only misunderstand or patronize.

The Minutes No One Owns

From *The Minutes No One Owns*, "Jumping the Grave-Sized Hole" not only presents Galvin's characteristic social archaeology of the New England town but also presents the problem of the outsider—summer people, progress, and suburbanization—that threatens the bonds of time-won intimacies and thus the essence of the town. While Galvin's impulse is to value and protect that sense of community, he realizes that the other side of closeness is closed-ness, the easy falling into small-mindedness and prejudice. "Them" deals with those others, the minorities who remain strangers even within the town itself.

WINTER OYSTERS AND SEALS IN THE INNER HARBOR

Poems such as "August," "General Confession of the Ex-King of Hamburg," and "Mrs. McCandless" (all from *Winter Oysters*) reveal Galvin's ability to etch the contrasting values and styles of native and summer people, intrusions of progress, and the carefully balanced sense of community. "Rural Mailboxes" (from *Seals in the Inner Harbor*) expresses once again Galvin's understanding of the mixed private and public identities of small-town New England life as he imagines the "tinny speech" that spreads gossip among the isolated icons of privacy.

Each of these poems combines the wit, bite, and tenderness that so often mate in Galvin's work, although the proportions change from poem to poem. Almost every line suggests more than it literally says, but there is never a loss of clarity. The closed range of experience in Galvin's small towns allows people some sense of mastery over their condition that is lacking in city life. They can develop reliable habits that will serve them almost as well as instinct serves the creatures of the sky and sea that Galvin has studied so carefully. The journey of the mind in a poem such as "The Old Trip by Dream Train" (from *Atlantic Flyway*) is reminiscent of Galvin's treatment of the migratory patterns and the homing instincts of birds, a subject that occupies his attention in many poems. The seeming freedom of birds' flight, the majestic range, however, is another matter. In "The Migrants" and "The Birds" (from *The Strength of a Named Thing*), Galvin provides a humbling perspective too often masked by people's homocentric habits of mind. In "Transmigration" (from *Winter Oysters*), one of Galvin's most ambitious poems, that dream of birds' flight is imaginatively realized.

Galvin's largely successful search for clarity is a difficult enterprise. The songs he sings and the songs he echoes are songs that everyone needs to relearn. In part, the resourceful poet works like the title creature in "The Mockingbird" (from *Winter Oysters*), who knows that when "the voices fill you,/ you must say nothing wrong,/ but follow them back/ through the day, going phrase/ by phrase over hills. . . ." Over the years and through his many poems and collections, Galvin has been slowly putting together a viable myth: The myth of a vigorous, inspiring, forgiving world in which people may be permitted to thrive if they behave honorably and respectfully. However, in Galvin's work, this myth does not seem like a pagan dream, an impossible return to a version of humanity in a nature that never was. Galvin leads the reader to feel fully engaged and ready to carry that energy of engagement out of the poems and back to the world, having fitted the lens of Galvin's vision to his eye.

GREAT BLUE

The general direction of Galvin's career may be reflected in the general pattern of *Great Blue*. The progress of the poems here is from sky to sea to land, and from humans as social, historical, and economic creatures to explorations of the individual psyche. A pivotal poem in this progress is "Seals in the Inner Harbor" (which first appeared in the volume of the same name), in which a comprehensive vision of the connectedness of things is economically, powerfully, and yet gently and humorously, evoked. There is another progression as well: a progress of shifting genre emphasis from lyric to meditative-narrative to dramatic.

SAINTS IN THEIR OX-HIDE BOAT

In fact, Galvin's next effort after *Great Blue* is a book-length poem (his second), at once narrative and dramatic. *Saints in Their Ox-Hide Boat* deepens Galvin's penetration into his Irish roots as he gives voice to the exploits of his sixth-century namesake, Brendan the Navigator. Informed by history but in no way shackled by it, Galvin creates the characters of Saint Brendan and his monks, voicing the physical hardships of their journey, imagining their meditations on humanity's relationship to God, conjuring the hallucinations fostered by their long and hazardous voyage. Alternately pious and playful, this story in verse once again shows Galvin's mastery of a vigorous and rigorous poetic diction that is never merely or falsely poetic.

HOTEL MALABAR

Just as ambitious, though different in almost every other way, is *Hotel Malabar*. Conveyed through several first-person narrators, this novel in verse mixes espionage and contemporary history in a dark vision of late twentieth century America. Galvin examines the corruption and deceit that underpin imperialist intentions.

SKY AND ISLAND LIGHT

Sky and Island Light brings readers once again the Galvin who is a master at evocation of place. Ireland, the Outer Hebrides, the Orkneys, the Shetland Islands, and familiar Cape Cod are the main locales that his artistry first inhabits, then reveals. Perhaps as a consequence of his own aging, many of these poems deal with time's passage and with loss. However, the pulse of life and the joy of beholding is everywhere, as is the characteristic firmness of diction and felt form.

THE STRENGTH OF A NAMED THING

In *The Strength of a Named Thing*, Galvin mostly stays at home, doing what he does best. The title of this collection suggests it all: Named things are Galvin's meat, and the names themselves are his seasoning. The essential human project of naming things that lies behind the earliest speech is the miracle that poets endlessly celebrate. Crows, bats, slugs, scallops, fish, birds of all sorts, shifts in light, shades of weather, increments of seasons, vegetation, geological features, these are the subjects or supporting details of Galvin's most distinctive poems. Humans are a part of all this—but only a part. Galvin's poetry helps one to know this, to feel it to be true. One learns, as the subjects of "Young Owls" do, "how nothing in this world/ gets out of its life alive." Readers are led to bless this gift of life that they share: "You could be/ the least tern who plucks/ the edge of the sea's potlatch,/ or the egret in its pool/ like your spirit's sudden cry at sloughed confusion" ("The Birds"). In the clear beholding that Galvin's art provides, an interchange takes place and people's crippling separateness vanishes.

PLACE KEEPERS

In *Place Keepers*, as in many of Galvin's later volumes of poetry, he retains his interest in his previous subjects, yet allows his imagination to move ever outward. In "May Day," the love poem that opens the volume, the goldfinches and other birds arriving for another New England spring remind the poet and his wife, Ellen, that "it takes/ two of anything for something to happen." "The Gang from Ballyloskey" returns to his Irish origins. "Cold Water Elegy," a dream poem, vividly conjures local boatwright Avery Bearse, long renowned for his craftsmanship; "The Blue Woods" chronicles the poet's at-a-distance checkout-line encounter with a woman who once dived "through my hands like silk" in a skinny-dip pond. These and other poems in *Place Keepers* possess the same precision and inventiveness that marked earlier phases of his career; indeed, Galvin endows the themes he revisits with an inexhaustible variety, making them new again. In some entries, he moves toward a more playful, expansive voice. For example, "The Potatoes Have a Word to Say" endows tubers with a voice that describes their own subterranean transformations and boasts that "we can be multiplied/ by anyone, prepared more ways than bread./ You are tired of living when you're tired of us." A sense of joy and exhilaration pervades the book. In "Listening to the Courtship Delirium of the Great Horned Owls," the owls' calls lead the poet to his own musings on "Love":

> Those old Greeks had it wrong:
>
> to never have been at all, that would be worst,
> to have missed these moments that arrived
> unbidden merely because we were here,
> never to have woven a lifetime of these
> momentary joys into a life.

"Winter Stars," another poem for the poet's wife, anticipates the changes that winter will bring to the landscape they inhabit when the tourists are "dragged/ back under the weight of ambition/ that presses down on cities" and the pair becomes "the only light keepers/ on our square mile of the planet." If the alterations bring a welcome sense of relief—"no need for reservations when/ Orion climbs farther away from the bleeping// inane, the blather of honchos inventing/ themselves on cell phones"—an otherworldly sense of wonder also pervades the poem: "Starlight. Silence./ Our thirty-five years under winter stars together."

"Testament," the last poem of *Place Keepers*, reveals the poet's resolve to continue rendering the natural world with his own unique vision and language, to "keep shoving these fists/ full of sickle asters into your face," anticipating the objections of resistant listeners and readers, even as he provides them with something they cannot get anywhere else: "Nothing/ I can tell you will fatten your checking account,/ and there's nothing here to lionize. There's only/ unpretending life, present and accounted for,/ the cerulean warbler's brittle stance a moment/ on the railing, intrepid for the run to Ecuador." Here as elsewhere, the lives Galvin brings to the page continue to deepen and enrich those of others.

HABITAT

Habitat joins eighteen new poems with many of the finest poems written throughout Galvin's career. The volumes prior to 1990 have been culled more severely than for *Great Blue* to make room for the work from his four subsequent volumes, but the most recent poems never disappoint. Even as Galvin maintains an interest in his previous subjects, his imagination moves ever outward, in works as diverse as *Saints in Their Ox-Hide Boat* and "Captain Teabag and the Wellfleet Witches." Poems such as "Pondycherry," "Pococurante," and "Nimblejacks," give free play to associational language, as the poet delights in exhausting his own ingenuity. As *Habitat* demonstrates, Galvin continues to turn a practiced naturalist's eye and a conservationist impulse on the world around him. Among the newest poems, "Riffing Deciduous" trains his practiced naturalist's eye on the color of autumn trees: "not red/ but its modulations: solferino, murrey,// minium, not yellow but vitelline and those/ others nameless as the obscurer insects." In "A Few Local Names for the Double-Crested Cormorant," the poet takes an inventive joy in describing a bird that most locals consider a nuisance. In another new poem, "For the Raven's Return," the poet calls on the old sailors who live in his dreams for guidance in invoking and welcoming the bird: "Out of everything/ eastbound from Long Gone . . . it's you we need most" to set right a world that seems almost hopelessly, even comically, out of kilter: "From gilded perches in the capitols, our representatives/ sing the lobbyists' tunes." However, the speaker's supplication finds a new urgency in the poem's closing lines:

> Make of these trees taking our cornfields back
> your great hall again. Dumpsters multiply
> for you across the land; inside the hollow steeples
> of churches, the cell phone towers grow taller,
> reaching for that year when no one will stand
> in silence alone without punching the numbers in
> when no one will hanker to crack their wings
> and fly around cronking.

Other new poems capture the spirit of place through adept and entertaining sketches of local, small-town characters. "Ploesti" tells the story of the poet's uncle Red

McHugh, a World War II veteran and former police officer who is summarily dismissed from an assisted-living facility for senior citizens after attacking his roommate for endlessly whistling. A similar poem, "Byrum Between the Headphones," takes on the voice of a veteran who scavenges the beaches with a metal detector, searching for others' losses: "whatever/ puts the frosting on my Navy pension." As in his earlier works, Galvin remains a patient listener, on intimate terms with the universe, occasionally addressing its citizens directly: "A Warning to the Comet Hyakutake about the Olafsen Brothers" aptly brings together the natural world and the "alleged" carpenters who installed the poet's skylight.

Galvin's firm foothold in the natural world has allowed him to explore, better than any other contemporary American poet, what it means to be truly human. "A Cold Bell Ringing in the East" describes waking "to the full moon just pulling away/ from the skylight's pine." Here he clarifies his stance, separating himself not only from poets who would envy the moon's light but also from anyone who sees nature as something that can be bought and sold: "What joy in having been at all,/ in feeding the fire and knowing/ that everything isn't about us." Thus the poet praises the glory of humanness, the ability to see "where a deer/ is first air, then color of dusk/ in scrub, then dusk itself,/with its air of invisible mending."

OTHER MAJOR WORK

TRANSLATION: *Women of Trachis*, 1998 (of Sophocles).

BIBLIOGRAPHY

Barber, David. "Natural Wonder." *Boston Globe*, December 14, 2008. Includes a good synopsis of Galvin's later poems.

Callahan, Mary. "Singing What's Out There." *Boston College Magazine* 47 (Winter, 1988): 37-41. This personality profile offers material on Galvin's schooling, his work habits, and his inspirations and prejudices. Galvin admits proudly to consulting reference books to indulge his passion for accuracy. He believes in a poet's need for obsessions. Galvin's own "How I Wrote It" follows, with commentaries on the creative process behind four of his poems.

Christina, Martha, ed. *Outer Life: The Poetry of Brendan Galvin*. Bristol, R.I.: Ampersand Press, 1991. This first collection of essays on Galvin's work is remarkable for the high standard of critical prose and critical insight. Contributors include Thomas Reiter (on *Wampanoag Traveler*), Peter Makuck, and Neal Bowers. The latter's "Outside In: Brendan Galvin's Poetry" views Galvin's work as a precursor to the New Formalism in its attempt to avoid "an absurd self-involvement." Bowers uses New England countryman Robert Frost as a foil to highlight Galvin's temperament and method.

Collins, Floyd. "The Image in Recent American Poetry." *Gettysburg Review* 3, no. 4

(Autumn, 1990): 686-704. Places Galvin's work within the context of contemporary American poetry and includes an excellent discussion of *Great Blue*.

Galvin, Brendan. "A Conversation with Brendan Galvin." Interview by Philip Paradis. *Tar River Poetry* 27 (Fall, 1987): 1-12. This interview begins with comments on the proper (and improper) relationship between poet and critic, then goes on to explore the importance of the image to the genesis and texture of Galvin's poems. Paradis has Galvin describe his writing habits, his attitude regarding poetic diction, and the influence of other poets on his own development. The interview reveals Galvin's commitment to a writing life unencumbered by theory, fashion, or coterie.

Garrett, George. "This Business of Getting the World Right: The Poetry of Brendan Galvin." *Three Rivers Poetry Journal* 19-20 (1982): 7-18. This engaging appreciation presents important biographical material and includes Galvin's own comments elicited by interview. Garrett stresses Galvin's integrity and helps readers to find the poet in the work. He considers the ways in which "the discipline, method, and the language of the sciences" combine in Galvin's art.

Kitchen, Judith. "Simplicities." *Georgia Review* 52, no. 2 (Summer, 1998): 341-361. Part of this omnibus review attends to Galvin's *Sky and Island Light*, making an excellent case for Galvin's importance as a writer who can place intensely observed natural detail in the context of human history so that one informs the other. A fine appreciation not only of this book's virtues but also of Galvin's work as a whole.

Makuck, Peter. "Brendan Galvin's Sense of Otherness." *Sewanee Review* 117, no. 4 (Fall, 2009): 611-627. An excellent overview of Galvin's work.

_____. "Galvin's Outer Reaches." *Texas Review* 8 (Fall/Winter, 1987): 38-58. This comprehensive overview pays special attention to Galvin's humor, his love of the odd word, and his attachment to marginalized people (victims, immigrants). Makuck explores the design and coherence of several collections, tracing how the poet has set increasingly greater risks for himself. These include the movement toward formal sequences and long, even book-length, poems, as well as the imaginative re-creation of the past.

Smith, R. T. "The Light Through the Trees." In *Spreading the Word: Editors on Poetry*, edited by Stephen Corey and Warren Slesinger. Columbia, S.C.: Bench Press, 2001. Smith writes about the features of a particular poem, "May Day," and what led him to choose it for an issue of *Shenandoah*. Smith attends to the poem's imagery, its quality of observation, its "rich ambivalence," and its formal virtuosity. A fine appreciation of a representative Galvin poem.

Philip K. Jason
Updated by Caroline Collins

EAMON GRENNAN

Born: Dublin, Ireland; November 13, 1941

PRINCIPAL POETRY

Wildly for Days, 1983
What Light There Is, 1987
Cat Scat, 1988
Twelve Poems, 1988
As if It Matters, 1991
So It Goes, 1995
Relations: New and Selected Poems, 1998
Provincetown Sketches, 2000
Selected and New Poems, 2000
Still Life with Waterfall, 2002
Renvyle, Winter, 2003
The Quick of It, 2005
Out of Breath, 2007
Matter of Fact, 2008
Out of Sight: New and Selected Poems, 2010

OTHER LITERARY FORMS

Although Eamon Grennan (GREH-nahn) is celebrated principally for his poetry collections, he also is a respected critic and translator of Irish poetry. He has written reviews for *Dublin Magazine*, *Irish Times*, *Poetry Ireland Review*, *Poetry London*, *The New Republic*, and the *Times Literary Supplement* on various topics, including new Irish writing, the plays of George Fitzmaurice, medieval Irish lyrics, James Joyce, and Irish poetry since Patrick Kavanagh. He has penned a major work on Irish poetry in the twentieth century and translated several important poetic works.

ACHIEVEMENTS

Eamon Grennan is recognized by many fellow poets for his uncanny constructions of bicultural, international poetic works. In 2003, he received the Lenore Marshall Poetry Prize for his *Still Life with Waterfall*. Commenting on the award, poet Robert Wrigley referred to Grennan's ability to reward the reader by means of clarification across international and cultural barriers. Grennan also received the PEN Award for Poetry in Translation (1997), for *Selected Poems of Giacomo Leopardi* (1995). Leopardi is widely considered as the greatest lyric poet in the Italian literary tradition. Grennan is cited for his unique ability to translate Leopardi's work into a modern English form that exactly mimics the original intonation. Grennan has also received the James Boatwright III Prize for Poetry (1995) and Pushcart Prizes (1997, 2001, 2002, 2005), and "The Curve" was included in *The Best American Poetry, 2006*, edited by Billy Collins and David Lehman. He has made many personal appearances at poetic events, including the Writers Institute on March 13, 1997, for a Commemoration of the Irish Famine and Celebration of Irish Literature with Peter Quinn.

BIOGRAPHY

Eamon Grennan was born in Dublin in 1941. He attended a boarding school in a Cistercian monastery. He did his undergraduate studies at University College in Dublin, where he became acquainted with fellow poets Derek Mahon and Eavan Boland. Afterward, he spent one year in Rome before coming to the United States in 1964. He earned his doctoral degree at Harvard. In 1974, he became the Dexter M. Ferry, Jr., Professor of English at Vassar College, and remained in that position until his retirement in 2004.

Grennan published *Wildly for Days*, his first collection of poems, in 1983. He has a long and distinguished record of publications and is known for his attention to the lyrical and cerebral qualities of his works. Former U.S. poet laureate Collins has remarked on Grennan's generous, telluric, and sensual works, which deal openly and compassionately with the complexity of being human.

Grennan has settled in the United States but returns frequently to Ireland. Like his poetry, he shares components of both cultures, often blending American experience with Irish recollection. He twice returned to Ireland for limited periods, in 1977 and 1981. It was in Ireland that he began writing poetry, and he states that Gaelic poetry became a dominant force in his need to produce poems that echo this unique linguistic sound. Grennan embraces his status of alien resident in the United States, stating that he prefers to live at a distance from the land he occupies, as this gives his work an angle that cannot otherwise be achieved.

ANALYSIS

Eamon Grennan writes of a magical world that lies before the eyes of all his readers—the natural world of bugs, bees, deer, wind, dolphins, dunes, waves, and any other element in nature he chooses. He does so in a manner that interweaves a natural sensuality with the eroticism of humans and in nature. His poems combine his native and adopted lands, Ireland and the United States. His intimate descriptions of the occupants with whom all people share Earth are presented through a sort of memory looking-glass that views his world through his unique form of "bilingual" English.

Grennan leads the reader of his poems down a verbal and poetic nature trail that not only winds its way through the intricate lives of insects and animals and through earth and light, but also brings the reader face-to-face with the complexity of human nature and experience. The organic world he describes is seldom tranquil. His observations often remind the reader of the brutal realities that exist in the natural world. To the natural world, he juxtaposes the parallel human world, especially the erotic one, which is also sublime, but full of challenge, decay, and erosion. Whether Grennan speaks of the thick and frosty light that illuminates Cobble Bay, the lethal radiance of an errant star, or a dead otter rotting by the tide line, he sheds light on the human world and people's lives much as an inspirational sunrise lights up one's soul. That is, his poems illuminate people's lives by confirming the profound beauty and brutal reality of a world people often overlook. Grennan describes with sincere reverence the spirituality embedded in the natural world.

AS IF IT MATTERS

In *As if It Matters*, Grennan demonstrates the interconnectedness between the human realm and the natural world. The often violent human interaction with nature is asserted in his memory of the simple and subtle act of a friend chopping wood. The friend finds a sense of freedom in the act, but the tree, so violently split apart in providing the wood, is just one of various examples in this collection that point out the often tragic consequences of human domination of the natural world. Other poems reflect on how nature also participates, without regret, in the ongoing destruction of self and others that is the final and unavoidable means of balancing out day-to-day existence on earth. These poems of first-person meditations are often shrouded in references to various forms of light, wind, rain, flames, and vividly contrasted colors. In "Endangered Species," this mixture of elements from the natural environment mingles with the stark human gaze on that world. Typical of Grennan's works, it draws on seemingly unconscious human observation of an equally indifferent plant, animal, and climatological realm. Although the almost endless references to untold utopian happenings tend to blur Grennan's decisive descriptions, the poems are masterfully insightful.

STILL LIFE WITH WATERFALL

In *Still Life with Waterfall*, Grennan successfully combines astute comments on personal moments of love with an almost erotic gaze on the seemingly least important acts that occur within nature. He subtly links the love and necessity of human existence with the unconsciousness of nature and, by analogy, sheds light on people's unrealized connectivity with the natural world in which they live. The poems weave together a realm of frost, fire, marshland, tangled branches, and animal sounds (both gentle and alarming), and the interplay of predator and prey with human reality. In "Detail," the man hunting is juxtaposed to the hawk that simply snatches the robin in flight. Both acts, seemingly harsh, are presented as uncomplicated realities within the natural environment of humans and animals. The human becomes less human and, somehow, more natural. Grennan takes the reader to a point where trivial moments such as the nearly unheard hatching of bird eggs or the intimate gaze of a deer that looks for a reason to run become fused with human observation (in "Grid"). The poet filters these glimpses of reality with his bicultural and individual viewpoint and leaves the reader with a new way of integrating the outer world in which people live with the inner world that all people possess.

RELATIONS

In *Relations*, which collects poems from earlier volumes and presents new poems written between 1993 and 1995, the poet continues his observations of the analogy between human existence and that of the other realms of the planet: the flora, fauna, land, and climate of Earth. His words reflect a lifetime of scrutinizing the physical world. He infuses this surveillance of life's minor events with remarkable meaning. For example, in "Compass Reading," his description of a cat contemplating the slow death of its victim leads the reader to a very human analogy, that is, our own mortality. In this collection, Grennan includes many poems that examine human love in its more basic and physical forms. His reflection on the girl who remains in his memory by means of her connectedness with nature and physical love draws a powerful response from the reader. In "Muse, Maybe," he presents visions of the girl who was kissed in a graveyard, her warm skin beneath a raincoat, a woman of shadows and half-lights who is worn like a mask in his mind. The natural world of light, darkness, rain, and inevitable death is one of Grennan's most repeated themes. The poet remains faithful to his personal gazes of nature that reveal his inner self, and ours. For example, in "Swifts over Dublin," the swifts that twist, kiss, and soar are seen with human delight. Nonetheless, their cavorting in the full flush of summer is beyond the author's real-time life. They bring awareness of the human yearning for the eternal moment. This is a remarkable collection of poems that invite the reader to look within by means of lucidly presented examinations of the least remarkable events within the natural world.

OTHER MAJOR WORK

NONFICTION: *Facing the Music: Irish Poetry in the Twentieth Century*, 1999.

TRANSLATIONS: *Selected Poems of Giacomo Leopardi*, 1995; *Oedipus at Colonus*, 2004 (with Rachel Kitzinger; of Sophocles).

BIBLIOGRAPHY

Baker, Timothy. "'Something Secret and Still': Silence in the Poetry of Eamon Grennan." *Mosaic* 42, no. 4 (December, 2009): 45-63. Compares Grennan to Yves Bonnefoy and examines how his poetry "reveals the world through notions of silence and absence."

Boran, Pat. *Flowing, Still: Irish Poets on Irish Poetry*. Syracuse, N.Y.: Dedalus Press, 2009. The introduction presents a thoughtful and well-organized overview of Irish poets and poetry. It is quite useful for understanding the place of Irish poetry in the modern world. Grennan's section, "That Blank Mouth: Secrecy, Shibboleths, and Silence in Northern Irish Poetry," gives the reader insight into his unique ability to present the ordinary as extraordinary. Includes bibliographical references and index.

Brophy, James D. *Contemporary Irish Writing*. Boston: Twayne, 1983. The section by Grennan, "That Always Raised Voice," presents his own description of the poet's personal presence in his works. Contains a general review of modern Irish poetry and prose. Includes an extensive bibliography.

Fleming, Deborah. "The Common Ground of Eamon Grennan." *Éire-Ireland* 28, no. 4 (Winter, 1993): 133-149. Discusses Grennan's simple but profound approach to poetry that involves linking the natural world to that of human experience and aspiration. The viewpoint presented is distinctly Irish.

Greening, John. Review of *Selected and New Poems*. *Times Literary Supplement*, April 13, 2001. Gives the reader a brief but interesting review of Grennan's *Selected and New Poems*.

Grennan, Eamon. "When Language Fails." Interview by William Walsh. *Kenyon Review* 28, no. 3 (Summer, 2006): 125-141. Grennan talks about the craft of poetry and how living abroad has affected him.

Hacht, Anne Marie, and David Kelly, eds. *Poetry for Students*. Vol. 21. Detroit: Thomson/Gale, 2005. Analyzes Grennan's "Station," about leaving his son at the station. Contains the poem, summary, themes, style, historical context, critical overview, and criticism. Includes bibliography and index.

Johnston, Fred. Review of *So It Goes*. *Irish Times*, February 17, 1996, p. 9. Presents an insightful review. Again, the viewpoint is from Ireland, but the international mixture of Irish and American experience is examined.

Kenneally, Michael. *Poetry in Contemporary Irish Literature*. Gerrards Cross, Buckinghamshire, England: Colin Smythe, 1995. Grennan's segment, "Foreign Relations: Irish and International Poetry," explores the international and intercultural approach that he uses in much of his poetry. The introduction to the book provides an overview of modern Irish poetry. Includes bibliography and index.

Paul Siegrist

JOHN MEADE HAINES

Born: Norfolk, Virginia; June 29, 1924
Also known as: John Haines

OTHER LITERARY FORMS

Though his primary medium has been poetry, John Meade Haines has published several books of prose, three of them substantial works of nonfiction. *Living off the Country: Essays on Poetry and Place* (1981) collects writing about Alaska and the wilderness, poets and poetry, a long interview, and autobiographical sketches. *The Stars, the Snow, the Fire: Twenty-five Years in the Northern Wilderness—A Memoir* (1989) collects eighteen essays about aspects of life in hunting, trapping, foraging, exploring, and dwelling in a cabin. *Fables and Distances: New and Selected Essays* (1996) collects letters to journal editors, plus essays about literature, nature, living in the wilderness, and an interview.

ACHIEVEMENTS

John Meade Haines has won many awards for his poetry, largely in recognition of his focus on nature, humanity's relationship to the natural world, and social justice. These honors include two Guggenheim Foundation Fellowships (1965, 1984), a National Endowment for the Arts Fellowship (1967), an Amy Lowell Scholarship (1976-1977), the Alice Fay di Castagnola Prize, an Ingram Merrill Foundation Grant, the Lenore Marshall Poetry Prize (1991), the Poets' Prize (1991), a Lifetime Achievement Award from the Alaska Center for the Book (1994), an Academy Award in Literature from the American Academy of Arts and Letters (1995), an Academy of American Poets Fellowship (1997), and the Aiken Taylor Award in Modern American Poetry (2008). He served as poet laureate for the state of Alaska from 1969 to 1971. His focus on the wilderness in the West, especially Alaska and Montana, is suggested by the Alaska Governor's Award in the Arts for life contributions to literary arts in the state (1982) and the Western States Arts Federation Lifetime Achievement Award (1990).

BIOGRAPHY

Born in a prime U.S. Navy port to a naval-officer father, John Meade Haines moved around with his family a good deal: Vallejo, California; Long Beach, California; Bremerton, Washington; Honolulu, Hawaii; San Diego, California; Newport, Rhode Island; Portsmouth, New Hampshire; and Washington, D.C. After attending high school in Washington, D.C., Haines was on active antisubmarine duty in the U.S. Navy from 1943 to 1946. He subsequently attended two art schools (National Art School in Washington, D.C., and Hans Hoffman School of Fine Arts in New York City). Haines, who had visited Alaska in 1947, homesteaded there in 1954. He lived in a cabin seventy miles from Richardson for about twenty-five years. After publication of several poetry collections and essays, Haines assumed visiting faculty positions at several universities, including the University of Alaska, University of Washington, University of Montana, Ohio University, George Washington University (Washington, D.C.), University of Cincinnati, and Austin Peay State University (Tennessee). At the age of seventy, Haines married his fourth wife, Joy De Stefano, his first three marriages, to Jo Ellen Hussey (1960-?), Jane McWhorter (1970-1974), and Leslie Sennett (1978-1982), having ended in divorce. In addition to Alaska, Haines has lived in Montana and Ohio and has traveled in Europe.

ANALYSIS

The poems of John Meade Haines range from short verses of eight to nine lines to longer poems with multiple sections, the latter becoming more frequent in his later volumes. Most of the poems are stanzaic, often with a repeating variable pattern, such as repeating stanzas of five and two lines. In word choice and imagery, the poems also demonstrate the poet's range; some are direct and simple, while others are surrealistic.

A recurrent subject is the relationship of humanity to nature: harmony or disharmony (including ecology); hunting (people hunting animals, animals hunting people, animals hunting each other), indigenous peoples (especially Native Americans and prehistoric humans), pioneering, the seasons, astronomy, and the contrast between rural and urban. A number of poems focus on social criticism: stewardship of the environment or overviews of human history, war, and injustice in economics and politics, in the United States or internationally. Because of Haines's involvement in art and poetry, inevitably some poems deal with the visual arts (from prehistoric cave paintings to Native American art to Renaissance and modern artists) and literature. Other poems deal with the human concerns of romantic love, children (including child versus adult or the parent-child relationship), domestic life, and aging or death.

Recurrent images are those of nature: animals (several dozen kinds of mammals, alone, from bats to whales), plants (berries, trees—especially alder, aspen, birch, cypress, pine, and spruce), blood, caves, cold, dust, fire, mist (or fog or smoke), moon, stars, sun, roads or paths, shadows, snow, stone (or rock), sunrise or sunset, water, and wind. Associated with human ignorance or knowledge, good or bad behavior, are coins, dreams, mirrors, and rust. Haines's artistic sense evokes repeated references to certain basic colors: red (blood, fire, sunrise, sunset), blue (beauty, cold, the sky), yellow (sunlight, animals' eyes, tree leaves), green (springtime energy, growth, inexperience), and white (cold, the snowbound landscape).

HUMANITY IN RELATION TO NATURE

"I Am a Tree, Very Quiet Are My Leaves" (from *At the End of This Summer*) is one of several poems in Haines's corpus that use a nonhuman speaker or persona. The tree reveals parallels to human beings in quietness on a still day, a kind of talkativeness of the leaves on a windy day, and in the aging process; however, unlike human beings, it is unafraid of the world's end, aware only of the cycle of the seasons, and it will not die— "shall never stop growing." In "Snowy Night" (*Winter News*), nature's essential otherness is explored, its force in coldness being "like a place/ we used to know, but stranger" creating a "frozen/ sea" in which "the moon is anchored/ like a ghost in heavy chains." In "The Stone Harp" (title poem of *The Stone Harp*), winter's cold causes the sun to sink like a ship, while in the desolation only the wind is a poet "making a sound/ like a stone harp/ strummed/ by a handful of leaves." In "The Lake in the Sky" (*Cicada*), the speaker describes people in harmony with their landscape, along with beavers, swallows, and people, literally in harmony, "singing out of sunken campgrounds"; all these echo the speaker's relationship with his sweetheart, whose engagement or wedding ring catches the fire, light, and gradual darkening of the sunset. In "The Blood Lake" (*News from the Glacier*), the speaker's descriptions of a pool of blood from a deer felled by a hunter and a newly painted red barn suggest the struggle of humanity to establish itself in the wilderness. The fifteen sections of "In the Forest Without Leaves" (*New Poems*) repeatedly counterpose the processes and elements of nature with human technology and incursion. "Star Photo," "NEAR Travels Far to Find Eros," and "NEAR Dreams Quietly of Mars" (all from *For the Century's End*), like "Little Cosmic Dust Poem" (*New Poems: 1980-1988*), provide reminders, through references to astronomy, satellite probes, and rockets, that nature includes the cosmos as well as Earth, and that the miracles of human beings and of romantic love seem unique amid the vastness of the universe.

SOCIAL CRITICISM

In "Pickers" (*Winter News*), the speaker, a field hand, describes the harsh life of the farmworkers: "All day we were bent over,/ lifting handfuls of wind and dust." The wagon for the produce is "a coffin on wheels," on which "the skinned/ bodies of the harvest were loaded," suggesting how much is being exacted from this oppressed group. In *The Stone Harp*, Haines includes a section titled "America," which contains poems that look at the greater society. The implied metaphor of a deadly spider stridently condemns Lyndon Johnson in "The Man from Texas" and a corrupt political system in "Lies." The speaker sympathizes with revolutionaries in "In the Middle of America" and "Guevara," while Native Americans have "vanished,/ the children of wind and shadow,/ gone off with their rags/ and hunger" as the speaker peers from the window in "The Train Stops at Healy Fork." In "Things . . ." (*Cicada*), Haines criticizes the technological and material orientation of modern society, symbolized by the image of eroded telephone wires and the rolling back from a blocked summit of "an uncoupled train/ with no hand on the brake,/ gathering speed in the dark/ on the mountain grade." In "The Invaders" (*News from the Glacier*), newcomers to the Alaskan wilderness, disregarding ecology, have "armor" and have "hoisted a dirty flag to the dawn" and are "treading down forests, bruising/ the snows." All six sections of "Death and the Miser" (*New Poems*) condemn the materialist mentality that ignores nature and fellow human beings, concluding the imagistic motif of metal with the ironic reference to another miser, as the materialist will hear the "ringing,/ metallic shadows of Death,/ who is himself a miser." In "Spilled Milk" (*The Owl in the Mask of the Dreamer*), Haines uses milk spilled on a kitchen table to evoke "forest after forest/ stripped for paper cartons,/ the wax from millions of candles melting," with the consumer acting like a child "saying he never meant to do it," and in "Tar" from the same volume, he criticizes the waste from and addiction to petroleum: A "tar baby" adheres to all modern persons, "bits of tar/ cling to our footsoles," our "children are born/ with glittering faces" shining from tar, our "kisses/ are stained with petroleum," and whales become "iridescent" from the "black hand" of oil that "wrinkles in the wind." The twelve sections of "In the House of Wax" (*For the Century's End*), inspired by a trip to a wax museum, use images of famous figures in history to present a panorama of social injustice from ancient times to the present; a gloomy conclusion in imagery is that the melting down of wax figures to make new ones is like the repetition of such oppressors throughout history.

THE VISUAL ARTS

In "Totem" (*At the End of This Summer*), the speaker addresses the Native American totem, noting that the "loving and respectful hands/ that carved your deep-eyed force" contrast with the cruelty and violence of life and sacrificial religion of the time; likewise, in "Two Horses, One by the Roadside" from the same volume, a real horse is compared and contrasted with a stone horse statue the speaker had seen on the plains of China. In "The Cave of Animals" (*Winter News*), an early or prehistoric cave painting captures forever the spirit of animals alone or in groups, unencumbered by human beings. "Dürer's Vision" and "The Middle Ages" (both from *The Stone Harp*) explore the gloomy philosophical or religious implications of the paintings or engravings by the famous artist Albrecht Dürer. In "The Stone Bear" (*Cicada*), the decaying stone bear sculpture on a grave's pedestal evokes the speaker's identification with animal life in the harsh Alaskan climate, while the various artworks in "In the Museum Garden" (from the same collection) evoke comparison and contrast with the beauty but transitoriness of the living plants and persons surrounding them. In "A Winter Light" (*News from the Glacier*), the romantic addressee, sharing the speaker's life, has a face that "still holds/ a mystery that once/ filled caves with the color/ of unforgettable beasts," while in "The Eye in the Rock" (from the same collection), the art on stone by Native Americans suggests their spiritual unity with all nature, including what modern people would deem inanimate. In the nine-part "Meditation on a Skull Carved in Crystal" (*The Owl in the Mask of the Dreamer*), the speaker contrasts the artwork with nature (ice) and real people (who are transitory, as opposed to the art). In *New Poems*, "Days of Edward Hopper" suggests the relation between art and social criticism through the speaker's connection of Hopper's paintings and the sad life and environment they depict. Similarly, Michelangelo's Sistine Chapel ceiling and statue of David in "Of Michelangelo, His Question," Vincent van Gogh's paintings in "On a Certain Field in Auvers," and Pablo Picasso's cubist paintings in "Broken Mirrors" provoke meditations on religious or personal inspirations of the art, respectively. In *The Owl in the Mask of the Dreamer*, the religious implications of Hieronymous Bosch's art in "Tondo of Hell" parallel the social criticism of Auguste Rodin's sculpture in "The Burghers of Calais," which Haines finds symbolic of the plight of exiles and refugees throughout history. Photography as art, conveying social criticism, is the subject of "Kent State, May 1970" and "The Unemployed, Disabled, and Insane" (both from *For the Century's End*); the former is about the famous photo of a young woman grieving over the body of a student shot by a member of the Ohio National Guard, and the latter is about the photographs in Germany by German photographer August Sander. Just as nature includes Earth and the cosmos, so social criticism and art include past and present, as well as America and the rest of the world.

OTHER MAJOR WORKS
SCREENPLAY: *The River Is Wider than It Seems*, 1980.
NONFICTION: *Living off the Country: Essays on Poetry and Place*, 1981; *Stories We Listened To*, 1986; *The Stars, the Snow, the Fire: Twenty-five Years in the Northern Wilderness—A Memoir*, 1989; *Fables and Distances: New and Selected Essays*, 1996.

BIBLIOGRAPHY
Bezner, Kevin, and Kevin Walzer, eds. *The Wilderness of Vision: On the Poetry of John Haines*. Brownsville, Oreg.: Story Line; 1996. A substantial 252-page anthology containing an introduction, biographical time line, sixteen articles and reviews, plus primary and secondary bibliographies.

Hudson, Marc. "'Voice at Once Contemporary and Ancient': The Enduring Value of John Haines's *Winter News*." *Sewanee Review* 117, no. 4 (2009): 576-591. An in-depth analysis by a critic and poet, who was inspired by the book.

Mason, David. "The Tenacity of John Haines." *Sewanee Review* 106, no. 1 (1998): 103-111. Placement of the poet's work in the context of other modern poets, plus a comment on the Bezner and Walzer critical anthology.

Rogers, Steven B., ed. *A Gradual Twilight: An Appreciation of John Haines*. Fort Lee, N.J.: CavanKerry Press, 2003. A collection of essays that examine Haines's life and work.

Taylor, Henry. "A Form of Patience: The Poems of John Haines." In *Twayne Companion to Contemporary Literature in English, I: Ammons-Lurie*, edited by R. H. W. Dillard and Amanda Cockrell. New York: Twayne-Thomson Gale, 2002. Comprehensive coverage of all the poetry through 2001.

Trueblood, Valerie. "One to Whom the Great Announcements Are Made." *American Poetry Review* (January/February, 2001): 47-50. Brief but comprehensive coverage of the prose as well as poetry through 2001.

Wild, Peter. *John Haines*. Boise, Idaho: Boise State University Press, 1985. A pioneering fifty-one-page monograph covering the prose as well as poetry through 1982.

Norman Prinsky

JOY HARJO

Born: Tulsa, Oklahoma; May 9, 1951

Principal poetry
The Last Song, 1975
What Moon Drove Me to This?, 1980
She Had Some Horses, 1983
Secrets from the Center of the World, 1989
In Mad Love and War, 1990
The Woman Who Fell from the Sky, 1996
A Map to the Next World: Poetry and Tales, 2000
How We Became Human: New and Selected Poems, 1975-2001, 2002

Other literary forms

Joy Harjo (HAHR-jow) has published mainly volumes of poetry, though she also has written many essays. She edited, with Gloria Bird, *Reinventing the Enemy's Language: Contemporary Native Women's Writing of North America* (1997). She also wrote a screenplay, *Origin of Apache Crow Dance* (1985). In 2000, Harjo published her first children's book, *The Good Luck Cat*, illustrated by Paul Lee. She has published a play *Wings of Night Sky, Wings of Morning Light* (pr., pb. 2009), and her musical interests combine with poetry in several musical albums, including *Winding Through the Milky Way* (2009).

Achievements

Joy Harjo is known for her use of American Indian mythology in her work and for her heritage as a member of the Muskogee Creek Nation. She has earned many honors and awards, including the American Indian Distinguished Achievement Award (1990), the William Carlos Williams Award (1991), the Josephine Miles Award (1991), the American Book Award for *In Mad Love and War* (1991), Oklahoma Book Awards for *The Woman Who Fell from the Sky* and *How We Became Human* (1995 and 2003, respectively), the New Mexico Governor's Award for Excellence in the Arts (1997), the Lila Wallace-*Reader's Digest* Writers' Award (1997), the Arrell Gibson Lifetime Achievement Award from the Oklahoma Center (2003), and the Lifetime Achievement Award from the Native Writers Circle of the Americas. She was named Writer of the Year in Poetry by the Wordcraft Circle of Native Writers and Storytellers (2003-2004) for *How We Became Human*. She has received National Endowment for the Arts Fellowships (1978, 1992), a Woodrow Wilson Fellowship at Green Mountain College (1993), a Witter Brynner Poetry Fellowship (1994), and a United States Artists

Joy Harjo

Rasumson Fellowship (2008). Benedectine College conferred an honorary doctorate on her in 1992.

Besides being a talented poet, Harjo plays the saxophone and performs her poetry along with her band. In 1997, her album *Letters from the End of the Century* won the Musical Artists of the Year award from the Wordcraft Circle of Native Writers and Storytellers.

BIOGRAPHY

Joy Harjo was born Joy Foster in 1951 in Tulsa, Oklahoma, to Allen W. Foster and Wynema Baker Foster. Harjo's mother was of mixed Cherokee and French heritage, while her father was a full-blooded Creek Indian. Her mother was nineteen when Harjo was born and had three more children in the next six years. Harjo's childhood was not a happy one, as her father drank and had extramarital affairs. He abused his family physically and emotionally. Her mother divorced Foster and remarried another abusive man. Harjo eventually came into conflict with her stepfather and left the house.

Harjo spent her high school years at the Institute of American Indian Arts in Santa Fe, New Mexico. The school's population consisted of members of various tribes.

Though the school did not provide the best education, Harjo felt she benefited from the experience. She toured with an all-Native American dance troupe and became involved with a fellow student named Phil Wilmon. In 1968, the tour ended, and Harjo graduated, returned to Oklahoma, and gave birth to her son, Phil Dayn.

Harjo returned to Sante Fe without Wilmon and enrolled at the University of New Mexico. She eventually became an English and creative writing major. She also met poet Simon Ortiz. Ortiz and Harjo became lovers, and he fathered Harjo's daughter, Rainy Dawn. Harjo split with Ortiz and graduated in 1976.

Harjo then went to the University of Iowa Writers' Workshop. She faced difficulties as a single mother of two but eventually earned her M.F.A. She next studied filmmaking at the Anthropology Film Center in Santa Fe. She also taught at the college level, including at the University of New Mexico in Albuquerque. She later left New Mexico, living in Los Angeles and later Honolulu. Harjo took her last name when she became an enrolled member of the Muskogee tribe at the age of nineteen. Harjo was the surname of her paternal grandmother.

<h3 style="text-align:center">ANALYSIS</h3>

Joy Harjo is usually classified as a American Indian poet. A member of the Muskogee tribe, she uses American Indian imagery, folktales, symbolism, mythology, and technique in her work. She writes about women and women's issues and takes political stands against oppression and the government as well. Landscape and environment play an important part in her work. Many poems have a sense of location or place. Sometimes those places are specific, such as Kansas City or Anchorage. At other times, they are dreamscapes or psychic spaces the poet visits. Many of Harjo's poems detail journeys and finding a sense of place. This fits with both her personal history and the history of the indigenous Americans, such as the Muskogee, one of the tribes forced to relocate along the Trail of Tears. Connected with landscape and place is memory. Harjo writes from personal and tribal memories, often connecting them with the places she has lived or visited. Another recurring theme is her anger at being half Caucasian and fluent only in English, the language of the "enemies." Many of her poems articulate this anger.

WHAT MOON DROVE ME TO THIS?

Harjo's first book-length collection of poetry, *What Moon Drove Me to This?* contained the ten poems from the chapbook *The Last Song*, as well as many other poems. The book is divided into two sections, "Summer" and "Winter." The poems contain images and themes that Harjo would develop more in her later works.

One of the characteristics of Harjo's poetry is the use of imagery from American Indian mythology. Both coyotes and crows appear in this collection. Both animals are trickster figures, and Harjo uses them as such. "Kansas City Coyote" introduces a character who appears in two of the poems. The name later emerges in "Old Lines Which

Sometimes Work, and Sometimes Don't." In this second poem, Kansas City Coyote is an unreliable male figure.

> "I'll be back in ten minutes.
> Just going to get cigarettes."
> That was the last time I saw him,
> two years ago.

A more general male coyote reference appears in the poem "Lame Dear." Crows, or blackbirds, appear in several poems as well, though not always as gender specific as Harjo's coyote references.

The persona of Noni Daylight also appears for the first time in this collection. Some critics see the Noni Daylight persona as an alter ego of the poet. Also evident in this collection is an awareness of the problem of alcoholism among Native Americans, particularly men. For example, in "Conversations Between Here and Home," she writes:

> Emma Lee's husband beat her up
> this weekend.
> His government check was held
> up, and he borrowed the money
> to drink on.

Other poems such as "The Lost Weekend Bar" and "Chicago or Albuquerque" show similar imagery.

SHE HAD SOME HORSES

Harjo's second full-length volume, *She Had Some Horses*, is divided into four uneven parts. Many of the poems in this collection use rhythms and beats influenced by American Indian chants. The first section, "Survivors," contains twenty-five poems detailing survivors of a variety of things, such as Henry, who survived "being shot at/ eight times outside a liquor store in L.A." and "The Woman Hanging from the Thirteenth Floor Window," who may or may not survive—Harjo deliberately leaves the poem open-ended, not completing the story, which could be told about many women.

The second section, "What I Should Have Said," contains eleven poems. Since the last line of her previous collection was "That's what she said," this section of her second book could be considered a follow-up. This section of the book contains poems about the difficulties of connecting in a long-distance relationship.

In the third section, "She Had Some Horses," Harjo uses the horse as a symbol, as she does in many other poems as well. The horse is a powerful American Indian symbol signifying strength, grace, and freedom, among other characteristics. The title poem begins this section. It repeats the phrase "She had horses" throughout the poem. The horses are varied and vivid: "She had horses who threw rocks at glass houses./ She had horses who licked razor blades." Later in the poem, Harjo states, "She had some horses she loved./ She had some horses she hated./ They were the same horses." The other four poems in this section continue to use and build on the imagery and symbolism of horses.

The fourth section is just one poem, "I Give You Back." In this poem, the speaker is giving fear back to those who caused it. It is a political poem, as Harjo gives the fear "back to the white soldiers/ who burned down my home, beheaded my children,/ raped and sodomized my brothers and sisters."

SECRETS FROM THE CENTER OF THE WORLD

In *Secrets from the Center of the World*, Harjo published poems that were inspired by the photographs of astronomer Stephen Strom. The collection is almost solely prose poems of very short length. Harjo makes a great use of landscape since all the photos by Strom are of southwestern landscapes. Harjo uses what is in the photos as well as what she imagines may be in the photos for her poems.

> A summer storm reveals the dreaming place of bears. But you cannot see their shaggy dreams of fish and berries, any land signs supporting evidence of bears, or any bears at all.

IN MAD LOVE AND WAR

Harjo's fifth book, *In Mad Love and War*, is a mixture of styles. Although some poems seem traditional, with line breaks and stanzas, just as many are prose poems. Several have brief explanatory notes or dedications, such as the poem "For Anna Mae Pictou Aquash . . . ," a poem written about a young Micmac woman who was murdered and her body dismembered by the Federal Bureau of Investigation. "Strange Fruit" is dedicated to Jaqueline Peters, a writer and activist murdered by the Ku Klux Klan.

As in previous books, Harjo divides this one into subsections—"The Wars" and "Mad Love"—after introducing the book with the poem "Grace." "Grace" speaks again of separation and the hurt and anger of a dispossessed people. These themes are continued throughout "The Wars" section. For example, in the poem "Autobiography," Harjo says, "We were a stolen people in a stolen land. Oklahoma meant defeat."

"Mad Love" changes the tone slightly with poems about Harjo's grandfather and daughter, as well as poems about musicians such as Nat King Cole and Billie Holiday. Harjo's growing interest in music is evident in this section. Both sections again contain poems rooted in place and landscape, such as "Climbing the Streets of Worcester, Mass." and "Crystal Lake."

THE WOMAN WHO FELL FROM THE SKY

In her sixth book, *The Woman Who Fell from the Sky*, Harjo shows herself as much the storyteller as poet. The collection's prose poems are story centered, often retellings of American Indian myths, such as the title poem and "The Creation Story." Each poem is followed by a brief story about how the poem was written. The book is divided into two parts, "Tribal Memory" and "The World Ends Here." Harjo focuses attention on the condition of American Indians and other oppressed peoples in such poems as "Witness" and "A Postcolonial Tale." Other familiar themes, such as love of music and American Indian spirituality, are also evident. As in her previous book, she looks at the atrocities committed by humans as well as the concept of love. She says in the explanation for "The Myth of Blackbirds," "I believe love is the strongest force in this world, though it doesn't often appear to be so at the ragged end of this century."

A MAP TO THE NEXT WORLD

A Map to the Next World is an ambitious collection containing forty-eight poems in 136 pages. Split into four sections—"Songline of Dawn," "Returning from the Enemy," "This Is My Heart; It Is a Good Heart," and "In the Beautiful Perfume and Stink of the World"—the book lives up to its title. While again cataloging the horrors of history, Harjo also offers spiritual guidance to the next world. "The End" describes the death of Pol Pot, the notorious leader of the Khmer Rouge in Cambodia. The next poem, "Compassionate Fire," links Pol Pot with Andrew Jackson, the "hero" of the American Indian wars, who later became president of the United States. This collection also contains the fourteen-part poem "Returning from the Enemy," a poem tracing her own coming to terms with her father. In "Preparations," Harjo says, "We should be like the antelope/ who gratefully drink the rain,/ love the earth for what it is—their book of law, their heart."

HOW WE BECAME HUMAN

How We Became Human has seven sections, the first six of which are made up of selected poems from Harjo's previous books. The seventh section, "New Poems, 1999-2001," contains thirteen new poems. The volume begins with fourteen pages of acknowledgments and biographical and sociopolitical context in which Harjo reflects on her development from her days as a student and emerging poet. In these ruminations, Harjo connects personal and political events to demonstrate how her poetry emerges. Foundational themes of her poetry are evident here. For example: "This earth asks for so little from us human beings." Her poetry, throughout her career, celebrates an appropriate relationship between humans and other living beings. This close association also establishes her understanding of life and death. Many of these later poems suggest a spirituality and a continuation, an American Indian metaphysics, which the poet sees implicit within the creative process itself. She ends her reflection of her poetic development by saying "What amazed me at the beginning and still amazes me about the creative process is that even as we are dying something always wants to be born."

This collection also contains an index and thirty-six pages of notes that offer interesting and helpful explanations and contexts for terms and issues found in various poems in the seven sections. For example, from the poem titled "Rushing the Pali," the notes explain that "*Pali* means cliff in Hawaiian. The Pali is the name of the cliff over which Kamehameha's warriors pushed the O'ahu warriors in order to take over O'ahu and unite the islands by violence."

In these new poems, Harjo links both her Muskogee heritage, and more generally, American Indian culture with a concern for other cultures from other parts of the world. This fascinating blend posits a unique power within her poetry—an ability to speak credibly to a diverse audience while remaining firmly secure in her culture of origin. There is also an intensifying emphasis on spirituality in these new poems. The poet offers a mature, sophisticated view of life beyond this physical experience. In "The Everlasting," Harjo mixes dream and waking moments to negate the oppression of past experiences. In "Morning Prayers," she claims to "know nothing anymore" concerning her place in the next world even as the poem links the poet's faith to "a notion of the sacred in/ the elegant border of cedar trees/ becoming mountain and sky." In "Faith," Harjo respectfully contrasts European "spires of churches" built by the faithful "on their knees" with her own "limp" faith. However, this poem ends with Harjo's characteristic understanding of faith, earth, and the next life: "I might miss/ The feet of god/ Disguised as trees." Finally, in "Equinox," readers experience Harjo's requiem toward balance and renewal, despite historical injustice: ". . . from each drop of blood/ springs up sons and daughters, trees,/a mountain of sorrows, of songs" and ". . . crocuses have/ broken through the frozen earth." In powerful honest images, Harjo balances history with justice, the personal with the cultural, and war with peace. ". . . I have buried the dead// and made songs of the blood, the marrow" she concludes, and the notion of equality intrinsic to the poem is nothing cheap, nor something that begs easy assimilation.

OTHER MAJOR WORKS

SHORT FICTION: "Boston," 1991; "Northern Lights," 1991; "The Flood," 1991; "The Woman Who Fell from the Sky," 1996; "Warrior Road," 1997.

PLAY: *Wings of Night Sky, Wings of Morning Light*, pr., pb. 2009.

SCREENPLAY: *Origin of Apache Crown Dance*, 1985.

NONFICTION: *The Spiral of Memories: Interviews*, 1996 (Laura Coltelli, editor).

CHILDREN'S LITERATURE: *The Good Luck Cat*, 2000.

EDITED TEXT: *Reinventing the Enemy's Language: Contemporary Native Women's Writing of North America*, 1997 (with Gloria Bird).

BIBLIOGRAPHY

Andrews, Jennifer. "In the Belly of a Laughing God: Reading Humor and Irony in the Poetry of Joy Harjo." *American Indian Quarterly* 24, no. 2 (2000): 200-218. Analyzes humor in Harjo's poetry, an important characteristic that the author claims is seriously ignored in studies of American Indian literature.

Harjo, Joy. Interviews. *The Spiral of Memory: Interviews, Joy Harjo*. Edited by Laura Coltelli. Ann Arbor: University of Michigan Press, 1996. In these interviews, the poet offers insights into her method of working as well as the continuing concerns of her writing.

_____. "Joy Harjo." http://www.joyharjo.com. The official Web site and blog of Joy Harjo offers a short biography, interviews, and photographs, as well as information on readings and musical events, her books, and her albums.

Lang, Nancy. "'Twin Gods Bending Over': Joy Harjo and Poetic Memory." *Melus* 18, no. 3 (Fall, 1993): 41-49. This article examines poetic memory in Harjo's poems. Lang states that Harjo's poetry shows complex layers and voices of memory. These memories can be personal, ancestral, tribal, or mythical. Lang further studies the use of memory in conjunction with Harjo's use of urban landscapes and briefly discusses the Noni Daylight poems.

Ludlow, Jeannie. "Working (In) the In-Between: Poetry, Criticism, Interrogation, and Interruption." *Studies in American Indian Literatures* 6, no. 1 (Spring, 1994): 24-42. A feminist approach, looking at marginality and subjectivity within the American Indian experience. The article focuses on the poem "The Woman Hanging from the Thirteenth Floor Window" compared to Louise Erdrich's "The Lady in the Pink Mustang."

Nixon, Angelique V. "Poem and Tale as Double Helix in Joy Harjo's *A Map to the Next World*." *Studies in American Indian Literatures* 18, no. 1 (Spring, 2006): 1-21. Focuses on the American Indian circular view of reality, which is evident in storytelling and poetry.

Pettit, Rhonda. *Joy Harjo*. Boise, Idaho: Boise State University Western Writer Series, 1998. Pettit's work takes an insightful look at the way Harjo uses technique, style, and symbolism. She analyzes the use of edges in all of Harjo's major poetry except *A Map to the Next World*. Pettit includes biographical information on Harjo as well as analysis of her first four major books. Also included is a bibliography of secondary sources.

Scarry, John. "Joy Harjo." In *Smoke Rising: The Native North American Literary Companion*, edited by Janet Witalec. Detroit: Gale Research, 1995. Scarry's brief entry on Harjo recognizes her "need for remembrance and transcendence" and includes several poems demonstrating this duality, including the prose poems "Grace" and "Autobiography," both from *In Mad Love and War*.

Wilson, Norma C. "The Ground Speaks: The Poetry of Joy Harjo." In *The Nature of Native American Poetry*. Albuquerque: University of New Mexico Press, 2001. Wilson's book covers a variety of American Indian poets including Wendy Rose, Linda Hogan, Simon Ortiz, and others. In chapter 9, Wilson gives an overview of Harjo's life and poetry, discussing such themes as landscape, fear, and communication.

Womack, Craig S. "Joy Harjo: Creek Writer from the End of the Twentieth Century." In

Red on Red: Native American Literary Separatism. Minneapolis: University of Minnesota Press, 1999. Womack provides a different perspective on Harjo and other American Indian writers, being himself a Creek-Cherokee. His book looks at American Indian literature with tribally specific concerns. In his chapter on Harjo, he recognizes the strength of her voice. He also shows the Creek content and use of Creek history in her work.

P. Andrew Miller
Updated by Kenneth Hada

JIM HARRISON

Born: Grayling, Michigan; December 11, 1937

PRINCIPAL POETRY

Plain Song, 1965
Locations, 1968
Outlyer and Ghazals, 1971
Letters to Yesenin, 1973
Returning to Earth, 1977
Selected and New Poems, 1961-1981, 1982
Natural World, 1983 (includes sculpture by Diana Guest)
The Theory and Practice of Rivers, 1985
The Theory and Practice of Rivers, and New Poems, 1989
After Ikkyū, and Other Poems, 1996
The Shape of the Journey: New and Collected Poems, 1998
Braided Creek: A Conversation in Poetry, 2003
Saving Daylight, 2006
In Search of Small Gods, 2009

OTHER LITERARY FORMS

Although Jim Harrison began his career as a poet, it was the publication of his fourth fiction title, *Legends of the Fall* (1979), that brought him national recognition. The book, which consisted of three novellas, two of which had previously appeared in *Esquire*, proved so successful that Dell Publishing Company reissued his previously published novels in paperback editions. The book became the basis of two films, *Revenge* (1990) and *Legends of the Fall* (1994). Harrison has published numerous other volumes of fiction, some of which also are three-novella collections. His *Farmer* (1976) became the basis for the film *Carried Away* (1996), and *Dalva* (1988) became a 1996 television movie. Harrison also wrote screenplays, including *Cold Feet* (1988, with Thomas McGuane) and *Wolf* (1994). *The Boy Who Ran to the Woods* (2000) is his first book for children. Harrison's novels and novellas, like his poetry, are often marked by a lyrical imagination, intelligence, and passion for living.

Harrison has also published numerous essays dealing with sports, cooking, wine, fishing, farming, and hunting; these articles complement the tone and thrust of his other writing and offer further evidence of his commitment to the natural environment and the code of ethics necessary for its maintenance. *Just Before Dark* (1991) is a collection of his nonfiction prose pieces. In 2002, he published *Off to the Side: A Memoir*.

Jim Harrison
(Library of Congress)

ACHIEVEMENTS

Jim Harrison has long been recognized as a talented and important voice in American letters. He has received National Academy of Arts grants (1967, 1968, 1969), a Guggenheim Fellowship (1969-1970), and the Spirit of the West Award from the Mountain and Plains Booksellers Association (2000). He was also elected to the Academy of Arts and Letters in 2007.

Harrison has combined a unique blend of elements, uniting the American vernacular with a distinctly Eastern metaphysics and widely reaching references to European culture. He consistently fuses primitive and naturalistic images with the arcane and ponderous and draws on both gothic and surreal conventions. By refusing to limit himself to a single genre and by attending to "audible things, things moving at noon in full raw light," Harrison has been able to appeal to a diversified audience and to promulgate an integrated vision that embodies the subtler nuances of the physical and natural world.

Relying on what T. S. Eliot called "the auditory imagination," he enables the reader to hear and feel simultaneously the meaning and motion of objects and experiences and to take part in the poet's personal journey toward self-discovery.

BIOGRAPHY

James Thomas Harrison was born in Grayling, Michigan, in 1937, to Winfield Sprague Harrison, a county agricultural agent, and Norma Olivia (Wahlgren) Harrison, and has spent much of his life in and around northern Michigan. He lost sight in his left eye when a child. Harrison received a B.A. (1960) and M.A. (1965) in comparative literature from Michigan State University. His father and sister died in an automobile accident when he was twenty-one years old. In 1959, he married Linda King; the couple would have two daughters. He became an assistant professor of English at State University of New York, Stony Brook (1965-1966), but he realized he was not suited for an academic career, moved back to Michigan, and became a freelance writer. His poetry gained favorable reviews, but he did not gain commercial success until *Legends of the Fall* was published.

As the allusions that pepper Harrison's writing make clear, he is a prodigious reader, and although he writes about Michigan's Upper Peninsula, he considers himself an internationalist. He peoples his writings with figures drawn from his German and Swedish ancestral lines and incorporates elements from Native American culture and Zen Buddhism. His love of hunting, fishing, and food are also evident. Harrison bought and moved to a farmhouse near Montana's Paradise Valley and began dividing his time between Montana and his winter home in Patagonia, Arizona, near the border with Mexico.

ANALYSIS

Jim Harrison is one of the twenty-first century's most stunning, original, and introspective poets. His poetry, while extremely tactile, is not quickly apprehended but yields vast rewards. Reading through any Harrison collection is a bit like traveling through a museum of the subconscious filled with pungent, piercing, beautiful, sexually charged, and tortured imagery drawn from the natural world and human experience. Using the natural world as a springboard, he infuses it with mystic correspondences, Zen allusions, and multiple layers of meaning. His preferred forms are the lyric, the haiku, the suite, and the ghazal, all of which involve loose assemblages of stanzas that are related largely by free associations. Hence, what may appear to be arbitrary suspensions of narrative sequences are, instead, highly crafted movements through the poet's preconscious mind.

Harrison is an iconoclast whose thought patterns, even in his more traditional narratives, tend to be elliptical. In the suites and ghazals, this tendency culminates in violent disruptions of linear connection and the compounding of discordant images. His poetry requires that the reader transcend the limits of the rational mind and follow the poet on his personal explorations, which have their own indigenous logic. Harrison is reaching directly for the experiences he is rendering in verse.

PLAIN SONG

Plain Song is Harrison's first published collection and an underrated book that attempts more than is readily apparent. Donald Jones, one of the few reviewers to treat the book apart from other collections, aptly applies the concept "numinous surds" to convey the craftsmanship of the best of these poems. What is most striking about this volume is Harrison's capacity to fuse his northern Michigan sensibility with an almost mystic sense of cosmic unity and a host of old European, Central American, and modern allusions. What reviewers see as his devotion to "the thing-in-itself" is but the surface of the work. Behind all of these poems is an organic consciousness unfettered by logical dictums and intent on immersing the reader in the elemental flux.

Plain Song begins with a modest *ars poetica*, "Poem," which reveals Harrison's poetic credo and his affinity for the natural world. Using the woods as a correlative for poetic form and a stalking bobcat to represent content, Harrison pictures structures as mere backdrops that, by definition, "yield to conclusion they do not care about or watch." In "Word Drunk," Harrison explains that poems are living creatures "suffused with light," essences yielding their "own dumb form—weight raw, void of intent." Herein lies the source of Harrison's predisposition toward suites and ghazals; both facilitate experimentation with form and transport the reader into "another field, or richer grain."

Already evident in these early pieces is his attention to sensory detail. Quite overtly in such poems as "Exercise" and "Park at Night," Harrison invites the reader to hear the almost muted sounds of nature: grass moving to create passageways, soil shifting, and fire selecting new wood. It is a keen ear, indeed, which can, as Harrison does in "Sounds," communicate the "loud weight of birds" capable of drowning out the carpenter's hammer, and can, in "February Suite," convey the sounds of soldiers breaking "like lightbulbs in a hoarse cry of dust." In other poems, such as "Northern Michigan" and "Returning at Night," he transforms what a casual observer might see as unkempt properties into wildlife sanctuaries. Often, as in "Dusk," what emerges is a gestalt of the visual, the olfactory, and the auditory.

The dominant point of view, rather too baldly stated in "Trees," is that people's utilitarian perspective senselessly discounts that which is superfluous to their materialistic ends. Clearly, Harrison's sentiments lie with the victims of civilization's onrush. This is most obvious in his depiction of the wolf in "Traverse City Zoo" and his wry commentary in "Fox Farm," but also present in "Kinship," which captures the nobility of the senile Uncle Wilhelm.

Harrison's romantic attachment to the woods and wilds is balanced by his capacity for irony and self-mockery. In "Lisle's River," for example, after establishing a resonance with the surroundings, he reverses himself, recounting a drunken violation of the spirit of place. In a very different vein, the persona that emerges from "Sketch for a Job Application Blank" is simultaneously self-abasing and proud. Compounded images of childhood and ancestry culminate in a series of oxymorons that transform sex into sacrament and darkness into a medium for growth. This tendency to shift gears and undercut his own affections is what saves Harrison from sentimentality.

Elemental images of darkness and death play a prominent part in these poems. The young boy in "David" can see through the antiseptic haze of words and the profusion of flowers that surround his father's casket and can confront the reality of death. In "John Severin Walgren, 1874-1962," a muted elegy to his maternal grandfather, Harrison describes death as an inevitable process "when the limit's reached" and yet captures the terror of "the blood of the young, those torn off earth in a night's sickness"—a terror that leads to the pronouncement of a bitter nihilistic credo in "New Liturgy" and a similarly virulent renunciation in "Malediction."

As a first volume, *Plain Song* is important; at its best, it reveals Harrison's ability to forge connections between objects. It also hints at the techniques and philosophies that have come to characterize his work. It is not, however, a representative collection in that he seems to rein in his imagination and content himself with presentation rather than probing.

LOCATIONS

The nascent strengths found in *Plain Song* come to fruition in *Locations*. Movement and process are dominant in these poems. Gone is even a residual tendency to focus on the "thing-in-itself"; instead, a single act or object is introduced and its implications unfolded through a process of accretion. "Walking," for example, fuses memories and immediate stimuli in such a way as to capture the incessant natural rhythms that enable nature to renew itself and humans to perceive even the familiar as notable. That "Walking" calls to mindHenry David Thoreau's essay is not surprising; throughout the book Harrison is, effectively, reconquering the land much as Thoreau suggested that the saunterer must.

The three poems labeled "suites" in this volume are most representative of Harrison's means of building on the significance of an image. Just as "Suite to Fathers" employs an ambiguous and shifting sense of "fathers," "Suite to Appleness" and "War Suite" convey multiple levels of meaning associated with the dominant image. The effect in all three cases is not to convolute, but to clarify through transmutation.

"Suite to Fathers," which constitutes a tribute of sorts to past masters in the field of arts and letters, is framed by two references to night as a "blind woman" and as a woman staring with a "great bruised eye." The "countless singulars" that the poem unveils are coupled with a pervasive sense of gothic horror culminating in the image of the poet's brain as a "glacier of blood, inching forward . . . silt covered but sweet." A similar movement pervades "Suite to Appleness," which transforms the destruction of an apple into a working metaphor capable of suggesting the callousness that induces war atrocities, suicides, ecological disruption, and "all things bruised or crushed as an apple." This thread is continued in "War Suite," which interweaves references to various orders and kinds of wars, not to equate them but to distinguish those that are propelled by necessity and those that are gratuitous and often fought out of vanity. The slaughter of whales and hawks that is lamented in "Natural World" is clearly in the latter class.

"The Sign," though structured in a way similar to the suites, is less intense. Harrison indulges in a dream-induced reverie over the astrological significance of having been born under the sign of Sagittarius, situated between the eagle (Scorpio) and the seagoat (Capricorn), and contemplates the patterned luminosity that somehow makes the infinite black more poignant. Significantly, however, these are indulgences permissible only at night, and he therefore concludes this meditation with the sobering realities of digging a well and the certifiable majesty of a stag "bounding away into his green clear music."

"American Girl" is similarly playful and freewheeling. Beginning with references to Helen of Troy and other temptresses, Harrison shifts his focus to his own rites of passage, which dispelled his idealism and revealed that media's images of women were "calcined, watery, with air-brushed bodies and brains." The experiential elements in this piece as well as in "Night in Boston" and "Locations" are rendered with a levity absent in much of *Plain Song*, suggesting that Harrison has achieved a needed distance.

What lies at the heart of Harrison's perspective is a respect for the natural world. The majesty of the red-tailed hawks in "Cold August" has the capacity to restore his spirits despite the metallic cast that has transformed the once verdant fields. This and other poems demonstrate that he is keenly attuned to seasonal variations as they are manifest in both landscape and animal life. While in "Cold August" and "Thin Ice," he uses a single phenomenon as a touchstone against which to measure the change, in "A Year's Changes," he provides a catalog of sense experiences and registers the sounds and silences that characterize the various seasons.

OUTLYER AND GHAZALS

Outlyer and Ghazals marks a turning point in Harrison's poetic career. The first seven poems (the outlyers) continue themes and techniques found in the earlier volumes. The remainder of the pieces (the ghazals) are groundbreaking and infectious. The title of the opening piece, "In Interims: Outlyer," suggests the point of view employed throughout this volume. "Interims" suggests the breaking space needed to contemplate those phenomena that are too easily dismissed as peripheral, while "outlyer" can be translated as a reference to the poet who has the task of contemplating buried connections. There is also the sense of the poet as the marginal man inhabiting the proverbial outback in the company of the aborigines. With such a frame, it is not surprising to find the epigraph drawn from Guillaume Apollinaire, another innovator and iconoclast.

"In Interims: Outlyer" properly sets the tone for the volume; it testifies to the poet's refusal to take aim at institutional pretense, asserting the need for a higher ordering of principles. Most overtly in this poem, the poet is charged with celebrating the bittersweet in order to resurrect the animistic spirit, the "Numen of walking and sleep," an end that he accomplishes in "Hospital," which captures the archetypal sounds of agony, and "Awake," which transforms a catalog of various anxieties and complaints into a workable backdrop against which to graft his ax-hewn wood metaphor.

Harrison is most effective when he discards the tough hunter-outdoorsman persona and allows his mystic sensibility to merge with his ironic wit. It is this that allows him in "She Again" to recast what was at best a simpering machismo in "Cowgirl" and "Drinking Song" into a gestalt of emotions that is winsome and lyrical. This combination also gives him the distance to explain that "in interims all journeys end in three steps with a mirrored door, beyond it a closet and a closet wall." Death is accepted as a constant, not as something to fear; it is celebrated as the completion of the circle and the prerequisite for the next procession.

At his best, Harrison's sense of relationships allows him to forge analogies that are surprisingly appropriate. Incongruities are blended in such a way that the shift from the "diamond head caught in crotch of branch" to his sister who died in an automobile accident debases neither phenomenon. This ability to relate dissimilar objects and events lies at the heart of the ghazals that dominate the book. In these sixty-five poems, Harrison gives his mind's eye full rein and repeatedly surprises his reader into taking a second look. Whether he is describing the screams of ecstatic stones becoming thinner, as in the opening poem, or exploring the implications of non-Euclidean geometry, as in the forty-fifth, his vision is always fresh and clear.

Ghazals, Harrison points out in his prefatory note, are essentially lyrics dating from the thirteenth century. They are akin to suites in that both proceed by means of metaphorical leaps of faith, but they are considerably shorter than suites, being limited to twelve couplets. Both the brevity and the couplet form serve Harrison well, allowing him "to regain some of the spontaneity of the dance, the song unencumbered by any philosophical apparatus, faithful only to its own music." Throughout the volume, poetry is equated with music, "scattered, elliptical, needing to be drawn together and sung," and thus it is appropriate that in the twenty-first ghazal, Harrison assembles a series of universal sounds into a consciously orchestrated medley that is dissonant but captivating. Insisting that "Poetry must die so poems will live again," Harrison is constantly experimental, pushing back the strictures of his chosen form.

The tempo of these poems is brisk and the tone lilting. He fuses together the lyric and the gothic and ruthlessly burlesques human foibles in order "to be finally sane and bow to all sentient creatures," as he explains in the thirty-second ghazal. However, he recognizes that "Apollinaire fertilizer won't feed the pigs or chickens" and that poetry "won't raise the dead or stir the living or open young girls' lips to jubilance." Hence, he is often self-mocking, calling himself, in the second poem, "a poet and a liar," saying, in the sixth, that he "writes with a putty knife and goo" and lamenting, in the thirty-fourth, that the "modal chord I carried around for weeks is lost for want of an instrument." It is this kind of circumspection that prevents him from taking himself too seriously and disarms the reader.

Again, the tightest of these pieces are securely moored to rural embankments. The rural emerges not simply as a purifier but as an essential antidote to the rapacity of the urban. He does not romanticize the rural, rejecting what he terms the "befouled nostalgia about childhood" and launches more than an occasional barb at the provincialism and hardships of rural life. In the second poem, he imagines what might happen if there were poetry competitions at the county fairs, and in the third, he captures the wearisome lot of a country girl who is hired out in the off-season.

These poems are replete with references to the slaughter of predators and other wild creatures; with quiet irony, Harrison debunks the logic of the rancher and the hunter alike. In the sixteenth poem, he neatly understates the plight of the "tamed" bear strapped to a bicycle "with straps of silver and gold straps inlaid with scalps." This image signals his overall moral stance, which prompts him to envision Spiro Agnew, vice president during Richard Nixon's administration, "retired to a hamster farm" and the wild animals "spying on the geologists" in the fourteenth poem and to complain about "vicious horses kicking when I bite their necks" in the twenty-seventh.

He relentlessly lampoons the world of politics. Art becomes, in the fifteenth poem, a miracle needed "to raise those years which are tombstones carved out of soap by the world's senators," and, in the sixteenth, the drama of "civic theater" emerges as "interminable with unconvincing geometric convulsions." In the eighteenth, the pathos of the migrant worker functions as a concertina, undercutting the pretense of literary groupies and the perniciousness of the Department of Defense. Still, Harrison eschews activism, refusing to become another "tremulous bulls-eye for hog fever" or "a poisoned ham in the dinner room of Congress."

As part of a disaffected generation, Harrison is wary of all institutions and, in the final analysis, holds nothing sacred other than the human capacity for wonder. Thus, religion emerges as a target because it has become institutionalized. Gone are the legends that were once central to an understanding of the cosmos. He rues the loss in both the fifty-second and fifty-third ghazals, implying that it is the magic—the "serpent becoming dragon and twelve moons lost at sea"—that has been sacrificed in the name of civilization. No longer does one find "Small people who hitch rides on snakes or ancient people with signs"; instead of being vital, religion has been sanitized and become entropic, as he suggests in the forty-ninth poem. The displacement of wonder by guilt leads him to note wryly in the first ghazal that "Jesus *will* return and the surprise will be fatal."

LETTERS TO YESENIN

Just how important wonder is for Harrison becomes clear in *Letters to Yesenin*. As he says in the twenty-seventh poem, "We learn to see with the child's delight again and perish." The book shows Harrison working though a dark period in his life and harking back to a fascination with an anthology of Russian poetry. The poet traveled in Russia in 1972, searching for the roots of some of his favorite writers who had led difficult lives after the Russian Revolution. Having struggled to make a living himself, Harrison identified with the soul-searching and discontent expressed by many Russian poets. In this volume, there is little of the youthful bravado that characterized his earlier works. He is deadly serious in this, his most consistently crafted book; his voice is honest and compelling. The disaffection evident in the ghazals has been sharply intensified as he does battle with the ghosts and killing realities of the past and present and tries to arrive at a credible reason for rejecting suicide as a proper response to life's absurdity.

The volume, which includes thirty meditative letters directed to Sergei Esenin, the Russian poet who hanged himself after writing his farewell poem in his own blood, teems with mordant critiques of the human condition. As Harrison admits in the twenty-ninth letter, the poems "often resemble a suicide note to a suicide." What prevents the constant presence of death from overwhelming these poems is Harrison's indomitable wit, his capacity to draw away from his target and mock his own reveries. In the fifteenth letter, he rhetorically asks whether this is a time for joking, and responds unequivocally: "Yes. Always." What results is a curious blend of backwoods and gallows humor, which fuels Harrison's ironic perspective. For the most part, his attempts at levity are confined to parenthetical remarks that lighten his otherwise dark imagery, but he also includes a few extended spoofs of the "triumphs" that make life bearable. The most effective, the ninth letter, is a mock ode to paper clips.

Harrison's ironic perspective allows him to cut through the veneer and depict the Russian revolution as "a red tinged glory, neither fire nor sun, a sheen without irony on the land" in the thirteenth letter, and to debunk the romance associated with Esenin's career. Noting the way in which Esenin's displacement and despair fed on each other and were exacerbated by his tumultuous marriage to Isadora Duncan, Harrison sums up the cost in the twenty-eighth poem: "One body and soul net, one brain already tethered to the dark, one ingenious leash never to hold a dog, two midwinter eyes that lost their technicolor."

In an effort to come to terms with Esenin's meteoric rise, which he compares to a "proton in an accelerator," and the motivation for his death, he alludes to countless others who were, to varying degrees, victims of their own genius. Among those he would like to "dream back to life" are Osip Mandelstam, Bella Akhmadulina, Waslaw Nijinski, Aleksandr Blok, and Hart Crane. Also present are Chief Joseph, who nobly "led a thousand with a thousand horses a thousand miles" during the Nez Perce War, and those who were senselessly slaughtered at the 1972 Olympics. Chief Joseph "was very understanding, incidentally, when the Cavalry shot so many of the women and children.

It was to be expected"; Harrison has also become inured to the violence and destruction of contemporary life.

It is clear, especially in the nineteenth and twenty-seventh poems, that he is tired of putting on a show and contenting himself with "those pure empty days with all the presence of a hole in the ground," and yet, unlike Esenin, he refuses to allow circumstances to overwhelm him. He remains capable of "helpless sensual wonder" and readily partakes of the "libidinal stew that calls us to life however ancient and basal," as he phrases it in the twenty-ninth letter. Further, as he makes clear in the twenty-fifth poem, he places a good deal of stock in the poet's mandate to speak for those who are condemned to suffer voicelessly. The poet emerges from the sixteenth poem as a "sorcerer bored with magic who has turned his attention elsewhere" and is capable of capturing "wonders that psilocybin never conceived of in her powdery head."

By the time he reaches the "Postscript," he has not only effectively vented the angst that threatened to dislodge his tenuous grip, but has also recast his view of Esenin's suicide, causing him to comment that it lacked the dignity of an animal's death and to announce his own decision to stay. The final piece, "A Domestic Poem for Portia," reaffirms this decision and acts as a completion of the circle begun in the first letter. It is not an optimistic piece by any stretch of the imagination, but the recurrent chorus of "nothing" that weighted the first piece has been replaced by variants of "This is all it is." He has, effectively, settled; what seemed about to overwhelm him has been accepted, leading him to conclude: "I'm hanging onto nothing today and with confidence, a sureness that the very air between our bodies, the light of what we are, has to be enough."

RETURNING TO EARTH

Returning to Earth, which followed on the heels of *Letters to Yesenin*, invites disappointment. Although both works display the same finely honed poetic imagination, they are markedly dissimilar. *Returning to Earth* is a loosely structured compendium of poems and sense-impressions that is keynoted by an incessant playfulness and a tendency to scramble metaphors. (Harrison also published a novel with the same title in 2007; it shares the themes of aging, death, and the cruelty of civilization.) While it is laced with telling insights, it is not as compelling as *Letters to Yesenin*. When Harrison says "I widowed my small collection of magic until it poisoned itself with longing," one cannot help feeling that he is referring to the time devoted to novels in lieu of poetry.

The title itself sets this work apart from *Letters to Yesenin*. The poet has left the literary realm and reentered northern Michigan. This meaning is suggested by his vignette about his fat pet bird with a malformed wing and a penchant for drink; when the bird, like the poet, drinks, he "flies in great circles miles wide, preferring bad days with low cold clouds looking like leper brains." After howling his pain, he "drags himself through air mostly landing near a screen door slamming, a baby's cry, a dog's bark, a forest fire, a sleeping coyote. The fabulous memories of earth!"

The point that is most insistently made in this volume is that life on earth is replete with agonies and events that leave scars that are only significant, finally, to the individual who suffered them. With a much more buoyant tone than that found in previous works, Harrison chronicles his own litany of complaints without dwelling on any particular one for too long. The net result is akin to reading a well-written journal that teems with insight but stops short of fleshing out the whole. That this may well have been Harrison's intent is suggested by his reference to the almost solipsistic nature of poetry— "brain moving as a river, governed precisely by her energies"—and by his desire to have his life "in cloud shapes, water shapes, crow calls, marsh hawk swooping over grass and weed tips." It is this desire that leads him to endorse the impressionistic and elliptical, claiming, "No music in statement, the lowest denominator by which our fragments can't find each other."

SELECTED AND NEW POEMS, 1961-1981

The publication of *Selected and New Poems, 1961-1981* made much of Harrison's earlier work, which had gone out of print, readily accessible. The volume includes about half of the poems from *Plain Song*, all but four of the poems from *Locations*, and all but one of the "outlyers" found in *Outlyer and Ghazals*. It also reprints *Letters to Yesenin* and *Returning to Earth* in their entirety and includes about twenty pages of new poems. Both the editorial selection and the accompanying imagistic drawings by Montana artist Russell Chatham reveal the care that went into its production.

Because it includes Harrison's best poems, this collection highlights his range and complexity, establishing him as a major voice in American poetry. The new poems again demonstrate his ability to use form as a liberator and to resist the tendency to write stylized or predictable poetry; Harrison is a master of the double entendre and again reveals not only the breadth of his knowledge but also the volatility of his imagination. He moves back and forth between concrete and abstract images as he eschews the narcissism of so many of the meditative, confessional poets as well as the self-effacement of the formalists.

These poems do not fall neatly into any particular pattern. Harrison includes two ghazals, both of which reinforce the notion that this is a form that suits him well. "The Chatham Ghazal" includes in each couplet an objective observation, which is then confounded by an unexpected addition that acts back on the initial image and casts it in a fresh light. "Marriage Ghazal" proceeds somewhat more sequentially with each couplet preparing the way for the next. In "Marriage Ghazal," Harrison moves from the image of a "sea wrack" seeking shore, through the image of a disembodied soul reentering its body and heading inland, and to an image of the drifter uniting with another, with whom he builds a new boat presumably to set sail on a different sea.

Operative in the best of these pieces is a multiple perspective that is explained in the final poem, "After Reading Takahashi." Beginning with the relatively mundane thought that "nothing is the same to anyone," Harrison energizes this idea with a series of counterpoints that leads finally to the resolve "to look at all creatures and things with a billion eyes, not struggling with the single heartbeat that is my life." The same point is more obliquely suggested in "Rooster." After an extended debate with himself, he realizes that "the worthless rooster" with his magnificent, wavering crow is "the poet's bird brother" (a sobering thought) and decides he cannot kill the bird without first sitting down and talking it over with him.

While poems like "Frog" are relatively straightforward and convey sensory memories economically and directly, the bulk of the new poems reach beyond the concrete, becoming almost ethereal. The opening poem, "Not Writing My Name," is a case in point. It begins with the poet's fantasy of etching his name in the snow with each letter being hundreds of yards long, but he dismisses this as the idea of a "star-crossed jock ego" and turns his attention instead to the visible signs and tactile sensations that accompany a northern Michigan winter. Following a series of conventional images, he suddenly introduces the mastodon floating through the trees, uses a metaphorical flashback to Africa, and thus lays the groundwork for the final image: "I have become the place the crow didn't appear." Similarly, in "My First Day as a Painter," he begins with a list of things to paint in which "nude women" initially seem to be an obsession but are abruptly transformed into a metaphor that encompasses both the regenerative powers of nature and the ethereal beauty resident in all things.

In several of the poems, he reverses the process by beginning with an abstraction and gradually grounding it with an infusion of concrete images. A variant of this technique is found in "Epithalamium," in which a gothic description of the wind blowing straight down from the heavens is used to signify a once-in-a-lifetime experience, a miracle of sorts. By the end of the poem, he has pulled away from this epiphany and begun to doubt that it ever occurred.

Absent in these poems is the self-absorption that in previous volumes has crept into Harrison's voice. He has, "Walter of Battersea" suggests, chosen to dance rather than allow his complaints to overwhelm him or his poetry. Poems such as "A Redolence for Nims," "Noon," and "Birthday" imply that he has come to accept the changes that accompany aging and the losses that punctuate life as part of a cyclical process through which the old skin is shed and a new set of dreams is formulated to provide the needed quotient of warmth. He has, in this sense, gained the necessary distance to transform private preoccupations into artistic statements and to transport the reader into his northern clime so as to share both the romance and the struggle of living in close contact with the environment.

NATURAL WORLD

Natural World, a collaborative venture between Harrison and Diana Guest, combines poetry and sculpture to celebrate the richness and diversity that is to be found beyond the beaten path. As in previous Harrison collections, however, the celebration is muted by acknowledgments of the waste and suffering that humankind has inflicted on the animal kingdom and by references to the inherently painful process of natural selection. The majority of the poems included in this volume are reprinted from previous Harrison collections, most notably from *Plain Song* and *Locations*. In this volume, however, the poems assume an even more poignant resonance because of their juxtaposition with Guest's sculptures. The whales and hawks mourned in "Natural World," for example, emerge as creatures to be revered, as creatures that "alter the universe" and make life a little more livable. Similarly, the foxes of "Fox Farm" and the wolf in "Traverse City Zoo" invite the reader to question the ethics that allow humans to exploit animals for the sake of vanity and commercial gain.

As in his other works, there is a tension between Harrison's naturalist proclivities and his tacit justification of humankind's sporting use of animals. This tension is clearly expressed in "Scrubbing the Floor the Night a Great Lady Died," an ode of sorts following the death of a three-year-old filly. On one hand, Harrison condones the use of animals in the sporting arena by noting that "A great creature died who took her body as far as bodies go toward perfection," but on the other hand, he empathizes with the horse, noting that "if I cannot care about a horse, I cannot care about earth herself. For she was so surely of earth, in earth, once so animate, sprung in some final, perfect form. . . ."

THE THEORY AND PRACTICE OF RIVERS

Perhaps the clue to Harrison's sometimes ambiguity lies in his belief in eternal essences and perpetual flux. These ideas, nascent in "Horse" and "Cobra," come to fruition in *The Theory and Practice of Rivers*, in which he muses that he will "assume the water mask, to finish my life disguised as a creek . . . to swallow myself in ceaseless flow." *The Theory and Practice of Rivers* is consummate Harrison. It reflects not only the breadth of his immense talent and interests but also his ability to control metaphors that would overwhelm lesser writers. The volume is made richer still by a liberal infusion of sketches by Chatham, who did the sectional illustrations for *Selected and New Poems*.

Dedicated to his deceased niece, the book opens with a wide-ranging poem devoted both to her memory and to the possibility that her spirit continues to inhabit the rivers in which she once played. In this poem, Harrison uses water imagery as a recurrent metaphor, but he also broaches countless other subjects as he allows his mind's eye to reflect on past adventures in all corners of the globe. Despite the diversity of subject matter, however, Harrison is constantly attuned to the mysterious ebb and flow that characterizes the life process, a process akin to a voyage across uncharted waterways. As with the other poems in this collection, the tone of the title poem ranges from the deadly serious to the playful. In fact, it is the vacillations of mood that make these pieces so compelling and readable. Poetry, Harrison implies in the title poem, must shun equilibrium and systematic formulas, for these are not the things of life. "Life often shatters in schizoid splinters" and defies easy categorization.

Harrison's sardonic wit peppers this volume, as in "The Brand New Statue of Liberty," in which he describes a customized necklace made of representative skulls of those who have been sacrificed for the American Dream. Equally ironic are "Looking Forward to Old Age," "The Times Atlas," and "Rich Folks, Poor Folks, and Neither," each of which critiques the banalities and posturing that have come to characterize modern civilization.

As in his previous works, Harrison relies heavily on allusions and stream-of-consciousness techniques that make the reader see commonplace phenomena in new lights. At the same time, however, he maintains a childlike capacity for wonder and occasionally, as in "My Friend the Bear," when he asks the reader to suspend disbelief and imagine a very different world, a world in which human being and beast form a tentative partnership that serves both their ends.

AFTER IKKYŪ, AND OTHER POEMS

After Ikkyū, and Other Poems is a collection inspired by Harrison's many years of Zen study. The influence of Ikkyū Sojun, the fifteenth century Japanese Zen priest and poet, has energized and freshened Harrison's vision and style. Though Harrison does not consider himself a traditional practitioner of Zen nor of Buddhism, he admires the Eastern style of thinking that cultivates detachment and awaits a flash of insight. The title sequence is composed of fifty-seven lyrics following in the footsteps of Ikkyū, who was the illegitimate son of an emperor and the wild man of Zen. Ikkyū lived outside Kyoto and patronized prostitutes. He liked to challenge people and to question their comfortable apathy, writing poetry about his wandering lifestyle and hatred of hypocrisy. His poetry and lifestyle in some ways resemble that of Harrison. The title poem is the product of an imagination on fire with life, suffering, and questioning reality. The book has other great poems with common Harrison forms and themes: "Time Suite" is a brilliant reflection on the quick passage of days and lives; "Return to Yesenin" is another tribute to the troubled Russian poet who committed suicide.

THE SHAPE OF THE JOURNEY

The Shape of the Journey brings together work from eight previous books plus a new section, "Geo-Bestiary," which contains thirty-four poems on various topics somewhat like the medieval poetic collection of beasts. In this final section, Harrison writes short lyrics inspired by assorted animals and natural scenery: beloved dogs, Mexican blue jays, wildflowers, farm animals, geese, cows, bears, and rural scenes in northern Michigan and Montana. It is clear in this collection looking back over more than thirty years that Harrison still regards himself as a poet first and a novelist a distant second. He was drawn to the novella and novel forms out of the sheer brutal requirement of making a living, which led him to scriptwriting in Hollywood and some brushes with fame. In the introduction, Harrison describes himself as temperamentally unsuited to teaching but from a young age profoundly drawn to the deep European and American tradition of letters with his devotion to the poetry of Theodore Roethke, Robert Lowell, Ezra Pound, Robert Duncan, Robert Bly, Gary Snyder, Charles Olson, William Carlos Williams, Apollinaire, Arthur Rimbaud, and Walt Whitman. Writing poetry was almost a religious calling for Harrison, who tried the assorted occupations of teaching, farming, construction work, and book wholesaling for the sole purpose of giving himself an income and the time to write poetry.

Harrison regards the impetus to write poetry as emanating from the same force that led prehistoric humans to etch paintings in cave ceilings or carve petroglyphs in rocks. There is a bardic, neoprimitive voice in many of his best poems such as "The Theory and Practice of Rivers" and the poems of *After Ikkyū, and Other Poems. The Shape of the Journey* shows Harrison's many flights of imagination in all directions and his bouts with clinical depression and a frenzied, ecstatic joy of living. His obsessions run the gamut from obscure Zen Buddhist practices to the folk medicine of American Indians and Mexicans. The visual scenery is often stunning and informed by the rural beauty of northern Michigan, southern Arizona, or small-town Montana, places where Harrison could pursue his muse. He seems unfazed by the lack of material success (though he has experienced it) and uninterested in the lack of attention paid to twenty-first century poets; Harrison belongs to an older world in which bards spoke for the community and were acknowledged as shamans and wise people, not insane mystics. The sweep and raw power of this collection shows Harrison at his best: honest, wry, humorous, self-deprecating, and visionary. Harrison is a poet who is blind in one eye and physically ugly, yet deeply attuned to beauty in nature and the human (especially female) form.

BRAIDED CREEK

In *Braided Creek*, Harrison and fellow poet Ted Kooser embark on a dialogue in the form of three- and four-line haiku-like effusions. These conversational, wry, and offbeat lyrics have an honest, earthy tone and are often vigorous and funny. Some of them are aphoristic puzzles resembling Zen koans, which do not reveal their meaning on the first reading but eventually bring forth distilled experience and even wisdom. The poems sometimes pose a question or make a sharp observation of particulars: the moon's shadow over the backyard, the mouse drowned in the toilet, or the beauty of a girl wearing blue shorts while walking a dog. The book is an attempt to distill the essence of friendship and acute observation through hard times. After Kooser was diagnosed with cancer, Harrison witnessed his friend's poems becoming more vivid. Each poem reads like the traditional seventeen-syllable haiku but does not follow the format precisely. The collection reads quickly but does not seem immediately meaningful. Oddly suited for an age of short attention spans, *Braided Creek* lacks any introduction and annotation so that the reader is forced to guess which author wrote each short poem. The two poets together ponder growing old and realizing that the best days are past, but they also embrace life, good food, cheap wine, and the thrill of watching a dog chase a jackrabbit through wet grass. The book is full of the mysteries of living, the wonder of the natural world, and the language of relationships and dreams. *Braided Creek* is testimony to the richness of friendship and common interests of two accomplished poets.

SAVING DAYLIGHT

Many of the poems in *Saving Daylight*, Harrison's first collection of new poems since *After Ikkyū, and Other Poems*, first appeared in a wide variety of periodicals such as *American Poetry Review*, *The New York Times Book Review*, and *Men's Journal*, which published "Bars," a typical Harrison evocation. The title poem, "Saving Daylight," refers to people not changing their clocks but preferring God's time, which means listening to any crazy voice giving them extreme directions such as to go to war or to avoid sexual activity. In his own life, Harrison claims to be following a school without visible teachers. The book is testimony to a veteran writer's continued productivity and creative genius. Some new topics and techniques appear, such as four poems in Spanish; in one of these poems, the narrator claims that the world should speak Spanish because English is the language of conquest and murder. The book occasionally wanders into political satire, with poems containing justifications of war and descriptions of politicians who prevent newspapers from printing photographs of American war casualties. The strongest poem in the book is "Livingston Suite," a return to a familiar form that allows Harrison the narrative space to reflect on life in small-town Montana, where the drowning of a boy in a river caused the poet to look back over his lifetime and what it means to reach the end of long journey, the eventual destination of all life on Earth.

At his best, Harrison uses his elliptical thought patterns and Eastern influences to make connections that would not otherwise be obvious and to force the reader to stretch intellectually. Although his segues are not always easy to follow given the syntactical and grammatical liberties that he takes, they are generally insightful and worthy of pursuit, connecting not only with one another but with the reader as well. His ability to capture the sounds and movements of the woods and rural environs, no less than his ability to translate the pathos of the dispossessed and disaffected, should surely earn him a hearing among all those who are concerned with what has been sacrificed in the name of civilization. Harrison, regrettably, represents a dying breed; he is a poet sufficiently attuned to the natural environment to tally the losses and to do it with a remarkable native wit. He may not be the most famous or well known, but Harrison is certainly one of the most accomplished and skilled American poets of the later twentieth and early twenty-first centuries.

OTHER MAJOR WORKS

LONG FICTION: *Wolf: A False Memoir*, 1971; *A Good Day to Die*, 1973; *Farmer*, 1976; *Legends of the Fall*, 1979 (collection of three novellas: *Revenge, The Man Who Gave Up His Name*, and *Legends of the Fall*); *Warlock*, 1981; *Sundog: The Story of an American Foreman*, 1984; *Dalva*, 1988; *The Woman Lit by Fireflies*, 1990 (collection of three novellas: *Brown Dog, Sunset Limited*, and *The Woman Lit by Fireflies*); *Julip*, 1994 (collection of three novellas: *Julip,.The Seven Ounce Man*, and *The Beige Dolorosa*); *The Beast God Forgot to Invent*, 2000 (collection of three novellas: *The Beast God Forgot to Invent, Westward Ho*, and *Forgot to Go to Spain*); *True North*, 2004; *The Summer He Didn't Die*, 2005 (collection of three novellas: *The Summer He Didn't Die, Republican Wives*, and *Tracking*); *Returning to Earth*, 2007; *The English Major*, 2008.

SCREENPLAYS: *Cold Feet*, 1988 (with Thomas McGuane); *Revenge*, 1989; *Wolf*, 1994 (with Wesley Strick).

NONFICTION: *Just Before Dark: Collected Nonfiction*, 1991; *The Raw and the Cooked: Adventures of a Roving Gourmand*, 2001; *Conversations with Jim Harrison*, 2002 (Robert DeMott, editor); *Off to the Side: A Memoir*, 2002.

CHILDREN'S LITERATURE: *The Boy Who Ran to the Woods*, 2000.

BIBLIOGRAPHY

Davis, Todd. "A Spiritual Topography: Northern Michigan in the Poetry of Jim Harrison." *Midwest Quarterly* 42, no. 1 (Autumn, 2000): 94-104. Examines the spiritual topography in the poetry of Harrison, specifically how his quest for life's meaning is influenced by the natural world, particularly the landscape of northern Michigan.

Harrison, Jim. Interviews. *Conversations with Jim Harrison*. Edited by Robert DeMott. Jackson: University Press of Mississippi, 2002. This collection of interviews with Harrison includes bibliographic references and an index.

_____. "Pleasures of the Hard-Won Life: An Interview with Jim Harrison." Interview by Charles McGrath. *The New York Times Book Review*, January 25, 2007, p. 27-28. Discusses how Harrison's love of food and hard drinking led to health problems that have altered his lifestyle but not his zest for living.

Orr, Gregg, and Beef Torrey. *Jim Harrison: A Comprehensive Bibliography, 1964-2008*. Introduction by Robert De Mott. Lincoln: University of Nebraska Press, 2009. This bibliography lists all the works of Harrison, whether print or other media, as well as reviews and interviews, both by and of the writer.

Pichaske, David R. *Rooted: Seven Midwest Writers of Place*. Iowa City: University of Iowa Press, 2006. The chapter on Harrison is entitled "Reluctant Postmodernist," and looks at how the upper Michigan region plays a part in Harrison's writings.

Reilly, Edward C. *Jim Harrison*. New York: Twayne, 1996. In this book of Harrison criticism, Reilly discusses the ways in which Harrison uses his writing as a medium for social commentary, among other topics.

Seaman, Donna. Review of *In Search of Small Gods*. *Booklist* 105, no. 13 (March 1, 2009): 15. This review of Harrison's poetry collection finds the poet creating a self-deprecating self-portrait. The poems deal with death, mortality, nature, and Harrison's daily life.

Smith, Patrick A. *The True Bones of My Life*. East Lansing: Michigan State University Press, 2002. With this collection of essays, Smith explores Harrison's fiction in terms of such ideas as the American myth, the American Dream, postmodernism, and the importance of place. Includes several photographs, an index, a critical bibliography, and a bibliography of Harrison's work that lists many of his published essays.

Taylor, Henry. "Next to Last Things." *Poetry* 176, no. 2 (May, 2000): 96-106. As part of an omnibus review, Taylor applies his considerable critical skills to an appreciation of Harrison's *The Shape of the Journey*.

Veale, Scott. "Eat Drink Man Woman." Review of *The Shape of the Journey*. *The New York Times Book Review*, January 3, 1999, p. 15. In this brief review, Veale finds this collection to have "a meandering feeling." He praises Harrison's grounding in the natural world, especially in those poems set in rural Michigan. He also values Harrison's colloquial style.

C. Lynn Munro; Philip K. Jason
Updated by Jonathan Thorndike

ROBINSON JEFFERS

Born: Allegheny (now in Pittsburgh), Pennsylvania; January 10, 1887
Died: Carmel, California; January 20, 1962

OTHER LITERARY FORMS

Robinson Jeffers explained his own work and expressed his ideas on society and art in some detail in the forewords to the Modern Library edition (1935) of *Roan Stallion, Tamar, and Other Poems* and *The Selected Poetry of Robinson Jeffers*. Other important prose statements are "Poetry, Gongorism, and a Thousand Years" (*The New York Times Book Review*, January 18, 1948); *Themes in My Poems* (1956); and *The Selected Letters of Robinson Jeffers, 1897-1962* (1968, Ann N. Ridgeway, editor).

In addition, the poet William Everson has collected, from various forgotten pages, two volumes of poetry that Jeffers had discarded. These volumes reconstitute the work of the transitional period from 1916 to 1922. They are *The Alpine Christ, and Other Poems* (1973) and *Brides of the South Wind* (1974).

ACHIEVEMENTS

Many years after his death, Robinson Jeffers remains probably the most controversial American poet, with the exception of Edgar Allan Poe, who has never been termed major. A number of important writers and critics have ranked him with Walt Whitman and invoked the Greek tragedians in trying to suggest his somber power. In the early years of his fame, his books typically went into several editions, and he was the subject of a *Time* magazine cover story. In 1947, his free translation of *Medea* for the New York stage brought him new acclaim as a dramatic poet. Since the early years of his fame, however, some critics, few but influential, were hostile, and others found Jeffers merely uninteresting as the subject of critical examination. The deep division over Jeffers's importance as a poet is seen today in college anthologies: He is given generous space in some and omitted entirely from others. The weight of criticism, however, has been consistently on the positive side. Serious studies have been published about his work that, while strongly favorable, avoid the extravagant praise of some of Jeffers's early admirers. All but the most hostile critics are agreed that he had an unmistakably original voice, strong dramatic talents, and great descriptive ability. He is the only American poet of note since Edwin Arlington Robinson—who praised him highly—to write a large quantity of narrative poetry. Some of Jeffers's short lyrics, moreover, notably "Hurt Hawks," "The Eye," "The Purse-Seine," and "Shine, Perishing Republic," seem destined to become classics. In addition to his poetic gifts, and indeed inseparable from them, is the force of a worldview that is unusual, coherent, and challenging, a set of reasoned attitudes that justifies classifying him as a philosophical poet of unusual interest. Jeffers's radical skepticism about the human race, embodied in his doctrine that humans should "uncenter" themselves from the universe, is expressed in poetry that draws on considerable scientific and historical study, on thorough knowledge of religious and classical literature, and on deep resources of myth and ritual. It is the combination of poetic power and philosophical stance that argues strongly for Jeffers's place in a twentieth century pantheon of American poets. Jeffers won a number of awards, including the Levinson Prize (1940), the Eunice Tietjens Prize (1951), and a Union League Civic and Arts Poetry Prize from *Poetry* magazine; the Borestone Mountain Poetry Award (1955); the Academy of American Poets Fellowship (1958); and the Shelley Memorial Award (1961). He was never given the Pulitzer Prize, even though Edna St. Vincent Millay and Louis Untermeyer, among others, repeatedly pressed his case. He served as chancellor for the Academy of American Poets from 1946 to 1955 and was a member of the American Academy of Arts and Letters from 1937 to 1962.

BIOGRAPHY

John Robinson Jeffers's life, milieu, and work are of one piece. From his early adulthood, one can see him choosing a place of living and a way of life that are strongly reflected in his poetry and in his occasional prose statements about his work.

When Jeffers was born in Pittsburgh in 1887, his father was forty-nine, his mother twenty-seven. His father's occupation as well as his age set the boy apart; the senior Jeffers had been a Presbyterian minister and was professor of Old Testament literature and exegesis at Western Theological Seminary. Young Robin was an only child for seven years, and he spent much of his time in solitary wandering or reading on the relatively isolated family property. He was later educated in Switzerland for nearly four years, in schools in which the language of instruction was either French or German. His father had introduced him to Greek at the age of five, and he also acquired Latin and some Italian. After his parents moved to Los Angeles, he entered Occidental College, where he continued his classical and literary education and supplemented his childhood religious training with courses in biblical literature and theology.

Although popular with his fellow students, Jeffers already was establishing the pattern of his life through his interest in camping and mountain climbing on one hand, and in reading and writing on the other. Graduating at eighteen, he then pursued medical studies at the University of Southern California, and later studied forestry, hoping to find a way to support himself amid nature that would permit him time for poetry. A small legacy, however, enabled him to settle, with his bride Una Call Custer, in Carmel, California, in 1914. The whole area, then uncrowded, had a dramatic beauty, and Jeffers called it his "inevitable place." He was profoundly affected by its massive simplicity of elements: huge, treeless mountains plunging directly into the Pacific, broken by occasional narrow canyons in which little groves of redwoods grew; the constant pound and swirl of the sea against bare granite shore-rocks; hawks soaring above the headlands where cattle were pastured. In this setting, Jeffers helped masons construct a simple stone house on Carmel Point, looking directly seaward; and later, he built with his own hands, using boulders that he laboriously rolled up from the shore, his famous Hawk Tower. Evoking with its name the fierce independence of the birds that were one of his favorite subjects, the tower became symbolically for him a place beyond time, a psychological vantage point for his often apocalyptic and prophetic stance in the world.

With his wife, to whom he was devoted, Jeffers reared twin sons (a daughter, born previously, lived only a day), and lived quietly in Carmel, departing only for vacations in Taos, New Mexico, and for rare trips to the East Coast or the British Isles. With a very few exceptions, he did not participate in the round of readings, book reviews, or campus appearances that characterizes the life of so many American poets.

When Jeffers died in 1962, it was in the seaward bedroom of his own house. There, in the poem "The Bed by the Window," he had many years earlier envisioned the day when a ghostly figure would appear, rap with his staff, and say, "Come, Jeffers."

ANALYSIS

Robinson Jeffers's central concept of the universe and of humankind's place in it, all-important in understanding his poetry, is grounded in his respect for scientific thought and in his own historical observations, but strongly colored in its expression by emotion. From science, he took a cool, analytical view of the human race as one species that evolved in one stage of an ever-evolving, dynamic universe—a mere "fly-speck" in the scheme of things. Perhaps because of his interest in astronomy (his younger brother, Hamilton, was for many years a scientist at the Lick Observatory in California), he took an extraterrestrial view even of Earth. The first photograph taken by the astronauts of Earth from the vicinity of the moon represented a view that Jeffers had achieved in his imagination long before: "It is only a little planet/ But how beautiful it is. . . ." In "The Double Axe," Jeffers paid tribute to one of the scientists who helped him to achieve this view, Copernicus, hailing him as the first who "pushed man/ Out of his insane self-importance."

A second factor that influenced Jeffers's outlook was his study of history. From the British archaeologist Flinders Petrie and the Italian philosopher Giovanni Battista Vico, Jeffers drew the concept of cultural cycles and the conviction that cultural or national groupings are inherently unstable and social progress temporary. This view, again, was bolstered by his observations of the inevitable cycles of growth, flowering, and decay in nature. It was given special force by Jeffers's belief, influenced by Oswald Spengler, that Western civilization was already on the downgrade.

Many scientists share Jeffers's objective view of the world but not the intensity of his feeling for the insignificance of humanity or the "beauty of things," his often-used phrase for natural loveliness. The roots of Jeffers's feeling seem to be in the Calvinistic teachings of his father's religion, which proclaimed the glory of God and the nothingness of humans. Rejecting his father's Christian God, Jeffers transferred his religious feeling to a new object, a universe whose parts are all "expressions of the same energy," a dynamic universe, ever in strain and struggle, and ever in that process discovering its own nature. In a letter outlining his views, Jeffers wrote, "This whole is in all its parts so beautiful, and is felt by me to be so intensely in earnest, that I am compelled to love it, and to think of it as divine." He went on to say that he felt there was "peace, freedom, I might say a kind of salvation, in turning one's affections toward this one God, rather than inward on one's self, or on humanity, or on human imagination and abstractions. . . ." Jeffers's sole admission of the possibility that humans could have a positive effect was to say that one may "contribute (ever so slightly) to the beauty of things by making one's own life and environment beautiful." Although he granted that such action could include moral beauty, which he called one of the qualities of humanity, for the most part the weight of his emotions was on the side of sad resignation where the human race was concerned, or actual disgust with its frequent moral ugliness.

Jeffers's intensity of feeling for natural beauty and especially for the dynamism of nature was profoundly affected by his lifelong residence on the spectacular Carmel coast. The area not only is ruggedly beautiful but also is wracked by periodic events reminding one of the awesome power of nature and of humans' uncertain tenure on Earth: brush fires that sweep the dry hills in late summer and sometimes destroy farms and homes, earthquakes that shudder along the San Andreas fault, fierce winds that torture the picturesque Monterey cypresses, and drenching rains that bring floods and dangerous mudslides. These natural events, recalling the fire, earthquake, wind, and deluge of the biblical apocalypse, appear as major instruments of destruction in many of the narratives, and are centrally important, too, in some of the lyrics. Most important, probably, was the sheer beauty of the surroundings, beauty that Jeffers identified as one of the six major themes in his poems in a talk given in 1941 at the Library of Congress. It is possible to imagine Jeffers living on the coast of Ireland, or in the Scottish Hebrides, or on a mountainside, but not in a quiet New England meadow or an industrial city. He chose his landscape, his "inevitable place," and it in turn formed him and became a major actor in his dramas. Today the Carmel/Big Sur area is known as Jeffers country.

The expression of his basic attitudes, to which Jeffers eventually gave the name "Inhumanism," took three major forms in poetry: dramatic, narrative, and, loosely considered, lyric. The dramatic poetry includes not only a play primarily intended for stage production, an adaptation of Euripides' *Medea* (pb. 1946), but also dramas primarily intended to be read, a Japanese Nō play, and a masque. The narratives and dramas range in length to well above one hundred pages. The lyrics include some poems that are of substantial length—several pages or more. Some poems are mixtures of elements and defy classification.

The narratives and dramas reveal metaphorically—and occasionally through interposed comments—the poet's preoccupation with the self-concern and solipsism of the human race. At the same time, they express Jeffers's sense of the historical cycles of human behavior and of the larger cycle of death and rebirth that Jeffers called, in "Cawdor," the "great Life." To embody these attitudes, Jeffers chose a number of often shocking subjects: incest, murder, rape, self-mutilation because of guilt, suicide, and the sexual feelings of a woman for a horse.

TAMAR

One of the best of the long narratives, the one that caused the greatest initial sensation when it was published with other poems in 1924, is *Tamar*. The setting is an isolated part of the California coast, where the Cauldwell family lives. Circumstances lead the daughter, Tamar, and her brother, Lee, into incest. Later, Tamar learns that her father had committed the same sin with his sister, now long dead. In one strange scene on the beach at night, Tamar is possessed sexually by the ghosts of the Indians who once occupied the area; the scene is a kind of descent into death, and after it Tamar is a "flame," self-destructive and demoniac, feeling herself doomed because of her breaking of natural laws. She then tempts her father sexually, as if to prove her depravity, although she commits no sexual act with him. Finally, the entire family is consumed in a fire from which they could have saved themselves had not Tamar, her brother, and her suitor, Will Andrews, been acting out the climax of fierce sexual jealousy.

This seemingly fantastic and occasionally lurid drama was based on one or both of the two biblical Tamar stories, and on Percy Bysshe Shelley's *The Cenci: A Tragedy in Five Acts* (pb. 1819), all of which include incest. These tales in turn, however, are overshadowed by the Greek myth of the creation of the human race: the incest of Heaven and Earth to produce Titan, and Titan's ensuing incest with his mother, Earth, to produce a child. Thus Jeffers has created a modern story based on layers of myth, reminding readers of the powerful libidinal forces that have been repressed by millennia of taboos but never, as Sophocles and Sigmund Freud noted, eliminated from human nightmares. Further, the isolated home of the Cauldwells on Point Lobos allegorically suggests the entire world, and the initial incest has strong overtones of Adam's fall. Thus humans' failure to relate themselves humbly to their environment, obeying natural laws such as the ban on incest, is comparable to Adam and Eve ignoring God's command to know their place in the scheme of things. The expulsion of Adam and Eve from paradise is comparable to the troubles visited on the little world of the House of Cauldwell. The story, moreover, is a chapter of apocalypse, with fire—persistently invoked throughout as an agent of cleansing destruction—accomplishing the destruction of Judgment Day. It is prophecy inasmuch as it warns against humankind's self-concern. It is also persistently evocative, as Robert J. Brophy has pointed out (*Robinson Jeffers: Myth, Ritual, and Symbol in His Narrative Poems*, 1973), of the monomyth of the seasonal cycle of death and rebirth. Yet only in relatively recent years have critics paid systematic attention to the complexity of *Tamar* and Jeffers's other narratives.

NARRATIVES

Jeffers's other narratives similarly explore recurrent patterns of human conduct as expressed in folklore, myth, or religion. "Roan Stallion," the poet's most powerful short narrative, is a modern version of the myth of God uniting with a human. This pattern is seen not only in the Christian story of the fatherhood of Jesus, but also in myths from various cultures, especially the Greek tales of Zeus and his sexual encounters—with Leda, when he took the form of a swan; with Antiope, as a satyr; with Europa, as a bull; and others. "The Tower Beyond Tragedy," one of Jeffers's most successful long poems, is a free adaptation of the first two plays of Aeschylus's *The Oresteia* (458 B.C.E.). In "Cawdor," the poet reworks the Hippolytus story of Euripides, adding an element—self-mutilation—from Sophocles' *Oedipus the King* (429-401 B.C.E.). "The Loving Shepherdess," another relatively early narrative that was well received, is imaginatively based on the Scottish legend of "Feckless Fannie." "Such Counsels You Gave to Me" is built on suggestions from the Scottish ballad "Edward, Edward," which in turn, like all true ballads, invokes deep folk memories. Other narratives explore age-old problems. "Give Your Heart to the Hawks" explores the question of who should administer justice; "Thurso's Landing" considers when, if ever, it is right to take another's life out of pity.

THE WOMEN AT POINT SUR

In one of his early long poems—the longest, in fact, at 175 pages—Jeffers did not base his story on myth or folklore, but created a poem that has become itself a kind of literary legend of magnificent failure: *The Women at Point Sur*. It is a violent, brilliant, chaotic, and difficult-to-comprehend story of a mad minister who collects disciples by telling them that there are no more moral rules and that they can do as their hearts, or bodies, desire. The poem did not generally achieve one of its main purposes, which, as Jeffers put it, was to show "the danger of that 'Roan Stallion' idea of 'breaking out of humanity,' misinterpreted in the mind of a fool or a lunatic." The prologue and other parts are impressive, nevertheless, and the poem has a curiously prescient character. Barclay, who commits an incestuous rape to prove that he is beyond good and evil himself, leads his followers into sex orgies. Not very many years later, the Big Sur area of the poem was the scene of sometimes tragic experimentation in sexual behavior amid some of the more extreme communes and "sensitivity institutes." Further, Barclay's corrupting influence on those around him prefigured the monstrous sway that Charles Manson held over the young women who went out from his remote California hideaway to do murder at his bidding.

SECOND PERIOD

The nature of the narratives and dramas changed somewhat through the years. In Jeffers's first mature period (his youthful work, when he produced two volumes of conventional verse, is of interest only to specialists), the concentration was on writing modern versions of myths, such as *Tamar*. In the second period, ranging from the late 1920's to about 1935, the narratives were realistic, though still based on older stories. Such scenes as the violation of Tamar by ghostly Indians were no longer written. "Cawdor," "Thurso's Landing," and "Give Your Heart to the Hawks" were in this vein, while "Dear Judas," chronologically a part of the period, a play in the Japanese Nō form, was based on myth and religion. In the late 1930's, Jeffers again concentrated on myth. In two of his least successful narratives, "Solstice" and "Such Counsels You Gave to Me," he focused on what Frederick I. Carpenter (*Robinson Jeffers*, 1962) has called "case histories in abnormal psychology." In the same period Jeffers wrote "At the Birth of an Age," a philosophical poem, partly in dramatic form, which has as a central figure a self-torturing Hanged God of the universe. One of the most interesting of Jeffers's poems, it is also one of the most complex and difficult, often appealing primarily to the mind, and having some of the same virtues and faults as Shelley's *Prometheus Unbound: A Lyrical Drama in Four Acts* (pb. 1820).

"THE DOUBLE AXE"

Jeffers again ventured into the mythic and the supernatural in "The Double Axe," a two-part poem published in 1948. In the first part, "The Love and the Hate," he took an idea from his earlier "Resurrection," a short narrative (1932) about a World War I soldier returned miraculously from the grave. In "The Love and the Hate," Hoult Gore has similarly returned from death in World War II. His denunciation of war and his presentation of the facts about who actually suffers for the pride of patriots and politicians are sometimes eloquent, but the ghoulishness of the central figure, the walking corpse, is so naturally repellent that it is difficult for the reader to sympathize with the hero emotionally, much less to identify with him. Additionally, there are moments when the writing comes close to unintentional humor, as when Gore's widow, first seeing him, says he looks "dreadful." The violence of the action, even though it is meant to be cleansing, is not properly prepared for by the buildup of emotions, so that it seems exaggerated and gratuitous. The second half of the poem, "The Inhumanist," is much more successful. In this poem, Jeffers creates a new mythical hero, an old man armed with Zeus's double-bitted axe, which is a symbol both of divine destruction and procreation. This Inhumanist has various adventures in the course of a complex and sometimes supernatural story. Despite its flaws, which include prosy passages of bitter political ranting, it is one of the essential poems for anyone wishing to achieve a full knowledge of Jeffers's thought.

"HUNGERFIELD"

"The Double Axe," which dealt a heavy blow to Jeffers's reputation, was succeeded by one other major narrative, another excursion into the supernatural, but this time a generally successful one—"Hungerfield." Written after the crushing blow of Una Jeffers's death, "Hungerfield" tells the story of a man who wrestled with death to save his mother from cancer. This violation of natural laws causes all kinds of other natural disasters to occur, recalling the way that the "miracle drugs" and chemical sprays with which people and farmlands are treated cause unforeseen and often disastrous side effects. The Hungerfield story, which also has mythic references (Hungerfield is a Hercules figure), is framed by Jeffers's personal meditation on the death of his wife, and ends with his reconciliation with it. These framing passages lack the compactness and intense poetic power of Jeffers's best lyrics, but their directness, tenderness, and simplicity carry them past the danger of sentimentality and make them moving and effective.

"THE PLACE FOR NO STORY"

The lyric poems, which are here taken to include all the shorter poems that are not basically narratives or dramas, celebrate the same things and denounce the same things as the narratives. Being primarily meditations on one subject, they are more intense and unified, and are free of the problems of multilayered poems such as *The Women at Point Sur*. Typically, a Jeffers lyric describes an experience and comments on it; and it does this in the simple, declarative voice that stamped every poem with his unique signature.

"The Place for No Story," although exceptionally short, is an excellent example. Jeffers opens with a simple description: "The coast hills at Sovranes Creek:/ No trees, but dark scant pasture drawn thin/ Over rock shaped like flame." Then he describes the "old ocean at the land's foot, the vast/ Gray extension beyond the long white violence." Jeffers describes a herd of cattle on the slope above the sea, and above that "the gray air haunted with hawks. . . ." Ending this section with a colon, he draws, figuratively and spiritually, a deep breath and simply states:

> This place is the noblest thing I have ever seen
> No imaginable
> Human presence here could do anything
> But dilute the lonely self-watchful passion.

There are many qualities to notice in this simple poem, qualities that will stand for those of scores of other lyrics, meditations, mixed-mode poems, and sections of the narratives and dramas. First, there is the voice. It is simple and colloquial, as characteristically attuned to the rhythms of everyday American speech as anything by Robert Frost. The word order is natural. The diction is simple and dignified, but not formal. It reflects Jeffers's conscious decision to focus on things that will endure. It would have been easily comprehensible in sixteenth century England, and will almost certainly be so for centuries to come. The poem is written in the typical style of the mature Jeffers: no rhyme, no regular metrical pattern.

As Jeffers explained, however, he had a sense of pattern that made him disagree with those who called his lines free verse. His feeling, he once wrote, was for the number of beats to the line and also for the quantitative element of long and short syllables. Most of his poems break up into recurring patterns of beats per line—ten and five, six and four, five and three alternations being common. In this poem, less regular than many, there is still a recurrence of four-beat lines, culminating in a pair at the end to make a couplet effect. The longer lines run mostly to six stresses, depending on how the poem is read. Binding the whole together is a subtle pattern of alliteration, a device that Jeffers used with full consciousness of his debt to the strong-stress lines of Anglo-Saxon verse.

In the first few lines, for example, the hard "c" of "coast" is repeated in "Creek" (and picked up much later in another stressed word, "cows"); the "s" in "Sovranes" reappears in "scant" and "shaped"; the "d" in "dark" reappears in "drawn"; the "f" of "flame," in "foot"; the "v" of "vast" in "violence"; the "h" in "hills" appears five lines later in "herd," six lines later in "hardly," seven lines later in "haunted" and "hawks." A notable assonance is "old ocean," which works to slow down its line with its long syllables.

In this short lyric, too, are embodied some of Jeffers's key ideas. The ocean's "violence" reminds the reader of the struggle ever present in the natural world. The contrast between rock, a symbol of endurance, and flame, a symbol of violent change, suggests that even rocks undergo change from the same process of oxidation that produces flame. Above, the hawks are Jeffers's preferred symbol of independence and of the inexorable violence of nature. The poem simply and unaffectedly celebrates beauty and at the end reminds the reader of the insignificance of human beings in a universe still discovering itself in the "passion" of its dynamic life.

The qualities found in this short lyric are found in abundance in many other poems of varying length. Among the most notable of the short poems not already cited are "To the Stone-Cutters," "Night," "Boats in a Fog," "Noon," "Rock and Hawk," "Love the Wild Swan," "Return," "All the Little Hoofprints," "Original Sin," "The Deer Lay Down Their Bones," and "For Una."

LONGER LYRICS

Among the longer lyrics, several are important for a full understanding of the poet. Chief among these is *Apology for Bad Dreams*, Jeffers's *ars poetica*. "Meditation on Saviors" and "De Rerum Virtute" are also important philosophical poems, as is "Margrave," a short narrative framed by an approximately equal amount of meditative lyric. Two large sections of "Cawdor" contain particularly powerful lyric sections. These, "The Caged Eagle's Death-Dream" and "The Old Man's Dream After He Died," have been reprinted in *The Selected Poetry of Robinson Jeffers* (1938).

THE BEGINNING AND THE END

After passing through a period (1938-1948) during which many of his poems were bitter political harangues, Jeffers achieved a quieter tone in the poems that were posthumously printed in *The Beginning and the End*. They lack the close texture and the intensity, however, of his better poems from earlier years, and tend to become prosy. At the same time, in their increasing concern with astrophysics, the origins of human life, and the terrible prospect that all may end in a nuclear catastrophe, they explore new territory and provide a fitting, relatively serene end to an enormously productive career.

LEGACY

In seeking to place Jeffers in the continuum of American poets, one is drawn to generalizations that often apply surprisingly well to Walt Whitman, who was temperamentally and sometimes philosophically Jeffers's polar opposite. Like Whitman, Jeffers was a technical innovator, developing a typically long, colloquial line and a voice that can be mistaken for no other. Like Whitman, he was often charged, with some justification, with using inflated rhetoric and exaggeration to achieve his effects, and with repetitiveness. Like Whitman, he was a poet of extremes, and for that reason perhaps he will be best appreciated when some of the political and social passions that he stirred have been forgotten. Like Whitman, too, Jeffers had a well-developed set of attitudes toward society and the world. These views put both men in the prophetic stance at times. Like

Whitman, Jeffers was deeply religious in a pantheistic way, and so profoundly conscious of the cycle of birth and regeneration that he thought of death as a redeemer.

Many of these characteristics are those of a public poet, a person in a dialogue with his nation and the world about its life and the right way of living. Beyond these qualities, Jeffers had other attributes of the public poet. He was not only prophetic, admonishing and seeking reform in attitudes and behavior, but also apocalyptic, standing apart and reminding his readers of the immanence and possible imminence of worldly destruction. He was historical, reminding them that cultures and nations had risen and fallen before them. He was an early environmentalist, reminding Americans that they were part of a complex cycle of life, and castigating them for their sins against the earth. He was an explorer of the depths probed by Freud and Carl Jung—and thus a psychological poet. He was also a mystical poet—the "Caged Eagle's Death-Dream" constituting a supreme illustration.

The process of sifting out and properly appraising the poems in which Jeffers succeeded in his various roles has begun. No single long narrative has been acclaimed by all favorable critics as entirely successful, but it is certain that at least half a dozen, probably led by "Roan Stallion," will survive. Many lyrics and shorter mixed-mode poems, however, are generally esteemed, and it is these poems that already have assured Jeffers a place among the honored writers of the century. Finally, the quality that seems most likely to ensure Jeffers's future stature is his very lack of timeliness. His references are not to ephemera but to rock, hawk, sea, and mountain—things that will be with the world as long as humans are there to perceive their beauty and their significance.

OTHER MAJOR WORKS

PLAYS: *Medea*, pb. 1946 (adaptation of Euripides' play); *The Cretan Woman*, pr. 1954 (adaptation of Euripides' play *Hippolytus*).

NONFICTION: *Themes in My Poems*, 1956; *The Selected Letters of Robinson Jeffers, 1897-1962*, 1968 (Ann N. Ridgeway, editor).

BIBLIOGRAPHY

Brophy, Robert J. *Robinson Jeffers: Myth, Ritual, and Symbol in His Narrative Poems*. Reprint. Hamden, Conn.: Archon Books, 1976. This basic study, often referred to by critics, thoroughly establishes the grounding of Jeffers's narrative works in—among others—Judeo-Christian, Greek, Norse, and Hindu mythologies. Contains illustrations, an index, notes, and a bibliography.

_____, ed. *The Robinson Jeffers Newsletter: A Jubilee Gathering, 1962-1988*. Los Angeles: Occidental College, 1988. A collection of the best articles from the first twenty-five years of the journal devoted to the poet and his works. Includes illustrations.

Everson, William. *The Excesses of God: Robinson Jeffers as a Religious Figure*. Stanford, Calif.: Stanford University Press, 1988. The author, himself a poet, sees Jeffers as a bardic and prophetic man and relates him to the thought of such modern theologians as Mircea Eliade. Contains notes and an index. Everson is also the author, under his previous pen name of Brother Antoninus, of an earlier study on the same subject, *Robinson Jeffers: Fragments of an Older Fury* (1968).

Hamilton, Ian. *Against Oblivion: Some Lives of the Twentieth-Century Poets*. London: Viking, 2002. This collection contains biographies and short assessments of poets that Hamilton feels deserve to be remembered for their work, including Jeffers.

Karman, James. *Robinson Jeffers: Poet of California*. Brownsville, Oreg.: Story Line Press, 1995. A revised and expanded edition of Karman's critical biography, which gives insight into the life of Jeffers, his family, and the honor he gave to hard work, self-reliance, and conservation of the environment.

Nolte, William H. *Rock and Hawk: Robinson Jeffers and the Romantic Agony*. Athens: University of Georgia Press, 1978. Relates Jeffers to the traditions of European, English, and American Romantic philosophy and poetry. Includes notes and an index.

Thesing, William B. *Robinson Jeffers and a Galaxy of Writers*. Columbia: University of South Carolina Press, 1995. A collection of critical essays by various authors dealing with Jeffers's life and work. Includes bibliographical references and index.

Vardamis, Alex A. *The Critical Reputation of Robinson Jeffers: A Bibliographical Study*. Hamden, Conn.: Archon Books, 1972. A chronological annotated bibliography of all the books, articles, and reviews about Jeffers from the beginning of his career to 1971. Contains a critical introduction.

Zaller, Robert. *The Cliffs of Solitude: A Reading of Robinson Jeffers*. New York: Cambridge University Press, 1983. An interpretation of Jeffers's entire career, with particular emphasis on the long narratives. Combines the psychoanalytic and mythic viewpoints. Contains chronology, index, notes, and bibliography.

Edward A. Nickerson

W. S. MERWIN

Born: New York, New York; September 30, 1927

OTHER LITERARY FORMS

A talented translator, W. S. Merwin has translated numerous works including *The Poem of the Cid* (1959), Persius's *Satires* (1961), *The Song of Roland* (1963), *Voices*, by Antonio Porchia (1969, 1988), *Transparence of the World*, by Jean Follain (1969), Dante's *Purgatorio* (2000), and poetry by Pablo Neruda and Osip Mandelstam. He has also written plays: *Rumpelstiltskin*, produced by the British Broadcasting Corporation

(BBC) in 1951; _Pageant of Cain_, produced by BBC Third Programme in 1952; and _Huckleberry Finn_, produced by BBC television, 1953. _Darkling Child_ was produced in London by Arts Theatre in 1956, _Favor Island_ was produced by Poet's Theatre in Cambridge, Massachusetts, in 1957, and _The Gilded West_ was produced in 1961 in Coventry, England, by the Belgrade Theatre. Merwin's prose works include _The Miner's Pale Children_ (1970), _Unframed Originals_ (1982), _Regions of Memory: Uncollected Prose, 1949-1982_ (1987, edited by Cary Nelson), _The Lost Upland_ (1992), _The Ends of the Earth: Essays_ (2004), and _Summer Doorways: A Memoir_ (2005).

ACHIEVEMENTS

W. S. Merwin received early recognition for his poetry with the selection in 1952 of _A Mask for Janus_ for publication in the Yale Series of Younger Poets, and he went on to receive many grants, fellowships, and awards. He won two Pulitzer Prizes, for _The Carrier of Ladders_ (1971) and _The Shadow of Sirius_ (2009). He was the recipient of a Kenyon Review Fellowship (1954), a National Institute of Arts and Letters Award (1957), an Arts Council of Great Britain bursary (1957), a Rabinowitz Research Fellowship (1961), a Ford Foundation Grant (1964), a Rockefeller grant (1969), the Academy of American Poets Fellowship (1973), and a National Endowment for the Arts Grant (1978). His many awards and honors include the Bess Hokin Prize (1962), the Chapelbrook Award (1966), the Harriet Monroe Memorial Prize from _Poetry_ magazine (1967), a PEN Translation Prize for _Selected Translations, 1948-1968_ (1969), the Shelley Memorial Award (1974), a Bollingen Prize (1979), the Governor's Award for Literature of the State of Hawaii (1987), and the Aiken Taylor Award in Modern American Poetry (1990). In 1994, he received the Lenore Marshall Poetry Prize for _Travels_, the Theodore Roethke Prize from _Poetry Northwest_, the Wallace Stevens Award, and the Lila Wallace-_Reader's Digest_ Writers' Award. He won the Ruth Lilly Poetry Prize (1998), the Gold Medal for poetry from the American Academy of Arts and Letters (2003), the Harold Morton Landon Translation Award (2003), the Lannan Lifetime Achievement Award (2004), the National Book Award for _Migration_ (2005), and the Bobbitt National Prize for _Present Company_ (2006). He was elected a member of the American Academy of Arts and Letters in 1972 and was a special bicentennial consultant (poet laureate) to the Library of Congress along with poets Rita Dove and Louise Glück in 1999-2000. He served as chancellor for the Academy of American Poets from 1998 to 2000. In 2010, Merwin was named poet laureate consultant in poetry to the Library of Congress.

BIOGRAPHY

William Stanley Merwin was born in New York City on September 30, 1927, and grew up in Union City, New Jersey (where his father was a Presbyterian minister), and in Scranton, Pennsylvania. From his own account, his parents were strict and rather cheerless. His earliest poems, written as a child, were austere hymns for his father. He received his bachelor's degree in English from Princeton University in 1947. In 1947, he married Dorothy Jeanne Ferry, the secretary to a Princeton physicist. While at Princeton, he was befriended by the critic R. P. Blackmur and became very interested in the work of Ezra Pound. Like Pound, he was a student of romance languages and began to value translation as a means of remaking poetry in English. As a student, he even grew a beard in imitation of Pound and eventually went to visit Pound at St. Elizabeths Hospital. In 1949, he followed Pound's example and left the United States to become an expatriate. His sojourn was to last some seven years. From 1949 to 1951, he worked as a tutor in France and Portugal. In 1950, he lived in Mallorca, Spain, where he was tutor to Robert Graves's son, William. Graves's interest in myth became one important influence on the younger poet. In Europe, he met Dido Milroy, whom he married in 1954; they would separate in 1968. After that he made his living for several years by translating from French, Spanish, Latin, and Portuguese. From 1951 through 1953, he worked as translator for the BBC's Third Programme. During 1956 and 1957, Merwin was playwright-in-residence for the Poets' Theatre in Cambridge, Massachusetts, and in 1962, he served as poetry editor for *The Nation*. He was an associate at the Théâtre de la Cité in Lyons, France, during 1964-1965. In 1971, he won a Pulitzer Prize for his collection *The Carrier of Ladders*.

In 1976, Merwin moved to Hawaii to study Buddhism. There he met Paula Schwartz; they were married in 1983. Merwin has made Maui his home base, traveling to the mainland United States to lecture and give readings. He has become an ecological advocate, lending his support to Hawaii's environmental movement.

ANALYSIS

The achievement of W. S. Merwin is both impressive and distinctive. His body of work encompasses a wide range of literary genres and includes poetry, plays, translations, and prose. His development as a poet has spanned great literary distances, from the early formalism of *A Mask for Janus* to the spare, simple language and openness of the verse form he refined in *The Lice*. His poetry has often displayed a prosaic, almost conversational quality, as in "Questions to Tourists Stopped by a Pineapple Field," from *Opening the Hand*.

Although Merwin himself has carefully avoided making in-depth comments or pronouncements about his poetry and has not engaged in the often fussy critical debate that has shadowed his career, his work continues to show evidence that the exploration of the power and enigmatic nature of language is one of his great concerns. His many remarkable translations have perhaps been a stimulating influence on his own innovations of poetic form. In moving away from the rather mannered style of his early verse with its reliance on myth, rhyme, and punctuation to a poetry of silence and absence, Merwin, according to Sandra McPherson, began "researching the erasures of the universe."

Beginning with his first book of poetry, *A Mask for Janus*, Merwin has explored how language structures and creates experience. He has also been devoted to myth, or mythmaking, as a way of making sense of experience. While experimenting with language and myth, he has examined the possibilities of developing poetic forms suited to expressing what language can reveal about the mind and existence. In his search, Merwin has had rich resources to draw from, such as the other languages of his many translations and his firm grounding in earlier poetic traditions. His background led him first to master orthodox forms and later to move beyond them.

His devotion to poetry and his life as a wandering poet have given him a folk hero's aura. Being of the generation that began writing in the 1940's and 1950's, he had his poetic roots in more classically influenced, technically controlled verse forms. His disaffection with the formal poetic styles of his predecessors was shared by other poets of his generation such as James Wright and Robert Bly. What he had to say required new ways of communicating, new vessels that would journey toward new realms of perception. By immersing himself in the literature of other cultures, both as a student of languages and as a translator, Merwin has been able to bring a sense of the archetypal source of all poetic expression to his work. His ability to look at a tree and describe the space between its leaves may be unique among contemporary poets. Merwin has referred to his poems as houses that he makes out of virtually anything and everything he can find. These houses made of words are places where the reader can enter and experience "the echo of everything that has ever/ been spoken."

A MASK FOR JANUS

Published in 1952, *A Mask for Janus* used myth and traditional prosodic forms to explore such themes as the birth-death cycle and the isolated self. In "Meng Tzu's Song," the speaker meditates on concerns of identity and solitude:

> How can I know, now forty
> Years have shuffled my shoulders,
> Whether my mind is steady
> Or quakes as the wind stirs?

At first reading, this poem has the flavor of a translation. Ed Folsom, writing in *W. S. Merwin: Essays on the Poetry* (1987), notes that while the verse in *A Mask for Janus* was seen by some critics as an example of traditional craftsmanship, it was also stiff at times, wordy, and overwrought. In recalling and using the structures and tonalities of a more formal poetry, however, Merwin was able to develop his mastery of those elements and earn his release from them.

THE DANCING BEARS

Merwin continued his use of myth and the narrative form in *The Dancing Bears*. In "East of the Sun and West of the Moon," Merwin uses the myth of Psyche and Cupid to explore the problem of identity. Through language that is often elegant and precisely shaped into neat thirteen-line stanzas, he offers clues to the enigma of inner and outer reality. In what may be read as a clarifying statement, Merwin reveals his belief that "all metaphor . . . is magic," and "all magic is but metaphor." Here, he employs his magic to explore the hidden realms of being.

THE DRUNK IN THE FURNACE

The preoccupation with myth and a formal, poetic style followed in his next two works, *Green with Beasts* and *The Drunk in the Furnace*. However, there is also a strange new energy working as Merwin begins moving away from Greco-Roman myths and toward the creation of his own.

In "The *Portland* Going Out" (from *The Drunk in the Furnace*), the apparent randomness of the disaster that strikes a passing ship recalls to the poet the mystery of life and death and thus of existence itself. The *Portland* had passed close by the poet's ship on its way out of the harbor to an ill-fated rendezvous with a storm, where it put "all of disaster between us: a gulf/ Beyond reckoning." This glimpse into the abyss works ironically as a reaffirmation of life.

There are several other poems in this collection that revolve around images of the sea. Alice N. Benston, writing in *Poets in Progress* (1962), calls the sea the "perfect symbol for Merwin." The duality inherent in the sea as both life-giver and symbol of nature's indifference to humanity provides Merwin with a metaphor for the unknown.

The poems in *The Drunk in the Furnace* take some other new and significant directions. For example, several examine the poet's youth and the family members who helped shape his early experiences. These poems are not reverential but sober, almost bitter reflections on his memories of "faded rooms," his grandfather left alone to die in a nursing home, and his grandmother's failure to see her worst sins as she reminisces about her life. The sarcastic tone of "Grandfather in the Old Men's Home" seems directed at the society in which Merwin was brought up—a society that he would later reject.

The family poems in *The Drunk in the Furnace* and others such as "Home for Thanksgiving" and "A Letter from Gussie" in *The Moving Target* allowed Merwin to explore his past further before turning away to begin a new journey. It is as if these poems generate and voice his realization and declaration that he will no longer be bound by the expectations of the culture into which he was born. Nor will he recognize any longer the restraints of the poetic forms that served as his early models.

THE LICE

The new style toward which Merwin was moving in *The Moving Target* emerges more fully realized in *The Lice*. Here he abandons narrative, adopts open forms, and eliminates punctuation:

> The nights disappear like bruises but nothing is
>   healed
> The dead go away like bruises
> The blood vanishes into the poisoned farmlands
> Pain the horizon
> Remains

With *The Lice*, in effect, Merwin leaves the shore, lifts off the launching pad, and enters a new realm where the poem becomes the vessel for voyages toward "nameless stars." While numerous critics have pointed to the overall negativism and pessimism of *The Lice*, hope is undeniably evident in the very act of poetic discovery, as Merwin sheds his skin and emerges as something born not only "to survive," but indeed "to live."

In *The Lice* lie keys to an understanding of the work that will follow. The stark, even dumbfounding silences in a poem such as "December Among the Vanished"—in which "the old snow gets up and moves taking its/ Birds with it"—attract Merwin away from a world that seems to be in the process of self-destruction and toward a new, strange sensibility. A new spareness, a new simplicity and immediacy inform these poems. Gone are the earlier elaborate, formal structures. According to Ed Folsom and Cary Nelson in their introduction to *W. S. Merwin: Essays on the Poetry*, Merwin had begun to lose, at this stage, his faith in language and for a time was not even sure he could write words to articulate experience. In an interview with Edward Hirsch in 1987, Merwin explained how he came to distrust language, believing that experience cannot be articulated.

The Lice also reveals a new, more serious concern with the deadly corrosiveness of politics and the wanton destruction of the environment by greedy corporations. Behind the poet's initial anger and numbing frustration over mass environmental destruction, however, is a recognition of the potential for other responses to Earth's tragedy. He listens carefully, trying to hear the hidden voices in nature. These voices, and the voices emanating from his inner self, offer the possibility of discovering new consciousness— new poems—as long as he does not allow his anger to deafen him or the state of the world to distract him.

In listening for these other voices, the poet remains open to the discovery not only of the world but also of himself. In "For a Coming Extinction," he asks the reader to join voices with "the sea cows the Great Auks the gorillas" and, using the speech of innocents, to testify to the inherent significance of all life.

THE CARRIER OF LADDERS

A new tone emerges in Merwin's poetry in *The Carrier of Ladders*, which was awarded the Pulitzer Prize in 1971. The tone is one of rebirth and reaffirmation. Thus far he has stared into the dark night of his disillusionment with a world corrupted by human beings and has seen only his own reflection. However much he regrets the alienation that such a vision brought forth, he realizes at this stage that to live and create he must seek the renewal of his own spirit.

To do so, the poet will have to step into the darkness, the unknown, and accept both what is there and what is not there. In "Words from a Totem Animal," Merwin writes,

> My eyes are waiting for me
> in the dusk
> they are still closed
> they have been waiting a long time
> and I am feeling my way toward them

The language and form of *The Carrier of Ladders* are perfectly suited to the poet's task of trying to see things with new eyes. This poetry is less judgmental and more open to the experiences of being alive. The simplicity of the diction, and the clear, fresh immediacy of tone draw the reader into the poems. There the poet waits, "standing in dry air" and "for no reason"—praying simply that his words may be clear.

NATURE

During the 1970's, Merwin continued his search for oneness with nature and the knowledge of self such a quest promises. The childlike innocence achieved in the poems of *The Carrier of Ladders* continues to characterize much of the poetry in *Writings to an Unfinished Accompaniment*, *The Compass Flower*, and *Finding the Islands*. Scattered throughout these books are references to the sea, fish, owls, dogs, cows, stones, mountains, clouds, the moon, and the stars. In "Gift" (*Writings to an Unfinished Accompaniment*), Merwin comes to realize that the revelation he seeks must be found through trust in what is given to him. An almost mystical stillness resides in these poems, as if one could hear the "sound of inner stone."

OPENING THE HAND

With *Opening the Hand*, Merwin looks outward toward more familiar landscapes and situations and fixes his hermetic gaze on them. In a poem about the death of his father, told as through a dream, the poet hallucinates images that seem to haunt him like ominous premonitions. His concern with ecology is also evident in this collection. In "Shaving Without a Mirror," he seems to be waking up from a night outdoors, listening for forest voices. The awe he feels, and his urge to surrender to the experience of being alone in the wilderness, confirms his sense of the interrelatedness of all things, a sense that first emerged in *The Lice*.

"What Is Modern" is a poem charged with irony. Merwin comments on the American culture's ridiculous preoccupation with defining modernity. An undeniable sense of humor and a refreshing looseness characterize the poem: "is the first/ tree that comes/ to mind modern/ does it have modern leaves." While grounded in the particular, the recognizable and commonplace, the poetry of *Opening the Hand* still achieves the same obsidian polish of earlier poems whose spare diction and mutedness gave an ethereal rather than concrete quality to things.

THE RAIN IN THE TREES

The Rain in the Trees combines many of the qualities in the work of the 1960's and 1970's, while continuing Merwin's experiments in style and form. The subjects include his family, nature, travel, John Keats, language, the Statue of Liberty, Hawaii, and love. In such diversity of subjects come surprise and freshness. The poems mirror his wanderings and his restlessness in pursuit of the ineffable.

In "Empty Water," Merwin uses incantatory speech to invoke the spirit of a toad whose eyes were "fashioned of the most/ precious of metals." He chants for the toad's return:

> come back
> believer in shade
> believer in silence and elegance
> believer in ferns
> believer in patience
> believer in the rain

A joy in the primal unity and the inherent beauty of all life is evident throughout *The Rain in the Trees*. In "Waking to the Rain," the poet wakes from a dream "of harmony" to find rain falling on the house, creating the one sound that reveals the silence that surrounds him.

TRAVELS

Travels shows Merwin continuing to experiment with syllabic lines and formal structures of his own devising. As the title suggests, the themes are varied, as are the locales. Meditations on his parents are among the most successful poems collected here, but what seem most fresh are the narratives that deal with historical figures: "Rimbaud's Piano," "The Blind Seer of Ambon," and "The Real World of Manuel Cordova" are likely to become classics of this kind of poem.

THE VIXEN

The Vixen, with its uniformity of style, can be read almost as a book-length poem. At once lyrical, narrative, and meditative, these pieces portray the landscapes and the people of the region in southwest France that Merwin knows so well and that are the subject of his *The Lost Upland*. Merwin's long, unpunctuated breaths of sinuous syntax wrap around line ends, twisting corners of thought and emotion in mesmerizing ways. Many of these pieces are quite short, and, though separately titled, they blend into one another to form a large, richly embroidered tapestry of sensation and a prayer-like celebration of interaction with place.

THE FOLDING CLIFFS

More clearly designed as a book-length poem, *The Folding Cliffs* is a sustained historical narrative about the exploitation of nineteenth century Hawaii. It is a major act of homage to that place that has been Merwin's home since 1976. Though many poems in his earlier collections deal with damage to Hawaii's ecosystems and to its culture, this poem serves as a capstone to Merwin's efforts. It is another in his ongoing testimonies to the experience of loss.

THE RIVER SOUND

Loss remains a theme, as well, in *The River Sound*, a fascinating if somewhat demanding collection that demonstrates Merwin's great vitality as he moves into old age. Stylistically, it is more varied that any of Merwin's other collections, as if, having tried it all, he can now pull from his long experience whatever suits the matter at hand. Although most of the poems here are short, there are three long ones that center and focus the book. "Testimony," with its 229 eight-line stanzas rhyming (though not mechanically) *ababbcbc*, is an ambitious memoir in verse, ranging back over key experiences and people in Merwin's life. "Lament for the Makers," set in fifty-two tidy couplet quatrains, is his tribute to fellow poets now gone. "Suite in the Key of Forgetting" is more associative, conjuring various states of absence and loss.

THE PUPIL

Hawaii and memories of his boyhood on the Atlantic coast take a backseat in *The Pupil*. Instead Merwin turns his poetic eye toward astronomy and the night sky, which allow for reflections on mortality, transience, and the void, delivered in Merwin's familiar fluid sentences. One poem remembers "the year of the well of darkness/ overflowing with no/ moon and no stars"; others portray "the darkness thinking the light" or "the white moments that had traveled so long." Other disparate themes are explored, including government-sponsored torture of bears in Pakistan and 1998's homophobic beating death of Matthew Shepherd in Wyoming.

PRESENT COMPANY

Present Company is a collection of 101 poems that address topics ranging from the prosaic to the profound. Many touch on the act of writing, which the elderly Merwin knows intimately well, and many others reflect on the constant changes that are a fact of old age. The poems are often stark in their portrayals—as if time has stripped away the concealing punctuation and metaphoric language in which younger poets indulge—but they are rarely brutal. Rather, Merwin's voice has become almost gentle in its reflective observation of long-deceased people and distant places. As in earlier works, Merwin embraces a delicacy of touch that demands the full attention of the reader. "To a Falling Leaf in Winter," for example, is a poem that takes a common symbol of the passage of time in the natural world—a falling leaf—and imbues it with a fresh viewpoint. Rather than watching the "fall" with ambivalence or fear, the poet looks on the appearance of winter with a calm assurance that he has intentionally not been fully mindful of the passage of his own years. "To Forgetting," as another example, describes the loss of memory as a rather desired state of affairs. The poet wistfully recalls the quiet vacuity of early life because he finds that his memories are increasingly interfering with the peaceful enjoyment of the physical pleasures inherent in a good meal, a stimulating conversation, or the view of a pretty face. All of these experiences end up reminding him of people and places that have long since ceased to be—a situation that makes his life seem fraught with sadness and defined by loss.

MIGRATION

Merwin was born in Scranton, Pennsylvania, but has spent his old age in the appropriately named town of Haiku. Given the vast geographical distance of Merwin's beginnings and endings, it should be no surprise that one of his later collections of verse should be named *Migration*. Merwin selected verses from fifteen of his previous volumes for *Migration*, seeking to make a collection that would be diverse in both topic and form. *Migration* is also a volume that celebrates Merwin's mastery of unstructured verse. Few poets have had poetic careers as long as that of Merwin, which makes the creation of a comprehensive collection of verse particularly challenging. On one hand, there is a vast and comprehensive range of poems to choose from; on the other, coming to any final decision on which works are to be included and which works are to be left out is a painful exercise in economy of scale. So many of Merwin's poems seem to engage in an intertextual dialogue that one hates to exclude any of them. The archaic forms of his earliest verse—lines that suggest the epic poetry of William Butler Yeats—are succeeded with increasingly spare, image-dependent lines that lack punctuation and traditional language, but there remains a consistency of purpose—the examination of one's conscience and one's definitions of self—within both types of poetry. For example, "For the Anniversary of My Death," Merwin moves outside linear time to be able to perceive the past and the future with equal clarity. Like Merlin, the wizard trapped in a crystal prison by his former student Morgan le Fay, Merwin's omniscient view is both a gift and a curse. He occupies every moment of his existence equally and is equally appalled and entranced by what he sees before him.

THE SHADOW OF SIRIUS

Even in his eighties, Merwin's poetic vision never seems to falter. *The Shadow of Sirius*, which earned Merwin his second Pulitzer Prize, demonstrates the ever-present agility of his trademark deft handling of free verse. Old age and mortality, once things to be feared, are studied with a kind of breathless intensity. "Still Morning," for example, relates the tireless flight of birds who are so accustomed to the support of myriad breezes and currents that they have ceased to notice their movement in space. Aging is a similar process, Merwin notes, as he travels time without allowing its passage to dim the ecstasy of his journey. Merwin recalls the formation of his childhood self with the sharpness of a much younger man, but his analyses have a greater depth and sensitivity tempered by the perspective that only intervening decades of self-reflection could provide. One of the ironies of Merwin's half-century of poetic work has been that his penchant for spinning multiple interpretations of a memory's significance has been developed into a finely honed skill by his actual longevity. Merwin is not only a poet shaped by memory, but also a poet who has much memory yet to shape. The simplicity of the form and structure of the poems in *The Shadow of Sirius* belies a thematic complexity that surprised even the poet himself. The poems came together easily, betraying connections that Merwin described as almost taking shape unconsciously. For the creator of *A Mask for Janus*, an unseen secondary persona that underlies a deceptively open form is nothing new. Paradoxically, Merwin can appear to lay his themes out before one like an open book while still concealing a deeper meaning under the deceptively simple images.

OTHER MAJOR WORKS

SHORT FICTION: *The Miner's Pale Children*, 1970; *Houses and Travellers*, 1977; *The Lost Upland*, 1992.

PLAYS: *Darkling Child*, pr. 1956; *Favor Island*, pr. 1957; *The Gilded Nest*, pr. 1961.

TELEPLAY: *Huckleberry Finn*, 1953.

RADIO PLAYS: *Rumpelstiltskin*, 1951; *Pageant of Cain*, 1952.

NONFICTION: *Unframed Originals*, 1982; *Regions of Memory: Uncollected Prose, 1949-1982*, 1987 (Cary Nelson, editor); *The Ends of the Earth: Essays*, 2004; *Summer Doorways: A Memoir*, 2005.

TRANSLATIONS: *The Poem of the Cid*, 1959; *Satires*, 1961 (of Persius); *Spanish Ballads*, 1961; *The Song of Roland*, 1963; *Selected Translations, 1948-1968*, 1968; *Products of the Perfected Civilization: Selected Writings of Chamfort*, 1969 (of Sébastian Roch Nicolas Chamfort); *Transparence of the World*, 1969 (of Jean Follain); *Twenty Love Poems and a Song of Despair*, 1969 (of Pablo Neruda); *Voices*, 1969, 1988 (of Antonio Porchia); *Asian Figures*, 1973 (of various Asian pieces); *Selected Poems*, 1973, 1989 (of Osip Mandelstam; with Clarence Brown); *Iphigenia at Aulis*, 1978 (of Euripides; with George E. Dimock, Jr.); *Selected Translations, 1968-1978*, 1979; *Four French Plays*, 1985; *From the Spanish Morning*, 1985 (of Spanish ballads, Lope de Rueda's prose play *Eufemia*, and *Vida de Lazarillo de Tormes*); *Vertical Poetry*, 1988 (of Roberto Juarroz); *East Window: The Asian Translations*, 1998; *Purgatorio*, 2000 (of Dante); *The Life of Lazarillo de Tormes: His Fortunes and Adversities*, 2005; *Spanish Ballads*, 2008.

BIBLIOGRAPHY

Byers, Thomas B. *What I Cannot Say: Self, Word, and World in Whitman, Stevens, and Merwin*. Urbana: University of Illinois Press, 1989. Byers's chapter on Merwin, "W. S. Merwin: A Description of Darkness," focuses primarily on *The Lice* and attempts to define Merwin's place in the American poetic tradition descended from Ralph Waldo Emerson and Walt Whitman. According to Byers, Merwin sees, as Stevens did, the self as inevitably isolated, even though his poetics recognize the need to see oneself as related to other people and other things in order to become more ecologically aware. Includes notes, a bibliography, and an index.

Christhilf, Mark. *W. S. Merwin, the Mythmaker*. Columbia: University of Missouri Press, 1986. Christhilf discusses Merwin's contributions to the postmodernist movement (with *The Moving Target*) and his assumed role of mythmaker, noting that the poet became ambivalent toward this role in the 1980's. In a useful discussion, Christhilf traces the mythmaking concern in American poetry across four decades.

Davis, Cheri. *W. S. Merwin*. Boston: Twayne, 1981. This study makes the poetry and prose of Merwin accessible to the reader new to his work. While well aware of the variety in Merwin's writing, Davis attempts to reveal what gives it unity. She examines his attitudes toward language and silence, his concern for animals and ecology, and his beliefs about poetry and nothingness. Chapters 1 through 5 look at his books of poetry, from *A Mask for Janus* through *The Compass Flower*. Chapter 6 discusses the prose poetry of *The Miner's Pale Children* and *Houses and Travellers*.

Felsteiner, John. *Can Poetry Save the Earth? A Field Guide to Nature Poems*. New Haven, Conn.: Yale University Press, 2009. Contains a chapter "W. S. Merwin's Motion of Mind," which deals with Merwin's concern for the environment.

Frazier, Jane. *From Origin to Ecology: Nature and the Poetry of W. S. Merwin*. Madison, N.J.: Fairleigh Dickinson University Press, 1999. An anlysis of images of nature in Merwin's poetry. Includes bibliographical references and an index.

Hix, H. L. *Understanding W. S. Merwin*. Columbia: University of South Carolina Press, 1997. Hix argues that despite its reputation for difficulty, Merwin's verse is clear and direct. Close readings of Merwin's verse reveal the emergence of such dominant themes as apocalypse, ecology, society, and place.

Nelson, Cary, and Ed Folsom, eds. *W. S. Merwin: Essays on the Poetry*. Urbana: University of Illinois Press, 1987. The editors provide a good introductory essay, comparing Merwin to Ezra Pound (both students of romance languages), William Carlos Williams, and Wallace Stevens. William H. Rueckert's notes are a help to readers of *The Lice*, and Folsom discusses Merwin's change in style beginning with *The Compass Flower*. Includes comprehensive bibliographies, full notes, and a thorough index.

O'Driscoll, Bill. "Legendary Poet W. S. Merwin Returns to Pittsburgh." Review of *Mi-*

gration. CP: Pittsburgh City Paper, November 9, 2006, p. C1. O'Driscoll's review is particularly interesting because it highlights the return of the western Pennsylvanian poet to the regions of his youth. O'Driscoll celebrates Merwin as a poet of "silence" and find the poet's reserve to echo the quiet ruminations of generations of Pennsylvanian pacifists and environmentalists.

Scigaj, Leonard M. *Sustainable Poetry: Four American Ecopoets*. Lexington: University Press of Kentucky, 1999. The chapter on Merwin traces how the poet's initial "poetics of absence" has slowly transformed "into an ecological poetics of wakefulness." Scigaj connects Merwin's growing understanding of stressed ecosystems to his aesthetic experimentation.

Francis Poole; Philip K. Jason; Sarah Hilbert
Updated by Julia M. Meyers

MARY OLIVER

Born: Cleveland, Ohio; September 10, 1935

PRINCIPAL POETRY

No Voyage, and Other Poems, 1963, 1965
The River Styx, Ohio, and Other Poems, 1972
The Night Traveler, 1978
Sleeping in the Forest, 1978
Twelve Moons, 1979
American Primitive, 1983
Dream Work, 1986
Provincetown, 1987
House of Light, 1990
New and Selected Poems, 1992-2004 (2 volumes)
White Pine, 1994
West Wind, 1997
The Leaf and the Cloud, 2000
Why I Wake Early, 2004
Thirst, 2006
Red Bird, 2008
Evidence, 2009
Swan: Poems and Prose Poems, 2010

OTHER LITERARY FORMS

Mary Oliver has written collections of essays: *Blue Pastures* (1995) and *Winter Hours* (1999). Although the essays are mainly prose meditations, some are written in poetic form. The subject matter is the creation of poetry, by Oliver herself or by poets who have influenced her. *Blue Pastures* celebrates the creative power of imagination, its capacity to reorder circumstances and to enter the natural world to find comfort, community, and joy. The meditations center on ponds, trees, animals, and seasons and on Romantic writers who looked to nature: Walt Whitman, John Keats, Percy Bysshe Shelley, William Blake, and Edna St. Vincent Millay, in whose house Oliver lived periodically for several years after college, serving as an assistant to Millay's sister.

Winter Hours takes up the same lines but offers essays and prose poems more sharply focused on the making of poems. Three essays consider the qualities that make powerful writing in the work of Edgar Allan Poe, Robert Frost, and Whitman.

Long Life: Essays and Other Writings (2004) is a collection of essays and other writings in which Oliver intersperses personal reflections in poetry and essay form. Oliver has also published two works that instruct readers concerning the writing and reading of poetry: *A Poetry Handbook* (1994) and *Rules for the Dance: A Handbook for Writing and Reading Metrical Verse* (1998). Oliver also provided text to accompany the photographs of the late Molly Malone Cook in *Our World* (2007).

ACHIEVEMENTS

Mary Oliver is known for her graceful, passionate voice and her ability to discover deep, sustaining spiritual qualities in moments of encounter with nature. Her vision is ecstatic, arising from silence, darkness, deep pain, and questioning—a searching sensibility acutely aware and on the lookout everywhere for transformative moments. Her central subject is the difficult journey of life and the capacity of the human imagination to discover energy, passion, compassion, and the light of conscious being in the very places where the difficult is encountered.

Acts of deep attention enable a crossing over into nature's consciousness for a time to revitalize bodily awareness. The poet imaginatively disappears into nature, merges with it, and reemerges transformed in experiential fire. Whitman is her great forebear, although instead of an ever-present "I" seeking a merging intimacy, Oliver seeks instead a dissolving oneness in which the reader displaces her in order to enter more directly the experience she renders. Ordinary diction and syntax coupled with startlingly fresh images fuse in a passion that seems ordinary yet extraordinarily tender and liquid.

Among Oliver's awards are the Shelley Memorial Award (1970), the Poetry Society of America's Alice Fay di Castagnola Award (1973), two Ohioana Book Awards for Poetry (1973, 1993), an Academy Award in Literature from the American Academy and Institute of Arts and Letters (1983), the Pulitzer Prize (1984) for *American Primitive*, the Christopher Award and the L. L. Winship/PEN New England Award (both 1991) for *House of Light*, the National Book Award (1992) for *New and Selected Poems*, and the James Boatwright III Prize for Poetry and the Lannan Literary Award for Poetry (both 1998). She also received a National Endowment for the Arts Fellowship (1972) and a Guggenheim Fellowship (1980-1981).

BIOGRAPHY

Mary Oliver's poetry bears witness to a difficult childhood, one in which she was particularly at odds with her father, a teacher who died without their being reconciled. Her childhood experience profoundly influenced her poetry, as the body of her work develops a journey of healing from the effects of trauma. In "Rage," she writes of a childhood incest scene, detailing its damaging and continuing effects on daily adult life. Her poetry is remarkable for its limited focus on herself as a personality while showing a path out of terror and sorrow to acceptance, safety, joy, and freedom.

Oliver attended Ohio State University for one year, then transferred to Vassar College, but left after a year. She has taught at several institutions: the Fine Arts Workshop in Provincetown, Massachusetts; Case Western Reserve as Mather Visiting Professor; Sweet Briar College in Virginia as Banister Writer-in-Residence; and Bennington College in Vermont as Catherine Osgood Foster Chair for Distinguished Teaching (1996-2001).

ANALYSIS

Mary Oliver's presence in her poems is most often a clear-sighted moving of eye and mind while staying physically still. She disappears, in a sense, by projecting her sense and moral life onto precise and compelling images that draw the reader into the "I" as experiencer. Through the projection of sensibility in the scene of nature, she can be harsh but accepting and express responsibility for her own life. For example, in "Moccasin Flowers" (from *House of Light*), the plant and human merge in spiritual ecstasy:

> But all my life—so far—
> I have loved best
> how the flowers rise
> and open, how
>
> the pink lungs of their bodies
> enter the fire of the world
> and stand there shining
> and willing—the one
>
> thing they can do before
> they shuffle forward
> into the floor of darkness, they
> become the trees.

In her characteristic step-down lines, which give a feel of graceful floating, Oliver expresses the nature and work of beings to be fully and joyfully in the world before they move on to their merging in death.

Although Oliver began writing in the midst of the confessional movement of Robert Lowell, Anne Sexton, and Sylvia Plath, she never took on a victim persona. To the contrary, all her effort has gone toward entering the deepest truths of what is within reach of human consciousness. Thus she embraces the totality, from people's wild and animal nature—joyful and painful—to their storied and moral questionings. Most often looking to nature for experiential knowledge, she is deeply Romantic in the American vein, taking as her models Henry David Thoreau, Ralph Waldo Emerson, and Whitman. The opening of "The Buddha's Last Instruction" (from *House of Light*) succinctly states her aim: "'Make of yourself a light.'" The closing line, "He looked into the faces of that frightened crowd," speaks of the terrifying difficulty of that journey. Between these lines, Oliver sees existence as a gift of "inexplicable value," and to see this fact, which is imaged in the sun, is to become oneself a light. The way of healing and spiritual awareness is through entering what nature knows.

NO VOYAGE, AND OTHER POEMS

Oliver's first five volumes of poetry, published over sixteen years, show the poet beginning with a lyrical "I" who is, like Whitman, awake, watching and listening to nature, simultaneously an individual person grounded in a scene of mythic resonance and "at ease in darkness" of creative natural life. In "Being Country Bred," from her first collection, *No Voyage, and Other Poems*,

> Spring is still miles away, and yet I wake
> Throughout the dark, listen, and throb with all
> Her summoning explosions underground.

The dark underside of nature is the unconscious coming to light, bringing danger and the excitement of possibility. In "No Voyage" (the title poem), she refuses to leave her own identity, determining instead to stay and "make peace with the fact" of her grief.

The poems of *No Voyage, and Other Poems* and *The River Styx, Ohio, and Other Poems* are conventionally versified, and many are narrative-based vignettes of people from Oliver's childhood. "At Blackwater Pond" (collected in *New and Selected Poems*), however, is a short nine-line lyric that presages her mature work. In a baptism-communion-resurrection scene, the poet dips her hands in water and drinks.

> . . . It tastes
> like stone, leaves, fire. It falls cold
> into my body, waking the bones. I hear them
> deep inside me, whispering
> *oh what is that beautiful thing*
> *that just happened?*

The mystery of ecstatic awakening precisely matches the flow of rapturous experience.

TWELVE MOONS

The subject and technique develop further in *Twelve Moons*—for instance, in "Mussels," with its short, step-down lines resisting, like the shelled animals, her grip. In "Sleeping in the Forest," the poet finds herself imaginatively transformed as she becomes a dark, fluid consciousness, one with the night's beings and businesses: "By morning/ I had vanished at least a dozen times/ into something better." James Wright's influence is evident (three poems are dedicated to him) in the leaving of the body in ecstatic moments to "break into blossom."

AMERICAN PRIMITIVE

With *American Primitive*, Oliver achieved a fully developed vision of return to the earth for healing and a reciprocal healing of the earth. The acute perceptiveness and radiant clarity presaged in some earlier poems arrive strong and sustained. Using nature and Native American themes, the poet shows the body becoming firmly the locus of mind and spirit. However, there is a clear separation; Oliver is fully aware that boundaries can be crossed but must be crossed back again. Knowledge is brought back from the visions of nature.

Poems such as "Lightning" and "Vultures" acknowledge the journey into the other world as fearful and painful: Sorrow and death are part of nature, and the only way to heal is to accept this and go the difficult path straight through terror. "Mushrooms" accepts nature's poisonous aspects but engages respect versus fear as the helpful knowledge. "Egrets" traces the journey into the dark interior. The traveler is "hot and wounded" but comes suddenly to an empty pond out of which three egrets rise as "a shower/ of white fire!" She sees that they walk through each moment patiently, without fear, "unruffled, sure/ by the laws/ of their faith not logic,/ they opened their wings/ softly and stepped/ over every dark thing." In "The Honey Tree," she boldly ascends into ecstatic joy of the body as a result of the difficult work of acceptance for her other poems. Ecstasy, she writes, results from so long hungering for freedom to be oneself unrestricted by pain of the pain. "Oh, anyone can see/ how I love myself at last!/ how I love the world!"

However, there is mourning for beings who did not survive. "Ghosts" is an elegy for the plains buffalo. This long poem ends with a dream in which a cow tenderly attends her newborn calf like "any caring woman." In a characteristic prayerful image, the poet kneels and asks to become part of them. It is a gesture toward death, which so many of Oliver's poems make, expressing simultaneously sorrow and ecstasy balanced in empathic tenderness. In "University Hospital, Boston," she mourns a friend who is dying, and one she did not know who is gone suddenly from his bed.

DREAM WORK

Dream Work is the darkest of Oliver's work, as she goes back to consider and repair major losses. Continuing in the vein of *American Primitive* and the Deep Image poets, she uses shamanist and other mythic vehicles to enter the otherness of consciousness to understand and absorb the power she wants to incorporate while shedding what is outworn or harmful. There is a new probing of the personal and the political as she delves into the suffering human beings cause each other.

"Rage," "The Journey," and "A Visitor" revisit the effects of abusive childhood experience in order to name harm and reclaim active responsibility. Perhaps the best known of these poems is "Wild Geese," which honors the experience of "the soft animal of your body" as essential to moving out of blame, guilt, and isolation and back to connection with the world. Other poems, such as "Stanley Kunitz," honor those she has learned from and express that learning is the result not of magic but of hard, patient digging, weeding, pruning, and "coaxing the new."

NEW AND SELECTED POEMS

New and Selected Poems contains thirty new poems and generous selections from the twenty-year span of Oliver's poetry up to 1992. The volume makes Oliver appear to be more of a nature writer than she is, as the majority of poems selected are engagements with nature but are without their full context of the healing journey. The new poems find Oliver on the other side of pain, having resolved grief and moved past terror, so that she is able to cross with ease "that porous line/ where my own body was done with/ and the roots and the stems and the flowers/ began" ("White Flowers"). "Alligator Poem" relates a terrifying encounter with the animal while drinking on her knees. The lesson is in how the water "healed itself with a slow whisper" after the alligator has sunk out of sight, how she "saw the world as if for the second time/ the way it really is." She gathers a token of wild flowers to hold in her shaking hands—a gesture that is an emblem of her poetic enterprise, nature giving both dark and light, fear and comfort, death and life. She chooses to gather and hold life and beauty.

THE LEAF AND THE CLOUD

A long epigraph from John Ruskin's *Modern Painters* (1843-1860) explains the leaf as a veil between the darkness of natural being and humankind, and the cloud as a veil between God and humankind. *The Leaf and the Cloud* is a single long poem, a seven-lyric sequence that progressively swells higher into ecstatic union with the world. Oliver writes the journey of a person who is sixty, who looks back on her painful childhood, buries her parents, but will not "give them the kiss of complicity" or "the responsibility for my life." She declares "glory is my work" and imaginatively becomes all creatures and parts of the earth, hunter as well as hunted. The poet is part of the world, its radiant witness, not separate: Words "sweet and electric, words flow from the brain/ and out the gate of the mouth."

Whitman is evident everywhere in voice, style, subject, and theme. The "I" ranges from the personal to the universal, gives bits of personal history to set the record down and then moves beyond them, lists objects of nature as divine life, declares prophetically, asks rhetorical questions, and embraces death as part of life.

WHY I WAKE EARLY

Oliver demonstrates increasing attention to religious devotion, questions of faith and mystery, while maintaining her signature style of close observations of nature. In this regard, her later poetry follows the tradition of William Wordsworth and Emerson—the known informing about the unknown. How these two factors work together in Oliver's imagination affects much of her later work. Many poems in *Why I Wake Early* present a happy affirmation of human experience within this world. One is defined by looking into the mirror of nature. With ultimate reality in mind, the increasing spiritual contemplation contrasts with unnecessary, trivial trinkets of materialism. Oliver's ecopoetic attitude challenges assumptions of consumerism: "Impossible to believe we need so much/ as the world wants us to buy," and again she contrasts all "this buying and selling" with the "beautiful earth in [her] heart," a heart that "grow[s] sharp" and "cold" given the context of seeing "what has been done to [the earth]" ("What Was Once the Largest Shopping Center in Northern Ohio Was Built Where There Had Been a Pond I Used to Visit Every Summer Afternoon").

Oliver's collection asks readers to hear the mysterious word that precedes human activity. "Accept the miracle," she writes (in "Logos"), "and don't worry about what is reality,/ or what is plain, or what is mysterious." Here logos joined with imagination constitutes the miraculous: "If you can imagine it, it is all those things." In a manner similar to Emily Dickinson's style when writing about God, Oliver draws insight from small, apparently insignificant creatures, such as a cricket "moving the grains of the hillside" in "Song of the Builders." This activity is compared to the speaker ". . . think[ing] about God—/ a worthy pastime." Both cricket and human are "inexplicable" as they are busy "building the universe."

THIRST

Thirst continues the spiritual introspection seen in the previous volume. Both collections are dedicated to Oliver's late beloved partner, Molly Malone Cook. *Thirst* offers a grieving persona trying to balance happy memories with an unknown future. Intense grief and loss are accentuated, although the larger context of nature as a reliable, friendly guide toward consolation and insight remains constant. The tone is set by the epigram quoting *The Sayings of the Desert Fathers*: "you can become all flame." This hinting toward transformation, signaling a longing for reunion and participation in the force beyond life's mysteries, marks this volume. Loss leaves Oliver thirsty for the ultimate and causes her to seek the mystical all around her. The prose poem "Thirst," presented as an epilogue to the volume, explains the genesis of the preceding poems: "Love for the earth and love for you are having such a long conversation in my heart."

Sadness and serious contemplation, marked by poems inspired by the Psalms and other biblical books, are balanced by lighter interactions with the affectionate, willful dog Percy, whose presence seems to help the poet negotiate her way through grief. Percy, as chief signifier of the natural, nonhuman world around the poet, functions something like a spiritual guide whose curiosity and independent joy help Oliver reacquaint herself with the steady consolation to be found in nature and to remind readers that life is precious in all its forms. Here Oliver realizes that darkness also "was a gift" ("The Uses of Sorrow") and that "weeds in a vacant lot" as well as "the blue iris" ("Praying") may serve to deliver one to silence, to prayerful thanksgiving and transformation.

RED BIRD

Oliver's next collection, *Red Bird*, displays renewed vitality. The poems suggest a healthy balance of enjoying life's often overlooked gifts while being acutely aware of death and danger within nature. Here, though, grief is not emphasized along with death. The poet says it is time for the heart ". . . to come back/ from the dark" ("Summer Morning"). The dangerous is beautiful, like a panther with "a conscience/ that never blinks" ("With the Blackest of Inks"). Oliver's poetry celebrates a fullness of earth by one whose heart is full and whose mind is aware not only of goodness but also of the injustice of power and dangers of materialism. Her voice proclaims the triumph of knowledge and refuses to give in to fear.

The controlling metaphor, Red Bird, serves as a messenger whose announcements frame the collection. In the first poem, "Red Bird," Red Bird comes in winter, as a reminder that it is possible to endure cold death. At the same time, he suggests that other joyful seasons will follow. In the last poem, "Red Bird Explains Himself," Red Bird, like a Platonic philosopher, teaches that bodies need "a song, a spirit, a soul" and that the "soul has need of a body."

This volume sings with energy. Oliver communes with the "heaven of earth" ("Luke"). She is concerned less with processing grief or theological consummation (as in the previous two books) than with a frank recognition that the natural order exhibits a kindness if it is sought and understood. This includes foxes killing mice: ". . . the fear that makes/ all of us, sometime or other,/ flee for the sake/ of our small and precious lives" ("Make of All Things, Even Healings"). Within this context, Oliver asserts, "someday we'll live in the sky," but for now "the house of our lives is this green world" ("Boundaries"). Like an ancient sage, Oliver understands that this green world is subject to change and death: ". . . lilies/ in their bright dresses// cannot last/ but wrinkle fast/ and fall" ("Another Everyday Poem"). Given this, she emphasizes the "small, available things" of the world, like the hummingbird, whose free existence negates human striving for "pieces of gold—/ or power" ("Summer Story"). Oliver wonderfully contrasts the healthy natural order with "the terrible debris of progress" ("Meadowlark Sings and I Greet Him in Return").

EVIDENCE

Oliver's *Evidence* collects her themes. The poems present evidence of good and bad, beauty and harm, God and humanity, earth and sky in an artistic, realistically balanced combination. Human choice corresponds to the potential of each category. "Beauty without purpose is beauty without virtue," as the title poem, "Evidence," asserts. Another line, "There are many ways to perish, or to flourish," displays the parameters of choice and consequence. Within this same poem, the capacity for human consequence is contrasted with symbols from nature, such as swans, among whom ". . . there is none called the least, or/ the greatest" and ". . . pine trees that never forget their/ recipe for renewal."

Oliver's poetry offers a frank realization of approaching death, but there is a profound determination to live naturally, simply (like Thoreau and others), and happily within the mysterious bonds of nature. Some choices lead to despair and destruction, and others lead to positive outcomes, but true peace and deep joy seem to be found by understanding that not all knowledge or power is available to humans. The ability (and necessity) to humbly accept limitation, as eternally signified by nature, is Oliver's legacy.

OTHER MAJOR WORKS

NONFICTION: *A Poetry Handbook*, 1994; *Blue Pastures*, 1995; *Rules for the Dance: A Handbook for Writing and Reading Metrical Verse*, 1998; *Winter Hours*, 1999.

MISCELLANEOUS: *Owls and Other Fantasies: Poems and Essays*, 2003; *Blue Iris: Poems and Essays*, 2004; *Long Life: Essays and Other Writings*, 2004; *Our World*, 2007 (photographs by Molly Malone Cook); *The Truro Bear and Other Adventures: Poems and Essays*, 2008.

BIBLIOGRAPHY

Bryson, J. Scott. *The West Side of Any Mountain: Place, Space, and Ecopoetry*. Iowa City: University of Iowa Press, 2005. One of the examples of growing interest in ecocriticism and scholarship. A good portion concerns Oliver and environmental concerns evident in her poetry.

Burton-Christie, Douglas. "Nature, Spirit, and Imagination in the Poetry of Mary Oliver." *Cross Currents* 46, no. 1 (Spring, 1996): 77-87. Examines Oliver's poetry as the work of spiritual attention and acceptance versus the will to change and domesticate.

Constantakis, Sara, ed. *Poetry for Students*. Vol. 31. Detroit: Thomson/Gale Group, 2010. Contains an analysis of Oliver's poem "The Black Snake."

Fast, Robin Riley. "Moore, Bishop, and Oliver: Thinking Back, Re-Seeing the Sea." *Twentieth Century Literature* 39, no. 3 (Fall, 1993): 364-379. Considers Oliver in the line of Marianne Moore's and Elizabeth Bishop's concern with death and the unconscious as background context for poetic imagination.

Graham, Vicki. "'Into the Body of Another': Mary Oliver and the Poetics of Becoming Other." *Papers on Language and Literature* 30, no. 4 (Fall, 1994): 352-372. An extensive treatment of Oliver as a postmodern feminist poet for whom, contrary to male Romantic poets, merging with consciousness regarded as other is a fuller apprehension of multiplicity instead of a loss of subjectivity.

McNew, Janet. "Mary Oliver and the Tradition of Romantic Nature Poetry." *Contemporary Literature* 30, no. 1 (Spring, 1990): 59-77. A fascinating treatment of Oliver as a feminist Romantic poet writing against the tradition of male Romantics, who imagined nature as feminine, to be both desired and feared. Critiques mainline Romantic criticism as gender-biased.

Mann, Thomas W. *The God of Dirt: Mary Oliver and the Other Book of God.* Cambridge, England: Cowley, 2004. Connects and comments on the religious language and imagery in Oliver's poetry.

Voros, Gyorgyi. "Exquisite Environments." *Parnassus: Poetry in Review* 21, nos. 1/2 (1996): 231-250. An omnibus review of three of Oliver's books and two by Gary Snyder, who is used to show what Oliver should be doing. An interesting perspective that understands Oliver's work narrowly as simply nature poetry, the kind of opinion that Janet McNew critiques.

Rosemary Winslow
Updated by Kenneth Hada

SIMON ORTIZ

Born: Albuquerque, New Mexico; May 27, 1941
Also known as: Simon J. Ortiz

PRINCIPAL POETRY

Naked in the Wind, 1971
Going for the Rain, 1976
A Good Journey, 1977
Fight Back: For the Sake of the People, for the Sake of the Land, 1980 (poetry and prose)
From Sand Creek: Rising in This Heart Which Is Our America, 1981
A Poem Is a Journey, 1981
Woven Stone, 1992
After and Before the Lightning, 1994
Telling and Showing Her: The Earth, the Land, 1995
Out There Somewhere, 2002

OTHER LITERARY FORMS

Even before the publication of his first book of poetry in 1971, Simon Ortiz (ohr-TEEZ) had begun to write short fiction, publishing his first short stories in the 1960's. "I've known 'story'—or stories—all my life," Ortiz observed in the preface to *Men on the Moon: Collected Short Stories* (1999). He has also edited several volumes devoted to the writing of Native American authors, most notably *Earth Power Coming: Short Fiction in Native American Literature* (1983) and *Speaking for the Generations: Native Writers on Writing* (1998), and has contributed to many books concerned with the heritage and cultural history of indigenous people, including *Toward a National Indian Literature* (1981) and *I Tell You Now: Autobiographical Essay by Native American Writers* (1987). *The People Shall Continue* (1977) is designed for young readers, as is *The Good Rainbow Road = Rawa 'Kashtyaa'tsi Hiyaani: A Native American Tale in Keres and English, Followed by a Translation into Spanish* (2004), a trilingual children's book.

Ortiz has made a number of recordings of his work and has appeared on radio programs and videos. *Nothing but the Truth: An Anthology of Native American Literature* (2001) contains an extensive contribution by Ortiz.

ACHIEVEMENTS

Simon Ortiz, along with Leslie Marmon Silko, N. Scott Momaday, and Louise Erdrich, was one of the people most directly responsible for the elevation of Native

American literature to a position of prominence in American literary life during the 1970's. In his poems and short fiction, Ortiz draws on the vibrant styles and subjects of the oral tradition that has endured for millennia in Native American cultural communities and brings them into a contemporary context as a written record of a people's experience. His poetry, in conjunction with the stories that deal with a complementary range of psychic conditions, social considerations, and geophysical phenomena, moves from an individual's encounters with life in the United States to the ways in which that person's life is presented as a reflection and representation of the cultural patterns and values of a clan or extended family within an ethnographic matrix.

Ortiz has remained closely connected to the increasingly complex and varied world of Native American writing since the initial publication of his own work, teaching at numerous institutions and editing and collecting the work of his peers. His efforts have been recognized with many awards, including a National Endowment for the Arts Discovery Award (1969), a Pushcart Prize (1981), a White House Salute to an Honored Poet (1981), the New Mexico Humanities Council Humanitarian Award (1989), a Lifetime Achievement Award from the Native Writer's Circle of the Americas (1993), the Lila Wallace-*Reader's Digest* Writers' Award (1996), the Wordcraft Circle Writer of the Year Award (1998), and a New Mexico Governor's Award for Excellence in the Arts (2000). In 2002, he received an honorary doctor of letters degree from the University of New Mexico.

BIOGRAPHY

Simon Joseph Ortiz grew up in the town known as McCartys, New Mexico, but known as Deetseyamah to the people of the Acoma (or Aacqumeh) Pueblo, his community (or *hanoh*). Both his parents connected him to his culture and his later enthusiasm for describing it. His father, who later worked for the railroad, was a tribal elder and woodcarver, and his mother was a potter and storyteller. Like most of the residents, he spoke the Acoma language at home and English at the McCartys Day School he attended, a place that Ortiz describes as carrying out a national policy designed to "sever ties to culture, family, and tribe," and to "make us into American white people." In spite of this, Ortiz recalls that "it was exciting, however, to go to school," and that "reading was fun" because he "loved language and stories."

In 1954, when Ortiz was in the fifth grade, his family moved to Skull Valley in Arizona, where his father was employed by the Santa Fe Railway, and Ortiz became aware of a world beyond his local community. He contrasted his family's lives with the lives of the family he read about in the Dick and Jane readers. He and his younger sister and brothers were the only Native Americans at the school, and his curiosity about the other students led him to "read voraciously just about anything I could get my hands on," authors ranging from H. G. Wells to Mark Twain. His first publication, a Mother's Day poem, appeared in the Skull Valley School newspaper.

At the St. Catherine's Indian School in Sante Fe, Ortiz was encouraged by nuns to read beyond the minimal grade requirements, and he began to keep a diary, which led to his lifelong habit of writing in a personal journal. Ortiz continued to write poetry and began to compose "brief, cursory passages" of description, character sketches, plot outlines, and other elements of fiction. When he transferred to Albuquerque Indian School closer to his family's home, Ortiz registered for a program in vocational training to "become employable," but at Grants High, an integrated school, he began to take his writing more seriously, seeing himself "as a writer later in life" and becoming "even more of a reader, heavily into recent and current poets and novelists," an eclectic grouping including Dylan Thomas, Sinclair Lewis, and Flannery O'Connor, as well as "a lot of the American and European classics."

While he took part in athletics and other school activities, Ortiz emphasizes that he "wanted to read and read and read and think." As a kind of pivotal point in his development as a writer, he cites a growing "awareness that our Acoma people and culture were in a fateful period in our destiny," and he resolved to direct himself as a writer to the preservation and presentation of his cultural heritage. His earliest fiction, which he concentrated on more than poetry, was about people struggling with poverty, social discrimination, and ethnic dispersion.

Unsure of how to become a writer, Ortiz went to work for Kerr-McGee, an energy corporation mining uranium, and began to develop characters modeled on the working men he met. The limits of their lives, and the restrictions that constrained members of the Acoma community, fed an anger that had been "seething for years," and Ortiz began drinking heavily to "exert the independence [he] wanted." He justified this by using the examples of Ernest Hemingway and Malcolm Lowry: He "believed in their greatness and in drinking as a part of that." Alcoholism did not prevent Ortiz from entering Fort Lewis College in 1961, serving in the U.S. Army from 1962 to 1965, then attending the University of New Mexico and winning a fellowship in the writing program at the University of Iowa, from which he received a master of fine arts degree in 1969.

His first book of poetry, *Naked in the Wind*, was published in 1971, and Ortiz worked as a newspaper editor for the National Indian Youth Council from 1970 to 1973. Despite positive early reception of his work, Ortiz experienced many periods of anger and disillusionment often fed by abuse of alcohol. He underwent treatment for alcoholism during 1974-1975 but was able to begin a teaching career at San Diego State University in 1974. He has also taught at the College of Marin, the University of New Mexico, Sinte Gleska University, the University of Toronto, and Arizona State University. Ortiz published *Going for the Rain* with Harper and Row in 1976, marking his emergence as an important American writer.

Ortiz has three children (Raho Nez, Rainy Dawn, and Sara Marie) and was married to Marlene Foster from 1981 to 1984. He has served as lieutenant governor of the Acoma Pueblo and presented his work at numerous conferences, university readings, and other literary gatherings throughout the North American continent. The strength and resonance of his writing has earned him the kind of respect that has given him the status of a wisdom figure or sage, who, as he says, has worked to make "language familiar and accessible to others, bringing it within their grasp and comprehension."

ANALYSIS

Simon Ortiz has reiterated throughout his writing life that at the core of his poetry is the idea that "Indians always tell a story" because this is the "only way to continue." His concern for the survival of a cultural heritage that has been threatened with extinction and his deep grounding in the oral tradition that has enabled it to endure in spite of efforts at suppression provide the purpose and direction for his work. Ortiz identifies the oral tradition as the key to the "epic Acoma narrative of our development," an ongoing expression of the fundamental consciousness of the Acoma *hanoh*. His poetry has been charged with the energy of a living language that draws on songs, chants, spoken tales, and intimate speech for sustenance, its essence, which he has labored to capture and convey in written forms. While his works have often reflected feelings of anger and despair, they have just as frequently moved toward an appreciation of the physical world and community as sources of peace and hope.

GOING FOR THE RAIN

Ortiz recalls that when he was working on the manuscript that was eventually published as two separate collections since "I was told three-hundred-page first major poetry collections weren't a good idea," he came to the realization that the oral tradition was more than a "verbal-vocal manifestation in stories and songs." In the largest sense, it "evokes and expresses a belief system, and it is a specific activity that confirms and conveys that belief." Consequently, he structured his first substantial book of poems, *Going for the Rain*, as a narrative of discovery, a journey on the *heeyaanih* (road of life) in which the poetic voice presents a series of incidents that lead toward an understanding of the belief system at the center of the Acoma community.

It is a book of origins, with seven poems exploring the mythic trickster/shape-shifter Coyote, an archetypal figure in Native American cultural history, as well as a record of geographic immersion, with poems located in many places in the United States, and a book of portraits in which the poet describes his encounters with people within and outside First Nations settlements. The journey is divided into four sections, "Preparation," which is rooted in family life; "Leaving" and "Returning," a journal of life on the road; and "The Rain Falls," a kind of summary of previous experience and a tentative presentation of a philosophic position that links metaphysical speculation with natural and ultranatural phenomena. The book is patterned after an Acoma myth that involves a ceremonial trek in which the motion of the *schiwana* (or Cloud People) encourages the return of the rain, which is necessary for the continuing life of the *hanoh*.

The poet's voice is primarily conversational, often addressed to a specific person, sometimes turned inward as a dialogue placed within the narrative consciousness. Ortiz tends to focus on the small details of a person's existence, finding something vital in the familiar, as in the poem "21 August '71 Indian":

> Fire burns the thin shavings quickly
> and soon dies down under larger pieces.
> The red coals are weak, have to watch
> and put smaller pieces on next time.
> Get knife and splinter larger into smaller
> and feed the coals, being patient.
> Will have a late supper tonight;
> maybe the clouds will part some by then
> and let me see some stars.

A GOOD JOURNEY

The second part of Ortiz's initial manuscript was published in the following year as *A Good Journey*, and he describes it as being based on "an awareness of heritage and culture," with "the poetry in the book styled as a storytelling narrative ranging from a contemporary rendering of older traditional stories to current experience." As Ortiz says in the preface, he writes so that he may have a "good journey" on his way home, and in a larger context, "Because Indians always tell a story." Ortiz has explained that he wanted to try to get something of the styles of the stories preserved in the oral tradition into print form, and he uses various devices, including multiple voices, direct address to the reader, quotations in several languages and intertextual commentary to produce some of the effect of oral performance. There are five parts to the journey of the title, beginning with "Telling," a section containing many versions of traditional stories, epitomized by the poem "And there is always one more story," whose title is a paradigm for the philosophical position that informs the narrative.

Further sections are titled "Notes for My Child," which picks up similar thoughts in "Going for the Rain; How Much He Remembered," which continues the idea of a travel journal; "Will Come Forth in Tongues of Fury," which focuses on political issues; and "I Tell You Know," which returns to family, community and the poet's universal beliefs. The appearance of Coyote in many poems suggests a correspondence of sorts between the legendary figure and aspects of the poet's own soul/spirit, with an ongoing dialogue between parties evolving through the book. A brief, cryptic poem, "How Much Coyote Remembered," states, "O, not too much./ And a whole lot./ Enough," an assertion of the vast span of time that constitutes the history of indigenous people on the North American continent that Ortiz is examining and rehearsing. Ortiz identifies with Coyote as a survivor who finds ways not only to survive, but also to thrive.

AFTER AND BEFORE THE LIGHTNING

Ortiz, operating in the largest conception of a "story," frequently combines what might be conventionally called poems with other rhetorical modes. In *From Sand Creek*, he placed narrative commentaries on facing pages with poems about what he described as "an analysis of myself as an American, which is hemispheric, a U.S. citizen, which is national, and an Indian, which is spiritual and human." He employed a similar structural technique in a more complex manner in *After and Before the Lightning*, a version of a journal/memoir of the time he spent on the Rosebud Sioux Indian Reservation through a long, harsh winter season.

Completely integrating prose narratives with poetic sections in many forms—lyrics, chants, songs, meditations—Ortiz developed an account of physical and psychic survival that paralleled a personal journey across a frozen landscape ("bitter cold nights, and endless wind") with legendary tales of survival on frigid terrain and against the assaults of governmental agencies. Ortiz found this poetry connecting his life to existence, so that a direct confrontation with fierce elemental forces provided a test as well as a source of inspiration. "The vast and boundless cosmos," Ortiz writes, was "vividly present, immediate, and foremost as context on the prairie." Moving from the universal in the first section, "The Landscape: Prairie, Time, and Galaxy," with entries marked by dates beginning in November, then moving toward the quotidian in the next section, "Common Trials: Every Day," followed by a visionary time, "Buffalo Dawn Coming," and on toward a revival in "Near and Evident Signs of Spring" in April, Ortiz assembles an exploration of and a tribute to the "Lakota friends" whom he celebrates as "the true caretakers of their beautiful prairie land."

OUT THERE SOMEWHERE

In *Out There Somewhere*, Ortiz continues developing poems that use familiar techniques, including the narrative-descriptive journal entry, the song, and the dialogue. Asserting his identity as a man of the Acoma people, he writes a few poems in his native language, which he then transcribes into English. Through these forms, he further explains the place of indigenous people in American culture, reaffirming native Acoma values presented in earlier volumes. Aggregating poems into subsections—"Margins," "Images," "Gifts," "Horizons," "Ever," and "Connections After All"—he describes a journey, this time an interior journey from anger to a renewed appreciation of his people's facility for valuing the earth and its treasures, as well as the community and its stories.

Poems in "Margins" reflect first on his feelings of bitterness for the circumstances in which he has often found himself. Awakening in jail, recovering from a hangover, coping with rehabilitation, and aching with loneliness remind him of the many times he has felt himself to be a marginal part of society, and he recognizes that this feeling is in fact the reality. He determines to cope with this feeling as well as the unwelcome pity of observers who insensitively question how American Indians ever survived. He struggles to identify something to disengage him from this destructive preoccupation. He instinctively heads for the beach, where he knows that he will find poetry in the stones, the seagulls, and the foamy water.

The second section, "Images," presents more examples of being disenfranchised or being a tourist attraction. He sees the United States at times as the land of the mall. He hears someone proudly assert that she has chosen not to raise consumer-oriented children—an arrogant assertion, he thinks, that prompts him to contrast her privileged life to the lives of his people and all the poor people struggling to survive. Thinking of all native people speaking their own languages who come together in an understanding of their shared humanity, he asks rhetorically what the Europeans saw when they arrived in America. The implicit answer is that they saw themselves as superior and saved.

In "Gifts," though, he develops images of special moments that have elicited peace, harmony, thankfulness. In an April light, he shows his children the nest of a sparrow and its five delicate eggs, a shared observation that connects them all with the earth, the sparrow, and each other. A moment of looking at a photograph with his mother, a remembered story, and the experience of planting together all become the grist for thoughts that enable him and his people to transcend the negative and reaffirm their connection with all life—the earth, their ancestors, and one another.

"Horizons," "Ever," and "Connections After All" expand on this appreciation of gifts. The poet recognizes the gifts even more broadly as the mountains, the prairie, the stars, the river, and finally, a personal connection with others. These gifts, collectively and individually appreciated by his people, enable continuance (his term for cultural survival) and a mode of prevailing developed in courage and hope and shared in stories.

OTHER MAJOR WORKS

SHORT FICTION: *Howbah Indians*, 1978; *Fightin': New and Collected Stories*, 1983; *Men on the Moon: Collected Short Stories*, 1999.

NONFICTION: *Traditional and Hard-to-Find Information Required by Members of American Indian Communities: What to Collect, How to Collect It, and Appropriate Format and Use*, 1978 (with Roxanne Dunbar Ortiz); *The Importance of Childhood*, 1982.

CHILDREN'S LITERATURE: *The People Shall Continue*, 1977; *Blue and Red*, 1982; *The Good Rainbow Road = Rawa 'Kashtyaa'tsi Hiyaani: A Native American Tale in Keres and English, Followed by a Translation into Spanish*, 2004.

EDITED TEXTS: *A Ceremony of Brotherhood, 1680-1980*, 1981 (with others); *Earth Power Coming: Short Fiction in Native American Literature*, 1983; *Speaking for the Generations: Native Writers on Writing*, 1998.

MISCELLANEOUS: *Song, Poetry, and Language: Expression and Perception*, 1977.

BIBLIOGRAPHY

Allen, Chadwick. "Simon Ortiz: Writing Home." In *The Cambridge Companion to Native American Literature*, edited by Joy Porter and Kenneth M. Roemer. New York: Cambridge University Press, 2005. Looks at Ortiz's writings with emphasis on his writing about his physical and spiritual home.

Brill de Ramírez, Susan Berry. "Walking with the Land: Simon J. Ortiz, Robert J. Conley, and Velma Wallis." *South Dakota Review* 38, no. 1 (Spring, 2000): 59-82. Shows ways that Ortiz intertwines oral and written literary traditions to develop stories promoting faith and courage.

Brill de Ramírez, Susan Berry, and Evelina Zuni Lucero, eds. *Simon J. Ortiz: A Poetic Legacy of Indigenous Continuance*. Albuquerque: University of New Mexico Press, 2009. Essays examine the writings of Ortiz, noting his emphasis on the culture in which he was raised.

Fitz, Brewster E. "Undermining Narrative Stereotypes in Simon Ortiz's 'The Killing of a State Cop.'" *MELUS* 28, no. 2 (Summer, 2003): 105-121. Explores Ortiz's complex and suggestive use of narrative.

Litz, A. Walton. "Simon J. Ortiz." In *The American Writers*. New York: Charles Scribner's Sons, 1996. A retrospective by an experienced critic that emphasizes Ortiz's early life as a key to his work.

Rader, Dean. "Luci Tapahonso and Simon Ortiz: Allegory, Symbol, Language, Poetry." *Southwest Review* 82, no. 2 (Spring, 1997): 75-92. Useful comparisons of the similarities in technique between two Native American writers.

Schein, Marie-Madeline. "Simon J. Ortiz." In *Updating the Literary West*, edited by Thomas J. Lyon. Fort Worth: Texas Christian University Press, 1997. Discusses themes in his work, especially survival humor.

Smith, Patricia Clark. "Coyote Ortiz: *Canis Iatrans Iatrans* in the Poetry of Simon Ortiz." In *Studies in American Indian Literature*, edited by Paula Gunn Allen. 5th ed. New York: Modern Language Association of America, 1995. A study of the importance of the mythic figure Coyote as legend, symbol, and poetic voice.

Wiget, Andrew. *Simon Ortiz*. Boise, Idaho: Boise State University Press, 1986. A study by a recognized American Indian scholar.

_____, ed. *Handbook of Native American Literature*. New York: Garland, 1996. Contains a concise overview of Ortiz's life and early works.

Leon Lewis
Updated by Bernadette Flynn Low

PATTIANN ROGERS

Born: Joplin, Missouri; March 23, 1940

OTHER LITERARY FORMS

Pattiann Rogers is best known for her poetry. In *The Dream of the Marsh Wren: Writing as Reciprocal Creation* (1999), a work of prose studded with poetry, Rogers describes the aims of her most admired verse and suggests how and why she writes. The book was published by Milkweed Editions as part of its Credo series, which explores the techniques, interests, and goals of contemporary American writers whose work focuses on natural history and the idea of place.

ACHIEVEMENTS

Pattiann Rogers has received many awards and honors, including two grants from the National Endowment for the Arts, a Guggenheim Foundation Fellowship, the Theodore Roethke Prize from *Poetry Northwest* in 1981, and Lannan Literary Awards for Poetry in 1991 and 2005. *Firekeeper* was a finalist for the Lenore Marshall Poetry Prize offered by the Academy of American Poets for the most outstanding poetry collection published in the United States in 1994 and received the Natalie Ornish Poetry Award from the Texas Institute of Letters. *Song of the World Becoming*, which contains all her previously published collections and includes forty new poems, was a finalist for a *Los Angeles Times* Book Prize. Individual poems have been awarded the Bess Hokin Prize (1982) and the Frederick Bock Prize (1998) from *Poetry*, the Theodore Roethke Poetry Prize from *Poetry Northwest* (1981), five Pushcart Prizes, and publication in *The Best American Poetry of 1996*, as well as in *Best Spiritual Writing* in 1999, 2000, and 2001.

In 2004, she served as a judge for the National Poetry Series. She was also awarded a residency at the Rockefeller Foundation's Bellagio Study and Conference Center in Italy.

BIOGRAPHY

Pattiann Rogers was born Pattiann Tall into a poor family headed by William Tall and Irene C. Tall. Her mother was a homemaker, and the family was dependent on what her father could earn as an inventor. When she was twenty, she married John Robert Rogers. She graduated Phi Beta Kappa from the University of Missouri in 1961, with a B.A. in English literature. After graduation, she worked as an English teacher to support her husband through graduate school. He became a geophysicist, giving Rogers a connection to science that informs much of her poetry. When her first son was born, she stayed home to take care of him, and another son soon followed. Rogers developed her poetry career while she was raising her two children.

In 1981, she earned an M.A. from the University of Houston and embarked on a career as an academic. She has taught at the University of Texas, the University of Montana, Washington University of St. Louis, and Mercer University as the Ferrol Sams Distinguished Writer-in-Residence. She was associate professor and taught at the University of Arkansas in the M.F.A. creative writing program at the University of Arkansas during spring semesters from 1993 to 1997. She and her husband settled in Colorado.

ANALYSIS

Pattiann Rogers is most often seen as the literary heir to such American poets as Ralph Waldo Emerson, Walt Whitman, Marianne Moore, and Wallace Stevens. She weaves together a scientific and theological vocabulary and writes about subjects variously informed by botany, zoology, geology, astronomy, and physics. One of the main concerns of her poetry is to use observations of nature to arrive at religious conclusions. Many poems give examples of phenomena that seem to signal a divine order beyond what is obvious. As well as using traditional images from natural history, Rogers also uses modern discoveries such as the motion of electrons around atoms. Whether they are frightening as a thunderstorm or comforting as a still sky full of stars, the objects of nature are presented with a discerning eye and as the key to another world beyond the physical.

LEGENDARY PERFORMANCE

In Rogers's *Legendary Performance*, a group of children play and interact in some undefined country place. Their conversation in the poem "After Dinner" centers on their different conceptions of natural phenomena, from weaver ants to the exploding supernova. The poems follow the group of children, who are sometimes joined by an Indian boy, Kioka, who may or may not be real, in their real or imagined adventures. The poems are tied together by the children and by recurring themes such as the color violet and the boys riding naked on ponies. The children are joined briefly by other relatives, such as Felicia's old, sick uncle and Cecil's second cousin, who has a handicap. The tone is conversational and processional, in the style of reflective prose. One of the most moving poems in the collection is "A Seasonal Tradition," describing a concert that Felicia's music teacher gives every year for Sonia, Cecil, Albert, Gordon, Felicia, and her insane uncle. The music teacher traditionally ends the concert with a piece on her violin in a register so high that no one can hear the music; instead, each child imagines a different melody, theme, or unspoken speech. Significantly, the unheard melody is the one most discussed afterward at tea.

SPITTING AND BINDING

Two years after *Legendary Performance*, the collection *Spitting and Binding* appeared, containing poems that more directly relate to Rogers's religious sensibility. The theme here is death, starting with the opening poem, "The Next Story," in which Rogers describes how she spent the whole morning watching a group of five jays darting and screaming over one of their dead that has been killed by a cat. She sees the pattern of their noisy distress matching the broken body of the dead bird. From this, she requests a denial of death, but will only accept a denial that is more convincing than the five wheeling jays she watches in their perfect lament. These poems of death are interspersed with poems of prayer, from "The Answering of Prayers," concerning the prayers of a field of iris, to the final poem of the book, "Before I Wake." The title of this poem is taken from the widely known children's prayer that ends, "But if I die before I wake/ I pray thee, Lord, my soul to take," and is slightly more formal than most of Rogers's poems, with the three stanzas ending in variations on a line from the original child's prayer.

GEOCENTRIC

Geocentric, from *geo*, an ancient Greek prefix meaning earth, and "centric," pertaining to the center, refers to being centered on the earth, as Rogers is. The volume is divided into four sections, each with its own emphasis. The first, "Earthrise," contains poems of marvel at how the world works, and the second, "Sea Saviors," looks to ocean phenomena for inspiration. The title poem, "Geocentric," is a thirty-two-line poem that describes many of Earth's most malodorous and disgusting excrescences, but ends up, in the last two lines, with the surprising comment: ". . . nobody/ loves you as I do." This might be taken as Rogers's comprehensive credo, since every poem revels in the physical phenomena of Earth, no matter how disgusting. Among the most unusual work in the second section is "What the Sea Means to a Rock Barnacle in a Tidal Pool." After three substantial stanzas enumerating the minute activities the rock barnacle is able to perform and the myriad concepts he cannot realize, the poem ends with a positive belief in the power of the barnacle to somehow know, in its quivering stalk, the power and abundance of the great sea that nightly engulfs him.

In the third section, "Good Heavens," the poet turns her eyes skyward and meditates on the stars and churning galaxies. In the title poem of this section, the words "good heavens" take on a double meaning: They are the old exclamation of surprise that is commonly used but also make use of a trope that is typical of Rogers's work. Taken literally, the word "good" to describe heavens is a use of personification: attributing human tendencies to utterly senseless objects or, in this case, systems. The fourth stanza of the poem explains this personification; after most of the poem describes the churning, whipping, spewing, suffocating, and bombarding actions of the galaxies and beyond, the poet finds that the universe is indeed "good"—because for so long its more violent actions have stayed "far, *far* away from our place."

GENERATIONS

With *Generations*, Rogers's work leaves the small-press publishing world of Milkweed for that of the major trade publisher Penguin, yet continues with her examination of the natural world's abundance, its dark side, and its connections with the human mind. She uses graphic violence that she finds throughout nature to connect generations of animals, human and nonhuman.

Generations refers to the many groups of living things born about the same time, yet because the title is plural, it refers to all the generations born in succession. The poems concern themselves not only with the generations of living things but also with the energy, duplications, and origins, in the sense of bringing into being, of generation itself. Divided into six parts, five sections are numbered stories ("The First Story," "The Second Story," and so on), but the final section is "The Following Story." The assumption is that each section contains a different story, but in the first part of the collection, there is the poem "Creating a Pillar to Heaven," which describes the different layers of the pillar. The reader cannot help wondering if these "stories" are really the layers of the pillar (as in a skyscraper).

Although most of her poems are rooted in realistic detail, Rogers is always aware of the unseen, the invisible world that people can only sense. She tackles this topic in the wonderful poem "The Soul of Subtlety," in which she describes the way plants, animals, and even fog are so present in the moment, yet unaware at the same time. In the poem "In Another Place," she plays with the idea of mutability, the possibility that one might be something else entirely, although in one passage Rogers questions whether people even have the proper vocabulary to describe such a thing: ". . . one might be the fire itself/ if *be* is the right word for such a state,/ if *state* has definition in such a realm." There seems to be no possibility that Rogers does not consider.

OTHER MAJOR WORK

NONFICTION: *The Dream of the Marsh Wren: Writing as Reciprocal Creation*, 1999.

BIBLIOGRAPHY

Bryan, Sharon, ed. *Where We Stand: Women Poets on Literary Tradition*. New York: W. W. Norton, 1993. This is a collection of essays on tradition in poetry, with such well-known poets as Joy Harjo, Madeline DeFrees, Alicia Ostriker, and Rogers contributing.

Grider, Sylvia Ann, and Lou Halsell Rodenberger, eds. *Texas Women Writers: A Tradition of Their Own*. College Station: Texas A&M University Press, 1997. Contains an essay that places the poets Rogers, Betsy Feagan Colquitt, and Naomi Shihab Nye squarely in the region of Texas, yet finds vast differences among them.

Kutchins, Laura. Review of *Wayfare*. *Orion* 26, no. 7 (November/December, 2008): 77. This review praises *Wayfare*, finding it a work of "yearning and fulfillment, of folding and unfolding, of peering and pressing."

Rogers, Pattiann. "Breaking Old Forms: A Conversation." Interview by Gordon Johnston. *Georgia Review* 62, no. 1 (Spring, 2008): 154. Johnston interviews Rogers about *Generations* and its critical response, as the book was judged to be different from her earlier works. The same issue carries her poem "At Work."

_____. "The Poetry World of Pattiann Rogers." http://home.comcast.net/~pattiann_rogers/. The official Web site of Rogers provides a biography, information on events and readings, information on her works, and links to other sites of interest.

Seaman, Donna. Review of *Generations*. *Booklist* 100, nos. 19/20 (June 1-15, 2004): 1688. Seaman calls Rogers's poetry "ravishingly lyrical and imaginative" in its blend of science and the spiritual.

Sheila Golburgh Johnson

GARY SNYDER

Born: San Francisco, California; May 8, 1930

PRINCIPAL POETRY

Riprap, 1959
Myths and Texts, 1960
The Firing, 1964
Hop, Skip, and Jump, 1964
Nanao Knows, 1964
Riprap, and Cold Mountain Poems, 1965
Six Sections from Mountains and Rivers Without End, 1965
A Range of Poems, 1966
Three Worlds, Three Realms, Six Roads, 1966
The Back Country, 1967
The Blue Sky, 1969
Sours of the Hills, 1969
Regarding Wave, 1969, enlarged 1970
Manzanita, 1972
The Fudo Trilogy: Spel Against Demons, Smokey the Bear Sutra, The California Water Plan, 1973
Turtle Island, 1974
All in the Family, 1975
Axe Handles, 1983
Left Out in the Rain: New Poems, 1947-1986, 1986
No Nature: New and Selected Poems, 1992
Mountains and Rivers Without End, 1996
Danger on Peaks, 2004

OTHER LITERARY FORMS

Gary Snyder's pioneering journal of personal environmental discovery, *Earth House Hold: Technical Notes and Queries to Fellow Dharma Revolutionaries* (1969), was an invitation to examine the treasures of the planet and to consider how it might be employed for the benefit of all living species. It represents the culmination of the work Snyder began nearly two decades before when he conceived of a major in literature and anthropology at Reed College, and its somewhat tentative, propositional format expresses the spirit of a movement that recognized the destructive aspects of modern industrial society and sought alternative approaches to the questions of planetary survival. Although Snyder was sometimes referred to disparagingly as "a kind of patron saint of ecology" by critics trapped in more conventional social arrangements, his interest in the environment has proved to be as perceptive and enduring as his best poetry, and the publication of *The Practice of the Wild* (1990) has deepened the context of his interests, offering the wisdom and experience of a lifetime spent living in and thinking about the natural world. The book is a linked series of reflective essays, and its amiable, reasonable tone—similar to Snyder's conversational voice in his interviews, most notably those collected in *The Real Work: Interviews and Talks, 1964-1979* (1980)—permits the power of his intellectual insights, his scholarly investigations, and his political theories to reach an audience beyond the experts he hopes to equal in his argument. Combining energetic conviction and poetic eloquence, Snyder's essays are intended to be a "genuine teaching text" and "a mediation on what it means to be human." They demonstrate his philosophy of composition as it reveals a poetics of existence and have been written to stimulate "a broad range of people and provide them with historical, ecological and personal vision." *A Place in Space: Ethics, Aesthetics, and Watersheds* (1995) continues his exploration of these concerns, which are summarized and extended in *Back on the Fire: Essays* (2007).

ACHIEVEMENTS

Before "ecology" had become a password of political correctness, Gary Snyder was devising a program of study designed to create a language of environmental advocacy; after many trendy Westerners had long since recoiled from the rigors of Eastern thought, Snyder completed a curriculum of apprenticeship in Japan and went on to develop an American version of Zen applicable to his locality. As Native American life and lore gradually seeped into the area of academic interest, Snyder continued his examinations of the primal tribal communities that lived in harmony with the North American land mass for pre-Columbian millennia and worked to apply their successes to contemporary life. While hippies and dropouts returned to the button-down corporate culture after a brief dalliance with a counterculture, Snyder built his own home at the center of a small community that endures as an example of a philosophical position in action. Most of all, while some of the other voices that arose during the post-"Howl" renaissance of the new American poetry have become stale or quaint, Snyder's use of a clear, direct, colloquial but literature-responsive language made it possible for his concerns to reach, touch, and move a substantial audience through his poetry.

Snyder's varied interests have given him extensive material for his poems, but the appeal of his work does not depend on a program calculated to educate or persuade. Much more than argument, the poetry is an outgrowth of the processes of Snyder's life—his work, his family, his intellectual and athletic interests, his cultural convictions, and his rapport with the landscape. He has been able to illustrate effectively how art and life can be intertwined in a reciprocal interchange that does not depend on academic procedures or traditional schools (while not denying their usefulness), an interchange that enriches and expands both realms, and in this he joins Herman Melville (the sailor), Henry David Thoreau (the naturalist), Ralph Waldo Emerson (the philosopher and teacher), and Walt Whitman (the celebrator) in a line of American artists whose work was, in a profound sense, the spiritual and aesthetic expression of their life's focus.

Snyder won the Pulitzer Prize in 1975 for *Turtle Island*. He has received numerous other awards, including the Bess Hokin Prize (1964), an Academy Award from the National Institute of Arts and Letters (1966), the Levinson Prize (1968), the Shelley Memorial Award (1986), the American Book Award from the Before Columbus Foundation (1984), Silver Medals from the Commonwealth Club of California (1986, 2002), the Fred Cody Award for lifetime achievement (1989), the Robert Kirsch Award from the *Los Angeles Times* (1996), the Bollingen Prize (1997), the John Hay Award for Nature Writing (1997), the Lila Wallace-*Reader's Digest* Writers' Award (1998), the Masaoka Shiki International Haiku Grand Prize (2004), and the Ruth Lilly Poetry Prize (2008). He served as chancellor for the Academy of American Poets from 2003 to 2009.

BIOGRAPHY

Gary Sherman Snyder was born in San Francisco in 1930, the son of Harold Alton Snyder and Lois Wilkie Snyder. His parents moved back to their native Pacific Northwest in 1932, where they settled on a dairy farm near Puget Sound in Washington. Snyder's mother moved to Portland, Oregon, to work as a newspaper-woman when Snyder was twelve, and she reared Snyder and his younger sister Anthea as a single parent, insisting that Snyder commute downtown to attend Lincoln High, the most intellectually demanding school in the Portland system.

In 1947, he received a scholarship to Reed College, where he devised a unique major in anthropology and literature. Early in his college years, he joined the Mazamas and the Wilderness Society, both outdoors groups, and took up backcountry hiking and skiing and snow-peak mountaineering. His first poems were published in the Reed College literary magazine. He lived in an old house shared by a dozen other students similarly interested in art and politics, including the poets Philip Whalen and Lew Welch, who became his close friends. Snyder wrote for *The Oregonian* newspaper at night and spent the summer of 1950 on an archaeological dig at old Fort Vancouver in Washington. At about that time, he was briefly married to Allison Gass, a fellow student.

Upon graduation from Reed, Snyder completed one semester of graduate studies in linguistics at Indiana University before transferring to the University of California, Berkeley, to study Asian languages. During the summers of the years he pursued graduate work, he took a job first as a fire-watcher in the Cascade mountains and later, after he was fired in the McCarthy-era hysteria of 1954, as a choker-setter for the Warm Springs Lumber Company. Utilizing skills in woodcutting he had learned from his family and neighbors, Snyder "was often supporting himself" in his student years, and his first accomplished poems were related to these experiences as well as to his work on a trail crew in Yosemite in 1955.

That fall, Snyder met Allen Ginsberg and Jack Kerouac and became involved in the exploding art scene in San Francisco, where he took part in the historic Six Gallery reading where Ginsberg read "Howl" in public for the first time. Snyder followed this extraordinary performance with his own poetry in a very different vein and was also successful in capturing the attention of the audience. He and Kerouac shared a cabin in Mill Valley, California, through that winter and spring, and then Snyder traveled to Kyoto, Japan, to take up residence in a Zen temple, beginning a twelve-year sojourn in Japan that was broken by a nine-month hitch as a crewman on the tanker *Sappa Creek* and a brief return to San Francisco in 1958. His translations from the Chinese poet Han-shan, who lived in the seventh century, were published in the *Evergreen Review* in 1958 as "Cold Mountain Poems," and his first collection, *Riprap*, was published by Cid Corman's Origin Press in Japan in 1959.

Working as a part-time translator and researcher of Buddhist texts, Snyder eventually became a student of Rinzai Zen under Oda Sesso, Roshi (master), and established contacts with activist groups concerned with ecology, women's issues, and world peace. His next collection, *Myths and Texts*, was published in 1960, the same year he married the poet Joanne Kyger. In 1962, he traveled to India with Ginsberg, Peter Orlovsky, and Kyger, and his association with the poet Nanao Sakaki drew him into artistic circles in Tokyo in 1964. He returned to the United States to teach at Berkeley in 1965, won a Bollingen grant, and returned to Japan. His marriage with Kyger was over when he met Masa Uehara, a graduate student in English, and they were married in 1967.

With his wife and his son, Kai, who was born in Kyoto, Snyder returned to the Western Hemisphere, settling in the northern Sierra Nevada mountains, where he built a home (called "Kitkitdizze," meaning "mountain misery" in a local dialect) in 1970 with a crew of friends. His first book of poems reflecting his commitment to his native country, *Turtle Island* (from an old Native American name for the continent), was published in 1974 and won the Pulitzer Prize. During this time, Snyder was traveling to universities three or four months a year to read poetry, working on the needs of his immediate mountain community, and serving the state of California as the chairman of its Arts Council. At the end of the decade, he published a collection called *The Real Work*, and in 1983, he published *Axe Handles*, poems written during the previous ten years. In 1985, he joined the English department at the University of California, Davis, where he taught literature and ecological matters until his retirement in 2002. He began to travel widely, visiting Hawaii, Alaska, China, and parts of Europe to speak "on the specifics of Buddhist meditation, ecological practice, language and poetics, and bioregional politics." The poems he had written but left uncollected were published in *Left Out in the Rain: New Poems, 1947-1986*. In 1988, he was divorced from Masa Uehara and married

Carole Koda, and in 1990, he completed a book that presented a program for personal renewal and planetary conservation called *The Practice of the Wild*. That same year, a compilation of comments, reminiscences, poems, and assorted other statements was published by the Sierra Club under the title *Gary Snyder: Dimensions of a Life* in celebration of the poet's sixtieth birthday. Snyder completed his epic "poem of process" *Mountains and Rivers Without End* in 1996 and continued to train students at Davis to deal with environmental crises. In the first decade of the twenty-first century, Snyder traveled extensively, sharing his ideas about environmental advocacy to a worldwide audience that recognized him as one of the visionary founders of an increasingly widespread "deep ecology" movement. His good-natured, inspiring and enlightening comments about the ecosystems of the planet were gathered in the essays of *Back on the Fire*, while his first collection of poems in twenty years, *Danger on Peaks*, was both a recapitulation and reaffirmation of the themes and subjects of his life's work and a mature reflection and reassessment of his most personal concerns. The hero-figure Kerouac patterned after Snyder in *The Dharma Bums* (1958), "Japhy Ryder," has become the source of wisdom, as the poet Snyder has grown into an elder of the tribe.

ANALYSIS

Among many evocative statements about his life and work, a particularly crucial one is Gary Snyder's claim that

> As a poet, I hold the most archaic values on earth. They go back to the late Paleolithic; the fertility of the soil, the magic of animals; the power-vision in solitude, the terrifying initiation and rebirth; the love and ecstasy of the dance, the common work of the tribe.

The social and philosophical principles he has expressed are the fundamental credo of his convictions as a man and an artist. He uses the word "archaic" to suggest "primal" or "original"—the archetype or first pattern from which others may evolve. His citation of the late Paleolithic era as source-ground stems from his belief that essential lessons concerning human consciousness have been learned and then lost. Thus Snyder devotes much time to the study of ancient (and primitive) cultures. The values he holds stand behind and direct his poetry, as it is drawn from his studies and experiences. His values include a respect for land as the source of life and the means of sustaining it; a respect for all sentient creatures and for the animalistic instincts of humans; a recognition of the necessity for the artist to resist social pressure in order to discover and develop power from within; an acknowledgment of the necessity for participation in both communal ritual and individual exploration of the depths of the subconscious to transcend the mundane and risk the extraordinary; an acceptance of the body and the senses—the physical capabilities, pleasures, and demands of the skin; and a feeling for the shared labor of the community, another version of "the real work" that unites the individual with a larger sense and source of meaning. Neither the poet as solitary singer nor as enlightened visionary is sufficient without the complex of relationships that joins the local, the bioregional, and ultimately the planetary in an interdependent chain of reliance, support, and enlightened use of resources. It is with these values in mind that Snyder defines an ethical life as one that "is mindful, mannerly and has style," an attitude that is crucial to the accomplishment of "the real work."

Each of these precepts has an important analogue in the technical execution of the poems themselves. As Jerome Rothenberg has observed, "where I continue to see him best is as he emerges from his poems." Poetically, then, "the fertility of the soil" is worthless without the labor that brings it to fruition, and as Snyder has commented, "the rhythms of my poems follow the rhythms of the physical work I'm doing and life I'm leading at any given time—which makes the music in my head which creates the line." The linkage between the rhythmic movement of the body, the larger rhythmic cycles of the natural world, and the structure of words in a particular poem follows the precepts that Charles Olson prescribed in the landmark essay "Projective Verse" (1950), and Snyder, like Ginsberg, Robert Creeley, and others, has always favored the creation of a particular shape or form to suit the purpose of the poem under attentive development. The rhythms of a particular poem are derived from an "energy-mind-field-dance" that, in turn, often results from labor designed to capitalize on the life of the earth.

Similarly, when Snyder speaks of "the magic of animals," he is identifying one of his central subjects, and the images of many of his poems are based on his observations of animals in the wild. The importance of wilderness and the manner in which animals seem to interact instinctively with their natural surroundings are, for Snyder, keys to his conception of freedom. The magic of their existence is part of a mystery that humans need to penetrate. Thus, as image and subject, animals and their ways are an important part of the "etiquette of freedom" that Snyder's work serves.

The concept of the "power vision in solitude" is derived from both the shamanistic practices that Snyder has studied in primitive societies and the varieties of meditation he has explored in his research into and expressions of Buddhist thought. Its immediate consequence in poetry is the necessity for developing a singular, distinct voice, a language with which one is comfortable, and a style that is true to the artist's entire life. For Snyder, this has meant learning to control the mood of a poem through tonal modulation, matching mood to subject and arranging sequences of poems that can sustain visionary power as well as intimate personal reflection. "The terrifying initiation and rebirth" is a corollary of the power vision. It implies that once a singular voice has been established, it must be followed according to the patterns of its impulsive organization—in other words, to its points of origin in the subconscious. Snyder speaks of the unconscious as "our inner wilderness areas," and sees in the "depths of the mind" the ultimate source of the imagination. The exploration of the wilderness within is vital to the image-making function of poetry.

The "love and ecstasy" Snyder speaks of stems from the revolt that Snyder and his colleagues led against the stiff, formal, distant academic poetry favored by critics in the 1950's, and its application has been to influence the colloquial nature of his language, to encourage the use of primitive techniques such as chant to alter perceptive states, to permit the inclusion of casual data from ordinary existence to inform the poem, and, most of all, to confront the most personal of subjects with honesty and self-awareness. There is a discernible narrative consciousness present in Snyder's poetry even when he avoids—as he generally does—personal pronouns and definite articles. However, his resistance to cultural authority is balanced by his praise for the "common work of the tribe," the artistic accomplishment that he treasures. As he has said, "I feel very strongly that poetry also exists as part of a tradition, and is not simply a matter of only private and personal vision." Explaining his interests in Ezra Pound, William Carlos Williams, Wallace Stevens, John Milton, and others, Snyder says he wants "to know *what* has been done, and to see *how* it has been done. That in a sense is true craft." Almost paradoxically, considering his emphasis on originality, he advocates (and practices) extensive examination of multidisciplinary learning, explaining that knowledge of the past saves one "the trouble of having to repeat things that others have done that need not be done again. And then also he knows when he writes a poem that has never been written before."

RIPRAP

Snyder's first collection, *Riprap*, is evidence of the writing and thinking that Snyder had been doing through the mid-1950's. *Riprap* took shape while Snyder was working on a backcountry trail crew in 1955, and its title is at first a description of "stone laid on steep, slick rock to make a trail for horses in the mountains," then a symbol of the interlinkage of objects in a region and a figure for the placement of words in a poetic structure. It serves to connect language and action, reflective thought and the work that generates it. The poems in the collection are dedicated to the men Snyder worked with, the "community" of cohesion and effort he joined, men who knew the requirements of the land and who transmitted their skills through demonstration. *Riprap* includes elements of the oral tradition Snyder intersected, and the title "celebrates the work of the hands" while some of the poems "run the risk of invisibility" since they tried "for surface simplicity set with unsettling depths." Poems such as "Above Pate Valley" and "Piute Creek" begin with direct description of landscape and move toward an almost cosmic perspective concerning the passage of time across the land over geological epochs. The specific and the eternal coalesce:

> Hill beyond hill, folded and twisted
> Tough trees crammed
> In thin stone fractures
> A huge moon on it all, is too much.
> The mind wanders. A million
> Summers, night air still and the rocks

> Warm. Sky over endless mountains.
> All the junk that goes with being human
> Drops away, hard rock wavers.

Poetry, as Snyder put it in "Burning: No. 13" from *Myths and Texts*, is "a riprap on the slick road of metaphysics," helping one find meaning and explaining why one reads "Milton by Firelight" (the title of another poem) and finds new versions of hell and "the wheeling sky" in the Sierras.

MYTHS AND TEXTS

Myths and Texts is Snyder's first attempt to organize his ideas into an evolving, complex structural framework. In it, Snyder's wilderness experience is amplified by the use of Pacific Coast Indian texts, which are set as a kind of corrective for the exploitation and destruction of the environment that Snyder sees as the result of misguided American-European approaches to nature. The crux of the matter is the failure of Judeo-Christian culture to recognize the inherent sacredness of the land, and Snyder uses what he feels is a kind of Buddhist compassion and a Native American empathy as a corrective thrust. The three books of the collection are called "Logging," which uses the lumber industry as an example of "technological drivenness" that destroys resources and shows no respect for the symbolic or ritualistic aspect of the living wilderness; "Hunting," which explores the intricate relationship between the hunter and the quarry (and between mind and body) in primitive societies; and "Burning," which is somewhat less accessible in its intriguing attempt to find or chart a symbolic synthesis that integrates the mythic material Snyder has been presenting into a universal vision of timeless cycles of destruction and rebirth.

As Snyder defines the terms, in a preliminary fashion, the myths and texts are the "two sources of human knowledge—symbols and sense-impressions." The larger context at which he aims—the "one whole thing"—is built on the power of individual poems, and among the best are ones such as "Logging: No. 8," in which the logged ground is likened to a battlefield after a massacre; "Logging: No. 3," in which the lodgepole pine is treated as an emblem of nature's enduring vitality; "Logging: No. 13," in which a fire-watcher reports a fire ("T36N R16E S25/ Is burning. Far to the west") and seems more interested in the abstract beauty of the landscape than in any specific situation; and among several hunting songs, the exceptional "No. 6," which carries the dedication, *"this poem is for bear."*

Snyder read the original version of "The Woman Who Married a Bear" in an anthropology text in Reed College and was fascinated by the interaction of the human and animal cultures. He devotes a chapter to the story in *The Practice of the Wild*, lamenting that "the bears are being killed, the humans are everywhere, and the green world is being unraveled and shredded and burned by the spreading of a gray world that seems to have no end." His poem is placed at the convergence of several cultures and is structured by the different speaking "voices"—not specifically identified but clear from tone and context. First, in a quote from the anthropological text, the bear speaks: "As for me I am a child of the god of the mountains." Then, a field scientist, observing the data:

> You can see
> Huckleberries in bearshit if you
> Look, this time of year
> If I sneak up on the bear
> It will grunt and run.

This relatively matter-of-fact, outside position is replaced by a tale of the girl who married a bear: "In a house under the mountain/ She gave birth to slick dark children/ With sharp teeth, and lived in the hollow/ Mountain many years." A shift has been made to the Native American culture, and what follows is the burden of the legend, as the girl's tribe goes to reclaim her. The next voice is the hunter addressing the bear:

> honey-eater
> forest apple
> light-foot
> Old man in the fur coat, Bear! come out!
> Die of your own choice!

Now the poet enters, turning the tale (text) into poetry (myth): "Twelve species north of Mexico/ Sucking their paws in the long winter/ Tearing the high-strung caches down/ Whining, crying, jacking off." Then the tale continues, as the girl's brothers "cornered him in the rocks," and finally the "voice" of the bear-spirit speaks, as through a shaman perhaps, in the "Song of the snared bear":

> "Give me my belt.
> "I am near death.
> "I came from the mountain caves
> "At the headwaters,
> "The small streams there
> "Are all dried up.

In a deft conclusion, Snyder reduces the dramatic tension by the interposition of the disarmingly personal. As if inspired by the story, he begins to imagine himself a part of the Paleolithic hunter culture: "I think I'll go hunt bears." However, he is too solidly grounded in reality to go beyond a reading of the text: "Why s— Snyder,/ You couldn't hit a bear in the ass/ with a handful of rice." Although, of course, in the poem, he has hit the target squarely by assimilating the different voices (as different strands of culture) into his own modern version of the myth.

COLD MOUNTAIN POEMS

The *Cold Mountain Poems*, published together with *Riprap* as *Riprap and the Cold Mountain Poems*, are "translations" (in the Poundian sense) from Han-shan, a hermit and poet of the Tang dynasty, and they represent Snyder's identification with a kind of nature prophet at home in the wild as well as his inclination to isolate himself from those aspects of American (or Western) society he found abhorrent until he could fashion a program to combat the social ills he identified. As in most effective translations, there is a correspondence in sensibility between the two artists, and Snyder's comfort with the backcountry, as well as his growing sense of a cross-cultural and transepochal perspective, may be seen in lines like

> Thin grass does for a mattress,
> The blue sky makes a good quilt.
> Happy with a stone underhead
> Let heaven and earth go about their changes.

Calling Han-shan a "mountain madman" or "ragged hermit," Snyder expresses through the translations his admiration for a kind of independence, self-possession, and mindful alertness that he saw as a necessity for psychic survival in the Cold War era, a husbanding of strength to prepare for a return to the social struggle. "Mind solid and sharp," he says, he is gaining the vision to "honor this priceless natural treasure"—the world around him ("the whole clear cloudless sky")—and the insight ("sunk deep in the flesh") to understand the complementary wonder within.

REGARDING WAVE

With *Regarding Wave*, Snyder's work turned from the mythic and philosophical toward the intimate and immediately personal. He had begun a family (his son Kai was born in 1968) and returned to the United States, and the poems recall his last days in the Far East and his sense of how he had to proceed after returning to his native land at a time of strife and turmoil. The family poems are celebratory, written in wonder, open and exuberant in the first flush of parenthood, expressing his delight with his wife Masa and their infant son. There are poems that are like meditations on the sensual: "Song of the View," "Song of the Tangle," or "Song of the Taste," and poems that are drawn from the experience of rearing a child, like "The Bed in the Sky" or "Kai, Today," which is an awestruck reflection on the act of birth, or the supra-mundane "Not Leaving the House," in which Snyder admits "When Kai is born/ I quit going out," and justifies his inward angle of view by concluding "From dawn til late at night/ making a new world of ourselves/ around this life."

After returning to the United States, Snyder found that the political situation was troubling ("Off the coast of Oregon/ The radio is full of hate and anger"), and he was warned that "beards don't make money," so he began to plan a life as a poet and activist in the United States. The effects of his action become clearer in his next collection, but the cast of his mind is apparent in the transitional "What You Should Know to Be a Poet," which calls together what he had learned from his life to that point:

> all you can about animals as persons
> the names of trees and flowers and weeds
> names of stars, and the movements of the planets
> > and the moon.
>
> your own six senses, with a watchful and elegant mind

and then blends it with a kind of resolution to confront the bestial nature of humans to prepare to engage the evil at large in the world, as expressed in the crucial central stanza beginning, "kiss the ass of the devil." From that point, the poem alternates positive aspects of existence ("& then love the human: wives husbands and friends") with an acceptance of the trials and burdens of life ("long dry hours of dull work swallowed and accepted/ and livd with and finally lovd") until it concludes with an unsettling sense of the future, "real danger. gambles. and the edge of death."

THE FUDO TRILOGY

Snyder's ambivalent feelings about living in the United States are again expressed in the hilarious "Smokey the Bear Sutra," in which the familiar symbol of the forest service is depicted as a kind of Asiatic avenging demon protecting the environment and resisting polluters. Published in 1973 as a part of *The Fudo Trilogy*—a pamphlet that included "The California Water Plan" (a section of *Mountains and Rivers Without End*) and "Spel Against Demons"—it combines Snyder's serious concerns about the environment and his continuing pursuit of Asiatic culture with his characteristically engaging high good humor. The chant, "Drown their butts; soak their butts" is presented in mock seriousness as a mantra of righteousness, while Smokey is depicted more as a lovable child's pet than the fierce scourge of evil that the archetype suggests. The comic conception works to keep Snyder's considerable anger under control, so that he does not turn his poetry into polemic.

TURTLE ISLAND

By the early 1970's, Snyder had become fully involved in the bioregional movement and committed to the local community of San Juan Ridge, where he had built a home. He began to follow a dual course in his poetry. The overarching theme of his work was to protect and preserve "Turtle Island—the old/new name for the continent, based on many creation myths," and it was expressed in poems that "speak of place, and the energy-pathways that sustain life" and in poems that decry the forces of destruction unleashed by the stupidity of "demonic killers" who perpetrate "aimless executions and slaughterings."

The poems were published under the title *Turtle Island*, sold more than 100,000 copies, and won the Pulitzer Prize. Among the most memorable poems Snyder has written, the ones that explore the "energy pathways" sustaining life include "The Bath"—a Whitmanesque rapture in appreciation of the body that challenges the latent Puritanism and fear of the skin in American society by describing in loving detail the physical wonder of his son, his wife, and himself in a bath. The sheer glory of the body glowing with health and the radiant reflection of the natural world around them build toward a feeling of immense physical satisfaction and then toward a complementary feeling of metaphysical well-being. The frankness of the language may be difficult for some readers, but Snyder's tasteful, delicate, and comfortable handling of it makes his declaration "this is our body," an echoing chorus, an assertion of religious appreciation. In an even more directly thankful mode, the translation of a Mohawk "Prayer for the Great Family" unites the basic elements of the cosmos in a linked series of gemlike depictions, concluding with one of Snyder's essential ideas: that there is an infinite space "beyond all powers and thoughts/ and yet is within us—/ Grandfather Space/ The Mind is his Wife." Other expressions of "eternal delight" include "By Frazier Creek Falls," "Source," and "The Dazzle," as well as many poems in the book's last section, a kind of basic history primer called "For the Children," that convey considerable emotion without lapsing into obvious emotional tugging.

The more overtly political poems and sketches tend to be somber, frequently employing a litany of statistics to convey grim information that needs little additional comment, but in "The Call of the Wild," Snyder's anger is projected in language purposefully charged with judgmental fervor. Avoiding easy partisanship, Snyder condemns, first, "ex acid-heads" who have opted for "forever blissful sexless highs" and hidden in fear from what is interesting about life. His image of people missing the point of everything by living in trendy "Geodesic domes, that/ Were stuck like warts/ In the woods" is as devastating as his cartoon conception of advanced technology declaring "a war against earth" waged by pilots with "their women beside them/ in bouffant hairdos/ putting nail-polish on the/ gunship cannon-buttons."

AXE HANDLES

The poems in *Axe Handles* have a reflective tone, moving inward toward the life Snyder has been leading in his local community, to which he dedicated the collection. His concerns do not change, but in a return to the more spare, lyrical poems of *Riprap*, Snyder condenses and focuses his ideas into "firm, clean lines of verse reminiscent of Ezra Pound's *Rock-Drill* cantos," according to critic Andrew Angyal. The title has a typically dual meaning, referring to language as an instrument for shaping meaning and to the entire meaning of tools in human life. The theme of "cultural continuity" is presented in terms of Snyder's passing his knowledge on to his family, friends, and readers and is explicitly explained in the parable of the title poem. The book evokes an ethos of harmony in cycles of renewal and restoration, rebirth and reconsideration. Snyder moves beyond his specific criticism of human social organizations in the late twentieth century and toward, in Angyal's words, his "own alternative set of values in communal cooperation, conservation, and a nonexploitative way of life that shows respect for the land." The compression and density of Snyder's thinking are evident in the poem "Removing the Plate of the Pump on the Hydraulic System of the Backhoe," which reads in entirety

> Through mud, fouled nuts, black grime
> it opens, a gleam of spotless steel
> machined-fit perfect
> swirl of intake and output
> relentless clarity
> at the heart
> of work.

The pursuit of "relentless clarity" in everything characterizes Snyder's life and art, but the pressures of the search are alleviated by his congenial nature and sense of humor. While emphasizing the importance of Zen "mindfulness," Snyder has also stressed that "a big part of life is just being playful." In accordance with this approach, Snyder has kept dogmatic or simplistic solutions out of his work and has cherished the wild and free nature of humankind. In "Off the Trail," which he wrote for his wife, Koda, he envisions a life in which "all paths are possible" and maintains that "the trial's not the way" to find wisdom or happiness. "We're off the trail,/ You and I," he declares, "and we chose it!" That choice—the decision to go against the grain "to be in line with the big flow"—has led to a poetry of "deeply human richness," as Charles Molesworth puts it in his perceptive study of Snyder's work, in which "a vision of plenitude" leads to a "liminal utopia, poised between fullness and yet more growth."

MOUNTAINS AND RIVERS WITHOUT END

On April 8, 1956, Snyder began to work on a "poem of process" somewhat akin to Pound's *Cantos* (1970) or Williams's *Paterson* (5 volumes, 1946-1956) that he called *Mountains and Rivers Without End*. Initially inspired by East Asian brush painting (*sumi*) on a series of screens and by his own experiences with what he viewed as "a chaotic universe where everything is in place," Snyder brought in elements of Native American styles of narration, his continuing study of Zen Buddhism, Asian art and drama, and the varied landscapes that he traversed on several continents during the next four decades as the primary features of the poem. "It all got more complicated than I predicted and the poems were evasive," Snyder remarked in retrospect about the project. A particular problem involved the central narrative consciousness, since the traditional idea of an epic hero as a focal perspective seemed outmoded. As an alternate center of coherence, Snyder devised an elaborate structural arrangement built on ways in which "walking the landscape can be both ritual and meditation" so that the evolving perceptual matrix of the artist provided a fundamental frame for the materials of the poem.

Drawing on the "yogic implications" of mountains as representations of "a tough spirit of willed self-discipline" and rivers as a projection of "generous and loving spirit of concern for all beings" (as Snyder explained in "The Making of *Mountains and Rivers Without End*," an afterword to the poem), the epic is energized by the interplay between these elemental forces. The essential things of the poet's life—his practice of Zen meditation and action, his abiding concern for the "ark of biodiversity," his love and care for friends and family, his investigative interest in the previous inhabitants of the North American continent, and his sense of himself as an artist whose poetry is an extension of the patterns of his working world—provide the distinct subjects and incidents for the separately composed poems that constitute individual sections, written (as he notes in his signatory final line) from "Marin-an 1956" to "Kitkitdizze 1996."

Like Pound, whom Snyder calls "my direct teacher in these matters," Snyder wanted to include what he considered the most important intellectual, mythological, and cultural aspects of his times, but he noted that "big sections of the *Cantos* aren't interesting." To avoid the kind of obscurity that requires endless emendations, Snyder provided several pages of explanation in endnotes and included a record of publication of the individual parts, which functions as an accompanying chronology. Nevertheless, the technical strategies Snyder employs to "sustain the reader through it" are fairly intricate and designed to maintain a discernible structure that contributes to the cohesion of the poem. The guiding principle behind the entire enterprise depends on Snyder's conviction that, as he stated in an afterword to a 1999 reprint of *Riprap*, the whole universe can be seen as "interconnected, interpenetrating, mutually reflecting and mutually embracing." Therefore, while some individual parts may contain names, ideas, and references that appear esoteric or strictly personal, "there will be enough reverberations and echoes from various sections so that it will be self-informing." Since the poem's progress is not chronological, arranged according to place rather than period, there is no ultimate sense of completion. For Snyder, the poem is not "closed up" but ideally should continue to maintain a "sense of usefulness and relevance" as it offers "stimulation and excitement and imagination" for the reader.

In addition to the widest patterns of intersection, Snyder uses several prominent technical devices to tie things together. Initially, he expected to have twenty-five sections, each centering on a key phrase. While this plan was not maintained for every part of the poem, there are some especially important key phrases, as in the seventh poem ("Bubbs Creek Haircut"), in which the third line from the last, "double mirror waver," is described by Snyder as a "structure point" conveying infinite reflection. Similarly, in "Night Highway 99," the third poem, the image of a "network womb" is described by Snyder as a reference to the Buddhist concept of "the great womb of time and space which intersects itself." The poem "The Blue Sky," which concludes part 1, contains what Snyder describes as a "healing" word, "sky/tent/curve," an image of an arc that connects the disparate horizons of isolated nations. This sense of joining is a crucial philosophical precept in the poem, since the original idea of landscape paintings on screens or scrolls is exemplified by Snyder's remark that he "would like to have the poem close in on itself but on some other level keep going."

The final form of the poem is clarified by the publication record, which indicates an unleashing of energy in the 1960's followed by an ingathering of strength during the mid-1970's to mid-1980's, when Snyder's travels took him to "most of the major collections of Chinese paintings in the United States." His sense of the poem was also "enlarged by walking/working visits to major urban centers," which became important social complements to the portrayals of the natural world. In the 1990's, Snyder says, "the entire cycle clicked for me" and he wrote sixteen of the poem's sections while revising the typography of some earlier parts and reorganizing the placement of the poems in the final version. While each individual poem can function as an independent entity, the completed poem has, as poet Robert Hass has commented, "the force and concentration of a very shaped work of art."

An overview of the poem reveals Snyder's shaping strategies. The first of the four parts deals with the origins of a voyage, the inner and outer landscapes to be traveled, and the ways in which the features of the terrain can be gathered into a personal vision. "Night Highway 99," for instance, is Snyder's *On the Road*, embracing the Pacific Coast route where Snyder hitchhiked south from his home ground and met people like Ginsberg ("A. G."), a road brother. The second part extends the journey to the concrete bleakness and compulsive energy of giant urban complexes. "Walking the New York Bedrock" revels in the sheer magnitude of a great city, which still recalls the "manyfooted Manhatta" of Whitman's paean. The parallels Snyder draws here between geologic strata, canyons, and skyscrapers imply a commonality in disparate forms. The third part moves toward a reconciliation of forces and forms, while the fourth, containing poems written more recently, conveys the now mature poet's reflective estimate of enduring values. The poem for Snyder's wife, Koda, "Cross-Legg'd," is a kind of prayer of appreciation for the rewards of the journey, an expression of serenity and alertness. As a demonstration of the qualities he esteems, its conclusion, "we two be here what comes," celebrates the condition of mindful awareness Snyder sought when he began his study of Buddhist ways.

Toward the poem's conclusion, "The Mountain Spirit" reframes the conception of mountains and rivers that launched the journey. Its declaration, "Streams and mountains never stay the same," is like a motto for the poet's way of being, while its statement "All art is song/ is sacred to the real" reemphasizes his fundamental credo. His quote "nothingness is shapeliness" is at the core of Zen practice, also echoing Ginsberg's claim, "Mind is shapely/ Art is Shapely." The final poem, "Finding the Space in the Heart," explores the infinity of space, which Snyder sees as a symbol of freedom, ending the poem in an ethos of gratitude epitomized by the "quiet heart and distant eye," which he acknowledges as the supreme gift of "the mountain spirit." Even with all of the evocative, vividly descriptive passages illuminating the natural world, Snyder's poetry remains firmly grounded on the human values he sees as the fundamentals of existence. As he has said, "In a visionary way, what we would want poetry to do is guide lovers toward ecstasy, give witness to the dignity of old people, intensify human bonds, elevate the community and improve the public spirit."

Danger on Peaks

Danger on Peaks is both a reflective recollection of important incidents and moments from earlier years and a continuing demonstration of the kinds of energy and insight that have made Snyder's work as a poet and environmental visionary so impressive. The essays in *Back on the Fire*, which acts as a companion volume, explore some of the same subjects that have been Snyder's most enduring concerns and reveal some of the circumstances that shaped the poems. The essays recall and comment on earlier poems, and the poems often illuminate some of the situations that led toward the composition of the essays. Notably, at the close of *Back on the Fire*, Snyder bids farewell to his wife, to whom *Danger on Peaks* is dedicated:

Carole Lynn Koda

OCTOBER 3, 1947-JUNE 29, 2006

gone, gone,   gone beyond
gone beyond beyond

bodhi

svāhā

This deeply emotional statement, cast in direct, clear language imbued with the kind of personal philosophical perspective that has informed Snyder's work, exemplifies the tone and attitude that make the poems in *Danger on Peaks* so appealing for readers familiar with his work and an appropriate introduction for those reading him for the first time. The book is divided into six thematic sections, each one focused on a particular part of Snyder's life recalled and reconsidered for the pleasure of the memory and the revivified moment.

The first section, "Mount St. Helens," evokes the spirit of the landscape that drew Snyder into the wild when he was thirteen. Spirit Lake, when he first saw it, "was clear and still, faint wisps of fog on the smooth silvery surface," but the lake was obliterated when the volcano erupted, and the changes in the small span (in geologic terms) of time since then leads to a meditation on transformation and the value of what endures. The next section, "Yet Older Matters," is a gathering of short lyrics of appreciation for the infinite range and fundamental features of the natural world, followed by versions of haiku expressing the poet's psychological moods at a moment of awareness:

> Clumsy at first
> my legs, feet and eye learn again to leap
> skip through the tumbled rocks

The third section, "Daily Life," is a series of short poetic accounts, mostly on one page, on subjects such as "reading the galley pages of [James] Laughlin's *Collected Poems*," "working on hosting Ko Un great Korean poet," visiting "Mariano Vallejo's Library," and in a high-spirited, rollicking song of pleasure and praise, building an addition to his home, "Old Kitkitdizze." The good-humored, energy-charged, inclusive communal atmosphere that has made Snyder's company as well as his writing so appealing is evident in his use of rhyming in short stanzas, listing, naming, and celebrating. The fourth section, "Steady, They Say," is a gallery of portraits, Snyder's friends from the recent (Seamus Heaney) and distant past ("To All the Girls Whose Ears I Pierced Back Then").

The last two sections take a turn toward the contemplative as Snyder offers brief narratives leading toward a poems that is both a commentary on an incident and a kind of concluding thought. The narrations are set as an unfolding present, each poem like a step toward a wider arc of apprehension. In "One Day in Late Summer," Snyder relates how he "had lunch with my old friend Jack Hogan," part of a group who "hung out in North Beach back in the fifties." Then, thinking about a half-century passing, he remarks:

> This present moment
> that lives on
>
> to become
>
> long ago

The last section, "After Bamiyan" (the valley where the Taliban destroyed colossal statues of Buddha carved in caves in the sixth century) begins as an exchange with "A person who should know better" about the value of art and human life, leading Snyder to insist "Ah yes . . . impermanence. But this is never a reason to let compassion and focus slide, or to pass off the suffering of others." He supports this with Issa's great haiku about the "dew-drop world," in Japanese and then with his own translation, providing poetry and vivid prose in the service of the things Snyder regards as sacred. The volume, appropriately, does not close with a feeling of finality, as the last poem, "Envoy," is succeeded by one of Snyder's own photographs of Mount St. Helens in August, 1945, then two pages of explanatory notes, then "Thanks To" (another list as a poem), a page of acknowledgments, and lastly a photo of Snyder himself, smiling, a benediction and gift for the world to enjoy.

OTHER MAJOR WORKS

NONFICTION: *Earth House Hold: Technical Notes and Queries to Fellow Dharma Revolutionaries*, 1969; *The Old Ways*, 1977; *He Who Hunted Birds in His Father's Village: The Dimensions of a Haida Myth*, 1979; *The Real Work: Interviews and Talks, 1964-1979*, 1980; *Passage Through India*, 1983, expanded 2007; *The Practice of the Wild*, 1990; *A Place in Space: Ethics, Aesthetics, and Watersheds*, 1995; *Gary Snyder Papers*, 1995; *Back on the Fire: Essays*, 2007; *The Selected Letters of Allen Ginsberg and Gary Snyder*, 2009 (Bill Morgan, editor).

MISCELLANEOUS: *The Gary Snyder Reader: Prose, Poetry, and Translations, 1952-1998*, 2000.

BIBLIOGRAPHY

Gray, Timothy. *Gary Snyder and the Pacific Rim.* Iowa City: University of Iowa Press, 2006. An interesting study of the poet, his work, and his countercultural place in literary history.

Hunt, Anthony. *Genesis, Structure, and Meaning in Gary Snyder's "Mountains and Rivers Without End."* Las Vegas: University of Nevada Press, 2004. An intelligent interweaving of Snyder's aesthetic and environmental concerns and the development of his forty-year epic.

Murphy, Patrick. *A Place for Wayfaring: The Poetry and Prose of Gary Snyder.* Corvallis: Oregon State University Press, 2000. After three introductory chapters on themes in Snyder's work, especially mythological themes, Murphy offers close readings of a number of individual poems.

_____. *Understanding Gary Snyder.* Columbia: University of South Carolina Press, 1992. A useful overview, written for students and general readers, of Snyder's work and influences, with detailed explications of his work.

_____, ed. *Critical Essays on Gary Snyder.* Boston: G. K. Hall, 1990. A comprehensive, well-chosen collection of critical essays by one of Snyder's most intelligent critics. This book, which captures the earliest responses to the poet's work as well as the next three decades of criticism, is evidence of the variety of perspectives Snyder's work has brought forth.

Phillips, Rod. *"Forest Beatniks" and "Urban Thoreaus": Gary Snyder, Jack Kerouac, Lew Welch, and Michael McClure.* New York: P. Lang, 2000. Examines the attitudes toward nature, ecology, and conservation in the Beats' poetry, countering the notion that Beat poetry was a purely urban phenomenon.

Schuler, Robert Jordan. *Journeys Toward the Original Mind: The Long Poems of Gary Snyder*. New York: P. Lang, 1994. Close readings of *Myths and Texts* and *Mountains and Rivers Without End*, focusing on Snyder's concept of "original mind," in which the mind is purified of all its cultural baggage in order to comprehend the universe directly.

Scigaj, Leonard M. *Sustainable Poetry: Four American Ecopoets*. Lexington: University Press of Kentucky, 1999. Along with Snyder, discusses and compares A. R. Ammons, Wendell Berry, and W. S. Merwin and their treatment of nature and environmental concerns in their works. Bibliographical references, index.

Smith, Eric Todd. *Reading Gary Snyder's "Mountains and Rivers Without End."* Boise, Idaho: Boise State University Press, 2000. An extended close reading of Snyder's four-decades-long epic of individual environmental exploration and Asian aesthetic expression.

Suiter, John. *Poets on the Peaks: Gary Snyder, Philip Whalen, and Jack Kerouac in the North Cascades*. Washington, D.C.: Counterpoint, 2002. Examines the environmental influences on Snyder, Jack Kerouac, and Philip Whalen that occurred through living in the Pacific Northwest mountains. Includes thirty-five photographs of places where Snyder lived and worked.

Leon Lewis
Updated by Lewis

DAVID WAGONER

Born: Massillon, Ohio; June 5, 1926

OTHER LITERARY FORMS

Best known as a poet and novelist, David Wagoner (WAG-uh-nuhr) has also written plays—*An Eye for an Eye for an Eye* was produced in Seattle in 1973—as well as short fiction and essays. He edited and wrote the introduction to *Straw for the Fire: From the Notebooks of Theodore Roethke, 1943-1963* (1972).

ACHIEVEMENTS

It is possible that David Wagoner will be best remembered as one of the finest "nature" and "regional" poets of twentieth century America, and as one who has been instrumental in generating renewed interest in Native American lore. To categorize him so narrowly, however, does disservice to his versatility, and to the breadth of his talent and interests. Publishing steadily since the early 1950's, Wagoner has created a body of work that impresses not only for the number of volumes produced, but also for their quality. His novels have been praised for their energy and humor and in many cases for the immediacy of their Old West atmosphere. He received a Ford Fellowship for drama (1964), but it is as a poet that he has been most often honored: with a Guggenheim Fellowship (1956), a National Institute of Arts and Letters Grant (1967), and a National Endowment for the Arts Grant (1969). *Poetry* has awarded him its Morton Dauwen Zabel Prize (1967), its Oscar Blumenthal Prize (1974), its Eunice Tietjens Memorial Prize (1971), its Levinson Prize (1994), and its Union League Civic and Arts Poetry Prize (1997). *Sleeping in the Woods, Collected Poems, 1956-1976,* and *In Broken Country* were nominated for National Book Awards. He won Pushcart Prizes in 1979 and 1983. Wagoner served as a chancellor of the Academy of American Poets from 1978 to 1999, succeeding Robert Lowell. He received an Academy Award in literature (1987) from the American Academy of Arts and Letters. He was awarded the Ruth Lilly Poetry Prize (1991), the Ohioana Book Award (1997) for *Walt Whitman Bathing,* and two Washington State Book Awards in Poetry (2000, 2009).

BIOGRAPHY

David Russell Wagoner was born on June 5, 1926, in Massillon, Ohio, and was reared in Whiting, Indiana, the son of a steelworker. After receiving his B.A. degree from Pennsylvania State University in 1947 and his M.A. from Indiana University two years later, Wagoner began his teaching career at DePauw University, returning after a year to Pennsylvania State University. During this time, he was deeply influenced by Theodore Roethke, with whom he had studied as an undergraduate. In 1954, Roethke was instrumental in Wagoner's move to the University of Washington, where he taught until his retirement in 2002. X. J. Kennedy has speculated that perhaps "the most valuable service Roethke ever performed for Wagoner was to bring him to the Pacific Northwest and expose him to rain forests"—and to the culture of the Northwest Coast and Plateau Indians, one might add. Not only has Wagoner made use in his own poems of specific Native American myths and legends, but he has also absorbed the Indians' animistic spiritualism into his own philosophy. In the author's note to *Who Shall Be the Sun?,* he explains that Indians "did not place themselves above their organic and inorganic companions on earth but recognized with awe that they shared the planet as equals." Wagoner finds this equality "admirable and worthy of imitation," as much of his poetry indicates.

When not teaching, Wagoner has worked as a railroad section hand, a park police officer, and a short-order cook. He is a member of the Society of American Magicians. He served as editor of *Poetry Northwest* from 1966 until it ceased publication in 2002, and he has contributed poetry and commentary to a range of literary journals, including *Antioch Review, The Atlantic, Harvard Review, New England Review, Poetry,* and *Prairie Schooner.*

ANALYSIS

Despite David Wagoner's accomplishments and honors, and despite the fact that his poems appear regularly in mass-circulation magazines such as *The New Yorker* and *The Atlantic*, as well as the literary quarterlies, he is generally regarded as one of the most underappreciated of American poets. His works, with the exception of "Staying Alive," had not been included in major poetry anthologies until the early twenty-first century, when his poems began appearing in collections such as *The Best American Poetry* (2003, 2004, 2005, 2006). There are several possible explanations for this. First, he lives in Seattle and has chosen as his primary subject matter the land and people of the Pacific Northwest—thus giving rise to the dismissive "regional" label. It is also possible that some of his own best qualities may work against him. His subject matter is anything but trendy; the reader searches his poems in vain for the issues of the day. The only explicit social comment one is likely to find is contained in a half dozen or so poems addressing the Weyerhaeuser Company, a logging firm, and its practice of clear-cutting three-mile swaths of virgin forest.

Perhaps the major problem, as X. J. Kennedy suggests, is Wagoner's very "readability." Much of his poetry seems, at least on first encounter, curiously unpoetic, even prosy. His unpretentious language and casual, conversational tone frequently combine with his sense of humor to create a deceptively simple surface for his complex and serious ideas. This simplicity does make the work accessible; on the other hand, it may actually encourage the casual or first-time reader to dismiss Wagoner's work as lightweight.

Even in his most alienated and melancholy early poems, Wagoner's wit continually asserts itself. He is fond of puns, palindromes, and other forms of wordplay, and makes frequent use of colloquialisms, folk sayings, clichés, non sequiturs, and other lunacies of ordinary speech, often twisting words or phrases in such a way that they take on startling new meanings. Still, it is not as a semantic magician that Wagoner should be remembered; there are not a great many "quotable" lines—in the sense of the exquisite image of dazzling insight to be isolated for admiration out of context—in his work. Wagoner is at least as much philosopher as poet, and his poems, effective as they are when looked at individually, together take on cumulative power and meaning. Outwardly dissimilar poems are often interrelated below the surface to a marked degree. The result is a coherent, explicitly delineated philosophy, a "way" of life based on acceptance, self-reliance, and a profound reverence for the natural world.

Those who insist on calling Wagoner a regional or nature poet are certainly correct, to a point. From his earliest collection on, his work has amply indicated a sensitivity to the landscape around him. Later poems, in particular, have been praised for their descriptive qualities. The same can be said of many writers, but the use to which Wagoner has put his rain forests, mountains, rivers, and coastlines is uniquely his own. His wilderness, with its unsentimental, uncompromising beauty, serves on one level as a conventional metaphor: the landscape, physical and spiritual, through which one travels on one's life journey. Rather than seeing rocks, trees, and animals, however, as separate entities to be reacted to—climbed over, caught and eaten, run from—Wagoner views the natural world as the medium through which humans can best learn to know themselves. Put another way, if one can accept one's place as a part of the ongoing natural processes of life, death, decay, and rebirth, one begins to "see things whole." It is this sense of wholeness, this appreciation for the interrelatedness of all the "organic and inorganic companions on earth" to which Wagoner invites his reader, as if to a feast.

The way to this ideal state involves an apparent paradox: To find oneself, one must first lose oneself, shedding the subject/object, mind/body, spirit/intellect dualities typical of "rational" Western thought. In "Staying Alive," a traveler lost in the woods is faced not only with problems of physical survival but also with "the problem of recognition," by anyone or anything external that might be looking for him, as well as recognition of his own true nature. Unable to make contact with others, the traveler is advised that "You should have a mirror/ With a tiny hole in the back . . ." that will reflect the sun and flash messages, that will reflect one's familiar physical image and that, because of the aperture, will also allow one to see through one's physical self to the wholeness of the surrounding natural world.

It is clear that, in Wagoner's view, modern industrial society has created too many wastelands and polluted waterways, and more than enough fragmented citizens such as "The Man from the Top of the Mind," with "the light bulb screwed into his head,/ The vacuum tube of his sex, the electric eye." This gleaming creature of pure intellect can "Bump through our mazes like a genius rat" but is incapable of any human emotion except destructive rage. On every level, it would appear, one has become estranged—from oneself, from others and from one's environment.

HANDBOOK POEMS

In place of this fragmentation and alienation, Wagoner offers synthesis: the ability to see and experience things whole. In a remarkable series of poems, he not only extends the offer but also provides an explicit, step-by-step guide—a Scouts' handbook or survival manual for the reader to follow.

Although these handbook poems span several volumes (from *Staying Alive* through *In Broken Country*), they are best read as a single group. All are similar in language and tone; all address an unnamed "you," offering advice for coping with problems that might arise on a wilderness trip. Should one find oneself lost, one need only remember that "Staying alive . . . is a matter of calming down." Further poems instruct one on what to do when "Breaking Camp," or "Meeting a Bear" ("try your meekest behavior,/ . . . eyes downcast"), even after "Being Shot" ("if you haven't fallen involuntarily, you may/ Volunteer now . . ."). In each case, "you," the reader, are put in touch—in most cases both literally and figuratively—with something that has previously seemed foreign or outside the realm of ordinary human experience. In other words, lack of sensitivity to natural processes results in estrangement and isolation. By becoming more receptive, and perhaps less "top of the mind" rational, one allows for the possibility of "rescue" in the form of new understanding.

Frequently, since they typically involve a stripping away of the ego, these new insights prove to be humbling. Traveling "From Here to There," one can see the destination easily, while the distance deceives and one is confused by mirages: "Water put out like fire, . . . flying islands,/ The unbalancing act of mountains upside down." The problem of recognition resurfaces; nothing is what it seems. There is nothing to do but keep slogging: "One Damn Thing After Another," until finally, having "shrugged off most illusions" you "find yourself" in a place "where nothing is the matter/ . . . asking one more lesson." Still harder to accept are the lessons that teach acquiescence in mortality; lessons that teach that even a violent death is as much a part of the life process as birth. In "Being Shot," one finds oneself helpless on the forest floor, "study[ing]/ At first hand . . . the symptoms of shock." With Wagoner's open and accepting life view, death is as natural and therefore as necessary as birth, and "To burrow deep, for a deep winter," as "Staying Alive" advises, will result, come spring, in a renewal of some kind, if only because—should one not survive—one's decaying body will provide nutrients with which to feed other forms of life.

A series of poems in the final section of *In Broken Country* provide a guide to survival in the desert rather than the forest. Similar in tone and intent to the earlier handbook poems, these divert from "The Right Direction" past "The Point of No Return," where ". . . from here on/ It will take more courage to turn than to keep going." The process is what matters.

The "you" in these poems is never identified. There is a strong sense that the reader is being addressed directly, as if he or she has enrolled in an Outward Bound course and is receiving a curious mix of practical and cryptic last-minute advice before setting out on a solo adventure. There is also a sense of the poet talking to himself, working his own way both from the industrialized northern Indiana of his youth to the rain forests of Washington, and, in a parallel journey, from a sense of alienation to one of harmony.

DRY SUN, DRY WIND

In *Dry Sun, Dry Wind*, Wagoner's first collection, his affinity with nature is already apparent, but no real contact seems possible. The poet remains isolated, seeing about him images of destruction ("sun carries death to leaves"), decay, and uncertainty ("last year's gully is this year's hill"). Time flies; memory is unable to delay it. The natural environment, blighted though it is, is "Too much to breathe, think, see" ("Warning"). In the early poems, the relationship between humans and nature—or humans and anything or anyone else—was generally one of conflict, an ongoing struggle for control resulting in disillusionment: a war, rather than a reconciliation, of opposites. "Progress" was often best achieved through violence to the land, and the stillness that in later works will open the way to enlightenment has precisely the opposite effect in early poems such as "Lull." Recognition, and, by extension, synthesis, are possible only when "the wind hums or wheels," creating movement, a kind of artificial life.

It is perhaps significant that none of the poems from this first volume has been included in any subsequent collection. The suggestion is that Wagoner quickly moved beyond these early efforts, struggling with his own problem of recognition as he searched for a true voice of his own. The major themes are there, often apparent only in their negative aspects, as, for example, the fragmentation and conflict that will yield in later poems to synthesis. In addition, there is at least one poem that deserves reading on its own merit.

"Sam the Aerialist" is "sick of walking." He wants to fly. Like the poet, like the trickster of Native American myth, like dreamers everywhere, he hungers for the impossible and yearns to exceed his natural bounds. In this, Sam is like most of the human race. His crime is not so much his desire to fly as it is his attitude, which is aggressive, self-serving, exploitative: Sam has a "lust for air" that is anything but properly reverent. The birds, therefore, instead of sharing their secrets with him, "have kept/ Far from his mind." "Birds are evil," Sam concludes,

> they fly
> Against the wind. How many have I pulled
> Apart . . .
> To learn the secret?

Sam learns by destroying. He lacks the empathy that could move him toward true understanding, and he remains isolated, cut off from his own nature as well as that around him.

Although he is never again referred to by name, there is a sense in which Sam the Aerialist's presence is felt throughout Wagoner's later poetry. He represents a kind of high-technology Everyman; his failings are the failings of society at large. He makes a stubborn but useful pupil. If such a one can absorb the early wisdom of "The Nesting Ground," that sometimes standing still will gain one more than flight; if he can follow where the handbook poems lead and lose himself in the discovery that there is a bottom as well as a top to his mind, then perhaps all is not lost. Certainly, there is an aspect of Sam in the "you" to whom the handbook poems speak.

"SEVEN SONGS FOR AN OLD VOICE"

Another step beyond specific survival lore in Wagoner's progress from alienation to harmony is represented by several groups of poems based on the mythology of the Northwest Coast and the Plateau Indians. Wagoner's interest in Native American culture is longstanding. "Talking to the Forest," included in *Staying Alive*, responds to a Skagit tribesman's statement: "When we can understand animals, we will know the change is halfway. When we can talk to the forest, we will know the change has come." In *Riverbed*, "Old Man, Old Man" teaches that "Every secret is as near as your fingers."

It was in the 1974 collection *Sleeping in the Woods*, however, that the pivotal group, "Seven Songs for an Old Voice," first appeared. This Voice, still singing the ancient animistic wisdom as reverently as it did in the days before the Iron People (whites) arrived, offers hymns equally to Fire, which keeps enemies away, and to the Maker of Nightmares, who "eat[s] my sleep for . . . food." Other songs address death, the soul leaving the body and returning to it, and the First People, nonhumans who became rocks, animals, plants, and water when they learned of the coming of humankind. No matter what the subject, the tone is one of acceptance and awe. Death is part of life. Terrifying as they are, nightmares are not to be denied. The Voice promises to "drink what you bring me in my broken skull,/ The bitter water which once was sweet as morning."

WHO SHALL BE THE SUN?

These "Seven Songs for an Old Voice" are included in *Who Shall Be the Sun?* along with other previously collected poems, new groups of "Songs for the Dream-Catchers," "Songs of Only-One," "Songs of He-Catches-Nothing," and two groups of myths and legends—one each from the Plateau and Northwest Coast Indian tribes. Wagoner explains in his author's note that the myths and legends are retellings of existing stories. The songs are original works, but Wagoner stresses his debt to the Indians' spirit if not their words.

As Robert K. Cording points out, these Indian-lore poems allow Wagoner to blend several hitherto separate themes. For the Native American, the interrelationship of humans and nature has traditionally been a given, as has a belief in the power of various religious and quasi-religious rituals and practices that non-Indians might call magic. Magic, as a motif, appears fairly frequently in Wagoner's earlier work; in this collection, human beings "magically" converse with the spirits of the First People in the trees above them and the dust beneath their feet. It is not only the First People who are capable of such transformations. Animals also can take on human shapes; humans can put on different skins. In certain situations, the dead can return to earth and the living can cross in safety to the land of the dead. Magic here is more than sleight-of-hand and an Indian's dreams are tools more powerful than the technology of Sam the Aerialist, as the title poem shows. "Who Shall Be the Sun?" the People ask, and despite his apparent lack of suitability for the job, Snake's ability to dream, coupled with his seemly modesty, allows him to succeed where the assertive, egocentric Raven, Hawk, and Coyote (who can merely think) have failed.

"Who Shall Be the Sun?" and other poems in the myth and legend sections are written in a language that closely echoes the cadences of English prose translations of Indian legends with which the reader may be familiar. The song groups are distinct from one another, the tone and rhythm consistent with each singer's personality and the subject addressed. It should be noted that although the pervading attitude is one of reverence and peace, not all of these poems present such a harmonious picture. Coyote and Raven, classic tricksters, are as likely to cause harm with their pranks as they are to improve the lot of those they purport to help, as the Indian culture, like any other, has always had its share of misfits, liars, and thieves. There is disease, madness, and death, of course, as well as someone called Only-One, who, half-blinded by the beak of an injured heron he had attempted to heal, sees only halves of things. Scarred by smallpox, neither truly dead nor truly alive, Only-One is an isolated soul. He dances with Dead Man, and the half-girl he takes for his bride turns out to be the bird that blinded him.

IN BROKEN COUNTRY AND LANDFALL

Following *Who Shall Be the Sun?*, Wagoner returned to a more characteristic range of subjects. *In Broken Country* mixes poems about love, childhood memories, parents, poets (including a lovely elegy to Roethke), bums, and prisoners (Wagoner himself included). A dozen desert handbook poems are preceded by a series of self-parodying mock-handbook entries.

Landfall also covers a broad range, although a particularly strong unifying cord runs throughout. A number of the most moving poems are about making contact with one's past, not merely in the sense of looking back and remembering, but in trying for reconciliation with aspects of one's life that may have caused one pain. Over the years, Wagoner has written poems about his father—puttering around the house, building a wall—a pleasant-seeming man, drained by his job in the steel mill. A certain edgy ambivalence of tone in these poems has kept the elder Wagoner an insubstantial figure. "My Father's Garden" changes this, introducing the reader to a man who picked "flowers" for his family: "small gears and cogwheels/ With teeth like petals," found in the scrapheap he passed on his way to work, work which "melted" his mind to the point that all he retained of an education in the classics was enough Latin and Greek for crossword puzzles. Paired with this is "My Father's Ghost," an extraordinary piece based on a Midwestern folk saying and reminiscent in tone of the Indian songs. Having performed the proper rituals, the poet should be able to see his father's spirit; but the charms do not work. The room stays empty. It is necessary to "imagine him," then; "and dream him/ Returning unarmed, unharmed. Words, words. I hold/ My father's ghost in my arms in his dark doorway."

The final section, "A Sea Change," describes a journey with no destination, in which the poet and his wife leave forest, desert, and marsh behind and head out to sea. This sea voyage is more explicitly psychological than the handbook poems, but here, too, reconciliations take place. The travelers must come to terms with the unfamiliar element to which they have entrusted their lives; in doing so, they will discover that it is not so foreign as they thought. They must overcome their dread of the dimly seen monsters coiling in the depths. In doing so, they discover that the monsters never break through the "mirror" of the water's surface—suggesting, perhaps, that to accept one's demons as the Old Voice singer accepted nightmares and death is to rob them of much of their power. In contrast to Wagoner's explicitly instructive poems, the Sea Change group does not explain precisely by what means these primal fears are to be overcome or how other changes are to be brought about. At journey's end, "Landfall," the two travelers simply come "wallowing" ashore like their "hesitant helpless curious ancestors," having somehow been in touch with a past too dim for memory or rational understanding. On feet that "keep believing/ In the sea," they regain firm ground, asking, "Have we come home? Is this where we were born? . . . this place/ Where, again, we must learn to walk?"

Wagoner's own answer to this would be yes, over and over again, on all ground and in all weather, backward, on our hands, on water, and on air. Getting there means starting over; starting over means rebirth, renewal, a second chance to see things whole. In many ways, this is just what Wagoner has been doing throughout his career.

WALT WHITMAN BATHING

In *Walt Whitman Bathing*, Wagoner finds inspiration in American experience and landscape, translating it into stacked, searching clauses: "Above the river, over the broad hillside/ and down the slope in clusters and strewn throngs,/ cross-tangled and intermingled,/ wildflowers are blooming, seemingly all at once." Story and lyric take alternating turns at center stage, and his lines consistently find their breath—long and short, substantial and supple—as in "Mapmaking," from the compelling sequence on landscapes: "You fix your eyes on [landmarks], one at a time,/ And learn the hard way/ How hard it is to fabricate broken country."

The first half of the book consists of poems of nostalgic, personal reminiscence and public eulogies. He advises, in "In the Woods," that as "you" find "yourself" contemplating the trees,

> Now you may make yourself at home by doing without
> The pointless heroics of moving, by remaining
> Quiet, by holding still
> To take your place as they have taken theirs: by right
> Of discovery in this immanent domain,
> Simply by growing
> Accustomed to being here instead of nowhere.

The book's second half revisits many of Wagoner's familiar settings, themes, and stylistics: there is nature without trivial transcendence, flora and fauna, and verses heavy with pronouns, addressed to his ever-present and insistent "you." His insights run deep and are expressed with a soft-spoken directness intimately linked to his skepticism about humankind's role in the cosmos. Wagoner talks quietly with the reader—when not penned in the second-person singular, his poetry beckons the reader near—about the relativity of the self and about "Searching for more than you at the end of you."

Wagoner also presents moving poems about human affection, often set during his midwestern boyhood. "My Father Laughing in the Chicago Theater" memorably portrays "Two hundred and twenty horizontal pounds/ Of defensive lineman, of open-hearth melter" doubling over at the quips of vaudeville comics. Several poems also center on American Gothic-era memories (red-nosed cops, trained bears, boys who wear "nightgowns"), images kept from cliché by Wagoner's sure touch. Never folksy, the poems are plainspoken and display a formal virtuosity that allows Wagoner to penetrate beneath the surface, as when sketching his parents in three-stress lines: "They stand by the empty car,/ By the open driver's door,/ Waiting. The evening sun/ is glowing like pig-iron." The sum effect of the book is authoritative but detached, descriptive yet minimalistic.

TRAVELING LIGHT

Culling poems from forty-five years of published work, *Traveling Light*, a generous retrospective, calls on Wagoner's experiences of hiking and camping in mountain wilderness, comments on angst and paranoia based on his everyday urban existence, and provides a glimpse into his personal experience with literature, love, and death. His plain midwestern diction and even tone prevent him from moving into portentousness à la Carl Sandburg, whom he meets and raises stakes on in such poems as "A Day in the City" and "The Apotheosis of the Garbageman." With a nod to Robert Penn Warren, he masters the poetic sequence ("Landscapes" or "Traveling Light"), and in a series on his late father, a steel-mill worker, he colloquially recalls his own sympathetic gestures:

> I shook the dying and dead
> Ashes down through the grate
> And, with firetongs, hauled out clinkers
> Like the vertebrae of monsters.

THE HOUSE OF SONG

Poems in *The House of Song*, *Good Morning and Good Night*, and *A Map of the Night* carry forward Wagoner's extraordinary variety of poetic voices; his eye for significant concrete details; his ear for easy rhythms, deceptively prose-like but subtle in their placement of pauses and emphasis; his wit, manifested in puns, irony, and metaphor; and his themes of the integration of the self with nature, family, tradition, and the world.

In the title poem of *The House of Song*, a Gilbert Islander made a song out of his environment each year, taught his song to his community, and then sat silent "As the people became that song,/ As the whole village around him and around them/ Became the house of that song." Wagoner, like the Gilbert Island singer makes the world around him—around the reader—into poetry.

In "Arranging a Book of Poems" (from *Good Morning and Good Night*), Wagoner describes his care in ordering his poems, and in the first section of *The House of Song*, he moves from the house of song to the greater, mysterious, but enlightening world beyond song. "The Book of Moonlight" begins with a quotation from Wallace Stevens: "The Book of Moonlight is not written yet." Wagoner asks, "Why should we ever write it?" Our "illiterate fingers" cannot make sense of the mystery of its overflowing brightness.

"Elegy on the First Day of Spring" describes the flowers' struggle against the poor soil and the hard climate of Wagoner's mother's garden, paralleling her own later struggles with dementia, which erased even her recognition of her family, but let her still play and sing songs about flowers. Wagoner himself moved on to a place where flowers grow abundantly, where "The earth wants to make music," and where the sun can be ". . . as astonished as we are/ At everything we can still remember."

The last words of the last poem of *The House of Song*, written from a Native American point of view, bring the reader full circle from the collection's title poem: "We must become more than what is left of our bodies/ And will see and become what is always/ Rushing toward us and around us."

GOOD MORNING AND GOOD NIGHT

Good Morning and Good Night begins with Federico García Lorca dreaming a beautiful poem and awakening to hear it actually sung—as he discovers—by an illiterate street sweeper. Possessing the gift of literacy, García Lorca returns to his bed "To lie there stark awake as sleeplessly/ As a poet who'd been told he was immortal." The collection ends with a series of poems on the night and the morning, some of them ironic. The final poem, "At the Foot of the Mountain," set in the early morning, seems to have nothing to do with the night—actual or metaphoric—until the unexpected last word: at the end of the poem "you"—one of Wagoner's common subjects, here a reluctant climber—finally join other climbers in "their uninterrupted *chanting*" [emphasis added]. Perhaps, then, this too is not only a good morning but a good night poem and the climb a metaphor for mortality, seen as challenge, duty, and ritual.

This collection also contains several handbook poems, a set of which are military instructions, and a section of poems about poetry. In "Trying to Make Music," the poet confronts not only unsympathetic listeners but also his own self-doubts. In "Poetry in Motion," he questions whether poetry can ". . . move itself and more/ Than itself and not be here, flat on the page." In "A Date with the Muse," the poet finds the muse repeatedly unresponsive to his offers. However, in the metaphorical "On Being Asked to Discuss Poetic Theory," the poet describes finding snow falling in the mountains and following the snowmelt as it courses down to the ocean. Even if the white tops of the mountains disappear behind clouds, he knows that snow is falling again. Clouded in mystery, the sources of the poet's inspiration do not fail.

A MAP OF THE NIGHT

Many of the poems in *A Map of the Night* are companion pieces to poems previously published. For instance, "My Father's Dance" is a counterpart to "Elegy to the First Day of Spring" in *The House of Song*, "Thoreau and the Mud Turtle" and "Thoreau and the Quagmire" add to the set of Thoreau poems also in *The House of Song*, and several military "Handbook" poems extend those in *Good Morning and Good Night*.

Wagoner's wit is displayed in several poems: In "Trying to Write a Poem While the Couple in the Apartment Overhead Make Love," the rhythms of Wagoner's poem neatly match the rhythms of the subject. In "Attention" (a military "Handbook" poem), the typography of the short two-stress lines makes the poem stand at attention on the page. Wagoner's focus on decorum in this, as in all of his "Handbook" poems, tends to put readers in their places. In "On First Looking Through the Wrong End of the Telescope," a series of puns puts all humankind in its place.

This collection also includes "On a Glass of Ale Under a Reading Lamp," in which small flies, like the drinker, risk ". . . a desire/ . . . to drink without drowning// to touch the good bitterness/ again, not knowing why." Another memorable poem is "On an Island," the protagonist of which, once again "you," is on a beach, with the sea on one side and a "dense interior" on the other. Here "you" must ". . . reconsider the unromantic agony/ of change without progress . . . ," finding ". . . yourself/ beginning where you were and seeing/ what you tried your best to remember/ or dismiss and forget."

Wagoner's poetry is readily accessible, not overly formal, expressive, even emphatic, sometimes witty, sometimes metaphorical, and solidly based in concrete images. Wagoner continues to advance his worldview of humankind in harmony with the familial, social, and, above all, natural orders.

OTHER MAJOR WORKS

LONG FICTION: *The Man in the Middle*, 1954, 1955; *Money, Money, Money*, 1955; *Rock*, 1958; *The Escape Artist*, 1965; *Baby, Come On Inside*, 1968; *Where Is My Wandering Boy Tonight?*, 1970; *The Road to Many a Wonder*, 1974; *Tracker*, 1975; *Whole Hog*, 1976; *The Hanging Garden*, 1980.

PLAY: *An Eye for an Eye for an Eye*, pr. 1973.

EDITED TEXTS: *Straw for the Fire: From the Notebooks of Theodore Roethke, 1943-1963*, 1972; *The Best American Poetry 2009*, 2009 (with David Lehman).

BIBLIOGRAPHY

Boyers, Robert. "The Poetry of David Wagoner." Review of *Staying Alive*. *Kenyon Review* 32 (Spring, 1970): 176-181. An appreciative review noting that *Staying Alive* marks a turning point in Wagoner's development. Boyers states that from this point forward, Wagoner could claim to be a major figure in contemporary American poetry.

Durczak, Joanna. "David Wagoner: Instructor Against Instructors." *Treading Softly,*

Speaking Low: Contemporary American Poetry in the Didactic Mode. Lublin, Poland: Wydawnictwo Uniwersytetu, 1994. Uniquely useful as an extended analysis of Wagoner's "Handbook" poems.

Lieberman, Laurence. "David Wagoner: The Cold Speech of the Earth." In *Unassigned Frequencies: American Poetry in Review, 1964-1977*. Urbana: University of Illinois Press, 1977. Looks at how this poet maps out a topography through his choice of words and images. Compares the later poems with the earlier ones and cites the same imagination but with greater depth of vision. Offers strong, in-depth criticism of *Collected Poems, 1956-1976* and places Wagoner in the company of Walt Whitman, Robert Frost, Edgar Lee Masters, and William Stafford.

McFarland, Ronald E. *The World of David Wagoner*. Moscow: University of Idaho Press, 1997. Presents literary criticism and interpretation of Wagoner's writings and looks at the role of the American Midwest and Northwest in literature.

Peters, Robert. "Thirteen Ways of Looking at David Wagoner's New Poems." Review of *Landfall. Western Humanities Review* 35, no. 3 (Autumn, 1981): 267-272. A provocative review, unusual among commentaries on Wagoner's poetry in its stress on what Peters takes to be Wagoner's lack of imagination and risk-taking.

Waggoner, Hyatt H. *American Visionary Poetry*. Baton Rouge: Louisiana State University Press, 1982. Chapter 7, "Traveling Light," explores Wagoner's identity as a visionary poet through his nature poems. Examines Wagoner's portrayal of the wilderness and how he guards himself in his poems. A sympathetic critique that praises Wagoner's volume *The Nesting Ground*.

Wagoner, David. "David Wagoner." Interview by Nicholas O'Connell. In *At the Field's End: Interviews with Twenty Pacific Northwest Writers*, edited by O'Connell. Seattle: Madrona, 1987. The interviewer explores with Wagoner the subjects of his poems and how he has re-created the Northwest landscape on paper. Examines the structure and sense of rhythm in his poems. Of particular note is a discussion of *Who Shall Be the Sun?*, a collection of poems that Wagoner read aloud to the Blackfeet tribe.

_____. "David Wagoner." Interview by Sanford Pinsker. In *Three Pacific Northwest Poets: William Stafford, Richard Hugo, and David Wagoner*. Boston: Twayne, 1987. A useful and insightful introduction to Wagoner's poems, analyzing his choice of themes and techniques. Contains critical commentary on all of his major poems. Notes that among Wagoner's strengths is his "sense of the dramatic."

_____. "David Wagoner—Slightly Different Ways of Thinking: An Interview." Interview by Kate Gray. In *Page to Page: Retrospectives of Writers from the "Seattle Review,"* edited by Colleen J. McElroy. Seattle: University of Washington Press, 2006. An account of a wide-ranging interview, accompanied by photographs, a bibliography, and three poems by Wagoner.

Sara McAulay; Sarah Hilbert
Updated by David W. Cole

WALT WHITMAN

Born: West Hills, New York; May 31, 1819
Died: Camden, New Jersey; March 26, 1892

PRINCIPAL POETRY
"Song of Myself," 1855
Leaves of Grass, 1855, 1856, 1860, 1867, 1871, 1876, 1881-1882, 1889, 1891-1892
Drum-Taps, 1865
Sequel to Drum-Taps, 1865-1866
After All, Not to Create Only, 1871
Passage to India, 1871
As a Strong Bird on Pinions Free, 1872
Two Rivulets, 1876
November Boughs, 1888
Good-bye My Fancy, 1891
Complete Poetry and Selected Prose, 1959 (James E. Miller, editor)

OTHER LITERARY FORMS

Walt Whitman published several important essays and studies during his lifetime. *Democratic Vistas* (1871), *Memoranda During the War* (1875-1876), *Specimen Days and Collect* (1882-1883, autobiographical sketches), and the *Complete Prose Works* (1892) are the most significant. He also tried his hand at short fiction, collected in *The Half-Breed, and Other Stories* (1927), and a novel, *Franklin Evans* (1842). Many of his letters and journals have appeared either in early editions or as parts of the New York University Press edition of *The Collected Writings of Walt Whitman* (1961-1984; 22 volumes).

ACHIEVEMENTS

Walt Whitman's stature rests largely on two major contributions to the literature of the United States. First, although detractors are numerous and the poet's organizing principle is sometimes blurred, *Leaves of Grass* stands as the most fully realized American epic poem. Written in the midst of natural grandeur and burgeoning materialism, Whitman's book traces the geographical, social, and spiritual contours of an expanding nation. It embraces the science and commercialism of industrial America while trying to direct these practical energies toward the "higher mind" of literature, culture, and the soul. In his preface to the first edition of *Leaves of Grass*, Whitman referred to the United States itself as "essentially the greatest poem." He saw the self-esteem, sympathy, candor, and deathless attachment to freedom of the common people as "unrhymed

Walt Whitman
(Library of Congress)

poetry," which awaited the "gigantic and generous treatment worthy of it." *Leaves of Grass* was to be that treatment.

The poet's second achievement was in language and poetic technique. Readers take for granted the modern American poet's emphasis on free verse and ordinary diction, forgetting Whitman's revolutionary impact. His free-verse form departed from stanzaic patterns and regular lines, taking its power instead from individual, rolling, oratorical lines of cadenced speech. He subordinated traditional poetic techniques, such as alliteration, repetition, inversion, and conventional meter, to this expansive form. He also violated popular rules of poetic diction by extracting a rich vocabulary from foreign languages, science, opera, various trades, and the ordinary language of town and country. Finally, Whitman broke taboos with his extensive use of sexual imagery, incorporated not to titillate or shock, but to portray life in its wholeness. He determined to be the poet of procreation, to celebrate the elemental and primal life force that permeates humans and nature. Thus, "forbidden voices" are unveiled, clarified, and transfigured by the poet's vision of their place in an organic universe.

Whitman himself said he wrote but "one or two indicative words for the future." He expected the "main things" from poets, orators, singers, and musicians to come. They would prove and define a national culture, thus justifying his faith in American democracy. These apologetic words, along with the early tendency to read Whitman as "untranslatable," or barbaric and undisciplined, long delayed his acceptance as one of America's greatest poets. In fact, if judged by the poet's own test of greatness, he is a failure, for he said the "proof of a poet is that his country absorbs him as affectionately as he has absorbed it." Whitman has not been absorbed by the common people to whom he paid tribute in his poetry. However, with recognition from both the academic community and such poets as Hart Crane, William Carlos Williams, Karl Shapiro, and Randall Jarrell, his *Leaves of Grass* has taken its place among the great masterworks of American literature.

BIOGRAPHY

Walter Whitman, Jr., was born in West Hills, Long Island on May 31, 1819. His mother, Louisa Van Velsor, was descended from a long line of New York Dutch farmers, and his father, Walter Whitman, was a Long Island farmer and carpenter. In 1823, the father moved his family to Brooklyn in search of work. One of nine children in an undistinguished family, Whitman received only a meager formal education between 1825 and 1830, when he turned to the printing trade for the next five years. At the age of seventeen, he began teaching at various Long Island schools and continued to teach until he went to New York City to be a printer for the *New World* and a reporter for the *Democratic Review* in 1841. From then on, Whitman generally made a living at journalism. Besides reporting and freelance writing, he edited several Brooklyn newspapers, including the *Daily Eagle* (1846-1848), the *Freeman* (1848-1849), and the *Times* (1857-1859). Some of Whitman's experiences during this period influenced the poetry that seemed to burst into print in 1855. While in New York, Whitman frequented the opera and the public library, both of which furnished him with a sense of heritage and of connection with the bards and singers of the past. In 1848, Whitman met and was hired by a representative of the New Orleans *Crescent*. Although the job lasted only a few months, the journey by train, stagecoach, and steamboat through what Whitman always referred to as "inland America" certainly helped to stimulate his vision of the country's democratic future. Perhaps most obviously influential was Whitman's trade itself. His flair for action and vignette, as well as descriptive detail, surely was sharpened by his journalistic writing. The reporter's keen eye for the daily scene is everywhere evident in *Leaves of Grass*.

When the first edition of his poems appeared, Whitman received little money but some attention from reviewers. Included among the responses was a famous letter from Ralph Waldo Emerson, who praised Whitman for his brave thought and greeted him at the beginning of a great career. Whitman continued to write and edit, but was unemployed during the winter of 1859-1860, when he began to frequent Pfaff's bohemian restaurant. There he may have established the "manly love" relationships that inspired the "Calamus" poems of the 1860 edition of *Leaves of Grass*. Again, this third edition created a stir with readers, but the outbreak of the Civil War soon turned everyone's attention to more pressing matters. Whitman himself was too old for military service, but he did experience the war by caring for wounded soldiers in Washington, D.C., hospitals. While in Washington as a government clerk, Whitman witnessed Abraham Lincoln's second inauguration, mourned over the president's assassination in April, printed *Drum-Taps* in May, and later added to these Civil War lyrics a sequel, which contained "When Lilacs Last in the Dooryard Bloom'd."

The postwar years saw Whitman's reputation steadily increasing in England, thanks to William Rossetti's *Selections* in 1868, Algernon Swinburne's praise, and a long, admiring review of his work by Anne Gilchrist in 1870. In fact, Gilchrist fell in love with the poet after reading *Leaves of Grass* and even moved to Philadelphia in 1876 to be near him, but her hopes of marrying Whitman died with her in 1885. Because of books by William D. O'Connor and John Burroughs, Whitman also became better known in the United States, but any satisfaction he may have derived from this recognition was tempered by two severe blows in 1873. He suffered a paralytic stroke in January, and his mother, to whom he was very devoted, died in May. Unable to work, Whitman returned to stay with his brother George at Camden, New Jersey, spending summers on a farm at Timber Creek.

Although Whitman recuperated sufficiently to take trips to New York or Boston, and even to Colorado and Canada in 1879-1880, he was never again to be the robust man he had so proudly described in early editions of *Leaves of Grass*. His declining years, however, gave him time to revise and establish the structure of his book. When the seventh edition of *Leaves of Grass* was published in Philadelphia in 1881-1882, Whitman had achieved a total vision of his work. With the money from a centennial edition (1876) and an occasional lecture on Lincoln, Whitman was able by 1884 to purchase a small house on Mickle Street in Camden. Although he was determined not to be "house-bound," a sunstroke in 1885 and a second paralytic stroke in 1888 made him increasingly dependent on friends. He found especially gratifying the friendship of his secretary and companion, Horace Traubel, who recorded the poet's life and opinions during these last years. Despite the care of Traubel and several doctors and nurses, Whitman died of complications from a stroke on March 26, 1892.

ANALYSIS

An approach to Walt Whitman's poetry profitably begins with the "Inscriptions" to *Leaves of Grass*, for these short, individual pieces introduce the main ideas and methods of Whitman's book. In general, they stake out the ground of what Miller has called the prototypical New World personality, a merging of the individual with the national and cosmic, or universal, selves. That democratic principles are at the root of Whitman's views becomes immediately clear in "One's-Self I Sing," the first poem in *Leaves of Grass*. Here, Whitman refers to the self as a "simple separate person," yet utters the "word Democratic, the word En-Masse." Citizens of America alternately assert their individuality—obey little, resist often—and yet see themselves as a brotherhood of the future, inextricably bound by the vision of a great new society of and for the masses. This encompassing vision requires a sense of "the Form complete," rejecting neither body nor soul, singing equally of the Female and Male, embracing both realistic, scientific, modern humanity and the infinite, eternal life of the spirit.

LEAVES OF GRASS

Whitman takes on various roles to lead his readers to a fuller understanding of this democratic universal. In "Me Imperturbe," he is at ease as an element of nature, able to confront the accidents and rebuffs of life with the implacability of trees and animals. As he suggests in *Democratic Vistas*, the true idea of nature in all its power and glory must become fully restored and must furnish the "pervading atmosphere" to poems of American democracy. Whitman must also empathize with rational things—with humanity at large and in particular—so he constructs what sometimes seem to be endless catalogs of Americans at work and play. This technique appears in "I Hear America Singing," which essentially lists the varied carols of carpenter, boatman, shoemaker, woodcutter, mother, and so on, all "singing what belongs to him or her and to none else" as they ply their trades. In longer poems, such as "Starting from Paumanok," Whitman extends his catalog to all the states of the Union. He intends to acknowledge contemporary lands, salute employments and cities large and small, and report heroism on land and sea from an American point of view. He marks down all of what constitutes unified life, including the body, sexual love, and comradeship, or "manly love." Finally, the poet must join the greatness of love and democracy to the greatness of religion. These programs expand to take up large parts of even longer poems, such as "Song of Myself" or to claim space of their own in sections of *Leaves of Grass*.

Whitman uses another technique to underscore the democratic principle of his art: He makes the reader a fellow poet, a "camerado" who joins hands with him to traverse the poetic landscape. In "To You," he sees the poet and reader as passing strangers who desire to speak to one another and urges that they do so. In "Song of the Open Road," Whitman travels the highways with his "delicious burdens" of men and women, calling them all to come forth and move forever forward, well armed to take their places in "the procession of souls along the grand roads of the universe." His view of the reader as fellow traveler and seer is especially clear in the closing lines of the poem:

> Camerado, I give you my hand!
> I give you my love more precious than money,
> I give you myself before preaching or law;

> Will you give me yourself? will you come travel
>   with me?
> Shall we stick by each other as long as we live?

Finally, this comradeship means willingness to set out on one's own, for Whitman says in "Song of Myself" that the reader most honors his style "who learns under it to destroy the teacher." The questions one asks are one's own to puzzle out. The poet's role is to lead his reader up on a knoll, wash the gum from his eyes, and then let him become habituated to the "dazzle of light" that is the natural world. In other words, Whitman intends to help his reader become a "poet" of insight and perception and then release him to travel the public roads of a democratic nation.

This democratic unification of multiplicity, empathic identification, and comradeship exists in most of Whitman's poems. They do not depend on his growth as poet or thinker. However, in preparing to analyze representative poems from *Leaves of Grass*, it is helpful to establish a general plan for the various sections of the book. Whitman revised and reordered his poems until the 1881 edition, which established a form that was to remain essentially unchanged through succeeding editions. He merely annexed materials to the 1881 order until just before his death in 1892, then authorized the 1891-1892 version for all future printings. Works originally published apart from *Leaves of Grass*, such as *Drum-Taps* or *Passage to India*, were eventually incorporated in the parent volume. Thus, an analysis of the best poems in five important sections of this final *Leaves of Grass* will help delineate Whitman's movement toward integration of self and nation, within his prescribed portals of birth and death.

"SONG OF MYSELF"

"Song of Myself," Whitman's great lyric poem, exemplifies his democratic "programs" without diminishing the intense feeling that so startled his first readers. It successfully combines paeans to the individual, the nation, and life at large, including nature, sexuality, and death. Above all, "Song of Myself" is a poem of incessant motion, as though Whitman's energy is spontaneously bursting into lines. Even in the contemplative sections of the poem, when Whitman leans and loafs at his ease observing a spear of summer grass, his senses of hearing, taste, and sight are working at fever pitch. In the opening section, he calls himself "nature without check with original energy." Having once begun to speak, he hopes "to cease not till death." Whitman says that although others may talk of the beginning and the end, he finds his subject in the now—in the "urge and urge and urge" of the procreant world.

One method by which Whitman's energy escapes boundaries is the poet's ability to "become" other people and things. He will not be measured by time and space, nor by physical form. Rather, he effuses his flesh in eddies and drifts it in lacy jags, taking on new identities with every line. His opening lines show that he is speaking not of himself alone but of all selves. What he assumes, the reader shall assume; every atom of him, and therefore of the world, belongs to the reader as well. In section 24, he represents himself as a "Kosmos," which contains multitudes and reconciles apparent opposites. He speaks the password and sign of democracy and accepts nothing that all cannot share. To stress this egalitarian vision, Whitman employs the catalog with skill and variety. Many parts of "Song of Myself" list or name characters, places, occupations, or experiences, but section 33 most clearly shows the two major techniques that give these lists vitality. First, Whitman composes long single-sentence movements of action and description, which attempt to unify nature and civilization. The poet is alternately weeding his onion patch, hoeing, prospecting, hauling his boat down a shallow river, scaling mountains, walking paths, and speeding through space. He then follows each set of actions with a series of place lines, beginning with "where," "over," "at," or "upon," which unite farmhouses, hearth furnaces, hot-air balloons, or steamships with plants and animals of land and sea. Second, Whitman interrupts these long listings with more detailed vignettes, which show the "large hearts of heroes"—a sea captain, a hounded slave, a fireman trapped and broken under debris, an artillerist. Sections 34-36 then extend the narrative to tales of the Alamo and an old-time sea fight, vividly brought forth with sounds and dialogue. In each case, the poet becomes the hero and is actually in the scene to suffer or succeed.

This unchecked energy and empathy carry over into Whitman's ebullient imagery to help capture the physical power of human bodies in procreant motion. At one point Whitman calls himself "hankering, gross, mystical, nude." He finds no sweeter flesh than that which sticks to his own bones, or to the bones of others. Sexual imagery, including vividly suggestive descriptions of the male and female body, is central to the poem. Although the soul must take its equal place with the body, neither abasing itself before the other, Whitman's mystical union of soul and body is a sexual experience as well. He loves the hum of the soul's "valved voice" and remembers how, on a transparent summer morning, the soul settled its head athwart his hips and turned over on him. It parted the shirt from the poet's "bosom-bone," plunged its tongue to his "bare-stript heart," and reached until it felt his beard and held his feet. From this experience came peace and the knowledge that love is fundamental to a unified, continuous creation. Poetic metaphor, which identifies and binds hidden likenesses in nature, is therefore emblematic of the organic world. For example, in answering a child's question, "What is the grass?" the poet offers a series of metaphors that join human, natural, and spiritual impulses:

> I guess it must be the flag of my disposition, out of
>   hopeful green stuff woven.
> Or I guess it is the handkerchief of the Lord,
> A scented gift and remembrancer designedly dropt,
> Bearing the owner's name someway in the corners,
>   that we may see and remark, and say *Whose*?

The grass becomes hair from the breasts of young men, from the heads and beards of old people, or from offspring, and it "speaks" from under the faint red roofs of mouths. The smallest sprout shows that there is no death, for "nothing collapses," and to die is "luckier" than anyone had supposed. This excerpt from the well-known sixth section of "Song of Myself" illustrates how image making signifies for Whitman a kind of triumph over death itself.

Because of its position near the beginning of *Leaves of Grass* and its encompassing of Whitman's major themes, "Song of Myself" is a foundation for the volume. The "self" in this poem is a replica of the nation as self, and its delineation in the cosmos is akin to the growth of the United States in the world. Without putting undue stress on this nationalistic interpretation, however, the reader can find many reasons to admire "Song of Myself." Its dynamic form, beauty of language, and psychological insights are sufficient to make Whitman a first-rate poet, even if he had written nothing else.

CELEBRATION OF SELF AND SEXUALITY

The passionate celebration of the self and of sexuality is Whitman's great revolutionary theme. In "Children of Adam," he is the procreative father of multitudes, a champion of heterosexual love and the "body electric." In "From Pent-Up Aching Rivers," he sings of the need for superb children, brought forth by the "muscular urge" of "stalwart loins." In "I Sing the Body Electric," he celebrates the perfection of well-made male and female bodies. Sections 5 and 9 are explicit descriptions of sexual intercourse and physical "apparatus," respectively. Whitman does not shy away from the fierce attraction of the female form or the ebb and flow of "limitless limpid jets of love hot and enormous" that undulate into the willing and yielding "gates of the body." Because he sees the body as sacred, as imbued with divine power, he considers these enumerations to be poems of the soul as much as of the body.

Indeed, "A Woman Waits for Me" specifically states that sex contains all—bodies and souls. Thus, the poet seeks warm-blooded and sufficient women to receive the pent-up rivers of himself, to start new sons and daughters fit for the great nation that will be these United States. The procreative urge operates on more than one level in "Children of Adam"—it is physical sex and birthing, the union of body and soul, and the metaphorical insemination of the poet's words and spirit into national life. In several ways, then, words are to become flesh. Try as some early Whitman apologists might to explain them away, raw sexual impulses are the driving force of these poems.

"CALAMUS" POEMS

Whitman's contemporaries were shocked by the explicit sexual content of "Children of Adam," but modern readers and critics have been much more intrigued by the apparent homoeroticism of the poems in the "Calamus" section of the 1860 edition of *Leaves of Grass*. Although it is ultimately impossible to say whether these poems reflect Whitman's gay associations in New York, it is obvious that comradeship extends here to both spiritual and physical contact between men. "In Paths Untrodden" states the poet's intention to sing of "manly attachment" or types of "athletic love," to celebrate the need of comrades. "Whoever You Are Holding Me Now in Hand" deepens the physical nature of this love, including the stealthy meeting of male friends in a wood, behind some rock in the open air, or on the beach of some quiet island. There the poet would permit the comrade's long-dwelling kiss on the lips and a touch that would carry him eternally forth over land and sea. "These I Singing in Spring" refers to "him that tenderly loves me" and pledges the hardiest spears of grass, the calamus-root, to those who love as the poet himself is capable of loving.

Finally, two of Whitman's best lyrics concern this robust but clandestine relationship. "I Saw in Louisiana a Live-Oak Growing" is a poignant contrast between the live oak's ability to "utter joyous leaves" while it stands in solitude, without companions, and the poet's inability to live without a friend or lover near. There is no mistaking the equally personal tone of "When I Heard at the Close of the Day," probably Whitman's finest "Calamus" poem. The plaudits of others are meaningless and unsatisfying, says Whitman, until he thinks of how his dear friend and lover is on his way to see him. When his friend arrives one evening, the hissing rustle of rolling waves becomes congratulatory and joyful. Once the person he loves most lies sleeping by him under the same cover, face inclined toward him in the autumn moonbeams and arm lightly lying around his breast, he is happy.

Other short poems in "Calamus," such as "For You O Democracy," "The Prairie Grass Dividing," or "A Promise to California," are less obviously personal. Rather, they extend passionate friendship between men to the larger ideal of democratic brotherhood. Just as procreative love has its metaphorical implications for the nation, so too does Whitman promise to make the continent indissoluble and cities inseparable, arms about each other's necks, with companionship and the "manly love of comrades." Still other poems move this comradeship into wider spans of space and time. "The Moment Yearning and Thoughtful" joins the poet with men of Europe and Asia in happy brotherhood, thus transcending national and continental boundaries. "The Base of All Metaphysics" extends this principle through historical time, for the Greek, Germanic, and Christian systems all suggest that the attraction of friend to friend is the basis of civilization. The last poem in the "Calamus" section, "Full of Life Now," completes Whitman's panoramic view by carrying friendship into the future. His words communicate the compact, visible to readers of a century or any number of centuries hence. Each seeking the other past time's invisible boundaries, poet and reader are united physically through Whitman's poetry.

"CROSSING BROOKLYN FERRY"

"Crossing Brooklyn Ferry" is the natural product of Whitman's idea that love and companionship will bind the world's peoples to one another. In a sense it gives the poet immortality through creation of a living artifact: the poem itself. Whitman stands motionless on a moving ferry, immersed in the stream of life and yet suspended in time through the existence of his words on the page. Consequently, he can say that neither time nor place nor distance matters, because he is with each reader and each fellow traveler in the future. He points out that hundreds of years hence others will enter the gates of the ferry and cross from shore to shore, will see the sun half an hour high and watch the seagulls floating in circles with motionless wings. Others will also watch the endless scallop-edged waves cresting and falling, as though they are experiencing the same moment as the poet, with the same mixture of joy and sorrow. Thus, Whitman confidently calls upon the "dumb ministers" of nature to keep up their ceaseless motion—to flow, fly, and frolic on—because they furnish their parts toward eternity and toward the soul.

Techniques match perfectly with these themes in "Crossing Brooklyn Ferry." Whitman's frequent repetition of the main images—sunrise and sunset, ebb and flow of the sea and river, seagulls oscillating in the sky—reinforces the belief in timeless, recurring human experience. Descriptions of schooners and steamers at work along the shore are among his most powerful evocations of color and sound. Finally, Whitman's employment of pronouns to mark a shift in the sharing of experiences also shows the poem's careful design. Whitman begins the poem with an "I" who looks at the scenes or crowds of people and calls to "you" who are among the crowds and readers of present and future. In section 8, however, he reaches across generations to fuse himself and pour his meaning into the "you." At the end of this section, he and others have become "we," who understand and receive experience with free senses and love, united in the organic continuity of nature.

"SEA-DRIFT" POEMS

The short section of *Leaves of Grass* entitled "Sea-Drift" contains the first real signs of a more somber Whitman, who must come to terms with hardship, sorrow, and death. In one way, this resignation and accommodation follow the natural progression of the self from active, perhaps callow, youth to contemplative old age. They are also an outgrowth of Whitman's belief that life and death are a continuum, that life is a symphony of both sonatas and dirges, which the true poet of nature must capture fully on the page. Whereas in other poems the ocean often signifies birth and creation, with fish-shaped Paumanok (Manhattan) rising from the sea, in "Tears," it is the repository of sorrow. Its white shore lies in solitude, dark and desolate, holding a ghost or "shapeless lump" that cries streaming, sobbing tears. In "As I Ebb'd with the Ocean of Life," Whitman is distressed with himself for daring to "blab" so much without having the least idea who or what he really is. Nature darts on the poet and stings him, because he has not understood anything and because no man ever can. He calls himself but a "trail of drift and debris," who has left his poems like "little wrecks" on Paumanok's shores. However, he must continue to throw himself on the ocean of life, clinging to the breast of the land that is his father, and gathering from the moaning sea the "sobbing dirge of Nature." He believes the flow will return, but meanwhile he must wait and lie in drifts at his readers' feet.

"OUT OF THE CRADLE ENDLESSLY ROCKING"

"Out of the Cradle Endlessly Rocking" is a fuller, finally more optimistic, treatment of the poet's confrontation with loss. Commonly acknowledged as one of Whitman's finest works, this poem uses lyrical language and operatic structure to trace the origin of his poetic powers in the experience of death. Two "songs" unite with the whispering cry of the sea to communicate this experience to him. Central to the poem is Whitman's seaside reminiscence of a bird and his mate, who build and tend a nest of eggs. When the female fails to return one evening, never to appear again, the male becomes a solitary singer of his sorrows, whose notes are "translated" by the listening boy-poet. The bird's song is an aria of lonesome love, an outpouring carol of yearning, hope, and finally, death. As the boy absorbs the bird's song, his soul awakens in sympathy. From this moment forward, his destiny will be to perpetuate the bird's "cries of unsatisfied love." More important, though, Whitman must learn the truth that this phrase masks, must conquer "the word" that has caused the bird's cries:

> Whereto answering, the sea,
> Delaying not, hurrying not,
> Whisper'd me through the night, and very plainly
>   before daybreak,
> Lisp'd to me the low and delicious word death,
> And again death, death, death, death.

Whitman then fuses the bird's song and his own with death, which the sea, "like some old crone rocking the cradle," has whispered to him. This final image of the sea as an old crone soothing an infant underscores the central point of "Out of the Cradle Endlessly Rocking": Old age and death are part of a natural flux. Against the threat of darkness, one must live and sing.

DRUM-TAPS

Like the tone of the "Sea-Drift" section, darker hues permeate Whitman's Civil War lyrics. His experiences as a hospital worker in Washington, D.C., are clearly behind the sometimes wrenching imagery of *Drum-Taps*. As a wound dresser, he saw the destruction of healthy young bodies and minds at first hand. These spectacles were in part a test of Whitman's own courage and comradeship, but they were also a test of the nation's ability to survive and grow. As Whitman says in "Long, Too Long America," the country had long traveled roads "all even and peaceful," learning only from joys and prosperity, but now it must face "crises of anguish" without recoiling and show the world what its "children enmasse really are." Many of the *Drum-Taps* lyrics show Whitman facing this reality, but "The Wound Dresser" is representative. The poet's persona is an old man who is called on years after the Civil War to "paint the mightiest armies of earth," to tell what experience of the war stays with him latest and deepest. Although he mentions the long marches, rushing charges, and toils of battle, he does not dwell on soldiers' perils or soldiers' joys. Rather, he vividly describes the wounded and dying at battlegrounds, hospital tents, or roofed hospitals, as he goes with "hinged knees and steady hand to dress wounds." He does not recoil or give out at the sight of crushed heads, shattered throats, amputated stumps of hands and arms, the gnawing and putrid gangrenous foot or shoulder. Nevertheless, within him rests a burning flame, the memory of youths suffering or dead.

Confronted with these horrors, Whitman had to find a way to surmount them, and that way was love. If there could be a positive quality in war, Whitman found it in the comradeship of common soldiers, who risked all for their fellows. In "As Toilsome I Wander'd Virginia's Woods," for example, Whitman discovers the grave of a soldier buried beneath a tree. Hastily dug on a retreat from battle, the grave is nevertheless marked by a sign: "Bold, cautious, true, and my loving comrade." That inscription remains with the poet through many changeful seasons and scenes to follow, as evidence of this brotherly love. Similarly, "Vigil Strange I Kept on the Field One Night" tells of a soldier who sees his comrade struck down in battle and returns to find him cold with death. He watches by him through "immortal and mystic hours" until, just as dawn is breaking, he folds the young man in a blanket and buries him in a rude-dug grave where he fell. This tale of tearless mourning perfectly evokes the loss caused by war.

Eventually, Whitman finds some ritual significance in these deaths, as though they are atonement for those yet living. In "A Sight in Camp in the Daybreak Gray and Dim," he marks three covered forms on stretchers near a hospital tent. One by one he uncovers their faces. The first is an elderly man, gaunt and grim, but a comrade nevertheless. The second is a sweet boy "with cheeks yet blooming." When he exposes the third face, however, he finds it calm, of yellow-white ivory, and of indeterminable age. He sees in it the face of Christ himself, "dead and divine and brother of all." "Over the Carnage Rose Prophetic a Voice" suggests that these Christian sacrifices will finally lead to a united Columbia. Even though a thousand may have to "sternly immolate themselves for one," those who love one another shall become invincible, and "affection shall solve the problems of freedom." As in other sections of *Leaves of Grass*, Whitman believes the United States will be held together not by lawyers, paper agreements, or force of arms, but by the cohesive power of love and fellowship.

"WHEN LILACS LAST IN THE DOORYARD BLOOM'D"

"When Lilacs Last in the Dooryard Bloom'd," another of Whitman's acknowledged masterpieces, repeats the process underlying *Drum-Taps*. The poet must come to terms with the loss of one he loves—in this case, the slain President Lincoln. Death and mourning must eventually give way to consolation and hope for the future. Cast in the form of a traditional elegy, the poem traces the processional of Lincoln's coffin across country, past the poet himself, to the president's final resting place.

To objectify his emotional struggle between grief, on one hand, and spiritual reconciliation with death on the other, Whitman employs several vivid symbols. The lilac blooming perennially, with its heart-shaped leaves, represents the poet's perpetual mourning and love. The "powerful fallen star," which now lies in a "harsh surrounding could" of black night, is Lincoln, fallen and shrouded in his coffin. The solitary hermit thrush that warbles "death's outlet song of life" from a secluded swamp is the soul or spiritual world. Initially, Whitman is held powerless by the death of his departing comrade. Although he can hear the bashful notes of the thrush and will come to understand them, he thinks only of showering the coffin with sprigs of lilac to commemorate his love for Lincoln. He must also warble his own song before he can absorb the bird's message of consolation. Eventually, as he sits amidst the teeming daily activities described in section 14, he is struck by the "sacred knowledge of death," and the bird's carol thus becomes intelligible to him. Death is lovely, soothing, and delicate. It is a "strong deliveress" who comes to nestle the grateful body in her flood of bliss. Rapt with the charm of the bird's song, Whitman sees myriad battle corpses in a vision—the debris of all the slain soldiers of the war—yet realizes that they are fully at rest and no longer suffering. The power of this realization gives him strength to let go of the hand of his comrade. An ever-blooming lilac now signifies renewal, just as death takes its rightful place as the harbinger of new life, the life of the eternal soul.

MATTERS OF SPIRIT

Whitman's deepening concern with matters of the spirit permeates the last sections of *Leaves of Grass*. Having passed the test of the Civil War and having done his part to reunite the United States, Whitman turned his attention to America's place in the world and his own place in God's design. As he points out in "A Clear Midnight," he gives his last poems to the soul and its "free flight into the wordless," to ponder the themes he loves best: "Night, sleep, death and the stars." Such poems as "Chanting the Square Deific" and "A Noiseless Patient Spider" invoke either the general soul, the "Santa Spirita" that pervades all created life, or the toils of individual souls, flinging out gossamer threads to connect themselves with this holy spirit.

"PASSAGE TO INDIA"

Whitman was still able to produce fine lyrics in his old age. One of these successful poems, "Passage to India," announces Whitman's intention to join modern science to fables and dreams of old, to weld past and future, and to show that the United States is but a "bridge" in the "vast rondure" of the world. Just as the Suez Canal connected Europe and Asia, Whitman says, America's transcontinental railroad ties the eastern to the western sea, thus verifying Christopher Columbus's dream. Beyond these material thoughts of exploration, however, lies the poet's realm of love and spirit. The poet is a "true son of God," who will soothe the hearts of restlessly exploring, never-happy humanity. He will link all human affections, justify the "cold, impassive, voiceless earth," and absolutely fuse nature and humanity. This fusion takes place not in the material world but in the swelling of the soul toward God, who is a mighty "centre of the true, the good, the loving." Passage to these superior universes transcends time and space and death. It is a "passage to more than India," through the deep waters that no mariner has traveled, and for which the poet must "risk the ship, ourselves and all."

"PRAYER OF COLUMBUS"

Whitman also uses a seagoing metaphor for spiritual passage in "Prayer of Columbus," which is almost a continuation of "Passage to India." In the latter, Whitman aggressively flings himself into the active voyage toward God, but in "Prayer of Columbus" he is a "batter'd, wreck'd old man," willing to yield his ships to God and wait for the unknown end of all. He recounts his heroic deeds of exploration and attributes their inspiration to a message from the heavens that sped him on. Like Columbus, Whitman is "old, poor, and paralyzed," yet capable of one more effort to speak of the steady interior light that God has granted him. Finally, the works of the past fall away from him, and some divine hand reveals a scene of countless ships sailing on distant seas, from which "anthems in new tongues" salute and comfort him. This implied divine sanction for his life's work was consolation to an old poet, who, at his death in 1892, remained largely unaccepted and unrecognized by contemporary critics and historians.

LEGACY

The grand design of *Leaves of Grass* appears to trace self and nation neatly through sensuous youth, crises of maturity, and soul-searching old age. Although this philosophical or psychological reading of Whitman's work is certainly encouraged by the poet's tinkering with its structure, many fine lyrics do not fit into neat patterns, or even under topical headings. Whitman's reputation rests more on the startling freshness of his language, images, and democratic treatment of the common American citizen than on his success as epic bard. Common to all his poetry, however, are certain major themes: reconciliation of body and soul, purity and unity of physical nature, death as the "mother of beauty," and above all, comradeship or love, which binds and transcends all else. In fact, Whitman encouraged a complex comradeship with his readers to bind his work to future generations. He expected reading to be a gymnastic struggle and the reader to be a re-creator of the poem through imaginative interaction with the poet. Perhaps that is why he said in "So Long" that *Leaves of Grass* was no book, for whoever touches his poetry "touches a man."

OTHER MAJOR WORKS

LONG FICTION: *Franklin Evans*, 1842.

SHORT FICTION: *The Half-Breed, and Other Stories*, 1927.

NONFICTION: *Democratic Vistas*, 1871; *Memoranda During the War*, 1875-1876; *Specimen Days and Collect*, 1882-1883; *Complete Prose Works*, 1892; *Calamus*, 1897 (letters; Richard M. Bucke, editor); *The Wound Dresser*, 1898 (Bucke, editor); *Letters Written by Walt Whitman to His Mother, 1866-1872*, 1902 (Thomas B. Harned, editor); *An American Primer*, 1904; *Walt Whitman's Diary in Canada*, 1904 (William S. Kennedy, editor); *The Letters of Anne Gilchrist and Walt Whitman*, 1918 (Harned, editor).

MISCELLANEOUS: *The Collected Writings of Walt Whitman*, 1961-1984 (22 volumes).

BIBLIOGRAPHY

Canning, Richard. *Whitman*. London: Hesperus, 2010. Part of the Poetic Lives series, this is a basic biography that examines Whitman's life and poetry.

Folsom, Ed. *Re-scripting Walt Whitman: An Introduction to His Life and Work*. Malden, Mass.: Blackwell, 2005. A good starting point for readers of Whitman, delving into his life and literary works.

Genoways, Ted. *Walt Whitman and the Civil War: America's Poet During the Lost Years of 1860/1862*. Berkeley: University of California Press, 2009. Uses unpublished letters and manuscripts to explore Whitman's involvement in the war, debunking his supposed indifference.

Herrero-Brassas, Juan A., ed. *Walt Whitman's Mystical Ethics of Comradeship: Homosexuality and the Marginality of Friendship at the Crossroads of Modernity*. Albany: State University of New York Press, 2010. This collection of essays examines Whitman's mystical religious beliefs, his concept of comradeship, and his homosexuality.

Killlingsworth, M. Jimmie, ed. *The Cambridge Introduction to Walt Whitman*. New York: Cambridge University Press, 2007. A comprehensive work that covers Whitman's life and presents extensive analysis of his poetry, including his prewar poetry, *Leaves of Grass*, "Calamus," "Children of Adam," earth and body poems, and elegies. Also looks at critical reception of his works and the image that was created around him.

Kummings, Donald D., ed. *A Companion to Walt Whitman*. Malden, Mass.: Blackwell, 2006. These thirty-five essays by prominent scholars delve into the life and writing of Whitman. The essays are classified under four sections, concentrating on the author's life, the cultural and literary contexts of his writing, and the texts themselves. Topics such as nature, the city, gender, civil war, and pop culture are discussed at length in relation to Whitman and his writing. Readers will also find this book valuable for the publication history it provides, as well as the thorough bibliography of criticism of Whitman's prose.

Reynolds, David S. *Walt Whitman*. New York: Knopf, 2005. Part of the Lives and Legacies series, this work examines the life and work of Whitman. Reynolds calls Whitman the founder of free verse and the first poet to treat sex candidly.

Robertson, Michael. *Worshipping Walt: The Whitman Disciples*. Princeton, N.J.: Princeton University Press, 2008. In his later years, Whitman developed "disciples," people who admired and supported him. This work examines his disciples, including Anne Gilchrist, John Burroughs, John Addington Symonds, and Horace Traubel.

Stacey, Jason. *Walt Whitman's Multitudes: Labor Reform and Persona in Whitman's Journalism and the First "Leaves of Grass," 1840-1855*. New York: Peter Lang, 2008. Focuses on the political views of Whitman as expressed in his journalism and in the first edition of *Leaves of Grass*. Whitman wrote on artisans who had lost their economic status, blaming them in part for becoming involved in consumerism and affectation.

Williams, C. K. *On Whitman*. Princeton, N.J.: Princeton University Press, 2010. Part of the Writers on Writers series, this work looks at Whitman from the standpoint of another poet and delves into Whitman's influence.

Perry D. Luckett

WILLIAM WORDSWORTH

Born: Cockermouth, Cumberland, England; April 7, 1770
Died: Rydal Mount, Westmorland, England; April 23, 1850

OTHER LITERARY FORMS

In addition to his poetry, William Wordsworth's preface to the second edition of his *Lyrical Ballads* is the single most important manifesto of the Romantic position in English, defining his ideas of the primary laws of nature, the working of the imagination, the process of association of ideas, and the balance of passion and restraint in human conduct.

ACHIEVEMENTS

William Wordsworth was one of the leading English Romantic poets. Along with William Blake, Samuel Taylor Coleridge, Lord Byron, Percy Bysshe Shelley, and John Keats, Wordsworth created a major revolution in ideology and poetic style around 1800. The Romantic writers rebelled against the neoclassical position exemplified in the works of Alexander Pope (1688-1744) and Samuel Johnson (1709-1784). Although all such broad generalizations should be viewed with suspicion, it is generally said that the neoclassical writers valued restraint and discipline, whereas the Romantic poets fa-

William Wordsworth
(Library of Congress)

vored individual genius and hoped to follow nature freely. Wordsworth's poetry praises the value of the simple individual, the child, the helpless, the working class, and the natural man. Such sentiments were explosive in the age of the French Revolution, when Wordsworth was young. He helped to define the attitudes that fostered the spread of democracy, of more humane treatment of the downtrodden, and of respect for nature.

Biography

The northwestern corner of England, which contains the counties of Northumberland and Westmorland, is both mountainous and inaccessible. The cliffs are not as high as those in Switzerland, but they are rugged, and the land is settled mainly by shepherds and by isolated farmers. The valleys have long, narrow, picturesque lakes, and so the region is called the English Lake District. William Wordsworth was born and lived much of his life among these lakes. Many of the English Romantic writers are sometimes called lake poets because of their association with this area. Wordsworth was born in 1770 in the small town of Cockermouth in Cumberland. Although he later wrote about the lower classes, his own family was middle class, and the poet never actually worked with his hands to make his living. His father was a lawyer who managed the affairs of the earl of Lonsdale. The poet had three brothers (Richard, John, and Christopher) and a sister (Dorothy). For the first nine years of his life, the family inhabited a comfortable house near the Derwent River. William attended Anne Birkett's school in the little town of Penrith, where Mary Hutchinson, whom he married in 1802, was also a student. His mother died when he was seven. The two brothers, William and Richard, then boarded at the house of Ann Tyson while attending grammar school in the village of Hawkshead.

Apparently this arrangement was a kindly one, and the boy spent much time happily roaming the nearby fields and hills. He also profited from the teaching of his schoolmaster William Taylor, who encouraged him to write poetry. In 1783, his father died and the family inheritance was tied up in litigation for some twenty years. Only after the death of the earl of Lonsdale in 1802 was Wordsworth able to profit from his father's estate. With the help of relatives, he matriculated at St. John's College, Cambridge University. Although he did not earn distinction as a student, those years were fertile times for learning.

While he was a student at St. John's, between 1787 and 1791, the French Revolution broke out across the English Channel. During his summer vacation of 1790, Wordsworth and his college friend, Robert Jones, went on a walking tour across France and Switzerland to Italy. The young students were much impressed by the popular revolution and the spirit of democracy in France at that time. Wordsworth took his degree at St. John's in January, 1791, but had no definite plans for his future. The following November, he went again to revolution-torn France with the idea of learning the French language well enough to earn his living as a tutor. Passing through Paris, he settled at Blois in the Loire Valley. There he made friends with Captain Michael Beaupuy and became deeply involved in French Republican thought. There, too, he fell in love with Annette Vallon, who was some four years older than the young poet. Vallon and Wordsworth had an illegitimate daughter, Caroline, but Wordsworth returned to England alone in December, 1792, probably to try to arrange his financial affairs. In February, 1793, war broke out between France and England so that Wordsworth was not able to see his baby and her mother again until the Treaty of Amiens in 1802 made it possible for him to visit them. His daughter was then ten years old.

In 1793, Wordsworth must have been a very unhappy young man: His deepest sympathies were on the side of France and democracy, but his own country was at war against his French friends such as Captain Michael Beaupuy; he was separated from Annette and his baby, and his English family associates looked on his conduct as scandalous; the earl of Lonsdale refused to settle his father's financial claims, so the young man was without funds and had no way to earn a living, even though he held a bachelor's degree from a prestigious university. Under these conditions, he moved in politically radical circles, becoming friendly with William Godwin, Mary Wollstonecraft, and Thomas Paine. In 1793, he published his first books of poetry, *An Evening Walk* and *Descriptive Sketches*.

Wordsworth and his younger sister, Dorothy, were close friends. In 1795, the poet benefited from a small legacy to settle with her at Racedown Cottage in Dorset, where they were visited by Mary Hutchinson and Samuel Taylor Coleridge. In 1797, they moved to Alfoxden, near Nether Stowey in Somerset, to be near Coleridge's home. Here a period of intense creativity occurred: Dorothy began her journal in 1798 while Wordsworth and Coleridge collaborated on *Lyrical Ballads*. A walking trip with Dorothy along the Wye River resulted in 1798 in "Lines Composed a Few Miles Above Tintern Abbey." That fall, Coleridge, Dorothy, and Wordsworth went to study in Germany. Dorothy and the poet spent most of their time in Goslar, where apparently he began to write *The Prelude*, his major autobiographical work which he left unfinished at his death. Returning from Germany, he and Dorothy settled in Dove Cottage in the Lake District. In 1800, he completed "Michael" and saw the second edition of *Lyrical Ballads* published. With the end of hostilities in 1802, Wordsworth visited Vallon and their daughter in France, arranging to make an annual child-support payment. Upon his return to England, he married Mary Hutchinson. During that year, he composed "Ode: Intimations of Immortality from Recollections of Early Childhood."

In 1805, his brother John was drowned at sea. Wordsworth often looked on nature as a kindly force, but the death of his brother in a shipwreck may have been a powerful contribution to his darkening vision of nature as he grew older. In 1805, he had a completed draft of *The Prelude* ready for Coleridge to read, although he was never satisfied with the work as a whole and rewrote it extensively later. It is sometimes said that when Wordsworth was a "bad" man, fathering an illegitimate child, consorting with revolutionaries and drug addicts, and roaming the countryside with no useful occupation, he wrote "good" poetry. When he became a "good" man, respectably married and gainfully employed, he began to write "bad" poetry. It is true that, although he wrote prolifically until his death, not much of his work after about 1807 is considered remarkable. In 1813, he accepted the position of distributor of stamps for Westmorland County, the kind of governmental support he probably would have scorned when he was younger. His fame as a writer, however, grew steadily. In 1842 when his last volume, *Poems Chiefly of Early and Late Years*, was published, he accepted a government pension of three hundred pounds sterling per annum, a considerable sum. The next year, he succeeded Robert Southey as poet laureate of England. He died April 23, 1850, at Rydal Mount in his beloved Lake District.

ANALYSIS

When the volume of poetry called the *Lyrical Ballads* of 1798 was published in a second edition (1800), William Wordsworth wrote a prose preface for the book that is the single most important statement of Romantic ideology. It provides a useful introduction to his poetry.

LYRICAL BALLADS

Wordsworth's preface to *Lyrical Ballads* displays the idea of primitivism as the basis of the Romantic position. Primitivism is the belief that there is some primary, intrinsically good "state of nature" from which adult, educated, civilized humankind has fallen into a false or wicked state of existence. When Jean-Jacques Rousseau began *The Social Contract* (1762) with the assertion that "Man was born free, and yet we see him everywhere in chains," he concisely expressed the primitivist point of view. The American and French revolutions were both predicated on Romantic primitivism, the idea that humanity was once naturally free, but that corrupt kings, churches, and social customs held it enslaved. The Romantic typically sees rebellion and breaking free from false restraint to regain a state of nature as highly desirable; Wordsworth's preface shows him deeply committed to this revolutionary ideology. He says that he is going to take the subjects of his poems from "humble and rustic life" because in that condition humankind is "less under restraint" and the "elementary feelings" of life exist in a state of simplicity.

Many writers feel that serious literature can be written only about great and powerful men, such as kings and generals. Some writers apparently believe that wounding a king is tragic, while beating a slave is merely funny. Wordsworth's preface firmly rejects such ideas. He turns to simple, common, poor people as the topic of his poetry because they are nearer a "state of nature" than the powerful, educated, and sophisticated men who have been corrupted by false customs of society. Many writers feel that they must live in the centers of civilization, London or Paris, for example, to be conversant with new ideas and the latest fashions. Wordsworth turns away from the cities to the rural scene. He himself lived in the remote Lake District most of his life, and he wrote about simple shepherds, farmers, and villagers. He explains that he chooses for his topics

> humble and rustic life . . . because, in that condition, the essential passions of the heart find a better soil in which they can attain their maturity, are less under restraint, and speak a plainer and more emphatic language; because in that condition of life our elementary feelings coexist in a state of greater simplicity, and consequently may be more accurately contemplated.

He sees a correspondence between the unspoiled nature of humankind and the naturalness of the environment. Romantic ideology of this sort underlies much of the contemporary environmentalist movement: the feeling that humans ought to be in harmony with their environment, that nature is beneficent, that people ought to live simply so that the essential part of their human nature may conform to the grand pattern of nature balanced in the whole universe.

The use of the words "passion" and "restraint" in Wordsworth's quotation above is significant. English neoclassical writers such as Alexander Pope tended to be suspicious of human passions, arguing that anger and lust lead people into error unless such passions are restrained by right reason. For Pope, it is necessary to exercise the restraint of reason over passion for people to be morally good. "Restraint" is good; "passion" bad. Wordsworth reverses this set of values. Humans' natural primitive feelings are the source of goodness and morality; the false restraints of custom and education are what lead people astray from their natural goodness. In his preface, Wordsworth seems to be following the line of thought developed by Anthony Ashley-Cooper, the third earl of Shaftesbury (1671-1713) in his *An Inquiry Concerning Virtue or Merit* (1709). Shaftes-bury asks his readers to imagine a "creature who, wanting reason and being unable to re-flect, has notwithstanding many good qualities and affections,—as love to his kind, courage, gratitude or pity." Shaftesbury probably is thinking of creatures such as a faith-ful dog or a child too young to reason well. In such cases, one would have to say that the creature shows good qualities, even though he or she lacks reasoning power. For Shaftesbury, then, to reason means merely to recognize the already existing good im-pulses or feelings naturally arising in such a creature. Morality arises from natural feeling, evidently present in creatures with little reasoning power.

Wordsworth's preface is heavily influenced by Shaftesbury's argument. He turns to simple characters for his poems because they exhibit the natural, primary, unspoiled states of feeling that are the ultimate basis of morality. Wordsworth's characters are sen-timental heroes, chosen because their feelings are unspoiled by restraints of education and reason: children, simple shepherds and villagers, the old Cumberland Beggar, Alice Fell, and so on. While William Shakespeare often puts a nobleman at the center of his plays and relegates the poor people to the role of rustic clowns, Wordsworth takes the feelings of the poor as the most precious subject of serious literature.

The preface displays two kinds of primitivism. Social primitivism is the belief that humankind's state of nature is good and that it is possible to imagine a social setting in which humans' naturally good impulses will flourish. Social primitivism leads to the celebration of the "noble savage," perhaps an American Indian or a Black African tribesman, who is supposed to be morally superior to the sophisticated European who has been corrupted by the false restraints of his own society. Social primitivism was, of course, one of the driving forces behind the French Revolution. The lower classes rose up against the repression of politically powerful kings and destroyed laws and restraints so that their natural goodness could flourish. Unfortunately, the French Revolution did not produce a morally perfect new human being once the corrupt restraints had been de-stroyed. Instead, the French Revolution produced the Reign of Terror, the rise of Napo-leon to military dictatorship, and the French wars of aggression against relatively demo-cratic states such as the Swiss Republic. With unspeakable shock, Wordsworth and the other Romantics saw the theory of social primitivism fail in France. The decline of Wordsworth's poetic power as he grew older is often explained in part as the result of his disillusionment with revolutionary France.

A second kind of primitivism in the preface is psychological. Psychological primi-tivism is the belief that there is some level in the mind that is primary, more certain than everyday consciousness. In the preface, Wordsworth says that humble life displays "the primary laws of our nature; chiefly, as far as the manner in which we associate ideas." Here Wordsworth refers to a very important Romantic idea, associational psychology, which developed from the tradition of British empirical philosophy—from John Locke's *Essay Concerning Human Understanding* (1690), David Hume's *Enquiry Concerning Human Understanding* (1748), and especially David Hartley's *Observations on Man* (1749).

When Wordsworth speaks in the preface to the *Lyrical Ballads* about tracing in his poems the "manner in which we associate ideas," he is endorsing the line of thought of the associational psychologists. Poems trace the process by which the mind works. They help people to understand the origins of their own feelings about what is good and bad by demonstrating the way impressions from nature strike the mind and by showing how the mind associates these simple experiences, forming complex attitudes about what proper conduct is, what fidelity and love are, what the good and the true are. In *The Prelude*, one of Wordsworth's main motives is to trace the history of the development of his own mind from its most elementary feelings through the process of association of ideas until his imagination constructs his complex, adult consciousness.

Wordsworth's preface to the second edition of *Lyrical Ballads* set out a series of ideas that are central to the revolutionary Romantic movement, including both social and psychological primitivism, the state of nature, the "noble savage," the sentimental hero, the power of the imagination, and the association of ideas. These concepts are basic to understanding his poetry.

"LINES COMPOSED A FEW MILES ABOVE TINTERN ABBEY"

Wordsworth's "Lines Composed a Few Miles Above Tintern Abbey" (hereafter called simply "Tintern Abbey") was composed on July 13, 1798, and published that same year. It is one of the best-known works of the English Romantic movement. Its poetic form is blank verse, unrhymed iambic pentameter, in the tradition of John Milton's *Paradise Lost* (1667, 1674). In reading any poem, it is important to define its dramatic situation and to consider the text as if it were a scene from a play or drama and determine who is speaking, to whom, and under what circumstances. Wordsworth is very precise in telling the reader when and where these lines are spoken. Tintern Abbey exists, and the poet Wordsworth really visited it during a tour on July 13, 1798. Because the poem is set at a real point in history rather than once upon a time, and in a real place rather than in a kingdom far away, it is said to exhibit "topographic realism." The speaker of the poem reveals that this is his second visit to this spot; he had been there five years earlier. At line 23, he reveals that he has been away from this pleasant place for a long time and, at lines 50-56, that while he was away in the "fretful stir" of the world he was unhappy. When he was depressed, his thoughts turned to his memory of this natural scene, and he felt comforted. Now, as the poem begins, he has come again to this beautiful site with his beloved younger sister, whom he names directly at line 121. The dramatic situation involves a speaker, or persona, who tells the reader his thoughts and feelings as if he were addressing his younger sister, who is "on stage" as his dramatic audience. Although the poem is autobiographical, so that the speaker resembles Wordsworth himself and the sister resembles Dorothy Wordsworth, it is better to think of the speaker and his listener as two invented characters in a little play. When William Shakespeare's Hamlet speaks to Ophelia in his play, the audience knows that Hamlet is not the same as Shakespeare although he surely must express some of Shakespeare's feelings and ideas. So, too, the reader imagines that the speaker in "Tintern Abbey" speaks for Wordsworth, but is not exactly the same as the poet himself.

The poem displays many of the ideas stated in the preface to the *Lyrical Ballads*. It begins with a description of a remote rural scene, rather than speaking about the latest news from London. In this rustic setting, the speaker discovers some essential truths about himself. The first twenty-two lines describe the natural scene: the cliffs, orchards, and farms. This is a romantic return to nature, the search for the beautiful and permanent forms that incorporate primitive human goodness. The speaker not only describes the scene, but also tells the reader how it generates feelings and sensations in him. In lines 23-56, the speaker says that his memory of this pure, natural place had been of comfort to him when he was far away. Lines 66-90 trace the speaker's memory of his process of growing up: When he first came among these hills as a boy, he was like a wild animal. He was filled with feelings of joy or fear by wild nature. As a boy, nature was to him "a feeling and a love" that required no thought on his part. That childish harmony with nature is now lost. His childish "aching joys" and "dizzy raptures" are "gone by." As he fell away from his unthinking harmony with nature, his power of thought developed. This power is "abundant recompense" for the childish joys of "thoughtless youth." Now he understands nature in a new way. He hears in nature "The still sad music of humanity." At line 95, he explains that his intellect grasps the purpose and direction of nature, whereas his childish experience was more intense and joyous but incomplete. Now, as an adult, he returns to this natural scene and understands what he had only felt as a child, that nature is the source of moral goodness, "the nurse, the guide, the guardian of my heart, and soul of all my moral being."

At line 110, he turns to his younger sister and sees in her wild eyes his own natural state of mind in childhood. He foresees that she will go through the same loss that he experienced. She too will grow up and lose her unthinking harmony with the natural and the wild. He takes comfort in the hope that nature will protect her, as it has helped him, and in the knowledge that the memory of this visit will be with her when she is far away in future years. Their experience of this pastoral landscape is therefore dear to the speaker for its own sake, and also because he has shared it with his sister. He has come back from the adult world and glimpsed primitive natural goodness both in the scene and in his sister.

The poem employs social and psychological primitivism. The rural scene is an imagined state of primitive nature where human goodness can exist in the child, like Adam in the garden of Eden before the Fall of Man. The poem shows how the primitive feelings of the boy are generated by the forms of nature and then form more and more complex ideas until his whole adult sense of good and bad, right and wrong, can be traced back to his elementary childish experiences of nature. Reason is not what makes beauty or goodness possible; natural feelings are the origin of the good and the beautiful. Reason merely recognizes what the child knows directly from his feelings.

Critics of Wordsworth point out that the "natural" scene described in the opening lines is, in fact, not at all "natural." Nature in this scene has been tamed by man into orchards, hedged fields, and cottage farms. What, critics ask, would Wordsworth have written if he had imagined nature as the struggling jungle in the Congo where individual plants and animals fight for survival in their environmental niche and whole species are brought to extinction by the force of nature "red in tooth and claw"? If Wordsworth's idea of nature is not true, then his idea of human nature will likewise be false. While he expects the French Revolution to lead to a state of nature in joy and harmony, in fact it led to the Reign of Terror and the bloodshed of the Napoleonic wars. Critics of Romantic ideology argue that when the Romantics imagine nature as a "kindly nurse," they unthinkingly accept a false anthropomorphism. Nature is not like a kindly human being; it is an indifferent or neutral force. They charge that Wordsworth projects his own feelings into the natural scene, and thus his view of the human condition becomes dangerously confused.

"MICHAEL"

"Michael: A Pastoral Poem" was composed between October 11 and December 9, 1800, and published that same year. It is typical of Wordsworth's poetry about humble and rustic characters in which the sentiments or feelings of human beings in a state of nature are of central importance. The poem is written in blank verse, unrhymed iambic pentameter, again the meter employed in Milton's *Paradise Lost*. Milton's poem ex- plores the biblical story of the fall of Adam from the Garden of Eden. Michael's destruction in Wordsworth's poem shows a general similarity to the tragedy of Adam in *Paradise Lost*. Both Michael and Adam begin in a natural paradise where they are happy and good. Evil creeps into each garden, and through the weakness of a beloved family member, both Adam and Michael fall from happiness to misery.

The poem "Michael" has two parts: the narrative frame and the tale of Michael. The frame occupies lines 1-39 and lines 475 to the end, the beginning and ending of the text. It relates the circumstances under which the story of Michael is told. The tale occupies lines 40-475, the central part of the text, and it tells the history of the shepherd Michael; his wife, Isabel; and their son Luke. The frame of the poem occurs in the fictive present time, about 1800, whereas the tale occurs a generation earlier. The disintegration of Michael's family and the destruction of their cottage has already happened years before the poem begins. The frame establishes that the poem is set in the English Lake District and introduces the reader to the "I-persona" or speaker of the poem. He tells the story of Michael and knows the geography and history of the district. A "You-character" who does not know the region is the dramatic audience addressed by the "I-persona." In the frame, "I" tells "You" that there is a hidden valley up in the mountains. In that valley, there is a pile of rocks, which would hardly be noticed by a stranger; but there is a story behind that heap of stones. "I" then tells "You" the story of the shepherd Michael.

Michael is one of the humble and rustic characters whose feelings are exemplary of the natural or primitive state of human beings. He has lived all his life in the mountains, in communion with nature, and his own nature has been shaped by his natural environment. He is a good and kindly man. He has a wife, Isabel, and a child of his old age named Luke. The family works from morning until far into the night, tending their sheep and spinning wool. They live in a cottage far up on the mountainside, and they have a lamp that burns late every evening as they sit at their work. They have become proverbial in the valley for their industry, so that their cottage has become known as the cottage of the evening star because its window glimmers steadily every night. These simple, hardworking people are "neither gay perhaps, nor cheerful, yet with objects and with hopes, living a life of eager industry." The boy is Michael's delight. From his birth, the old man had helped to tend the child and, as Luke grew, his father worked with him always at his side. He made him a perfect shepherd's staff and gave it to his son as a gift. Now the boy has reached his eighteenth year and the "old man's heart seemed born again" with hope and happiness in his son.

Unfortunately, Michael suffers a reversal of his good fortune, for news comes that a distant relative has suffered an unforeseen business failure, and Michael has to pay a grievous penalty "in surety for his brother's son." The old man is sorely troubled. He cannot bear to sell his land. He suggests that Luke should go from the family for a time to work in the city and earn enough to pay the forfeiture. Before his beloved son leaves, Michael takes him to a place on the farm where he has collected a heap of stones. He tells Luke that he plans to build a new sheepfold there and asks Luke to lay the cornerstone. This will be a covenant or solemn agreement between the father and son: The boy will work in the city, and meanwhile the father will build a new barn so that it will be there for the boy's return. Weeping, the boy puts the first stone in place and leaves the next day for his work far away. At first, the old couple get a good report about his work, but after a time Luke "in the dissolute city gave himself to evil courses; ignominy and shame fell on him, so that he was driven at last to seek a hiding-place beyond the sea." After the loss of his son, Michael still goes to the dell where the pile of building stones lies, but he often simply sits the whole day merely staring at them, until he dies. Some three years later, Isabel also dies, and the land is sold to a stranger. The cottage of the evening star is torn down and nothing remains of the poor family's hopes except the straggling pile of stones that are the remains of the still unfinished sheepfold. This is the story that the "I-persona," who knows the district, tells to the "You-audience," who is unacquainted with the local history and geography.

The poem "Michael" embodies the ideas proposed in Wordsworth's preface to the *Lyrical Ballads*. He takes a family of simple, rural people as the main characters in a tragedy. Michael is a sentimental hero whose unspoiled contact with nature has refined his human nature and made him a good man. Nature has imprinted experiences on his mind that his imagination has built into more and more complex feelings about what is right and wrong. The dissolute city, on the other hand, is confusing, and there Luke goes astray. From the city and the world of banking and finance, the grievous forfeiture intrudes into the rural valley where Michael was living in a state of nature, like a noble savage or like Adam before his fall.

The poem argues that nature is not a neutral commodity to be bought and sold. It is man's home. It embodies values. The poem demands that the reader consider nature as a living force and demonstrates that once one knows the story of Luke, one never again can look on a pile of rocks in the mountains as worthless. That pile of rocks was a solemn promise of father and son. It signified a whole way of life, now lost. It was gathered for a human purpose, and one must regret that the covenant was broken and the sheepfold never completed. Likewise, all nature is a covenant, an environment, filled with human promise and capable of guiding human feelings in a pure, simple, dignified, and moral way. The function of poetry (like the "I-persona's" story of Michael) is to make the reader see that nature is not neutral. The "I-persona" attaches the history of Michael to what otherwise might be merely a pile of rocks and so makes the "You-audience" feel differently about that place. Likewise, the poem as a whole makes the reader feel differently about nature.

"Tintern Abbey" and "Michael" both explore the important question of how human moral nature develops. What makes humans good, virtuous, or proper? If, as the preface argues, people are morally best when most natural, uncorrupted by false custom and education, then the normal process of growing up in the modern world must be a kind of falling away from natural grace.

"ODE: INTIMATIONS OF IMMORTALITY FROM RECOLLECTIONS OF EARLY CHILDHOOD"

Wordsworth's "Ode: Intimations of Immortality from Recollections of Early Childhood" (hereafter called "Ode: Intimations of Immortality") is also concerned with the process of growing up and its ethical and emotional consequences. The poem is written in eleven stanzas of irregular length, composed of lines of varying length with line-end rhyme. The core of the poem is stanza 5, beginning "Our birth is but a sleep and a forgetting." Here the poet discusses three stages of growth: the infant, the boy, and the man. The infant at birth comes from God, and at the moment when life begins the infant is still close to its divine origin. For this reason, the newborn infant is not utterly naked or forgetful, "but trailing clouds of glory do we come from God." The infant is near to divinity; "Heaven lies about us in our infancy," but each day leads it farther and farther from its initial, completely natural state. As consciousness awakens, "Shades of the prison house begin to close upon the growing boy." In other words, the natural feelings of the infant begin to become constrained as man falls into consciousness. A boy is still near to nature, but each day he travels farther from the initial source of his natural joy and goodness. The youth is like a priest who travels away from his Eastern holy land, each day farther from the origin of his faith, but still carrying with him the memory of the holy places. When a man is fully grown, he senses that the natural joy of childish union with nature dies away, leaving him only the drab ordinary "light of common day" unilluminated by inspiration. This process of movement from the unthinking infant in communion with nature, through the stage of youth filled with joy and natural inspiration, to the drab adult is summarized in stanza 7, from the "child among his new-born blisses" as he or she grows up playing a series of roles "down to palsied Age."

The poem as a whole rehearses this progression from natural infant to adulthood. Stanzas 1 and 2 tell how the speaker as a child saw nature as glorious and exciting. "There was a time when meadow, grove, and stream . . . to me did seem apparelled in celestial light." Now the speaker is grown up and the heavenly light of the natural world has lost its glory. Even so, in stanza 3, his sadness at his lost childhood joys is changed to joy when he sees springtime and thinks of shepherd boys. Springtime demonstrates the eternal rebirth of the world, when everything is refreshed and begins to grow naturally again. The shepherd boys shouting in the springtime are doubly blessed, for they are rural characters, and moreover, they are young, near the fountainhead of birth. In stanza 4, the adult speaker can look on the springtime or on rural children and feel happy again because they signify the experience he has had of natural joy. Even though, as he says in stanza 10, "nothing can bring back the hour of splendour in the grass, of glory in the flower," the adult can understand with his "philosophic mind" the overall design of the natural world and grasp that it is good.

THE PRELUDE

The Prelude is Wordsworth's longest and probably his most important work. It is an autobiographical portrait of the artist as a young man. He was never satisfied with the work and repeatedly rewrote and revised it, leaving it uncompleted at his death. He had a fairly refined draft in 1805-1806 for his friend Coleridge to read, and the version he left at his death in 1850 is, of course, the chronologically final version. In between the 1805 and 1850 versions, there are numerous drafts and sketches, some of them of the whole poem, while others are short passages or merely a few lines. When a reader speaks of Wordsworth's *The Prelude*, therefore, he is referring not so much to a single text as to a shifting, dynamic set of sometimes contradictory texts and fragments. The best edition of *The Prelude* is by Ernest de Selincourt, second edition revised by Helen Darbishire (Oxford University Press, 1959), which provides on facing pages the 1805-1806 text and the 1850 text. The reader can open the de Selincourt/Darbishire edition and see side by side the earliest and the latest version of every passage, while the editors' annotations indicate all significant intermediate steps.

The 1805 version is divided into thirteen books, while the 1850 version has fourteen. Book 1, "Introduction, Childhood and Schooltime," rehearses how the poet undertook to write this work. He reviews the topics treated in famous epic poems, in Milton's *Paradise Lost*, Edmund Spenser's *The Faerie Queene* (1590, 1596), and other works. He concludes that the proper subject for his poem should be the process of his own development. He therefore begins at line 305 of the 1805 version to relate his earliest experiences, following the ideas explored above in "Tintern Abbey" and his "Ode: Intimations of Immortality." He traces the earliest impressions on his mind, which is like the tabula rasa of the associational psychologists. "Fair seed-time had my soul, and I grew up/ Foster'd alike by beauty and by fear." He tells of his childhood in the lakes and mountains, of stealing birds from other hunters' traps, of scaling cliffs, and especially a famous episode concerning a stolen boat. At line 372, he tells how he once stole a boat and rowed at night out onto a lake. As he rowed away from the shore facing the stern of the boat, it appeared that a dark mountain rose up in his line of vision as if in pursuit. He was struck with fear and returned with feelings of guilt to the shore. Experiences like this "trace/ How Nature by extrinsic passion first peopled my mind." In other words, impressions of nature, associated with pleasure and pain, provide the basic ideas that the imagination of the poet uses to create more and more complex attitudes until he arrives at his adult view of the world. The process described in the stolen boat episode is sometimes called the "discipline of fear."

Book 2 concerns "School-Time." It corresponds to the three stages of life outlined in "Ode: Intimations of Immortality": infant, youth, and adult. As in "Tintern Abbey," in *The Prelude*, book 2, Wordsworth explains that his early experiences of nature sustained him when he grew older and felt a falling off of the infant's joyful harmony with the created universe. Book 3 deals with his "Residence at Cambridge University," which is like a dream world to the youth from the rural lakes: "I was a Dreamer, they the dream; I roamed/ Delighted through the motley spectacle." He talks of his reading and his activities as a student at St. John's College, concluding that his story so far has been indeed a heroic argument, as important as the stories of the ancient epics, tracing the development of his mind up to an eminence, a high point of his experience.

Book 4 recounts his summer vacation after his first year of college, as he returns to the mountains and lakes of his youth, a situation comparable to the return of the persona in "Tintern Abbey" to the rural scene he had previously known. He notes the "inner falling-off" or loss of joy and innocence that seems to accompany growing up. Yet at line 344, he tells of a vision of the sun rising as he walked homeward after a night of gaiety and mirth at a country dance, which caused him to consider himself a "dedicated spirit," someone who has a sacred duty to write poetry. Later in this book, he recounts his meeting with a tattered soldier returned from military service in the tropics and how he helped him find shelter in a cottage nearby. Book 5 is simply titled "Books" and examines the role of literature in the poet's development. This book contains the famous passage, beginning at line 389, "There was a boy, ye knew him well, ye Cliffs/ And Islands of Winander." There was a youth among the cliffs of the Lake District who could whistle so that the owls would answer him. Once when he was calling to them the cliffs echoed so that he was struck with surprise and wonder. This boy died while he was yet a child and the poet has stood "Mute—looking at the grave in which he lies." Another recollection concerns the appearance of a drowned man's body from the lake.

Book 6, "Cambridge and the Alps," treats his second year at college and the following summer's walking tour of France and Switzerland. When the poet first arrived at Calais, it was the anniversary of the French Revolution's federal day. The young man finds the revolutionary spirit with "benevolence and blessedness/ spread like a fragrance everywhere, like Spring/ that leaves no corner of the land untouched." Frenchmen welcome the young Englishman as brothers in the struggle for freedom and liberty and they join in a common celebration. The Alps were a formidable barrier in the nineteenth century, seeming to separate the Germanic culture of northern Europe from the Mediterranean. Crossing the Alps meant passing from one culture to a totally different one. Ironically, the poet records his errant climb, lost in the fog and mist, as he approached Italy, so that the English travelers cross the Alps without even knowing what they had done. Perhaps the crossing of the Alps unaware is like his observation of the French Revolution. The poet *sees* more than he *understands*. Book 7 treats of the poet's residence in London. As one would expect, the city is unnatural and filled with all kinds of deformed and perverted customs, epitomized at the Bartholomew Fair, "a hell/ For eyes and ears! what anarchy and din/ Barbarian and infernal! 'tis a dream/ Monstrous in colour, motion, shape, sight, sound."

Book 8, "Retrospect—Love of Nature Leading to a Love of Mankind," is in contrast to book 7. Opposed to the blank confusion of the city, book 8 returns to the peaceful, decent rural scenes of the Lake District. It contrasts a wholesome country fair with the freak shows of London. Nature's primitive gift to the shepherds is beauty and harmony, which the poet first experienced there. Such "noble savages," primitive men educated by nature alone, are celebrated as truly heroic.

Book 9 tells of the poet's second visit to France and residence in the Loire Valley. It suppresses, however, all the real biographical details concerning Wordsworth's affair with Annette Vallon and his illegitimate daughter. As he passes through Paris, the poet sees "the revolutionary power/ Toss like a ship at anchor, rock'd by storms." He arrives at his more permanent home in the Loire Valley and makes friends with a group of French military officers there. One day as he wanders with his new friends in the countryside, he comes across a hunger-bitten peasant girl, so downtrodden that she resembles the cattle she is tending. His French companion comments, "'Tis against *that* which we are fighting," against the brutalization of humankind by the monarchical system. In later versions, at the conclusion of this book, Wordsworth inserts the story of "Vaudracour and Julia." This love story seems to stand in place of Wordsworth's real-life encounter with Vallon. Book 10 continues his discussion of his visit to France, including a second visit to Paris while the Reign of Terror is in full cry and the denunciation of Maximilien Robespierre takes place. This book also traces his return to England and the declaration of war by England against France, which caused the young Wordsworth deep grief. The French Revolution was probably the most important political event in the poet's life. His initial hopes for the French cause were overshadowed by the outrages of the Reign of Terror. His beloved England, on the other hand, joined in armed opposition to the cause of liberty. In the numerous reworkings of this part of his autobiography, Wordsworth steadily became more conservative in his opinions as he grew older. Book 10 in the 1805 text is split into books 10 and 11 in the 1850 version. In this section, he explains that at the beginning of the French Revolution, "Bliss was it in that dawn to be alive,/ But to be young was very heaven." Yet the course of the revolution, running first to despotic terror and ending with the rise of Napoleon, brought Wordsworth to a state of discouragement and desolation.

Book 11 in the 1805 text (book 12 in the 1850 version) considers how one may rise from spiritual desolation: Having lost the innocent joy of primitive youth and having lost faith in the political aims of the French Revolution, where can the soul be restored? At line 74, the poet tells how "strangely he did war against himself," but nature has a powerful restorative force. At line 258, he enters the famous "Spots of time" argument, in which he maintains that there are remembered experiences that "with distinct preeminence retain/ A vivifying Virtue" so that they can nourish one's depleted spirits. Much as in "Tintern Abbey," a remembered experience of nature can excite the imagination to produce a fresh vitality. Book 12 in the 1805 version (book 13 in the 1850) begins with a summary of nature's power to shape man's imagination and taste:

> From nature doth emotion come, and moods
> of calmness equally are nature's gift,
> This is her glory; these two attributes
> Are sister horns that constitute her strength.

The concluding book tells of the poet's vision on Mount Snowdon in Wales. On the lonely mountain, under the full moon, a sea of mist shrouds all the countryside except the highest peaks. The wanderer looks over the scene and has a sense of the presence of divinity. Nature has such a sublime aspect "That men, least sensitive, see, hear, perceive,/ And cannot choose but feel" the intimation of divine power. In this way, Nature feeds the imagination, and a love of nature leads to a sense of humankind's place in the created universe and a love for all humankind. The poem ends with an address to the poet's friend Coleridge about their mutual struggle to keep faith as true prophets of nature.

It is often said that Wordsworth's *The Prelude*, written in Miltonic blank verse, is the Romantic epic comparable to *Paradise Lost* of Milton. Other critics point to a similarity between *The Prelude* and the bildungsroman, or novel of development. *The Prelude* is subtitled "The Growth of a Poet's Mind" and bears considerable resemblance to such classic stories as Stendhal's *The Red and the Black* (1830), in which the author traces the development of the hero, Julien Sorel, as he grows up. Finally, most readers find an important pastoral element in *The Prelude*. The "pastoral" occurs whenever an author and an audience belonging to a privileged and sophisticated society imagine a more simple life and admire it. For example, sophisticated courtiers might imagine the life of simple shepherds and shepherdesses to be very attractive compared to their own round of courtly duties. They would then imagine a pastoral world in which shepherdesses with frilly bows on their shepherds' crooks and dainty fruits to eat would dally in the shade by fountains on some peaceful mountainside. Such a vision is termed pastoral because it contrasts unfavorably the life of the real author and audience with the imagined life of a shepherd. *The Prelude* makes such pastoral contrasts frequently: for example, in the depiction of rural shepherds in the Lake District compared with urban workers; in the comparison of the life of a simple child with that of the adult; and in the comparison of the working classes of France and England with their masters. The pastoral elements in *The Prelude* are a natural consequence of the primitivism in the poem's ideology.

Wordsworth is one of the recognized giants of English literature, and his importance is nearly equal to Milton's or Shakespeare's. Even so, his work has been the subject of sharp controversy from its first publication until the present. William Hazlitt in his *Lectures on the English Poets* (1818) argues that Wordsworth is afflicted with a false optimism and that his idea of nature is merely a reflection of the human observer's feelings. Aldous Huxley in "Wordsworth in the Tropics" in *Holy Face and Other Essays* (1929) attacks the unnaturalness of Wordsworth's view of nature. John Stuart Mill's *Autobiography* (1873), on the other hand, discusses the restorative power of Romantic poetry and the capacity of Wordsworth to relieve the sterility of a too "scientific" orientation. Later critics have continued the controversy.

The apparent decline of Wordsworth's poetic powers in his later years has occasioned much debate. Was he disillusioned with the course of the French Revolution so that he could no longer bear to praise humankind's primitive nature? Was he so filled with remorse over his affair with Annette Vallon that his inspiration failed? Was he a living demonstration of his own theory of the development of man from infant, to boyhood, to adult: that as man grows older he becomes more and more remote from the primitive feelings of the infant who comes into this world trailing clouds of glory, so that old men can never be effective poets? In any case, the young Wordsworth writing in the 1790's and the first decade of the nineteenth century was a voice calling out that life can be joyful and meaningful, that humankind's nature is good, and that people are not alone in an alien world, but in their proper home.

OTHER MAJOR WORKS

NONFICTION: *The Prose Works of William Wordsworth*, 1876; *Letters of William and Dorothy Wordsworth*, 1935-1939 (6 volumes; Ernest de Selincourt, editor).

BIBLIOGRAPHY

Barker, Juliet. *Wordsworth: A Life*. New York: Viking, 2002. This biography traces Wordsworth's life over eight decades, shedding light on his relationship with his family, his early poetic career, and his politics.

Bloom, Harold, ed. *William Wordsworth*. New York: Chelsea House, 2009. A collection of critical essays on Wordsworth, with an introduction by Bloom.

Bromwich, David. *Disowned by Memory: Wordsworth's Poetry of the 1790's*. Chicago: University of Chicago Press, 1998. Bromwich connects the accidents of Wordsworth's life with the originality of his works, tracking the impulses that turned him to poetry after the death of his parents and during his years as an enthusiastic disciple of the French Revolution.

Gill, Stephen. *William Wordsworth: A Life*. New York: Oxford University Press, 1989. This first biography of Wordsworth since 1965 makes full use of information that came to light after that time, including the 1977 discovery of Wordsworth's family letters as well as more recent research on his boyhood in Hawkshead and his radical period in London.

_____, ed. *The Cambridge Companion to Wordsworth*. New York: Cambridge University Press, 2003. The fifteen essays in this compilation provide excellent introductions to Wordsworth's works.

Johnston, Kenneth R. *The Hidden Wordsworth: Poet, Lover, Rebel, Spy*. New York: W. W. Norton, 1998. A thoroughgoing reexamination of the poet's life that places him far more firmly in the tradition of liberal Romanticism than previous twentieth century critics or even his own contemporaries might have thought.

Liu, Yü. *Poetics and Politics: The Revolutions of Wordsworth*. New York: Peter Lang, 1999. Liu focuses on the poetry of Wordsworth in the late 1790's and the early 1800's. In the context of Wordsworth's crisis of belief, this study shows how his poetic innovations constituted his daring revaluation of his political commitment.

Simpson, David. *Wordsworth, Commodification, and Social Concern: The Poetics of Modernity*. New York: Cambridge University Press, 2009. A discussion of Wordsworth and his works that looks at how his political and philosophical views affected his writings.

Sisman, Adam. *The Friendship: Wordsworth and Coleridge.* New York: Viking, 2007. An intimate examination of Wordsworth and Samuel Taylor Coleridge's friendship and its deterioration.

Worthen, John. *The Gang: Coleridge, the Hutchinsons, and the Wordsworths in 1802.* New Haven, Conn.: Yale University Press, 2001. Worthen describes the relationships among Samuel Taylor Coleridge and his wife, Sarah; William Wordsworth and his sister, Dorothy; and the Hutchinson sisters, Mary and Sara.

Todd K. Bender

BARON WORMSER

Born: Baltimore, Maryland; February 4, 1948

OTHER LITERARY FORMS

Baron Wormser (WURM-sur) has written essays and book reviews for various literary magazines. Two important book reviews, extensive analyses of the works of Polish poets Adam Zagajewski and Czesław Miłosz, reveal Wormser's extraordinary knowledge of Western poetry, history, and culture. He has published essays concerning William Blake, the spirit of poetry in a democracy, and the necessity of religious poetry in our time. In 2000, he melded his vast wisdom about poetry with his love of teaching into a book, written with David Cappella, titled *Teaching the Art of Poetry: The Moves*. His memoir of his years in rural Maine, *The Road Washes Out in Spring: A Poet's Memoir of Living Off The Grid*, appeared in 2006. Wormser published *The Poetry Life: Ten Stories* (2008), a book of ten short fictional narratives about poets from Blake in the eighteenth century to Sylvia Plath and Joe Bolton in the late twentieth century and how their work figured in the lives of imagined characters. The range of poets addressed—from formalists such as Weldon Kees to Beat poets such as Gregory Corso—helps Wormser imagine the significance of poetry in people's personal triumphs and struggles. *The Poetry Life* is vital for understanding Wormser's vision of what poetry is and can be.

ACHIEVEMENTS

Baron Wormser gained critical stature in the 1980's and 1990's, as evidenced by the honors he accrued during these decades. In 1982, he won the Frederick Bock Prize from *Poetry* magazine, and in 1996, he won the Kathryn A. Morton Prize in Poetry. In 2000, he was appointed Maine's poet laureate, a position in which he served until 2005. He also received fellowships from the National Endowment for the Arts and the John Guggenheim Memorial Foundation. His poems, reviews, and essays have appeared in literary magazines such as *Paris Review*, *Sewanee Review*, *Harper's*, *The New Republic*, and *Poetry*.

BIOGRAPHY

Born and reared in Baltimore, Baron Wormser grew up enjoying the city's rich ethnic diversity. He attended Baltimore City College, then a citywide public boys' school located near Memorial Stadium. In 1970, he was graduated from The Johns Hopkins University. He was married to Janet Garbose in 1969 in Brookline, Massachusetts. He briefly pursued graduate study at the University of California, Irvine, and the University of Maine. Toward the end of 1970, he and his wife chose rural living, homesteading on a one-hundred-acre parcel at the end of an old logging road in Mercer, Maine. There they reared a daughter, Maisie, and a son, Owen. In 1972, Wormser began work as the librarian of School Administrative District 54 in Madison, Maine, a mill town approximately twenty-five miles from his home. Wormser's living in a house with no electricity and no indoor plumbing reflects not only his deep commitment to the natural world but also his serious endeavor to live as much of a life of the spirit as is possible in contemporary America and his determination to renounce as far as possible the distractions of sophisticated life and the pretensions of the urban elite. Although Wormser left Maine in 1998 to live in Cabot, Vermont, he still remains strongly rooted in a rural and regional identity. However, his poems are not particularly in a local-color mode and possess a discursive quality that gives them a broad interrelation with poetry in English worldwide and through the centuries. Wormser's public and civic emphasis precludes his being a poet merely of his own region, and he does not write exclusively autobiographical or observational poetry.

While maintaining an active writing life and working as a high school librarian, Wormser began to teach creative writing to high school students and discovered his gift for teaching. From the late 1980's onward, Wormser was busy teaching the writing of poetry at the University of Maine at Farmington, serving in 2000 as a visiting professor at the University of South Dakota, and conducting workshops and seminars at the Frost Place in Franconia, New Hampshire. Wormser continues to lecture frequently in New England and in selected national and international venues. His poetry has gained new exposure through the determined championship of Philip Fried, editor of the *Manhattan Review*, who has been a persistent advocate of Wormser's work and has placed it in a world context. From 2000 to 2005, he served as Maine's poet laureate, even though at that point he no longer lived in the state. He has directed the Frost Place Conference on poetry and teaching in Franconia Notch, new Hampshire. He began teaching at the Stonecoast master of fine arts in writing program in 2002 and the Fairfield University master of fine arts program in 2009.

ANALYSIS

Baron Wormser's poetry offers a deeply sympathetic look at what it means to be human. His distinctive voice, intelligent observations of the particulars of existence, and sense of humor blend with superior technical skill to reveal the strange complexities that underlie people's actions. Addressing a broad range of topics in his poetry, Wormser brings a heightened awareness of life's predicaments by tackling its large truths, revealing what humans share as they live.

Wormser's poetry seems to represent a departure for American poetry. His intellectualism clearly reveals a multifaceted vision of the world; however, for him, intellect is not distant and cool, rather it is a passion, a mode of apprehending reality. His technical skill formalizes these glimpses of humanity. Wormser is an American poet with a sensibility that elevates his subject matter into a larger context. His imagination blends an eye for the obvious with intellectual perceptions about culture and civilization to create extraordinary insights into why people are the way they are. In this sense, Wormser's sensibility is quite distinguishable from that of his contemporaries and more akin to that of poets of Central and Eastern Europe such as Zagajewski, Miłosz, or Jaan Kaplinski.

Considered as a whole, Wormser's work epitomizes the idea of poetry as aspiring toward the status of a spiritual gift. It is a poetry of exuberance, alive with the wonder of being, and filled with a deep knowledge of the world. Beauty manifests itself in the daily drama enacted by the individual, replete with obvious experience and natural emotion. This celebration of the commonality of life's rich pageant reveals the essentially religious nature of Wormser's poetry. It is poetry that teaches the reader about human existence by articulating its source—the soul.

THE WHITE WORDS

In *The White Words*, the tension and irony created as the sublime rubs constantly against the everyday demonstrate the supreme beauty of life. It is people that act out this drama. "Passing Significance," taking place in the sitting room of an inn, brings travelers together, each involved in his own interior world. Some read, some write, the innkeeper's wife worries about who is going to pay, a baby cries, a woman quietly sings, and a clerk rustles a newspaper. Even a dog sighs. The chief assessor, however, barges into the room, stamping snow off his boots, and decides immediately that there is "no one of importance here." Such is not the case. The poem informs the reader that each of these people in the sitting room is significant, and that a special state of mind must inhere within an individual for him or her to understand this simple yet complex fact of life. Fittingly, the poem ends with an epigrammatic lesson: "To study other people/ You must be free and easy and remember nothing."

Wormser's poetry is a poetry of nuance; it sees through the obviousness of how people live. This quality is well exemplified in "Of Small Towns." Here the poet describes the mundane lives of the citizens of a small town, elevating them by revealing the nature of their humanity. In doing so, he dignifies not only the purpose of their lives but also the purpose of their town, showing how it ennobles the lives of its people. Ultimately, the town is its people, and vice versa.

What is distinctive about Wormser's poetry is this ability to exalt human experience, employing both the intellect and the imagination. While the heart and soul of New England gently seep into almost every one of Wormser's poems, his insights transcend place. For example, in "Cord of Birch," a typically New England problem becomes a quest. After cutting some birch, the narrator decides to ask around the neighborhood about how well birch burns. After seeking out and listening to various contradictory opinions, he wanders home, pouting and disgruntled about his pile of wood. Eventually, it is winter that frees him of his worries. He burns the birch because he has no choice: Need lends him wisdom. Wormser accomplishes this progression from the exterior to the interior, from summer to winter, through the use of tightly controlled rhyming couplets.

In "Letter from New England," an odd moment during a midwinter funeral and a comment by the narrator's daughter inspire a realization of what an image can conjure, of what it means for an individual even to be aware of an image. "Beech Trees," a meditation on human nature, not only addresses the fact that stingy beech leaves refuse to fall even in the dead of winter but also uses the image of their dangling on a sapling in January to initiate a rumination about the lingering as well as the ending of things—a rumination that concludes with the revelatory notion that people and leaves are not all that different.

Wormser's poetry is more than regional. Throughout *The White Words*, his wide-ranging intellect is brought to bear on political, social, philosophical, historical, and literary themes. Such themes emerge from specific contexts. In "Some Recollections Concerning the Exiled Revolutionary, Leon Trotsky," the poet sees Trotsky and even imagines his voice. Through the man's thinking, he elaborates on the essence of politics, providing a glimpse of what it means to be exiled and to be a revolutionary.

A poem such as "Report on the Victorians" displays Wormser's extensive knowledge of history and social mores. In a sharp narrative flow, anchored by a well-choreographed rhyme scheme, Wormser investigates the sensibility of Victorianism. For him, what is essential is how Victorians saw, felt, and responded to their times. Their manners, their prejudices, and their hopes and dreams interest him. In their customs and intellectual sensibilities, Wormser perceives an inherent archetype within humanity that is composed of a duality, in this case fiendishness and hope, each element of which is found within the other. This archetype is an indelible part of human nature that connects all eras.

Wormser also tackles the philosophical. His formal and intellectual approach to a subject, which is very European, separates him from most of his contemporaries. The finely woven sonnet titled "Hegel and Co." is an example of Wormser's gift for shaping substantive material and filtering it through his imaginative lens so that the reader freshly perceives Georg Wilhelm Friedrich Hegel's awareness of his intellectual climate. Wormser seeks to re-create within the reader's mind the internal workings of the philosopher. Similarly, "Henry James," which ues a formal stanza, ponders the novelist's milieu.

Wormser is very much a poet of the human environment. Setting and circumstance provide him with particular images that in turn allow him to probe the emotional domain. "Piano Lessons" is the quintessential example of how Wormser uses quotidian human activity to elicit a profound sympathy for and a deep understanding of the human predicament. Here the pathos of a young boy who cannot play the piano and of his teacher who cannot escape her lonely situation manifests itself in the last couplet, when, as the boy recalls, teacher and student "walked into the room where the piano stood/ For all that we wanted to do yet never would."

GOOD TREMBLING

With his second volume, *Good Trembling*, Wormser extends this sympathy for being human by fusing it with a larger cultural relevance. His brief statement "Words to the Reader" implicitly conveys a deepening concern for human conduct. His poems become paradigms of sharing, and they reveal the meaning in people's lives by allowing them to sympathize with one another. Poetry functions to lead its readers to understanding about being human.

The narrow settings of place and time within each poem of this volume widen into the larger realm of history and culture. Wormser uses the concrete in order to contemplate these broad forces that continually sweep over individuals' lives. This type of sensibility, the ability to see the universal in the particular, reveals Wormser's brilliant capacity to capture the essence of human existence. Again, such a sensibility seems more European than American. Thus, "Shards," for example, moves beyond a description of the remnants of an old homestead to become a reflection on what drives people to act the way they do.

Wormser envisions the sweep of history as a landscape shaped by the conduct of individuals. "By-Products," taking place in a stale, eerily lit Legion Hall, exposes the outcome of United States foreign policy through a legless Vietnam veteran's words and behavior. When the veteran Stan vocalizes his feelings, the force of history becomes a personal drama, not an abstraction.

In such poems as "Tutorial on the Metaphysics of Foreign Policy," "Europe," and "The Fall of the Human Empire," Wormser turns his intellectual and philosophic gaze toward the circumstances of being American. These circumstances are viewed from various perspectives that range from musing on U.S. government policies to delineating how the remnant sensibility of Europe resides in a small New England town to using a run-over dog to symbolize how people, as individuals, fit into the scheme of civilization.

One particular poem in this volume skillfully addresses the abstract nature of history and civilization alongside the concrete nature of life at the moment when they meet head-on. "I Try to Explain to My Children a Newspaper Article Which Says That According to a Computer a Nuclear War Is Likely to Occur in the Next Twenty Years" uses the common, all-too-real situation of a parent explaining the idea of death (with a wonderful use of personification) to his children as a means to stress the higher concern of how humankind has surrendered the natural world to the vastly indifferent world of politics.

ATOMS, SOUL MUSIC, AND OTHER POEMS

Atoms, Soul Music, and Other Poems, Wormser's third collection, represents the poet at his most ambitious and most visionary. As he deftly observes contemporary dilemmas, he explores the large ideas of history and civilization in terms of humankind's spiritual capacity. For him, the quality of being human in the present age can be measured by the depth of one's connection to this spirituality. Merely the titles of a group of poems in the first section of the book—"Kitchen, 1952," "1967," "1968,'"1969," "Dropping Acid at Aunt Bea's and Uncle Harry's 40th Wedding Anniversary Celebration," and "Embracing a Cloud: Rural Commune, 1971"—suggest Wormser's sense of history as he contemplates life in twentieth century America. His chronicling of Americans' spiritual state extends across a range of modern experiences, including an Otis Redding and Aretha Franklin concert and an anniversary celebration at which one celebrant has taken a psychedelic drug. Nothing is trivialized in these portraits of modern life. Wormser's explorations probe the heart of Americans' daily rites. A fine example of this process is "Married Sex." Here the poet unmasks the psyche of people's sexual selves through a nimble portrait of passion in marriage—the web of familiarity that steals spontaneity even while it creates a ritualized joy in a couple's sexual encounters.

The long poem "Atoms" constitutes the second and final section of Wormser's third volume. Using the voices of several characters, Wormser ponders the trajectory of American culture by exploring the darker side of the covenant (an unspoken one) that every culture makes with death. "Atoms" exposes how nations are really at war with themselves and thus with their own people. Through the poem's characters, Wormser demonstrates how foolish it is to think that having a nuclear arsenal has prevented nuclear war. As he discusses politics in a postnuclear age, Wormser delves into the manner in which a culture conceives of evil. According to the poet, American society has colluded with evil and has thus made death an unnatural danger. This collusion conceals itself in the political and social orthodoxy of the present—an orthodoxy that, although couched cunningly in rationalism as well as sincerity, inevitably results in war, death, and subjugation.

The central characters of "Atoms" give flesh to this crisis of modernity. They are pilgrims on a journey, and they contain the fire of atoms. Airman Hawkins wonders about the world he inhabits, a stranger in a strange landscape. John Lennon rocks and rolls for peace, his own messy soul a sad prophecy. The clergyman grounds his protests in a faith smothered by an indifferent, purgatorial world. The bureaucrat Keats, "an underdeputy for Nuclear Security Policy," and his superior, Horace, exemplify the granite officiousness of government policy. Wormser's description and juxtaposition of the characters' inner lives evoke the turbulence of contemporary America's spiritual state.

"Atoms" transcends its political observations to become an examination of spiritual worthiness. Only through a significant repentance of the internal, volitional kind, along with the nurturing of conscience, will Americans rescue themselves, Wormser seems to say. Atonement and humility become the means that allow people to accomplish the noblest of tasks—finding and speaking the truth. Thus, "Atoms" is one of America's few truly religious poems.

The cumulative power of "Atoms," derived from the poet's ability to modulate gnomic utterances, is built up through an incantatory rhythm that gives it the structure of an extended prayer. By using tight lines of uncommon clarity, Wormser keeps this rhythm pulsing through the varied depictions of each pilgrim character. Sharp images of human activity (at times ridiculously trite and indifferent) are continually contrasted with images of the innate, organic energy of life within all people. This multilayered texture of "Atoms" serves to illuminate the general theme of how the salvation of any civilization is, finally, determined by the spiritual actions of its members.

WHEN

In *When*, whether in Las Vegas, Sun City, or driving a Ford in 1978 on "The Nuclear Bullet Tour," Wormser beholds the myth of America: a myth of contradictions, covenants, and prayers for the unruly middle class—but a myth "you'd be a fool to refuse." The collection is a mix of autobiography and storytelling that never forgets a basic writerly tenet: Locality is the only universality. Alice Fulton, who selected this volume for the Kathryn A. Morton Prize in 1996, commented that Wormser does not succumb to "the emotional gush and self-dramatization that characterize much contemporary poetry," a sentiment that testifies to his primary focus on the lives of others. Wormser hones in on specific details of his characters' actions, whether the subject is Beethoven's maid hearing strange sounds, a deli waiter bemoaning his work, or Wormser as a boy walking through Pikesville, Maryland, and imagining it to be Charles Baudelaire's Paris. However, the insights the characters achieve and the emotions they feel are universal: A trucker who "skidded the better part of a quarter-mile/ toward a stopped school bus/ . . . and he said he saw himself as a boy." There are also a handful of extremely sensitive portraits and testimonials that again focus on other lives: a young man dead of acquired immunodeficiency syndrome (AIDS), a Jew imagining that Dachau will be peaceful countryside. Taken together, the poems of *When* present a menagerie of wonderfully familiar strangers.

MULRONEY AND OTHERS

Mulroney and Others revisits Wormser's unique perspective on the world around him and again calls forth a universality of experience. The collection provides glimpses of Wormser's childhood, adolescence, and adulthood, as well as accounts of Vietnam veterans, draft dodgers, socialites, and outcasts. In "Fatality," there is the finality of ending, not just in poetic structure but also with the thought woven into the fabric of the poem: the suddenness of death, followed by the quiet aftermath when life picks up and continues. Wormser's invitation to engage in seeing is irresistible, especially as he models the process with such impassioned interest. His poems tempt the reader to trade the obscurity of facile assumption for the powerful illumination of wonder. In Wormser's words, the universe is irrefutably personal.

SUBJECT MATTER

Subject Matter presents a more inward and perplexed mental state than readers have become accustomed to seeing in Wormser. A sense of change and peril is in the air, and the buff discursiveness present in Wormser's earlier poems is here as a kind of reassuring backbeat determined to see the reader through the storm, not the directly appealing credo it had been in his works of the 1980's and 1990's. "Bankruptcy" lambastes the rich and indolent, tacitly linking them to the policies of then-President George W. Bush in what the poet perceives as their uncaring hedonism. Wormser's mood is angry here, filled with a *saeva indignatio* (righteous indignation) associated with eighteenth century satirists such as Jonathan Swift:

> The *condottieri* of money emblazon
> their glad handed chicanery on frail paper
> monumentalize their visions in acronyms

When these plutocrats go bankrupt, the poet frankly exults. Most likely written in response to the Enron and other corporate scandals of 2002, the poem retained its impact when read in the light of the economic near-collapse of 2008. Wormser's wrath permits him to employ more elevated diction than he usually does, as if he is confident that the purity of his spleen will safeguard him against any sense of pretension or showing off.

"Anecdotes" is the first poem in *Subject Matter*. It is a seemingly slight but ultimately subtle poem, which comes to terms with poetry's ability to marshal ordinary experience into meaning while realizing that this can often be a way to attribute a false unity or facile overall leaning to aspects of experience that are in themselves disparate and autonomous. Wormser, though, in a sense provides the answer to his own dilemma here, as poetry not only can stitch events together but also testify and delight in their radical singularity. It can provide an umbrella philosophy of life, but it can also delight in anarchy and randomness. Unlike faith, poetry both gives and takes away; its innate property is to do both. Comparable to "Poetry and Religion" (1987, by the Australian poet Les Murray) in its rigorous diagnosis of what poetry can and cannot offer, Wormser's poem steals up on the reader, transmogrifying itself from trifle to illumination.

Both sides of this equation continue to be canvassed in two subsequent poems in the volume, "Israel" and "Genius." In "Israel," two dogs fight while two old men quibble about God. A boy notes sophomorically that "dog" is "God" spelled backward. Reverence, irreverence, and animal insensibility are all part of the same experiential field. There is a sense that spirituality lies beyond an affirmation of an explicit credo: The same boy who jokes about God's name assures his mother that he regularly talks with God privately at night. Wormser suggests that if finite things are let be and are allowed to reside in their own place on the continuum, the infinite can somehow be solicited and an impasse of the merely finite can be evaded.

In "Genius," Wormser recalls the definition of "extravagant" as "extra-vagant," wandering beyond appointed limits, going outside boundaries. Modernist art prided itself on extravagance, furled both its rebellion and its latent spirituality in its self-heralding of its own aesthetic innovation. Recalling a visit to the Museum of Modern Art in New York, the poet looks with both appreciation and a layer of irony at the way the museum becomes a temple of art. Wormser is not entirely spoofing the high aspirations of the modernists. Indeed, he greatly honors them, but he realizes that, at times, modernism took itself too seriously and became the sort of absolutism it had earlier opposed.

"Anti-Depressant" has one of the most bracing openings of all of Wormser's poems.

> "What a pig happiness is. Plus
> I'm a body living with an anti-body
> You probably don't know how that goes
> One of my hang-ups is trying to tell you

The sense of inward dissatisfaction and psychological incongruity is unusual in a Wormser poem, as most of his poems' themes customarily address nature or history rather than the experience of the self. However, Wormser's jaunty jocularity, and his ever-overt awareness of even the most private poetry as a public speech act, carries the reader through as if on a conveyor belt:

> The pills tell me to let sincerity lapse
> I used to talk a blue streak but now
> I honor mute science as dryly as
> the next atheist . . .

This poem most likely does not reflect any personal experience taking antidepressants on Wormser's part nor is it a comment on their effect on eloquence—the taking of antidepressants is believed to have enabled the British poet Geoffrey Hill to compose his later work—but rather how the impulse to always be comfortable leads people to give up too much. Another aspect of the poem is that Wormser, often seen as more a poet of equilibrium than of affect, is reminding himself and his readers how important a virtue affect is to poetry; that even the most responsible poetry relinquishes affect at great peril. It may be ridiculous for the poet to cry at "ratty English sparrows" foraging in the hay, but if the poet does not do this nobody will. If people all prevent themselves from feeling because they fear suffering, there will be no poetry.

CARTHAGE AND SCATTERED CHAPTERS

Carthage was a series of satiric poems echoing some of the political themes of *Subject Matter*, but in a much lighter vein in its satire of a George W. Bush-like president. *Scattered Chapters* was largely a compilation of Wormser's previous few volumes, along with new poems that continued Wormser's characteristic mix of pasionate ferocity and discursive responsibility.

The promulgation and furtherance of poetry has been the mission of Wormser's poetic career. As teacher, as prose writer, and pivotally, as wise, confident poet, he has, over three decades, made a forceful and steady dedication of his talent to poetry—its nuances, its dangers, its sense of an earned grace—a remnant saved from the flux of experience.

OTHER MAJOR WORKS

SHORT FICTION: *The Poetry Life: Ten Stories*, 2008.

NONFICTION: *Teaching the Art of Poetry: The Moves*, 2000 (with David Cappella); *A Surge of Language: Teaching Poetry Day by Day*, 2004 (with Cappella); *The Road Washes Out in Spring: A Poet's Memoir of Living Off the Grid*, 2006.

BIBLIOGRAPHY

Birkerts, Sven. *The Electric Life: Essays on Modern Poetry*. New York: William Morrow, 1989. This wide-ranging book includes a condensed discussion of Wormser, connecting the poet's sense of place and occasion with his ability to enlarge on the particular. A solid overview of the poet that hints at his larger, spiritual themes and the complex subtleties of his thinking process.

Boruch, Marianne. "Comment: The Feel of a Century." *American Poetry Review* 19 (July/August, 1990): 18-19. Included in this lengthy review of several poets is a discussion of Wormser's *Atoms, Soul Music, and Other Poems*. Despite the brief treatment of the book, two major points are made about his long poem "Atoms": that it tackles American culture and that it exemplifies the poet's attempt to capture the private and specific in a public manner.

Briggs, Edwin. "Poet Shapes an Image That's Fresh and True." Review of *The White Words*. *The Boston Globe*, May 29, 1983, p. D3. This review gives a succinct account of Wormser's attitude toward language and of his use of tone and images to control the subject matter. It is an insightful glimpse into the poet's stance.

Finch, Robert. "'Living Inside a Poem': A Meditation About Twenty Years in the Maine Woods, Thinking Deliberately, Working Creatively." *Boston Globe*, November 19, 2006, p. R6. Underlines important similarities and differences between Wormser's valuation of the land and the simple life described by earlier American writers, especially Henry David Thoreau.

Johnson, Greg. "Essential Themes: Elegant Variations." *Georgia Review* 67, no. 9 (Summer, 2009): 336-344. Discusses *The Poetry Life*, critiquing what Johnson sees as its overly essayistic quality but also conceding that this was perhaps necessary to bring home Wormser's ideas about how poetry actually mattered to people.

Mesic, Penelope. Review of *The White Words*. *Poetry* 144 (February, 1984): 302-303. In a balanced look at the poet's first book, this terse yet praiseworthy review commends the poet's wit, technical skill, and use of details.

Wormser, Baron. "Populous Worlds of a Quiet Laureate." Interview by Sally Read. *South Dakota Review* 39, no. 2 (Summer, 2001): 121-122. This interview conducted during Wormser's tenure as a visiting professor at the University of South Dakota is a crucial one for understanding issues of voice, tone, and reference in Wormser's oeuvre.

David Cappella; Sarah Hilbert
Updated by Nicholas Birns

WILLIAM BUTLER YEATS

Born: Sandymount, near Dublin, Ireland; June 13, 1865
Died: Roquebrune-Cap-Martin, France; January 28, 1939

PRINCIPAL POETRY

Mosada: A Dramatic Poem, 1886
Crossways, 1889
The Wanderings of Oisin, and Other Poems, 1889
The Countess Kathleen and Various Legends and Lyrics, 1892
The Rose, 1893
The Wind Among the Reeds, 1899
In the Seven Woods, 1903
The Poetical Works of William B. Yeats, 1906, 1907 (2 volumes)
The Green Helmet, and Other Poems, 1910
Responsibilities, 1914
Responsibilities, and Other Poems, 1916
The Wild Swans at Coole, 1917, 1919
Michael Robartes and the Dancer, 1920
The Tower, 1928
Words for Music Perhaps, and Other Poems, 1932
The Winding Stair, and Other Poems, 1933
The Collected Poems of W. B. Yeats, 1933, 1950
The King of the Great Clock Tower, 1934
A Full Moon in March, 1935
Last Poems and Plays, 1940
The Poems of W. B. Yeats, 1949 (2 volumes)
The Collected Poems of W. B. Yeats, 1956
The Variorum Edition of the Poems of W. B. Yeats, 1957 (P. Allt and R. K.
    Alspach, editors)
The Poems, 1983
The Poems: A New Edition, 1984

OTHER LITERARY FORMS

William Butler Yeats (yayts) was a playwright as well as a poet. During certain periods in his career, he devoted more time and energy to the composition, publication, and production of plays in verse or prose than to the writing of nondramatic poetry. These plays, excluding several early closet dramas, were republished singly or in various collections from 1892 through the year of his death. *The Collected Plays of W. B. Yeats* was

William Butler Yeats
(©The Nobel Foundation)

published in 1934, and a "new edition with five additional plays" appeared in 1952 (London) and 1953 (New York), the former being the "basic text." The genuinely definitive publication, however, is the admirably edited *Variorum Edition of the Plays of W. B. Yeats* (1966).

In addition to poems and plays, Yeats published prolifically during the course of his life in almost every imaginable genre except the novel. Numerous prose tales, book reviews, nationalistic articles, letters to editors, and so on far exceeded poems and plays in volume in the early stages of Yeats's career. In 1908, *The Collected Works in Verse and Prose of William Butler Yeats*—including lyrics, narrative poems, stories, plays, essays, prefaces, and notes—filled eight volumes, of which only the first contained predominantly nondramatic poetry. Previously, stories and sketches, many of them based wholly or in part on Irish folk tales, had been collected in *The Celtic Twilight* (1893) and *The Secret Rose* (1897). Rewritten versions of those tales from *The Secret Rose* that featured a roving folk poet invented by Yeats were later published as *Stories of Red Hanrahan* (1904). Similarly, relatively formal critical and philosophical essays were collected and published as *Ideas of Good and Evil* (1903), *The Cutting of an Agate* (1912), and *Essays, 1931-1936* (1937).

A slender doctrinal book, *Per Amica Silentia Lunae* (1918), is generally regarded as something of a precursor to *A Vision* (1925). The first edition of *A Vision* itself, an exposition of Yeats's mystical philosophy, appeared in 1925. A considerably revised edition first published in 1937 has revealed to scholars that while the book unquestionably owes much to his wife's "automatic writing," as avowed, more than a little of its content is generally based on Yeats's or his and his wife's earlier occult interests and contacts. In 1926, Yeats published a volume titled *Autobiographies*. In 1938, an American edition titled *The Autobiography of William Butler Yeats* was released, with the addition of several sections or units that had been published separately or in groups in the interim. Then, in 1955 a final British issue appeared with the original title and one sub-unit not included in the American edition. A posthumous supplement to *Autobiographies* is *Memoirs* (1972), combining the draft of an earlier unpublished autobiography with a complete transcription of the private journal from which Yeats had used only selected portions in the post-1926 versions of his original book. A large and carefully edited collection of Yeats's correspondence, *The Letters of W. B. Yeats*, was published in 1954, and various smaller collections of correspondence with certain people have been published from time to time since the poet's death.

Most of Yeats's major prose, other than *A Vision*, *Autobiographies*, and his editor's introduction to *The Oxford Book of Modern Verse* (1936), has been collected and republished in three volumes printed simultaneously in London and New York. *Mythologies* (1959) includes *The Celtic Twilight*, *The Secret Rose*, *Stories of Red Hanrahan*, the three so-called Rosa Alchemica stories from 1897 (which involve Yeats's fictional personae Michael Robartes and Owen Aherne), and *Per Amica Silentia Lunae*. *Essays and Introductions* (1961) incorporates *Ideas of Good and Evil*, most of *The Cutting of an Agate*, *Essays, 1931-1936*, and three introductions written in 1937 for portions of a projected edition of Yeats's works that never materialized. *Explorations* (1962) brings together a number of miscellaneous items, most of them previously not readily accessible. There are three introductions to books of legend and folklore by Lady Augusta Gregory, introductions to some of Yeats's own plays, a sizable body of his early dramatic criticism, the essay "If I Were Four and Twenty," *Pages from a Diary Written in Nineteen Hundred and Thirty* (1944), and most of the author's last prose piece *On the Boiler* (1939), a potpourri including late political philosophy.

As to fiction not already mentioned, two stories from 1891—a long tale and a short novel—have been republished in a critical edition, *John Sherman and Dhoya* (1969), and a fine scholarly edition of Yeats's early unfinished novel, *The Speckled Bird* (published in a limited edition in Dublin in 1974), was printed in 1976 as an item in the short-lived *Yeats Studies* series. In another highly competent piece of scholarship, almost all the previously mentioned early book reviews, nationalist articles, and so on, as well as some later essays, have been edited and republished in *Uncollected Prose by W. B. Yeats*, Volume 1 in 1970 and Volume II in 1976. Finally, the bewildering mass of Yeats's unpublished materials—thousands of pages of working drafts, notebooks, proof sheets, personal and family letters and papers, occult documents, automatic scripts, and the like—were made available on microfilm by the poet's son, Senator Michael Yeats, in 1975. Two sets of these films are housed, one each, at the National Library of Ireland and the State University of New York at Stony Brook. With the generous permission of Yeats's daughter and son, Anna and Michael, scholars are currently studying, transcribing, and editing many of these materials. Several books that employ or reproduce portions of them have been published. Several volumes of Yeats's letters, *The Collected Letters of W. B. Yeats*, trace his life and poetic influences between the years 1865 and 1904. Most of the letters included are from Yeats's twenties, when he was passionately involved with furthering two causes: his own career and Irish literature as a whole.

ACHIEVEMENTS

William Butler Yeats is generally regarded as one of the major English-speaking poets of the "modern" era (approximately 1890 to 1950). Some authorities go even further, designating him the most important twentieth century poet in any language. Although in his late career and for some time thereafter, he was overshadowed by the poetic and critical stature of T. S. Eliot, in the years since Eliot's death, Yeats's reputation has continued to grow whereas Eliot's has declined. Like most modern poets, writing in a period labeled the age of the novel, Yeats has been relatively obscure and inaccessible to the general reader, but among academicians his eminence has flourished, and, even more significant, his influence on other poets has been both broad and deep.

Even though he was never very robust, suffering from chronic respiratory problems and extremely poor eyesight throughout much of his adult life, Yeats lived a long, productive, and remarkably multifaceted life. How one person could have been as completely immersed in as many different kinds of activity as he was is difficult to conceive. Throughout his life, he was involved in occult pursuits and interests of one kind or another, a preoccupation that has long been considered by many authorities (especially early ones) as more an impediment than a contribution to his literary career. Of more "legitimate" significance, he was, with a handful of associates, a leading figure in the initiation of the related movements that have come to be known as the Irish Renaissance and the Celtic Revival. Especially as a cofounder and codirector of the Irish National Theatre—later the famous Abbey Theatre—he was at the center of the literary movement, even aside from his prolific publication of poems, plays, essays, and reviews and the editorship of his sisters' artistically oriented Cuala Press. Moreover, between 1903 and 1932, Yeats conducted or participated in a series of five theater or lecture tours in America, thereby enhancing his renown in English-speaking countries on both sides of the Atlantic.

Major expressions of national and international recognition for such endeavors and achievements were forthcoming in the last decades of Yeats's life in such forms as honorary degrees from Queen's University (Belfast) and Trinity College (Dublin) in 1922, Oxford University in 1931, and Cambridge University in 1933; appointment as senator for the newly established Irish Free State in 1922; and, most gratifying of all, the Nobel Prize in Literature in 1923. Furthermore, in 1935 Yeats was designated editor of the *Oxford Book of Modern Verse*, having declined previously an offer of knighthood in 1915 and an invitation to lecture in Japan in 1919. From young manhood, Yeats had lived and played out the role of the poet in society, gesturing, posing, and dressing for the part. In middle years and old age, he experienced genuine fulfillment of his dream and enjoyed self-realization as "the great man" of Anglo-Irish literature within his own lifetime.

Yeats's greatest accomplishment, however, was the achievement, in both his life and his work, of an astonishing singleness or oneness in the midst of myriad activities. Driven by an obsessive precept that he labeled "Unity of Being," he strove unceasingly to "hammer" his thoughts into "unity." Though never a masterful thinker in terms of logic or ratiocination, Yeats possessed unequivocal genius of the kind recognized by today's psychologists as imaginative or creative, if not visionary. In addition to an almost infallible gift for the precisely right word or phrase, he had a mind awesomely capacious in its ability to conceive and sustain complexly interwoven structures of symbolic suggestion, mythic significance, and allusive associations. He used these abilities to link poems to plays, and oeuvre to a self-consciously dramatic life, which was itself hardly other than a supremely sculpted *objet d'art*. By the time of his death at the age of seventy-three, Yeats had so completely interfused national interests, philosophical convictions, theories of symbolic art, and mythopoeic techniques of literary composition that he had indeed fulfilled his lifelong quest to master experience by wresting unity from multiplicity, achieving an intricately wrought identity of life and work in the midst of almost unimaginably manifold diversity.

BIOGRAPHY

The eldest son of an eldest son of an eldest son, William Butler Yeats was born on June 13, 1865, in Sandymount, Ireland, a small community on the outskirts of Dublin that has since been absorbed by that sprawling metropolis. His father, paternal grandfather, and great-grandfather Yeats were all graduates of Trinity College, Dublin, but only his father, John Butler Yeats, had begun his postcollegiate career in the city where he had studied. Both the great-grandfather and the grandfather had been clergymen of the Protestant Church of Ireland, the latter in county Down, near Northern Ireland, and the former at Drumcliff, near the west-Irish port town of Sligo, with which the poet is so thoroughly identified.

The reason for the identification with Sligo is that John Butler Yeats married the sister of his closest collegiate schoolmate, George Pollexfen, whose family lived in Sligo. Dissatisfied with the courts as a fledgling barrister, J. B. Yeats abandoned law and Dublin to follow in London his inclinations as a graphic artist in sketches and oils. The combination of limited finances and his wife's dislike of urban life resulted in numerous extended visits by her and the growing family of children back to Sligo at the home of the poet's maternal grandfather, a sea captain and partner in a shipping firm. Thus, Yeats's ancestral line doubled back on itself in a sense. In the Sligo area, he became acquainted with Yeats descendants of the Drumcliff rector, and in memory and imagination the west-Irish valley between the mountains Ben Bulben and Knocknarea was always his spiritual home.

Yeats's formal education was irregular, at best. His earliest training was in London at the hand of his father, who read to him from English authors such as Sir Walter Scott and William Shakespeare. He did not distinguish himself at his first school in London or at Erasmus High School when the family returned to Dublin in 1880. Declining to matriculate at Trinity in the tradition of his forebears, he took up studies instead at the Metropolitan School of Art, where he met George Russell (later Æ), who was to become a lifelong close acquaintance. Yeats soon found that his interests inclined more toward the verbal arts than toward the visual, however, and by 1885, he had discontinued his studies in painting and had published some poems. At this same relatively early time, he had also become involved in occult interests, being among the founders of the Dublin Hermetic Society.

In 1887, the family returned to London, where Yeats was briefly involved with the famous Madame Blavatsky's Theosophical Society. The years 1889 to 1892 were some of the most important in this crucially formative period of his life. He was active in the many diverse areas of interest that were to shape and color the remainder of his career. In rapid succession, he became a founding member of the Rhymers Club (a young group of Pateresque fin de siècle aesthetes) and of the Irish Literary Society of London and the Irish Literary Society of Dublin (both devoted to reviving interest in native Irish writers and writing). He also joined the newly established Hermetic Order of the Golden Dawn, a Rosicrucian secret society in which he became an active leader for a number of years and of which he remained a member for more than two decades. In 1889, Yeats published *The Wanderings of Oisin, and Other Poems* and became coeditor of an edition of William Blake's work, an experience that was to influence greatly much of his subsequent thought and writing. No event in this period, however, had a more dramatic and permanent effect on the rest of his life than his introduction in the same year to Maud Gonne, that "great beauty" of Ireland with whom Yeats fell immediately and hopelessly in love. The love was largely unrequited, although Maud allowed the one-sided relationship to continue for a painfully long time throughout much of the poet's early adult life—in fact, even after her marriage and widowhood.

From this point on, Yeats's life was a whirlwind of literary, nationalistic, and occult activity. In 1896, he met Lady Augusta Gregory and John Millington Synge, with both of whom he was later to be associated in the leadership of the Abbey Theatre, as well as in investigation of the folklore and ethos of west-Irish peasants. The purpose of the Abbey Theatre, as far as these three were concerned, was to produce plays that combined Irish interests with artistic literary merit. The acquaintance with Lady Gregory also initiated a long series of summer visits at her estate in Coole Park, Galway, where his aristocratic inclinations, as well as his frequently frail physical being, were nurtured. During parts of 1895 and 1896, Yeats shared lodgings in London briefly with Arthur Symons, of the Rhymers Club, who, as author of *The Symbolist Movement in Literature* (1899), helped to acquaint him further with the French Symbolist mode. Actually, however, through his intimate relationships with Hermetic lore and the English Romantics—especially Blake and Percy Bysshe Shelley—Yeats was already writing poetry in a manner much like that of his continental contemporaries. Later in 1896, Yeats moved in to 18 Woburn Buildings, Dublin, which came to be his permanent residence, except for rather frequent travels abroad, for an extended period.

At about the turn of the century and just after, Yeats abandoned his Pre-Raphaelite aestheticism and adopted a more "manful" style. Not wholly unrelated to this was his more outgoing involvement in the daily affairs of the nationalist theater movement. The fact should be remembered—for it is easy to forget—that at this time Yeats was in his late thirties, already moving into a somewhat premature middle age. In 1909 he met Ezra Pound, the only other major figure in the modernist movement with whom he was ever to develop an acquaintance to the point of literary interaction and influence. The relationship reached its apex in the years from 1912 to 1915, during which Pound criticized Yeats's romantic tendencies and, perhaps more important, encouraged the older poet's interest in the highly stylized and ritualistic Nō drama of Japan.

In the same years, another important aspect of Yeats's life and interests had been developing in new directions as well. Beginning about 1908-1909, his esoteric pursuits shifted from active involvement in the Order of the Golden Dawn to investigations in spiritism, séances, and "psychical research." This preoccupation continued until 1915 or 1916, at which point some biographers seem to indicate that it ended. Yet, in one sense, spiritism as an obsessive concern simply redoubled itself about this time on the occasion of Yeats's late-life marriage, for his wife turned out to be the "mystic" *par excellence*, through whose mediumship came the ultimate flowering of his lifelong prepossession with occult aspects of human—and superhuman—experience.

After Maud Gonne MacBride's husband was executed for his participation in Dublin's 1916 Easter uprising, Yeats visited Maud in Paris and proposed to her, only to be rejected as on previous occasions years before. He then became attracted to her daughter Iseult and proposed to her in turn. Once again rejected, he decided to marry an English woman whom he had known in occult circles for some years and who was a close friend of mutual acquaintances—Georgie Hyde-Less. On their honeymoon in 1917, Georgie began to experience the first of what came to be a voluminous and almost literally fantastic collection of "automatic writings," the basis of Yeats's famous mystic system, as elaborated in his book *A Vision*.

The various honors that Yeats received in the 1920's and 1930's have been outlined already under "Achievements." Ironically, from these same years, not earlier ones, came most of the poems and collections by which his importance as a major modern literary figure is to be measured. Two interrelated experiences were very likely the chief contributors to the newfound vigor, imagery, and stylistic devices characteristic of these late works—his marriage and the completion of his mystic system in *A Vision*. The nature and degree of indebtedness to the latter of these influences, however, has often been both misunderstood and overestimated. The connection can probably never be assessed with complete accuracy, whereas various other possible factors, such as his renewed interest in the writings of John Donne and Jonathan Swift, should not be ignored or minimized.

In 1926 and 1927, Yeats's health became a genuinely serious problem, and at times in the last dozen years of his life, to live seemed to him to be almost more difficult than to die. There can be little question that such prolonged confrontation with that ultimate of all human experiences is responsible for some of the combined profundity, choler, and—paradoxically—wit of his last poems and plays. During this period, winters were usually spent in various Mediterranean locales for climatic reasons. Death eventually came in the south of France in January, 1939. With characteristic doggedness, Yeats continued working to the very end; he wrote his last poem only a week before his death and dictated to his wife some revisions of a late poem and his last play after the onset of his final illness, only two days before he died. Because of transportation difficulties at the beginning of World War II, Yeats was initially buried at Roquebrune, France. His body was exhumed in 1948, however, and transported aboard an Irish corvette for reburial at Drumcliff Churchyard, as he had specified at the end of his valedictory poem, "Under Ben Bulben." As his friend and fellow author Frank O'Connor said on the occasion, that event brought to its appropriate and symbolic conclusion a life that was itself a work of art long planned.

ANALYSIS

The complexity and fullness of William Butler Yeats's life was more than matched by the complexity and fullness of his imaginative thought. There are few poets writing in English whose works are more difficult to understand or explain. The basic problems lie in the multiplicity and intricacies of Yeats's own preoccupations and poetic techniques, and all too often the reader has been hindered more than helped by the vagaries of criticism and exegesis.

A coincidence of literary history is partly responsible for the latter problem. The culmination and conclusion of Yeats's career coincided with the advent of the New Criticism. Thus, in the decades following his death, some of his most important poems became exercise pieces for "explication" by commentators whose theories insisted on a minimum of attention to the author's cultural background, philosophical views, personal interests, or even thematic intentions (hence their odd-sounding term "intentional fallacy"). The consequence has been critical chaos. There simply are no generally accepted readings for some of Yeats's major poems. Instead, there have been ingenious exegeses, charges of misapprehension, countercharges, alternative analyses, then the whole cycle starting over again—in short, interpretational warfare.

Fortunately, in more recent years, simultaneously with decline of the New Critical movement, there has been increasing access to Yeats's unpublished materials—letters, diaries, and especially the manuscript drafts of poems and plays—and more scholarly attention has been paid to the relationships between such materials and the probable themes or meanings in the completed works. Even so, critical difficulties of no small magnitude remain because of continuing widespread disagreement among even the most highly regarded authorities about the basic metaphysical vision from which Yeats's poetic utterances spring, variously interpreted as atheism, pagan theism, quasi-Christian theism, Theosophy, sheer aestheticism, Platonic dualism, modern humanist monism, and existentialism.

SHIFTING PHILOSOPHIES

Added to the problems created by such a critical reception are those deriving from Yeats's qualities as an imaginative writer. Probably the most obvious source of difficulty is the highly allusive and subtly symbolic mode in which Yeats so often expressed himself. Clearly another is his lifelong practice of infusing many of his poems and plays with elements of doctrine, belief, or supposed belief from the various occult sources with which he was so thoroughly imbued. Furthermore, as to doctrine or belief, Yeats was constantly either apparently or actually shifting his ground (more apparently than actually). Two of his better-known poems, for example, are appropriately titled "Vacillation" and "A Dialogue of Self and Soul." In these and numerous others, he develops and sustains a running debate between two sides of an issue or between two sides of his own truth-seeking psyche, often with no clear-cut solution or final stance made unequivocally apparent.

Related to this—but not simply the same—is the fact that Yeats tended to change philosophical or metaphysical views throughout a long career, again either actually or apparently, and, also again, sometimes more apparently than actually. One disquieting and obfuscating consequence of such mental habits is that one poem will sometimes seem flatly to contradict another, or, in some cases even aside from the dialogue poems, one part of a given poem may appear to contradict a different part of the same poem. Adjacent passages in the major piece "The Tower," involving apparent rejection of Plato and Plotinus alongside apparent acceptance of Platonic or Neoplatonic reincarnation and "translunar paradise," constitute a case in point.

To quibble at much length about Yeats's prevailing metaphysical vision is to indulge in delusive sophistry, however, if his more than moderate pronouncements on such matters in prose are taken at anything approaching face value. What emerges from the prose is the virtually unequivocal proposition that—having rejected orthodox Christianity—

the poet developed his own theistic "religion." His ontology and cosmology are made from many pieces and parts of that almost unimaginably multiplex body of lore—exoteric and esoteric—sometimes referred to as the *philosophia perennis*: Platonism, Neoplatonism, Hermetic symbolism, spiritual alchemy, Rosicrucianism, and certain elements of cabalism. Moreover, as Yeats stated in several essays, he found still further parallel and supporting materials at almost every turn—in Jakob Boehme, Emanuel Swedenborg, and William Blake; in the folklore of the Irish peasantry; in classical mythology, Irish legends, and the seasonal rituals examined by Sir James George Frazer; and in Asian religions, among other places. In two different senses Yeats found in all these materials convincing bases for the perpetuation of his obsession with extracting unity from multiplicity. For one thing, all the similarities and parallels in theme and motif from the many diverse sources constituted in themselves a kind of unity within multiplicity. Furthermore, the "philosophies" involved were largely oriented toward oneness—Plato's idea of the good, alchemy's distillation of the immutable *lapis* from the world of flux, Hermetism's theory of symbolic correspondences (as above, so below), Hinduism's Brahma, and so on.

In both thought and work, however, the unresolved opposites sometimes seem to loom as large as—or even larger than—the union itself. From this context came the so-called doctrine of the mask or anti-self (though not actually wholly original with Yeats). From that in turn, or alongside it, came the concept of the daimon, "guardian genius," or minor deity for each human being, a concept fundamental to a number of the traditional sources already cited. The greatest of all possible unions, of course, was the ultimate one of human beings with God, natural with supernatural, or temporal with eternal. Because of the *scintilla* principle, however, also inherent in parts of the tradition (the universe's permeation with tiny fragments of the godhead), the union of human being and daimon became virtually equivalent to the ultimate divine union. This concept helps to explain a handful of otherwise misleading passages where Yeats occasionally seemed to be rejecting his usually dominant dualism for a momentary monism: For example, in "The Tower," man creates everything in the universe from his own soul, and in "Two Songs from a Play" whatever illuminates the darkness is from man's own heart. Such human wholeness and power, however, are not possible, Yeats would probably say, without communion with daimon.

In spirit, doctrine, or belief, then, Yeats remained preponderantly a romantic and a nineteenth century spiritualist as he lived on into the increasingly positivistic and empirically oriented twentieth century. It was in form, not content, that he gradually allowed himself to develop in keeping with his times, although he abjured *vers libre* and never wholly relinquished his attachment to various traditional poetic modes. In the direction of modernism, he adopted or employed at various times irregular rhythms (writing by ear, declaring his ignorance of the technicalities of conventional metrics), approximate rhymes, colloquial diction, some Donnean or "metaphysical" qualities, and, most important of all, symbolic techniques much like those of the French movement, though not from its influence alone. The inimitable Yeatsian hallmark, however, remained a certain romantic rhetorical quality (despite his own fulminations against rhetoric), what he called passionate syntax, that remarkable gift for just the right turn of phrase to express ecstatic emotional intensity or to describe impassioned heroic action.

To suggest that Yeats consistently achieved great poetry through various combinations of these thematic elements and stylistic devices, however, would be less than forthright. Sometimes doctrinal materials are indeed impediments. Sometimes other aspects of content are unduly personal or sentimental. At times the technical components seem to be ill-chosen or fail to function as might have been expected, individually or conjointly. Thoroughly capable of writing bad poetry, Yeats has by no means been without his detractors. The poems for which he is famous, however—even those which present difficulties of understanding—are masterpieces, alchemical transformations of the raw material of his art.

"The Lake Isle of Innisfree"

Probably the most famous of all Yeats's poems, especially from his early period and with popular audiences, is "The Lake Isle of Innisfree." A modern, middle-income Dublin homemaker, chosen at random, has said on mention of Yeats's name: "Oh, yes; I like his 'Lake Isle of Innisfree'; yes, I always did like 'The Lake Isle of Innisfree.'" Such popularity, as well as its representative quality among Yeats's early poems, makes the piece a natural choice for initial consideration here.

On the surface, there seems to be little that is symbolic or difficult about this brief lyric, first published in 1890. The wavering rhythms, syntactical inversions, and colorful but sometimes hazy images are characteristic of much of Yeats's youthful verse. So too are the Romantic tone and setting, and the underlying "escape motif," a thematic element or pattern that pervades much of Yeats's early work, as he himself realized and acknowledged in a letter to a friend.

The island of the title—real, not imaginary—is located in Lough Gill near the Sligo of Yeats's youth. More than once he mentioned in prose a boyish dream of living on the wooded isle much as Henry David Thoreau lived at Walden Pond, seeking wisdom in solitude. In other passages, he indicates that while homesick in London he heard the sound of a small fountain in the window of a shop. The experience recalled Lough Gill's lapping waters, he says, and inspired him to write the poem. The most important factor for Yeats's emerging poetic vision, however, was his long-standing fascination with a legend about a supernatural tree that once grew on the island with berries that were food for the Irish fairy folk. Thus in the poet's imaginative thought, if not explicitly in the poem itself, esoteric or occult forces were at play, and in a figurative sense, at least, the escape involved was, in the words of the letter to his friend, "to fairyland," or a place much like it.

One of the most notable sources of praise for "The Lake Isle of Innisfree" was a letter from Robert Louis Stevenson in distant Samoa. Stevenson wrote that only two other passages of literature had ever captivated him as Yeats's poem did. Yeats himself said later that it was the earliest of his nonnarrative poems whose rhythms significantly manifested his own music. He ultimately developed negative feelings, however, about his autobiographical sentimentality and about instances of what he came to consider unduly artificial syntax. Yet in late life when he was invited to recite some of his own poems for radio programs, he more than once chose to include "The Lake Isle of Innisfree." Evidently he wished to offer to that audience what he felt it probably wanted to hear. Evidently he realized that the average Irish homemaker or ordinary working man, then as later, would say in response to the name Yeats: "Oh, yes, I like his 'Lake Isle of Innisfree.'"

"LEDA AND THE SWAN"

Technically, "Leda and the Swan" (1923) is a sonnet, one of only a few that Yeats ever composed. The spaces between quatrains in the octave and between the octave and the sestet—not to mention the break in line eleven—are evidently Yeats's innovations, characteristic of his inclination toward experimentation within traditional frameworks in the period of the poem's composition. The story from Greek mythology on which the poem is based is well known and much treated in the Western tradition. In the tale from antiquity, a Spartan queen, Leda, was so beautiful that Zeus, ruler of the gods, decided that he must have her. Since the immortals usually did not present themselves to humankind in their divine forms, Zeus changed himself into a great swan and in that shape ravished the helpless girl. The story has often been portrayed pictorially as well as verbally; Yeats himself possessed a copy of a copy of Michelangelo's lost painting on the subject. There has been considerable critical discussion of the degree of interrelationship between the picture or other graphic depictions and Yeats's poem, but to no very certain conclusion, except that Leda seems much less terrified in Michelangelo's visual version—where perhaps she might even seem to be somewhat receptive—than in Yeats's verbal one.

The poem has been one of Yeats's most widely praised pieces from the time of early critical commentaries in the first decade after his death. Virtually all commentators dwell on the power, economy, and impact of the poem's language and imagery, especially in the opening sections, which seem to be concerned predominantly, if not exclusively, with mere depiction of the scene and events themselves. The poem's apparent simplicity, especially by Yeatsian standards, however, is decidedly deceptive. The greatest problem in interpretation is with the sestet's images of Troy in flames and with Agamemnon's death.

To understand the importance of these allusions to Greek history—and the deeper meanings of the poem—the reader must realize that Yeats intended the poem to represent the annunciation of a new era of civilization in his cyclic vision of history, the two-thousand-year-period of pagan polytheism that preceded the present age of Christian monotheism. As emphasized in Giorgio Melchiori's book *The Whole Mystery of Art* (1961), the poet later imaginatively balanced a second poem against "Leda and the Swan": "The Mother of God," in which another woman, Mary, is visited by another deity, the Holy Ghost, in the form of another bird, the divine dove, to initiate another period of history, the Christian era. The conscious intention of such a parallel between the two poems is attested by Yeats's having printed "Leda and the Swan" at the head of the chapter in *A Vision* titled "Dove or Swan," with a sentence on the next page stating explicitly that he thought of the annunciation that began Grecian culture as having been made to Leda. Equally unequivocal evidences are Melchiori's citation of a letter in which Yeats called the poem a classic annunciation, Yeats's note for the poem that speaks of a violent annunciation, and the fact that the poem's first submission to a publisher was under the title "Annunciation."

This last-mentioned fact relates to another point of critical disagreement. In a note, Yeats says that the poem was written in response to a request from the editor of a political review. As he worked, though, the girl and the swan took over the scene, he says, and all politics fell away. Some commentators have accepted or reaffirmed this assertion, failing to realize that Yeats—intentionally or unintentionally—overstated the case. Bird and woman did indeed so dominate the poet's imagination in the first eight lines that one critical consequence has been undue attention to the language and imagery of the surface there. When one recalls, however, that the pre-Christian era in Yeats's system was governmentally monarchical or totalitarian while the present era was imagined (however erroneously) as predominantly democratic, the perception dawns that the affairs of Leda's progeny, especially Helen as a causal factor in the Trojan war and Clytemnestra as a figure involved in its aftermath, constitute, in truth, "politics" enough. Otherwise, the allusions to the burning city and deceased king would be gratuitous deadwood in the poem, unaccountable anomalies, which is just exactly what they remain in those analyses that disregard them or minimize their importance.

Even recognition and acceptance of the themes of annunciation and history do not reveal the poem's full complexity, however, as the average reader may well sense on perusal of the final interrogative sentence. This concluding question seems to constitute a third unit in the piece, as well as the basis of some third level of significance. The traditional octave-sestet relationship of the Italian sonnet created for Yeats a division into two parts with two different but related emphases. It is his unconventional break in line 11, however, which achieves a tripartite structure at the same time that it introduces the thematic bases for an amalgamating—if not resolving—unity for all three parts of the poem and for all their interrelated levels of symbolic implication.

If the octave can be said to focus predominantly on the "surface" level of "Leda and the Swan," with the allusions to antiquity adumbrating a historical level, then the final question—a real one rather than the rhetorical sort with which Yeats sometimes concluded poems—can be seen as the introduction of a philosophical or metaphysical level. Given the possibility of such consort or interaction between the human and the divine, what supernatural effects—if any—are consequent for the mortal party? This issue, so relevant to the rest of this poem, is raised not only here or a few times in related pieces like "The Mother of God," but rather over and over again throughout the entirety of Yeats's canon. More than that, it is frequently voiced in those other places in surprisingly similar terms.

SEEKING A TRANSCENDENT UNION

The possibility of union between humankind and God, between natural and supernatural, is probably the most persistent and pervasive theme in all of Yeats's oeuvre. It is the strongest of those threads woven throughout the fabric of his work that create the unity within multiplicity previously considered. It was also unquestionably the motivating factor in his relentlessly moving from one occult preoccupation to the other. Moreover, the conviction that artistic inspiration was one of the more readily observable manifestations of such divine visitation on the human sensibility was what made Yeats philosophically a confessed Romantic for life, regardless of what modernist elements of style or technique he may have allowed to emerge in the poetry of his later years.

A major emblem for such miraculous converse, elsewhere in Yeats just as in "Leda and the Swan," is sexual union. In several prose passages, for example, he draws explicit parallels between human interaction with the daimon or semidivine guardian spirit and a man's relationship with his sweetheart or lover. In another place, he conjectures that the "mystic way" and physical love are comparable, which is not surprising in the light of the fact that most of his occult sources employed the same analogy and frequently spoke of the moment of union—mortal with immortal—as the "mystic marriage." Yeats's utilization of this particular sexual symbology is apparent in pieces such as "Solomon and the Witch," "A Last Confession," "Chosen," and *The Player Queen*, among others. Equally relevant is the fact that Yeats repeatedly used birds as symbols of discarnate spirits or deities. Finally, the two motifs—sexual union as an analogue for supernatural union and avian symbolism for the divine—occur together in at least two works by Yeats other than "Leda and the Swan": the plays *At the Hawk's Well* (pr. 1916) and *The Herne's Egg* (pb. 1938), in the latter of which, copulation between a woman and a great white bird is similarly fundamental to the piece's philosophical implications.

In Yeats's imaginative thought, such moments of transcendent union leave behind in the physical world some vestige of the divine condescension—the art object's "immortality" in the case of inspiration, for example. In more portentous instances, however, such as those imaged in "Leda and the Swan" and "The Mother of God"—with clear metaphorical interplay between the phenomena of creation and procreation, even if not voiced in so many words—the remnant is the conception of some demigod or incarnate divinity such as Helen or Christ, whose beauty, perfection, or power is so great that its presence on earth inaugurates a whole new cultural dispensation.

What one ultimately finds in "Leda and the Swan," then, is Yeats hammering out, in the midst of manifold antinomy, two kinds of unity at a single stroke. The three somewhat separate parts of the poem are joined in unity with one another, and, simultaneously, the poem as a unified whole is united to some of the most important themes that recur throughout his canon. This unity within multiplicity is achieved through Yeats's ingeniously imaginative manipulation of a single famous myth chosen from many that involve—either or both—godhead manifested in avian form and divine visitation on humankind cast in the image of sexual conjugation.

"THE SECOND COMING"

Almost as synonymous with Yeats's name as "The Lake Isle of Innisfree" is the unusual and foreboding poem "The Second Coming," which was composed in January, 1919, and first published in 1920. It is one of Yeats's few unrhymed poems, written in very irregular blank verse whose rhythms perhaps contribute to the ominous effect created by the diction and imagery. The piece has had a strange critical reception, deriving in part from the paradox that it is one of Yeats's works most directly related to the system of history in *A Vision*, but at the same time appears to offer reasonably accessible meanings of a significant kind to the average reader of poetry in English.

The more obvious "meanings," generally agreed on, are implications of disorder, especially in the first section, in which the falcon has lost touch with the falconer, and impressions of horror, especially in the second section, with its vision of the pitiless rough beast slouching through the desert. In the light of the date of composition, the validity of such thematic elements for both Yeats and his audience is immediately evident. World War I had just ended, leaving the Western world in that continuing mood of despondency voiced also in T. S. Eliot's *The Waste Land* (1922) (which shares with Yeats's poem the desert image) and in Gertrude Stein's—and Ernest Hemingway's—epithet of "a lost generation." In other words, despite the author's considerable further concerns, the piece on this level "caught a wave," as it were, so that it quickly came to be regarded by commentators and the author alike as prophetic—an attitude enhanced, of course, by the richly allusive title.

HISTORY AS SPIRAL

On a deeper level, "The Second Coming" is directly related to the cyclical conception of history that Yeats delineated in *A Vision*. As seen in the discussion of "Leda and the Swan," Yeats envisioned history in terms of two-thousand-year eras, each of which was ushered in by a portentous annunciation of some sort. If Zeus's descent on Leda initiated the period from about 2000 B.C.E. to the year zero, and if the Holy Ghost's descent to Mary initiated the subsequent period from the year zero to approximately 2000 C.E., then in 1919, the poet could speculate that the next such annunciation might occur either just barely within his lifetime or else not very long thereafter. These two-thousand-year periods of culture were characterized, like so many other things in Yeats's imaginative thought, by opposition to each other, with the main oppositions in *A Vision* designated as antithetical (or "subjective") and primary (or "objective"). These labels, or tinctures as Yeats called them, are not always easy to define, but from reading *A Vision* one begins to sense their nature. In general, theantithetical is individualistic (self-centered), heroic, aristocratic, emotional, and aesthetic. It is concerned predominantly with inner being and is symbolized by a full moon. The primary, by contrast, is anti-individualistic (mass-oriented), saintly or sagelike, democratic, rational, and moral. It is associated mainly with external existence and is symbolized by either the sun or the dark of the moon. Yeats identified himself with the antithetical and associated many things that he disliked (such as democracy and "fact-finding" science) with the primary. Thus he favored the polytheistic era of Homeric and classical Greece (antithetical), whereas he rejected or spurned the moral and anti-individualistic monotheism (primary) which began with the birth of Christ.

Borrowing from Swedenborg and other esoteric sources, Yeats conceptualized the growth of these historical movements in terms of gyres or spirals, a feature of the system rather difficult to discuss without reference to diagrams. (One may see *A Vision* for diagrams in great sufficiency.) For the sake of convenience in depiction, the spirals (widening from vertex in larger and larger circles) are imaged as the outer "shells" surrounding them—that is, as cones. Furthermore, for purposes of two-dimensional representation on a book's page, each cone is usually regarded simply in terms of its profile—that is, as a triangle. However, since the entire system of *A Vision* is based on the proposition that the universe consists of numberless pairs of antinomies or contraries, no cone or triangle exists in isolation; instead, everyone is in locked interpenetration with an opposing cone or triangle, each with its vertex or narrowest point at the center of the other's widest expansion or base. Thus, Yeats conceived of the present two-thousand-year era not simply as one set of interlocked cones, but rather as two sets of one thousand years each, as is made quite explicit in the chapter that reviews history under the title "Dove or Swan." Thus, instead of the Christian gyre or cone sweeping outward toward its widest expansion at the year 2000 C.E., as most commentators seem to have assumed, the widest expansion of the triangle representing that primary religious dispensation occurred at about the year 1000 C.E., completely in keeping with the medieval Church's domination of virtually all aspects of life at that time. For the period following 1000 C.E., that religion's declining movement is represented by a contracting gyre, its base set against the base of its predecessor, forming, in two-dimensional terms, a figure that Yeats speaks of as shaped like an ace of diamonds. The Christian dispensation, then, is at dwindling to its cone's or triangle's narrowest point, at the center of the opposing gyre's widest expansion, completely in keeping with the post-Darwinian upheaval in Victorian England about science's undermining the foundations of the Church, subsequent notions of the "death of God," and so on.

What, then, is spiraling outward to its widest expansion in the twentieth century, the falcon's gyring flight having swept so far from the falconer that "the centre cannot hold"? The answer to this question lies in recognition of a point that appears rather clearly at various places in *A Vision*. In Yeats's system of history, every cone representing a religious dispensation has as its interlocking counterpart a cone that represents the secular culture of the same period. Thus, the two movements, religious and secular, live each other's death and die each other's life, to use an expression from Heraclitus that Yeats repeated time and again, in creative pieces as well as in his discursive prose. The birth of Christ came, then, as Yeats indicates with unequivocal clarity, at the time of an antithetical secular or political phenomenon at the very height of its development, at the widest expansion of its cone—the Roman Empire. As the gyre representing the primary Christian religious movement revolved outward toward its widest expansion in the Middle Ages, the power of the Roman Empire gradually declined until it vanished at about 1000 C.E. (Yeats uses the year 1050 in "Dove or Swan"). Then both movements reversed directions, with primary Christianity beginning to dwindle at the same time that a new secular life of antithetical nature started and gyred outward up to the present day. This—the widest expansion of an antithetical secular or political gyre in the twentieth century—is almost certainly what Yeats identified with fascism, not the new annunciation to come. Such a collapsing and reexpansion of the antithetical spirals in the two-thousand-year period since the birth of Christ—two one-thousand-year cones tip to tip—created what Yeats called an hourglass figure superimposed on (or, more accurately, interlocked with) the diamond shape of Christianity's primary religious dispensation.

TINCTURES

The crucial point in interpreting "The Second Coming" is that the annunciation of every new religious dispensation involves what Yeats calls an interchange of the tinctures. In other words, at 2000 B.C.E., at the year zero, and at 2000 C.E., religion changes from primary to antithetical in quality, or vice versa, while secular life and politics change tinctures just oppositely. (Yeats was explicit about identification of the secular with politics.) No such interchange occurs, however, at the initiation of new secular gyres, as at 1000 B.C.E. or 1000 C.E. At those points the expanding or collapsing gyres of both aspects of life—religious and secular—simply reverse directions without their tinctures changing from primary to antithetical or the other way around. The importance of this feature of the system for meanings in "The Second Coming" can hardly be over-stated. The interchange is sudden and cataclysmic, causing such strife in human history as the Trojan War soon after the annunciation to Leda from Zeus or the widespread battles of the Roman Empire soon after the annunciation from the Holy Ghost to the Virgin

Mary. The abrupt change near the end of the twentieth century, of the antithetical tincture from secular life's widely expanded cone to religion's extremely narrowed one (and, vice versa, of the primary tincture almost instantaneously from the nearly extinguished religious gyre to the widest expansion of the counterpoised secular or political gyre), could in and of itself be catastrophic enough to warrant most of the portentous imagery and diction in Yeats's poem. Fearful concerns even more specifically related to the system than that, however, were involved in the piece's genesis and evolution. The annunciation of a new religious dispensation, antithetical in nature, would not have been anticipated by Yeats with foreboding, for he simultaneously favored the antithetical tincture and held in low regard the existing primary religious movement which was to be displaced. The only disappointing thing for Yeats about the forthcoming antithetical religion was that it would have no more than its merest beginnings within his lifetime or shortly thereafter, reaching its fullest expansion as a historical gyre not until the year 3000 C.E. The sudden imposition on the world of a primary political system, on the other hand, at its widest expansion from the very outset, was quite another matter.

What might constitute such an ultra-primary or super-"democratic" political phenomenon for the aristocratic-minded Yeats as he looked about the European world in 1919? Other than the last stages of World War I, one particular violent upheaval had just occurred: the Bolshevik Revolution. Communism was for Yeats the horrifying rough beast slouching through the postwar wasteland to be born, its politically primary hour come round exactly as predicted by the gyres and cycles of history available to him from the "automatic scripts" that his wife had begun to write out more than a year before the poem's composition.

Although this interpretational conclusion can be reached through a careful reading of *A Vision*'s sections on history, its validity has been made virtually unequivocal by Jon Stallworthy's publication of the poem's manuscript drafts (originally in his book *Between the Lines: Yeats's Poetry in the Making*, 1963, and again with fuller transcription of some partially illegible passages in the journal *Agenda*, 1971/1972). Along with several other convincing clues in these drafts occurs one line that leaves little to the imagination: "The Germany of Marx has led to Russian Com." Working with these same unpublished drafts as well as other materials, Donald Torchiana has made a persuasive case for the proposition that what upset Yeats most of all was the possibility that Ireland's civil strife in this same period made his country a highly vulnerable tinderbox for the spread of Marxist factions or Communistic forces (*W. B. Yeats and Georgian Ireland*, 1966). A letter by Yeats written later in 1919 makes this thesis virtually incontrovertible. In it the poet states that his main concern was for Ireland to be saved from Marxist values, because he felt that their fundamental materialism could only lead to murder. Then he quotes a catch-phrase that seems to echo lines from "The Second Coming": "Can the bourgeois be innocent?"

The manuscripts reveal much else as well. They show, for example, that from its earliest inception—a brief prose draft of the opening portion—"The Second Coming" was a decidedly political poem, not one concerned with some antithetical religious annunciation. Even the highly effective—though intentionally ironical—religious allusions to Bethlehem and Christ's return emerged relatively late in the poem's development. Moreover, the politics of concern are plainly of the primary tincture; the word "mob" appears repeatedly. When the expression "surely" occurred for the first time, it was followed by "the great falcon must come." Yeats, however, having said in a much-quoted passage elsewhere that he often used large noble birds to represent the subjective or antithetical and beasts that run on the ground to symbolize the objective or primary, realized his momentary drift toward depiction of the birth of an antithetical religious entity and struck the line. Then later came the famous beast, with its blank solar (primary) gaze.

Although it might shock some readers to think that Yeats would identify Christ with a beast, and with a political ideology such as Marxism, the point that should not be overlooked is that while Christ may be alternately sacred or secular in Yeats's imaginative thought, he is always unalterably primary. *A Vision* is quite explicit in several places about Christ's being primary. The poem is therefore, about his second coming, although in a frighteningly unfamiliar secular guise: a mass-oriented and anti-individualistic political materialism that paradoxically corresponds to but simultaneously contravenes his previous mass-oriented and anti-individualistic spiritual teachings. After twenty centuries of religious equality urged by Christ the Lamb, a cataclysmic and leveling social anarchy is about to be loosed on the world by Christ the Lion.

"AMONG SCHOOL CHILDREN"

Composed in 1926 and published in 1927, "Among School Children" is another of Yeats's most widely acclaimed and extensively studied poems. The two most famous interpretative readings are by Cleanth Brooks in *The Well Wrought Urn: Studies in the Structure of Poetry* (1947) and John Wain in *Interpretations: Essays on Twelve English Poems* (1955). Although both essays are almost belligerently New Critical, each sees as the overall theme the relationships between natural and supernatural, or between matter and spirit, and the ravages wrought on humankind by the passage of time. Most other analyses tend to accept this same general meaning for the poem as a whole, although almost inevitably there have been some who see the subject as the triumph of art, or something of that sort. With this poem, the problems and difficulties of interpretation have been not so much with larger suggestions of significance as with individual lines or passages in their relationships—or supposed relationships—to the poem's broadest meanings. Such tendencies toward agreement about the piece's general thematic implications are fortunate since they are in keeping with Yeats's own comments in notes and letters: that physical or temporal existence will waste the youthful students and that the poem is one of his not infrequent condemnations of old age.

The inspirational matrix for the poem was literal enough—a visit by Yeats in his role as senator in the newly established Irish Free State to a quite progressive school administered by a Catholic convent. Given this information, the reader will have no problems with stanza 1. (Any analysis, incidentally, which suggests that Yeats felt that the children depicted were being taught the wrong kinds of things is open to question, for Yeats subsequently spoke to the Senate about the convent school in highly laudatory terms.) The next three stanzas, however, although they are generally thought to be less problematical than the last part of the poem, are somewhat more opaque than the casual-toned and low-keyed opening. In stanza 2, the sight of the schoolchildren suddenly brings to the poet-senator's memory (with little transition for the reader) a scene in which a beautiful woman had told him of some childhood chastisement, probably by a schoolteacher. That memory, in turn, evokes for him a vision of what she must have looked like at such an age, perhaps not too much unlike the girls standing before him in the convent's hall.

There can be little doubt that the beautiful woman in question is the one by whom Yeats's aching "heart" was "driven wild" for a large part of his adult life—Maud Gonne. Time and time again throughout his canon, Yeats compares that special woman's almost divine or superhuman beauty to the beauty of Helen of Troy, who, in Greek mythology, was born to Leda after her visitation by Zeus. This information, then, helps to clarify such characteristically allusive terms in stanzas 2 through 4 as "Ledaean body," "daughters of the swan," "every paddler's heritage," "Ledaean kind," and "pretty plumage." The alteration of Plato's parable (in the *Symposium*, probably one of the middle dialogues, where the basis of love is explained as the desire in divinely separated humankind for reunion in a sphere) to union in the white and yellow of a single egg, rather than the myth's division, also fits into this pattern of Ledaean imagery, at the same time that it looks forward to images and suggestions of generation or birth in subsequent stanzas.

Then, in stanza 4, with still another shift, the beautiful woman's present visage drifts before the poet's eyes. Surprisingly, despite the rather heavily connotative language of lines 3 and 4, along with Yeats's comparison in the second quatrain of his own youth with his present old age (not to mention similar thematic implications in the entire poem), there has been some controversy about line one. The issue is whether Yeats meant to convey a vision of the woman still young and beautiful or, instead, ravaged by time and decrepitude. The word "Quattrocento," denoting fifteenth century Italian art and artists, might be taken to substantiate either side of such a debate, depending on how it itself is construed; but along with virtually everything else in the stanza, the concluding—and later recurring—scarecrow image would seem to lend support to the suggestion of deterioration and decay.

If lines 2 through 4 of stanza 5 were removed, the stanza not only would be completely intelligible, but it would also be a rather concise statement of one of the poem's two main themes—the effects on humankind of time's passage. Since lines 2 through 4 were included, however, along with other characteristically Yeatsian elements akin to them in subsequent stanzas, the poem's real difficulties begin to manifest themselves in its second half. In a note to the poem, Yeats indicates that the honey of generation is an image that he borrowed from Porphyry's essay "The Cave of the Nymphs," almost certainly with an intended symbolic suggestion, on one level, of the pleasures of sexual union. The same note, however, also indicates explicitly that the recollection mentioned is the soul's memory—à la William Wordsworth's "Ode: Intimations of Immortality from Recollections of Early Childhood"—of a prenatal condition higher and freer than earthly incarnation. At this point, Yeats's occult and esoteric beliefs that so many critics have found difficult to accept enter the poem. Brooks's reaction, for example, is virtual incredulity. To make interpretational matters even worse, Yeats evidently employed the honey image ambiguously to relate also to "the drug," presumably physically procreated or temporal existence, which allows or causes the prenatal memory to fade. Both the note and the draft versions of the poem (reproduced in Thomas Parkinson's *W. B. Yeats: The Later Poetry*, 1964) suggest the likelihood of such intentional or semi-intentional ambiguity. All this, along with what is probably the poem's least felicitous line— "sleep, shriek, struggle . . ."—has led to considerable exegetical dispute about who or what was betrayed—mother or shape? The ambiguity seems less intentional in this particular case, however, and the drafts, along with a certain amount of common sense, tend to indicate the child, a soul entrapped in flesh by the mother's generatively honeyed act.

Stanza 6 is perhaps not too difficult once the reader realizes that the final line is, in effect, appositionally related to the main nouns in the other seven lines. In other words, the generally accepted thrust of meaning is that even the greatest and presumably wisest of men come to be, in time, like elderly poet-senators and everyone else, dilapidated old scarecrows. There is, however, a bit more wit and symbolism at work—or at play—in the stanza. For one thing, Yeats has chosen men who were teachers or students or—in two cases—both in turn: Plato, Aristotle, Alexander the Great, and Pythagoras. Furthermore, three of these four men spent their lives contemplating and theorizing about the same crucial and fundamental aspects of human experience which are the subjects of the poem—the relationships between spirit and matter and between being and becoming.

The second half of stanza 7 is the most problematical unit in the poem. The first quatrain, however, gives little trouble. With a pun on the word "images," Yeats refers both to pictures in the maternal mind's eye and to religious icons or statuary. The "Presences" of line 5 are what create interpretational difficulties, again because here Yeats's occult views become involved, views that too few exegetes have been willing to address even as accepted by the poet himself. Yeats's use of a capital *P* and the expression "self-born" (compare "self-sown," "self-begotten," and "miracle-bred" on the very next page of *The Collected Poems of W. B. Yeats*) should be clues that some kind of divinity is being apostrophized in this stanza about worship. That, in turn, can lead to recognition of a third level of meaning for the punword "images." The mask, the antiself, and especially the daimon (not synonymous terms, but kindred ones in Yeats's esoteric thought and vocabulary) were sometimes referred to as the image, for they are, like a mirror image, simultaneously like and yet exactly opposite to the human individual. Furthermore, with the daimon, that special semidivine guiding or misguiding spirit, each man or woman is involved in an exasperating attraction-repulsion relationship which explains the poet's emphasis upon heartbreak and mockery. Fleetingly known—in actuality or by analogy—through such heightened experiences as the earlier stanzas' sexual love (passion), religious love (piety), or maternal love (affection), these hatefully loving guardian geniuses draw man onward from the flesh toward spiritual glory at the same time that they do all they can to frustrate every inch of his progress or enterprise along the way.

The first half of the closing stanza would be much more readily comprehensible if Yeats had retained his draft's version of the opening line, which began with the word "all" instead of "labor." That would have agreed with a draft line relating to the dancer, "all so smoothly runs," and would justify the status *usually* attributed to the concluding quatrain: perhaps the most successful of Yeats's famous passages whose antinomy-resolving symbols or images lift poet, poem, and reader above the strife of physical existence to a condition of triumphant affirmation or realm of artistically perfected unity. Dance and dancer are indivisibly—almost divinely—one. The tree—and the poem—are supremely organic wholes, greater than the sums of their parts. This seems to be Romantic lyricism at its transcendent best.

Such a conclusion, however, is too hasty. When its initial word was "all," the first quatrain of the final stanza rather plainly meant something like "Life in this world is best when and where humankind achieves a balance between body and soul, between spirit and flesh." Yeats's eventual substitution of the word "labor," however, could well have been intended to add, among other things, the idea that such a balance is never easily come by nor readily sustained in this life. That would echo in one sense the feminine persona in "Adam's Curse," who says that women have to labor to become beautiful, as well as her interlocutor's rejoinder that subsequent to Adam's fall nothing very fine can be achieved or created without a great deal of labor. How, then, did the poet move so suddenly from the broken hearts and mockery of stanza 7 to some rhapsodically evoked unity or triumph in the last four lines of stanza 8? Perhaps the poem was never meant to suggest such a leap. There is, after all, no journey in this poem from one realm to another, as there is in "Sailing to Byzantium." The tree and the dancer are still very much in the sensuous physical realm. Perhaps the supposed transition has been only through some strange magic as unsavory to common sense as Yeats's occult inclinations were to the critics who have perpetrated this illusory transmutation. Perhaps, ironically, the un-Romantic critics have made Yeats much more Romantic in this particular poem than he ever intended to be. In all fairness, the point must be acknowledged, however, that

Brooks and Wain themselves read the final stanza in much more neutral or negative terms than many of the commentators who have written subsequently. Almost unquestionably the chief influence on numerous analyses of the final stanza in terms of transcendence and artistic unity has been Frank Kermode's book *Romantic Image* (1957), which takes the passage as a virtual epitome of the opposition-resolving powers of the symbolic mode, as the image of the Image.

"Among School Children" has a rather high incidence of puns and intentional ambiguities in addition to the ones already noted. The two most obvious further instances involve the words "labor" and "play," which have been commented on both separately and together. Perhaps insufficient attention has been given, however, to possibilities of multiple meanings in that salient feature, the title. Yeats, an inveterate reviser, was well capable of changing a title if it no longer best suited the interests of his poem. Why would he have retained the title here if it did not fit the finished piece—the whole work as well as the opening portions? Some continuing concern with the symbolic implications of students and teachers has already been observed in stanza 6. Why would not or could not the same kind of thing be appropriate for that very important portion of the poem, its conclusion? Suppose, in contrast to prevalent interpretations of the last quatrain, that the questions asked there are real questions, such as schoolchildren ask, rather than rhetorical ones implying some transcendence or triumph over the rest of the poem's concerns. Like a staring schoolchild, man might well ask—in fact, for centuries he has asked—where the material world ends and the spiritual world begins, and how, in this temporal realm, he can separate the one from the other. The great rooted blossomer, then, may be more an emblem of the puzzles and problems studied in life's schoolroom than of some artistically achieved solution to them. Is man the newborn infant, the adolescent pupil, the youthful procreator, or the white-haired elder statesman—or none of these or all of these or more than all of these? In the face of such conundrums, all men are "among school children," seeking and inquiring, frequently without finding or being given reassuring answers.

"SAILING TO BYZANTIUM" AND "BYZANTIUM"

No work in Yeats's canon has won more renown or elicited more controversy than the so-called Byzantium poems, "Sailing to Byzantium" (1927) and "Byzantium" (1930). Critical opinion as to which is poetically superior has been almost, if not quite, equally divided. There is almost universal agreement, however, that the earlier and more frequently reprinted piece, "Sailing to Byzantium," is the easier to understand.

Several authorities, in fact, have gone so far as to say that "Sailing to Byzantium" explains itself or needs no extensive clarification; but if such were actually the case, the amount of commentary that it has generated would clearly constitute an anomaly. If nothing else, the general reader ought to have some answer to the almost inevitable question, "Why Byzantium?" Though it does not provide every possible relevant response to such a query, a much-quoted passage from *A Vision* indicates some of the more important reasons why and how Yeats came to let that great Near Eastern city of medieval times represent in his imagination a cultural, artistic, and spiritual ideal. He believes, he says, that one might have found there "some philosophical worker in mosaic" with "the supernatural descending nearer to him than to Plotinus even," that in "early Byzantium" perhaps more than at any other time in history "religious, aesthetic and practical life were one." Artists of all kinds expressed "the vision of a whole people," "the work of many that seemed the work of one" and was the "proclamation of their invisible master."

Although there is no question whatever that "Sailing to Byzantium" is a richly symbolic poem, its genesis apparently involved a more or less literal level that, even though it has not been ignored, may not have been stressed in all its particulars as much as might be warranted. Yeats was first exposed to Byzantine art during a Mediterranean tour in 1907 that included Ravenna, where he saw mosaics and a frieze in the Church of San Apollinare Nuovo that is generally regarded as the chief basis of imagery in stanza 3 of "Sailing to Byzantium." Years later, however, two factors coincided to renew his interest, one of them involving a voyage in certain respects interestingly akin to that in the poem. In the first half of the 1920's, Yeats had read rather widely about Byzantium in connection with his work on the historical "Dove or Swan" section of *A Vision*. Then in 1924, nearing sixty years of age, he became somewhat ill and suffered high blood pressure and difficulty in breathing. He was advised to stop work and was taken by his wife on another Mediterranean tour, this time seeking out other Byzantine mosaics, and similar craftsmanship that sharply contrasted art with nature, at places such as Monreale and Palermo, Sicily. As at least one commentator has pointed out, Yeats had no great regrets about leaving home at this time because of dissatisfaction with the political situation and depression about his health. The first legible words in the drafts of "Sailing to Byzantium" are "Farewell friends," and subsequent early portions make unequivocal the fact that "That country" in the finished poem is (or at least originally was) Ireland. Thus, the imaginative and poetic voyage of a sick old man leaving one locale for a more desirable one very probably had at least some of its antecedents in a rather similar actual journey a few years earlier.

Two symbolic interpretations of "Sailing to Byzantium" have been predominant by a considerable margin: Either the poem is about the state of the poet's spirit or soul shortly before and after death, or it is about the creative process and artistic achievement. A choice between the two might be said to pivot on response to the question, "How ideal is the ideal?" In other words, does Byzantium represent this-worldly perfection on the aesthetic level or perfection of an even greater kind in a transcendent realm of existence? A not insignificant amount of the massive critical commentary on the poem (as well as on its sequel "Byzantium") has been in the way of a war of words about the "proper" reply to such a question, with surprisingly inflexible positions being taken by some of the combatants. Fortunately, however, a number of authorities have realized that there is no reason at all why both levels of meaning cannot obtain simultaneously and that, as a matter of fact, the poem becomes much more characteristically Yeatsian in its symbolic complexity and wealth of import if such a reading is accepted.

RETURN TO PHYSICALITY, SEXUALITY

About 1926 or 1927 and thereafter, an apparent major change—with emphasis on apparent—seems to have taken place in Yeats's attitude toward life. On the surface, "Sailing to Byzantium" may look and sound like the culmination of a long line of "escape" poems, while many poems or passages written after it (for example, "A Dialogue of Self and Soul") seem to stress instead a plunge into the physicality of this world, even a celebration of earthly existence. Even though Yeats continued to write poems very much concerned with transcendence, supernaturalism, and otherworldliness, he developed in his late career a "new" kind of poem. These poems were often short, were frequently presented in series or sequences, and were frequently—but not always—concerned with a particularly physical aspect of worldly existence, sex.

These poems also share other attributes, a number of them related to Yeats's revived interest at the time in the ballad form. One group is titled, for example, *Words for Music Perhaps, and Other Poems*, indicating their songlike qualities. In addition to the poems themselves being brief, the lines and stanza patterns are also short, the lines sometimes having as few as two stresses. Diction, syntax, and idiom are—again as in the ballad or folk song—colloquial and uncomplicated. Imagery, too, is earthy, sometimes stark or blunt. At times sound patterns other than rhyme contribute to the songlike effects, and some pieces, although not all, make effective use of the refrain as a device. In these verses, Yeats has come a long way from the amorphous Pre-Raphaelitism of his early lyrics. In them, in fact, he achieves some of the most identifiably "modern" effects in his entire canon.

Related to that modernity is the fact that these late-life songs are anything but simple in content and meaning. Their deceptiveness in this regard has led some early critics to label them—especially the scatological ones—as tasteless and crude. More recent and perceptive analysts, however, have found them to be, in the words of one commentator, more nearly eschatological. What Yeats is doing thematically in such pieces, in fact, is by no means new to him. As in "Solomon and the Witch," "Leda and the Swan," and some other earlier pieces, he is using the sexual metaphor to explore some of the metaphysical mysteries of human existence. One significant difference, however, is that now the sexual experience itself sometimes seems to be regarded as something of a mystery in its own right.

CRAZY JANE POEMS

Almost as well known as Yeats himself is his fictive persona Crazy Jane, evidently based compositely on two old Irish women from the poet's experience, one early, one late. Like Shakespeare's—and Yeats's—fools, however, Jane is usually "crazy like a fox." In her series of poems, in the "Three Bushes" sequence, and in poems such as "Chosen," "A Last Confession," "Her Anxiety," "Consolation," and "The Wild Old Wicked Man," Yeats considers or deals with sexuality and sexual imagery in some six or seven different, though frequently interrelated, ways. At times, the poet seems to vacillate or contradict himself from one poem to another, a habit that at first makes understanding these pieces rather difficult. After a while, however, the phenomenon can be recognized for what it is: Yeats's characteristic technique of shifting ground or altering angle of vision in order to explore his subject the more completely.

One basic use of the sexual image has already been seen: The union of man and woman is parallel to or representative of the union of natural with supernatural, human with divine, or man with daimon. In some of these poems, however, the union seems to be so overwhelming that it almost ceases to be mere symbol and becomes the thing in itself, as in the last stanza of "Chosen" or in an unpublished poem where even the gyres are laid to rest in the bed of love. On the other hand (and at the other extreme) are poems that suggest that sex just does not accomplish very much at all, as in "The Chambermaid's Second Song" (last in the "Three Bushes" sequence), where after mere physical pleasure, man's spirit remains "blind as a worm." A poem of this kind echoes a reported statement by Yeats that the most unfortunate thing about coitus is the continuing "virginity of the soul." In between the two extremes are poems that see sex as little better than a *pis aller*—"Consolation," for example, or "The Wild Old Wicked Man," whose protagonist chooses "the second-best" on "a woman's breast." Then there are poems that contemplate the pleasures or problems of sexuality in this life in the light of a Swedenborgian intercourse of the angels ("A Last Confession" and "Crazy Jane on the Day of Judgment") or the Hermetic paradigm—as above, so below ("Ribh Denounces Patrick," though this piece is not in the ballad tradition). Still other poems in the collection, instead of comparing bodies in this world with spirits in the other world, use sexual symbolism to ponder the conundrums of the body-soul relationship here on earth, a theme reminiscent of "Among School Children." The Lady's three songs in the "Three Bushes" series fall into this category. Finally, Yeats sometimes uses the transience of sexual experience to parallel the ephemeral nature of all human experience, especially such heightened moments as mystic vision or artistic inspiration. Such an ironic self-consuming quality inherent in the sex act is touched on in the first stanza of "Crazy Jane and Jack the Journeyman" and in "Her Anxiety," among other places.

"UNDER BEN BULBEN"

As indicated earlier in the biographical section, Yeats continued to work on poems and plays right down to the last day but one before his death. Although "Under Ben Bulben" was not his last poem, it was written quite consciously as a valedictory or testamentary piece in the summer and fall of 1938, when Yeats knew that death was not far away. Although such a status for the poem has been widely recognized by authorities from a very early date, surprisingly little has been written about it until relatively recently.

Ben Bulben is the impressive west-Irish headland "under" whose shadow Yeats specified that his body be buried in the churchyard at Drumcliff where his great-grandfather had been rector a century earlier. In draft versions, "Under Ben Bulben" had two previous titles: "His Convictions" and "Creed." Furthermore, the opening lines that read "Swear by" in the finished poem originally read "I believe." Here, then, presumably, if anywhere, one should be able to find Yeats's final views on life and the human condition. Because the poem goes on, however, to indicate quite candid belief in the existence of supernatural spirits and, further still, in reincarnation or transmigration of the soul, modern critics who do not accept such quasireligious views have evidently declined to take the piece very seriously. One apparent consequence has been that they have had little adequate basis for understanding or glossing the epitaph with which the poem concludes.

Ironically, the epitaph has been very often quoted: "Cast a cold eye/ On life, on death./ Horseman, pass by!" Exegetical commentary on these three lines, however, has been almost as rare as that on the larger poem. Explication has been so minimal and inconclusive, in fact, that as late as 1974 one spokesperson, Edward Malins, asserted that determination of the epitaph's meaning and its intended audience "is anybody's guess." In terms of the framing poem's thesis of transmigration, however, along with evidence from other sources, the horseman can be identified as Yeats himself, a cosmic journeyer engaged in a vast round of cyclical deaths and rebirths, as outlined in *A Vision*. A cold eye is cast on both life and death because the point of possible release from the wheel of reincarnation to some ultimate beatific state such as that imaged in "Sailing to Byzantium" is at such great distance that the grave is little more than a way station on the cosmic odyssey. Thus, there is time or place for little more than a passing nod or glance toward either life or death. In the words of a passage from *A Vision* that is virtually a prose counterpart of the epitaph's verse, man's spirit can know nothing more than transitory happiness either between birth and death or between death and rebirth; its goal is to "pass rapidly round its circle" and to "find freedom from that circle."

The means of passing rapidly around *A Vision*'s great wheel is to live each incarnation properly "in phase." Failure in this endeavor can cause rebirth again into the same phase, thus slowing progress toward "freedom" or release. From his youthful days as a disciple of Walter Pater, Yeats had long regarded the living of life itself as an art. With the coming of *A Vision*, teleological impetus was added to this aesthetic conviction. In a note on "Sailing to Byzantium" from a radio script and in several poems, Yeats exclaims that he must "make his soul." In the terms of *A Vision*, then, once he knew the prescribed qualities of his current incarnation or phase on the wheel, he must shape and sculpt his very life until it becomes a concrete manifestation of that phase, a mythopoeic *objet d'art*.

In *Autobiographies*, on the other hand, Yeats states that when great artists were at their most creative, the rest was not simply a work of art, but rather the "re-creation of the man through that art." Similarly, in a scrap of verse, he said that whenever he remade a poem, the real importance of the act was that, in the event, he actually remade himself. Thus emerged the ultimate unity. Yeats's life and his work became two sides of the one coin. The phenomena were mutually interdependent, the processes mutually interactive. As he forged his poems, Yeats also created his self. That created self, a living myth, was in turn the image reflected in his poetry, the center of vision embodied in the verbal constructs of his art.

OTHER MAJOR WORKS

SHORT FICTION: *John Sherman and Dhoya*, 1891, 1969; *The Celtic Twilight*, 1893; *The Secret Rose*, 1897; *The Tables of Law; The Adoration of the Magi*, 1897; *Stories of Red Hanrahan*, 1904; *Mythologies*, 1959.

PLAYS: *The Countess Cathleen*, pb. 1892; *The Land of Heart's Desire*, pr., pb. 1894; *Cathleen ni Houlihan*, pr., pb. 1902; *The Pot of Broth*, pr. 1902 (with Lady Augusta Gregory); *The Hour-Glass*, pr. 1903, 1912; *The King's Threshold*, pr., pb. 1903 (with Lady Gregory); *On Baile's Strand*, pr. 1904; *Deirdre*, pr. 1906 (with Lady Gregory); *The Shadowy Waters*, pr. 1906; *The Unicorn from the Stars*, pr. 1907 (with Lady Gregory); *The Golden Helmet*, pr., pb. 1908; *The Green Helmet*, pr., pb. 1910; *At the Hawk's Well*, pr. 1916; *The Dreaming of the Bones*, pb. 1919; *The Only Jealousy of Emer*, pb. 1919; *The Player Queen*, pr. 1919; *Calvary*, pb. 1921; *Four Plays for Dancers*, 1921 (includes *Calvary, At the Hawk's Well, The Dreaming of the Bones*, and *The Only Jealousy of Emer*); *The Cat and the Moon*, pb. 1924; *The Resurrection*, pb. 1927; *The Words upon the Window-Pane*, pr. 1930; *The Collected Plays of W. B. Yeats*, 1934, 1952; *A Full Moon in March*, pr. 1934; *The King of the Great Clock Tower*, pr., pb. 1934; *The Herne's Egg*, pb. 1938; *Purgatory*, pr. 1938; *The Death of Cuchulain*, pb. 1939; *Variorum Edition of the Plays of W. B. Yeats*, 1966 (Russell K. Alspach, editor).

NONFICTION: *Ideas of Good and Evil*, 1903; *The Cutting of an Agate*, 1912; *Per Amica Silentia Lunae*, 1918; *Essays*, 1924; *A Vision*, 1925, 1937; *Autobiographies*, 1926, 1955; *A Packet for Ezra Pound*, 1929; *Essays, 1931-1936*, 1937; *The Autobiography of William Butler Yeats*, 1938; *On the Boiler*, 1939; *If I Were Four and Twenty*, 1940; *The Letters of W. B. Yeats*, 1954; *The Senate Speeches of W. B. Yeats*, 1960 (Donald R. Pearce, editor); *Essays and Introductions*, 1961; *Explorations*, 1962; *Ah, Sweet Dancer: W. B. Yeats, Margot Ruddock—A Correspondence*, 1970 (Roger McHugh, editor); *Uncollected Prose by W. B. Yeats*, 1970, 1976 (2 volumes); *Memoirs*, 1972; *The Collected Letters of W. B. Yeats*, 1986-2005 (4 volumes); *Early Articles and Reviews: Uncollected Articles and Reviews Written Between 1886 and 1900*, 2004 (John P. Frayne and Madeleine Marchaterre, editors).

MISCELLANEOUS: *The Collected Works in Verse and Prose of William Butler Yeats*, 1908; *The Collected Works of W. B. Yeats*, 1989-2008 (13 volumes).

BIBLIOGRAPHY

Chaudhry, Yug Mohit. *Yeats, the Irish Literary Revival, and the Politics of Print.* Cork, Ireland: Cork University Press, 2001. A study of Yeats's political and social views as well as a critique of his writings. Bibliography and index.

Foster, R. F. *W. B. Yeats: A Life.* 2 vols. New York: Oxford University Press, 1997-2003. An excellent, extensive guide to Yeats and his work.

Greaves, Richard. *Transition, Reception, and Modernism in W. B. Yeats.* New York: Palgrave, 2002. In examining Yeats's poetry of 1902 to 1916, Greaves rejects the label of "modernist" and instead analyzes Yeats's poetry from the context of the poet's life.

Grene, Nicholas. *Yeats's Poetic Codes.* New York: Oxford University Press, 2008. Grene examines the key words and habits of speech that shape Yeats's poetry, focusing on poetic technique to understand the work.

Holdeman, David. *The Cambridge Introduction to W. B. Yeats.* New York: Cambridge University Press, 2006. Examines Yeats's poems, drama, and stories in their cultural, historical, and literary contexts.

Howes, Marjorie, and John Kelly, eds. *The Cambridge Companion to W. B. Yeats.* New York: Cambridge University Press, 2006. Yeats scholars from the United States, England, and Ireland contributed eleven essays to this work, illuminating the personal and political events in Yeats's life. Howes and Kelly chronicle his early interests in theater, politics, and the occult, along with the portrayal of these topics in his writing. Includes a detailed time line, bibliography, and index.

Jeffares, A. Norman. *W. B. Yeats: A New Biography.* New York: Continuum, 2001. A biography of Yeats by a leading scholar of the writer.

Ross, David. *Critical Companion to William Butler Yeats: A Literary Reference to His Life and Work.* New York: Facts On File, 2008. A reference work that provides information on his life and critical analysis of his writings.

Vendler, Helen. *Our Secret Discipline: Yeats and Lyric Form.* Cambridge, Mass.: Harvard University Press, 2007. A guide to Yeats' poetry that focuses exclusively on his use of form and the ways in which meaning is derived from it. Useful to scholars and students of poetry.

James Lovic Allen

CHECKLIST FOR EXPLICATING A POEM

I. The Initial Readings

A. Before reading the poem, the reader should:
1. Notice its form and length.
2. Consider the title, determining, if possible, whether it might function as an allusion, symbol, or poetic image.
3. Notice the date of composition or publication, and identify the general era of the poet.

B. The poem should be read intuitively and emotionally and be allowed to "happen" as much as possible.

C. In order to establish the rhythmic flow, the poem should be reread. A note should be made as to where the irregular spots (if any) are located.

II. Explicating the Poem

A. *Dramatic situation.* Studying the poem line by line helps the reader discover the dramatic situation. All elements of the dramatic situation are interrelated and should be viewed as reflecting and affecting one another. The dramatic situation serves a particular function in the poem, adding realism, surrealism, or absurdity; drawing attention to certain parts of the poem; and changing to reinforce other aspects of the poem. All points should be considered. The following questions are particularly helpful to ask in determining dramatic situation:
1. What, if any, is the narrative action in the poem?
2. How many personae appear in the poem? What part do they take in the action?
3. What is the relationship between characters?
4. What is the setting (time and location) of the poem?

B. *Point of view.* An understanding of the poem's point of view is a major step toward comprehending the poet's intended meaning. The reader should ask:
1. Who is the speaker? Is he or she addressing someone else or the reader?
2. Is the narrator able to understand or see everything happening to him or her, or does the reader know things that the narrator does not?
3. Is the narrator reliable?
4. Do point of view and dramatic situation seem consistent? If not, the inconsistencies may provide clues to the poem's meaning.

C. *Images and metaphors*. Images and metaphors are often the most intricately crafted vehicles of the poem for relaying the poet's message. Realizing that the images and metaphors work in harmony with the dramatic situation and point of view will help the reader to see the poem as a whole, rather than as disassociated elements.

1. The reader should identify the concrete images (that is, those that are formed from objects that can be touched, smelled, seen, felt, or tasted). Is the image projected by the poet consistent with the physical object?
2. If the image is abstract, or so different from natural imagery that it cannot be associated with a real object, then what are the properties of the image?
3. To what extent is the reader asked to form his or her own images?
4. Is any image repeated in the poem? If so, how has it been changed? Is there a controlling image?
5. Are any images compared to each other? Do they reinforce one another?
6. Is there any difference between the way the reader perceives the image and the way the narrator sees it?
7. What seems to be the narrator's or persona's attitude toward the image?

D. *Words*. Every substantial word in a poem may have more than one intended meaning, as used by the author. Because of this, the reader should look up many of these words in the dictionary and:

1. Note all definitions that have the slightest connection with the poem.
2. Note any changes in syntactical patterns in the poem.
3. In particular, note those words that could possibly function as symbols or allusions, and refer to any appropriate sources for further information.

E. *Meter, rhyme, structure, and tone*. In scanning the poem, all elements of prosody should be noted by the reader. These elements are often used by a poet to manipulate the reader's emotions, and therefore they should be examined closely to arrive at the poet's specific intention.

1. Does the basic meter follow a traditional pattern such as those found in nursery rhymes or folk songs?
2. Are there any variations in the base meter? Such changes or substitutions are important thematically and should be identified.
3. Are the rhyme schemes traditional or innovative, and what might their form mean to the poem?
4. What devices has the poet used to create sound patterns (such as assonance and alliteration)?
5. Is the stanza form a traditional or innovative one?
6. If the poem is composed of verse paragraphs rather than stanzas, how do they affect the progression of the poem?

7. After examining the above elements, is the resultant tone of the poem casual or formal, pleasant, harsh, emotional, authoritative?

F. *Historical context*. The reader should attempt to place the poem into historical context, checking on events at the time of composition. Archaic language, expressions, images, or symbols should also be looked up.

G. *Themes and motifs*. By seeing the poem as a composite of emotion, intellect, craftsmanship, and tradition, the reader should be able to determine the themes and motifs (smaller recurring ideas) presented in the work. He or she should ask the following questions to help pinpoint these main ideas:

1. Is the poet trying to advocate social, moral, or religious change?
2. Does the poet seem sure of his or her position?
3. Does the poem appeal primarily to the emotions, to the intellect, or to both?
4. Is the poem relying on any particular devices for effect (such as imagery, allusion, paradox, hyperbole, or irony)?

BIBLIOGRAPHY

GENERAL REFERENCE SOURCES

BIOGRAPHICAL SOURCES

Colby, Vineta, ed. *World Authors, 1975-1980*. Wilson Authors Series. New York: H. W. Wilson, 1985.

_____. *World Authors, 1980-1985*. Wilson Authors Series. New York: H. W. Wilson, 1991.

_____. *World Authors, 1985-1990*. Wilson Authors Series. New York: H. W. Wilson, 1995.

Cyclopedia of World Authors. 4th rev. ed. 5 vols. Pasadena, Calif.: Salem Press, 2003.

Dictionary of Literary Biography. 254 vols. Detroit: Gale Research, 1978-   .

International Who's Who in Poetry and Poets' Encyclopaedia. Cambridge, England: International Biographical Centre, 1993.

Seymour-Smith, Martin, and Andrew C. Kimmens, eds. *World Authors, 1900-1950*. Wilson Authors Series. 4 vols. New York: H. W. Wilson, 1996.

Thompson, Clifford, ed. *World Authors, 1990-1995*. Wilson Authors Series. New York: H. W. Wilson, 1999.

Wakeman, John, ed. *World Authors, 1950-1970*. New York: H. W. Wilson, 1975.

_____. *World Authors, 1970-1975*. Wilson Authors Series. New York: H. W. Wilson, 1991.

Willhardt, Mark, and Alan Michael Parker, eds. *Who's Who in Twentieth Century World Poetry*. New York: Routledge, 2000.

CRITICISM

Brooks, Cleanth, and Robert Penn Warren. *Understanding Poetry*. 4th ed. Reprint. Fort Worth, Tex.: Heinle & Heinle, 2003.

Classical and Medieval Literature Criticism. Detroit: Gale Research, 1988-   .

Contemporary Literary Criticism. Detroit: Gale Research, 1973-   .

Day, Gary. *Literary Criticism: A New History*. Edinburgh, Scotland: Edinburgh University Press, 2008.

Draper, James P., ed. *World Literature Criticism 1500 to the Present: A Selection of Major Authors from Gale's Literary Criticism Series*. 6 vols. Detroit: Gale Research, 1992.

Habib, M. A. R. *A History of Literary Criticism: From Plato to the Present*. Malden, Mass.: Wiley-Blackwell, 2005.

Jason, Philip K., ed. *Masterplots II: Poetry Series, Revised Edition*. 8 vols. Pasadena, Calif.: Salem Press, 2002.

Lodge, David, and Nigel Wood. *Modern Criticism and Theory*. 3d ed. New York: Longman, 2008.

Magill, Frank N., ed. *Magill's Bibliography of Literary Criticism*. 4 vols. Englewood Cliffs, N.J.: Salem Press, 1979.

MLA International Bibliography. New York: Modern Language Association of America, 1922-   .

Nineteenth-Century Literature Criticism. Detroit: Gale Research, 1981-   .

Twentieth-Century Literary Criticism. Detroit: Gale Research, 1978-   .

Vedder, Polly, ed. *World Literature Criticism Supplement: A Selection of Major Authors from Gale's Literary Criticism Series*. 2 vols. Detroit: Gale Research, 1997.

Young, Robyn V., ed. *Poetry Criticism: Excerpts from Criticism of the Works of the Most Significant and Widely Studied Poets of World Literature*. 29 vols. Detroit: Gale Research, 1991.

POETRY DICTIONARIES AND HANDBOOKS

Carey, Gary, and Mary Ellen Snodgrass. *A Multicultural Dictionary of Literary Terms*. Jefferson, N.C.: McFarland, 1999.

Deutsch, Babette. *Poetry Handbook: A Dictionary of Terms*. 4th ed. New York: Funk & Wagnalls, 1974.

Drury, John. *The Poetry Dictionary*. Cincinnati, Ohio: Story Press, 1995.

Kinzie, Mary. *A Poet's Guide to Poetry*. Chicago: University of Chicago Press, 1999.

Lennard, John. *The Poetry Handbook: A Guide to Reading Poetry for Pleasure and Practical Criticism*. New York: Oxford University Press, 1996.

Matterson, Stephen, and Darryl Jones. *Studying Poetry*. New York: Oxford University Press, 2000.

Packard, William. *The Poet's Dictionary: A Handbook of Prosody and Poetic Devices*. New York: Harper & Row, 1989.

Preminger, Alex, et al., eds. *The New Princeton Encyclopedia of Poetry and Poetics*. 3d rev. ed. Princeton, N.J.: Princeton University Press, 1993.

Shipley, Joseph Twadell, ed. *Dictionary of World Literary Terms, Forms, Technique, Criticism*. Rev. ed. Boston: George Allen and Unwin, 1979.

INDEXES OF PRIMARY WORKS

Frankovich, Nicholas, ed. *The Columbia Granger's Index to Poetry in Anthologies*. 11th ed. New York: Columbia University Press, 1997.

_____. *The Columbia Granger's Index to Poetry in Collected and Selected Works*. New York: Columbia University Press, 1997.

Guy, Patricia. *A Women's Poetry Index*. Phoenix, Ariz.: Oryx Press, 1985.

Hazen, Edith P., ed. *Columbia Granger's Index to Poetry*. 10th ed. New York: Columbia University Press, 1994.

Hoffman, Herbert H., and Rita Ludwig Hoffman, comps. *International Index to Recorded Poetry*. New York: H. W. Wilson, 1983.

Kline, Victoria. *Last Lines: An Index to the Last Lines of Poetry*. 2 vols. Vol. 1, *Last Line Index, Title Index*; Vol. 2, *Author Index, Keyword Index*. New York: Facts On File, 1991.

Marcan, Peter. *Poetry Themes: A Bibliographical Index to Subject Anthologies and Related Criticisms in the English Language, 1875-1975*. Hamden, Conn.: Linnet Books, 1977.

Poem Finder. Great Neck, N.Y.: Roth, 2000.

POETICS, POETIC FORMS, AND GENRES

Attridge, Derek. *Poetic Rhythm: An Introduction*. New York: Cambridge University Press, 1995.

Brogan, T. V. F. *Verseform: A Comparative Bibliography*. Baltimore: Johns Hopkins University Press, 1989.

Fussell, Paul. *Poetic Meter and Poetic Form*. Rev. ed. New York: McGraw-Hill, 1979.

Hollander, John. *Rhyme's Reason*. 3d ed. New Haven, Conn.: Yale University Press, 2001.

Jackson, Guida M. *Traditional Epics: A Literary Companion*. New York: Oxford University Press, 1995.

Padgett, Ron, ed. *The Teachers and Writers Handbook of Poetic Forms*. 2d ed. New York: Teachers & Writers Collaborative, 2000.

Pinsky, Robert. *The Sounds of Poetry: A Brief Guide*. New York: Farrar, Straus and Giroux, 1998.

Preminger, Alex, and T. V. F. Brogan, eds. *New Princeton Encyclopedia of Poetry and Poetics*. 3d ed. Princeton, N.J.: Princeton University Press, 1993.

Spiller, Michael R. G. *The Sonnet Sequence: A Study of Its Strategies*. Studies in Literary Themes and Genres 13. New York: Twayne, 1997.

Turco, Lewis. *The New Book of Forms: A Handbook of Poetics*. Hanover, N.H.: University Press of New England, 1986.

Williams, Miller. *Patterns of Poetry: An Encyclopedia of Forms*. Baton Rouge: Louisiana State University Press, 1986.

Maura Ives
Updated by Tracy Irons-Georges

GUIDE TO ONLINE RESOURCES

WEB SITES

The following sites were visited by the editors of Salem Press in 2010. Because URLs frequently change, the accuracy of these addresses cannot be guaranteed; however, long-standing sites, such as those of colleges and universities, national organizations, and government agencies, generally maintain links when their sites are moved.

Academy of American Poets

http://www.poets.org

The mission of the Academy of American Poets is to "support American poets at all stages of their careers and to foster the appreciation of contemporary poetry." The academy's comprehensive Web site features information on poetic schools and movements; a Poetic Forms Database; an Online Poetry Classroom, with educator and teaching resources; an index of poets and poems; essays and interviews; general Web resources; links for further study; and more.

Contemporary British Writers

http://www.contemporarywriters.com/authors

Created by the British Council, this site offers profiles of living writers of the United Kingdom, the Republic of Ireland, and the Commonwealth. Information includes biographies, bibliographies, critical reviews, and news about literary prizes. Photographs are also featured. Users can search the site by author, genre, nationality, gender, publisher, book title, date of publication, and prize name and date.

LiteraryHistory.com

http://www.literaryhistory.com

This site is an excellent source of academic, scholarly, and critical literature about eighteenth, nineteenth, and twentieth century American and English writers. It provides individual pages for twentieth century literature and alphabetical lists of authors that link to articles, reviews, overviews, excerpts of works, teaching guides, podcasts, and other materials.

Literary Resources on the Net

http://andromeda.rutgers.edu/~jlynch/Lit

Jack Lynch of Rutgers University maintains this extensive collection of links to Web sites that are useful to researchers, including numerous sites about American and English literature. This collection is a good place to begin online research about poetry, as it links to other sites with broad ranges of literary topics. The site is organized chronologically, with separate pages about twentieth century British and Irish literature. It also has separate pages providing links to Web sites about American literature and to women's literature and feminism.

LitWeb
http://litweb.net

LitWeb provides biographies of hundreds of world authors throughout history that can be accessed through an alphabetical listing. The pages about each writer contain a list of his or her works, suggestions for further reading, and illustrations. The site also offers information about past and present winners of major literary prizes.

The Modern Word: Authors of the Libyrinth
http://www.themodernword.com/authors.html

The Modern Word site, although somewhat haphazard in its organization, provides a great deal of critical information about writers. The "Authors of the Libyrinth" page is very useful, linking author names to essays about them and other resources. The section of the page headed "The Scriptorium" presents "an index of pages featuring writers who have pushed the edges of their medium, combining literary talent with a sense of experimentation to produce some remarkable works of modern literature."

Outline of American Literature
http://www.america.gov/publications/books/outline-of-american-literature.html

This page of the America.gov site provides access to an electronic version of the ten-chapter volume *Outline of American Literature*, a historical overview of poetry and prose from colonial times to the present published by the Bureau of International Information Programs of the U.S. Department of State.

Poetry Foundation
http://www.poetryfoundation.org

The Poetry Foundation, publisher of *Poetry* magazine, is an independent literary organization. Its Web site offers links to essays; news; events; online poetry resources, such as blogs, organizations, publications, and references and research; a glossary of literary terms; and a Learning Lab that includes poem guides and essays on poetics.

Poet's Corner
http://theotherpages.org/poems

The Poet's Corner, one of the oldest text resources on the Web, provides access to about seven thousand works of poetry by several hundred different poets from around the world. Indexes are arranged and searchable by title, name of poet, or subject. The site also offers its own resources, including "Faces of the Poets"—a gallery of portraits—and "Lives of the Poets"—a growing collection of biographies.

Representative Poetry Online

http://rpo.library.utoronto.ca

This award-winning resource site, maintained by Ian Lancashire of the Department of English at the University of Toronto in Canada, has several thousand English-language poems by hundreds of poets. The collection is searchable by poet's name, title of work, first line of a poem, and keyword. The site also includes a time line, a glossary, essays, an extensive bibliography, and countless links organized by country and by subject.

Voice of the Shuttle

http://vos.ucsb.edu

One of the most complete and authoritative places for online information about literature, Voice of the Shuttle is maintained by professors and students in the English Department at the University of California, Santa Barbara. The site provides countless links to electronic books, academic journals, literary association Web sites, sites created by university professors, and many other resources.

Voices from the Gaps

http://voices.cla.umn.edu/

Voices from the Gaps is a site of the English Department at the University of Minnesota, dedicated to providing resources on the study of women artists of color, including writers. The site features a comprehensive index searchable by name, and it provides biographical information on each writer or artist and other resources for further study.

ELECTRONIC DATABASES

Electronic databases usually do not have their own URLs. Instead, public, college, and university libraries subscribe to these databases, provide links to them on their Web sites, and make them available to library card holders or other specified patrons. Readers can visit library Web sites or ask reference librarians to check on availability.

Canadian Literary Centre

Produced by EBSCO, the Canadian Literary Centre database contains full-text content from ECW Press, a Toronto-based publisher, including the titles in the publisher's Canadian fiction studies, Canadian biography, and Canadian writers and their works series; *ECW's Biographical Guide to Canadian Novelists*; and *George Woodcock's Intro-*

duction to Canadian Fiction. Author biographies, essays and literary criticism, and book reviews are among the database's offerings.

Literary Reference Center

EBSCO's Literary Reference Center (LRC) is a comprehensive full-text database designed primarily to help high school and undergraduate students in English and the humanities with homework and research assignments about literature. The database contains massive amounts of information from reference works, books, literary journals, and other materials, including more than 31,000 plot summaries, synopses, and overviews of literary works; almost 100,000 essays and articles of literary criticism; about 140,000 author biographies; more than 605,000 book reviews; and more than 5,200 author interviews. It contains the entire contents of Salem Press's MagillOnLiterature Plus. Users can retrieve information by browsing a list of authors' names or titles of literary works; they can also use an advanced search engine to access information by numerous categories, including author name, gender, cultural identity, national identity, and the years in which he or she lived, or by literary title, character, locale, genre, and publication date. The Literary Reference Center also features a literary-historical time line, an encyclopedia of literature, and a glossary of literary terms.

MagillOnLiterature Plus

MagillOnLiterature Plus is a comprehensive, integrated literature database produced by Salem Press and available on the EBSCOhost platform. The database contains the full text of essays in Salem's many literature-related reference works, including *Masterplots, Cyclopedia of World Authors, Cyclopedia of Literary Characters, Cyclopedia of Literary Places, Critical Survey of Poetry, Critical Survey of Long Fiction, Critical Survey of Short Fiction, World Philosophers and Their Works, Magill's Literary Annual,* and *Magill's Book Reviews.* Among its contents are articles on more than 35,000 literary works and more than 8,500 poets, writers, dramatists, essayists, and philosophers; more than 1,000 images; and a glossary of more than 1,300 literary terms. The biographical essays include lists of authors' works and secondary bibliographies, and hundreds of overview essays examine and discuss literary genres, time periods, and national literatures.

Rebecca Kuzins
Updated by Desiree Dreeuws

GEOGRAPHICAL INDEX

CATEGORY INDEX

SUBJECT INDEX